Man's Most Dang

Man's Most Dangerous Myth

The Fallacy of Race

SIXTH EDITION
ABRIDGED STUDENT EDITION

Ashley Montagu

AltaMira Press
A Division of Sage Publications, Inc.
Walnut Creek • London • New Delhi

For information address:

AltaMira Press
A Division of Sage Publications, Inc.
1630 North Main Street, Suite 367
Walnut Creek, CA 94596
explore@altamira.sagepub.com

SAGE Publications Ltd.
6 Bonhill Street
London EC2A 4PU
United Kingdom

SAGE Publications India Pvt. Ltd.
M-32 Market
Greater Kailash 1
New Delhi 110 048 India

PRINTED IN THE UNITED STATES OF AMERICA

98 99 00 01 02 03 04 05   7 6 5 4 3 2

Library of Congress Cataloging-in-Publication Data

Montagu, Ashley, 1905–
   Man's most dangerous myth : the fallacy of race / Ashley Montagu.
—6th ed.
      p.   cm.
   Includes bibliographical references and index.
   ISBN 0-8039-4647-3 (cloth). — ISBN 0-8039-4648-1 (pbk.)
   1. Race.   2. Race relations.   I. Title.
GN280.M59   1998
599.97—dc21   97-21132
                                                                                CIP

Abridged student edition

Typeset by Letra Libre

Cover design by Joanna Ebenstein

Contents

Acknowledgments

To Leonard Lieberman, Professor of Anthropology at Central Michigan University, my heartfelt thanks for his devoted reading of and commentary on every chapter of this book, and for his always helpful suggestions. I am similarly indebted to Professor of Sociology Larry T. Reynolds at Central Michigan University. To John Stanfield, Professor of Sociology at the University of California at Davis, I am similarly obliged. Their gentle ministrations have made this book a much better one than it would have otherwise been. To Elaine and Harry Mensh I am indebted for their help in the revision of chapter 6.

To Louise Schaeffer, Librarian of the Biology Library at Princeton University, I am greatly indebted for bibliographical help; also to Mary Chaikin, Librarian of the Psychological Library at Princeton; to the reference librarians at Firestone Library of Princeton University; to Louise Yorke, Librarian of the Princeton Medical Center; to the reference librarians at the Princeton public library, all for their bibliographical help so generously given.

To Mitch Allen, my editor and publisher, I am most grateful for his advice and patience beyond the call of duty. To Erik Hanson I am similarly grateful. To Pattie Rechtman, my copyeditor, I am enormously indebted for her microscopic eye, and for keeping me in order, much to the benefit of this book.

Above all, my gratitude goes to my wife, Marjorie, for her heroic endurance, over the course of six years in the making of this revision, of the colossal untidiness of my study and its overflow into the adjoining dining room.

Ashley Montagu
Princeton, New Jersey
September 1997

About the Author

ASHLEY MONTAGU (1905–) ranks as one of the most influential public intellectuals of the twentieth century. Of British origin but an American resident since 1930 and a naturalized citizen since 1940, Montagu has written or edited over 80 books, many in multiple editions, and thousands of research articles, magazine pieces, book chapters, letters, commentaries, and lectures in a career that has spanned three-fourths of this century. Among his best known book-length works are *The Natural Superiority of Women, Touching,* and *The Elephant Man,* but he has also authored key professional volumes and textbooks in physical anthropology, cultural anthropology, human evolution, and anatomy. His intellectual contributions also have been felt in an enormous range of other fields including prenatal and infant development, aging, the role of culture in evolution, the evolutionary development of human behavior, the basic behavioral needs, human nature and genetics, education, history of science, human-animal relations, sociobiology, American culture, emotions, computers, and nuclear disarmament.

In the area of race relations, it can be argued that Ashley Montagu is the most important theorist of the twentieth century. The initial publication of *Man's Most Dangerous Myth,* at the height of Nazism in 1942, radically challenged the idea that race was a determinant of human behavior, a position he championed almost alone for decades until it became accepted wisdom. Through subsequent editions of the book, his other works on race, and his authorship of the seminal UNESCO *Statement on Race,* Montagu's work has become foundational for those who study the learned dimensions of human behavior.

Ashley Montagu received a Ph.D. from Columbia University, taught anthropology at New York University, Harvard University, Princeton University, Rutgers University, and other places, and is the recipient of honorary awards and degrees from organizations around the globe.

Foreword to the First Edition, 1942
by Aldous Huxley

Dr. Ashley Montagu's book possesses two great merits, rarely found in current discussions of human problems. Where most writers over-simplify, he insists on the principle of multiple and interlocking causation. And where most assume that "facts will speak for themselves," he makes it clear that facts are mere ventriloquists' dummies, and can be made to justify any course of action that appeals to the socially conditioned passions of the individuals concerned.

These two truths are sufficiently obvious; but they are seldom recognized, for the good reason that they are very depressing. To recognize the first truth is to recognize the fact that there are no panaceas and that therefore most of the golden promises made by political reformers and revolutionaries are illusory. And to recognize the truth that facts do not speak for themselves, but only as men's socially conditioned passions dictate, is to recognize that our current educational processes can do very little to ameliorate the state of the world. In the language of traditional theology (so much more realistic, in many respects, than the "liberal" philosophies which replaced it), most ignorance is voluntary and depends upon acts of the conscious or subconscious will. Thus, the fallacies underlying the propaganda of racial hatred are not recognized because, as Dr. Montagu points out, most people have a desire to act aggressively, and the members of other ethnic groups are convenient victims, whom one may attack with a good conscience. This desire to act aggressively has its origins in the largely unavoidable frustrations imposed upon the individual by the processes of early education frustrations imposed upon the individual by the processes of early education and later adjustments to the social environment.

Dr. Montagu might have added that aggressiveness pays a higher dividend in emotional satisfaction than does cooperation. Cooperation may produce a mild emotional glow; but the indulgence of aggressiveness can be the equivalent of a drinking-bout or sexual orgy. In our industrial societies, the goodness of life is measured in terms of the number and intensity of the excitements experienced. (Popular philosophy is molded by, and finds expression in, the advertising pages of popular magazines. Significantly enough, the word that occurs more frequently in those pages than any other is "thrill.") Like sex and alcohol, aggressiveness can give enormous thrills. Under existing social conditions, it is therefore easy to represent aggressiveness as good.

Concerning the remedies for the social diseases he has so penetratingly diagnosed, Dr. Montagu says very little, except that they will have to consist in some process of education. But what process? It is hoped that he will answer this question at length in another work.

Foreword to the Sixth Edition
by C. Loring Brace

Well over half a century ago—two full generations—the world was in the midst of the colossal armed conflict of World War II. The instigator of its European manifestation was Germany under the leadership of Adolf Hitler and his Nazi Party. The basic motive behind Germany's actions was the belief, repeatedly articulated by Hitler, that Germans were a "master race" which had the right to take precedence over their neighbors because of their innate superiority.[1] In this regard, World War II was a resumption of the aspirations that had led to the outbreak of World War I in 1914 and which had not been extinguished by the German defeat of 1918. In Germany, there had been no sense that their role in generating World War I had been unjustified, and there was a comparable failure to face the fact that the war had been fairly lost. Instead, the scenario was constructed that their inability to continue generating the weaponry and personnel necessary for victory had been caused by a "stab-in-the-back" on the part of the "international financial community," a code name for "the Jews," themselves stigmatized as an "inferior race."[2]

Adolf Hitler took full advantage of this current of "racial" mythology and, in a masterfully murderous ploy of mass psychology, mobilized the German state to cleanse itself from "the enemy within"—the Jews—and charge forth in an attempt to gain control of the rest of the world. As a part of this overall plan, Jews were rounded up and shipped to concentration camps in the eastern part of Germany, in Czechoslovakia, and especially in Poland where they were killed by the millions. The whole appalling phenomenon came to be known as "The Holocaust."[3] This marked the first time in human history that a whole segment of the human species was earmarked for systematic extermination solely on the basis of what was perceived to be its "race."

At the very time that this was being carried out, Ashley Montagu produced the first edition of what is arguably his most important book, *Man's Most Dangerous Myth: The Fallacy of Race*.[4] In this work, Ashley Montagu was the first to articulate in fully developed fashion the fact that, despite almost universal belief to the contrary, the concept of "race" as applied to

13

the picture of human biological diversity had absolutely no scientific justification. Among those who had checked the manuscript prior to publication was America's premier anthropologist, Franz Boas, who had been the author's doctoral dissertation mentor at Columbia University in the mid-1930s. Launched with a Foreword by Aldous Huxley, the author who subsequently became celebrated for his *Brave New World,* the book rode a wave of public reaction fueled by a growing awareness of the pervasive evil manifest in the Nazi uses of "race."

There is a curious double irony to this whole situation. First, when Montagu wrote the book, neither he nor the public for which he was writing had more than a partial realization of the magnitude of that lethal enormity being enacted by the Nazis. When the full extent of the Holocaust became known as the war came to an end three years later (1945), *Man's Most Dangerous Myth,* then in its second edition, achieved well-deserved public recognition as a warning against the horrors that could result from a belief in and application of the concept of "race."

The second irony is to be found in the fact that the public, while giving Ashley Montagu due credit for having raised the alarm, never really took to heart the fact that the foundation for that warning was located in his demonstration that "race" was invalid from the perspective of basic biology. At most, readers were willing to grant the fact that Jews are not really a definable biological unit, but they were not yet ready to face the fact that there simply is no valid biological entity that corresponds to what is meant by the term "race." They certainly recognized the inhumane consequences of the political usage of the concept, but they tended—then and since—to assume that the objections raised in *Man's Most Dangerous Myth* were solely based on the social and political stance of the author.[5]

This is not to say that it avoided any expression of social and political values. Far from it. The social values articulated were explicit and humanitarian, and were presented with forthright expressions of admiration for the democratic ideals contained in the United States Constitution and particularly in the wording of the Declaration of Independence. He also recalled, from his own childhood in London before the outbreak in 1914 of World War I, the furor caused by the publication of a glorification of war and an exhortation to Germany to embark on a campaign of conquest for the greater glory of people who were "racially" German and for the German nation. This was written by the former Prussian officer, Friedrich von Bernhardi, who had led the triumphal march of the conquering army into Paris in 1871 symbolizing the defeat of France in the Franco-Prussian War.[6] The unresolved issues that were left by that conflict led directly to the two world wars of the succeeding century. Among those issues was the belief that human "races" not only constitute real entities but also that they can be ranked in a hierarchy of worth, and that such differences warrant differences in treatment. The assumption that human groups must differ in cognitive as well as visually recognizable attributes can be designated "racialism," and the conversion of such beliefs into differential behavior directed towards such groups is what counts as "racism." As Todorov has recently concluded, "When . . . racism uses racialism to justify itself, the results are catastrophes: this was precisely the case with Hitler's racism."[7]

This was clearly understood by those who had prevailed over Hitler's intentions in World War II, and it was exactly this that earned Ashley Montagu such a sympathetic readership for *Man's Most Dangerous Myth* in the years immediately following the conclusion of that colossal conflict. Consistent with his admiration for the ideals expressed by Thomas Jefferson, he has regularly quoted the views of the latter in regard to those of varying background: "whatever be their degree of talent it is no measure of their rights."[8] This is the stance that underlay the political ideology of Jefferson's *Declaration of Independence,*[9] it was explicitly echoed by Abraham Lincoln at the time of the American Civil War, and it has been repeated in all five previous editions of this Ashley Montagu's most important book. Almost certainly this is why so many have felt that his position was based on political ideals alone.[10] It takes nothing away from the fundamental significance of his expressed ideals to note that there is a basic biological issue that often has been overlooked in the process.

That biological issue was at the bottom of the first edition of *Man's Most Dangerous Myth* in 1942, and Ashley Montagu's appreciation of it was so far ahead of his time that the anthropological world is only just now beginning to catch up. This is the idea that biological variation in a widespread species, where there is reproductive continuity from one group to another throughout the entire extent of the species range, is best understood by looking at the gradients in distribution of traits taken one at a time. The graded distribution of each such trait will be controlled by the distribution of the selective force to which it represents a response. In humans, the most easily perceived of such traits is the color of the skin. The descendants of populations who had resided in the tropics for a prolonged period of time will have heavily pigmented skin. The skin pigment, melanin, represents a defense against the cancer-causing effect of the intensive ultraviolet radiation in tropical sunlight. The degree of reduction in human skin pigmentation will be in proportion to the length of time that a given human group has lived north (and also south) of the portions of the earth included between the Tropic of Cancer and the Tropic of Capricorn. The selective force that controls the degree of skin pigmentation is the intensity of ultraviolet radiation which is at its maximum in the Tropics.[11]

Other traits, such as blood groups for example, will be controlled by selective forces such as diet and disease that are distributed without any regard to the distribution of ultraviolet intensity.[12] The configuration formed by the intersection of such traits then will have no meaning in and of itself. In fact, if we focus on such configurations rather than the distribution of each trait separately and in terms of its own selective force, then we will have lost the ability to make any kind of sense out of the meaning of human biological variation.[13]

Ashley Montagu understood this in theory in 1942, although the full range of basic biological data necessary to sustain such a theory had yet to be collected. The idea was not entirely original with him as he was the first to note. As he explicitly pointed out, the viewpoint was laid out by Lancelot Hogben over a decade earlier,[14] and it was also behind the stance taken by Alfred Cort Haddon and Julian Huxley in their insightful work, *We Europeans*.[15] Right after that book had appeared, Julian Huxley—the literate scientist brother of the scientifically literate writer, Aldous—articulated the concept of "cline" which went on to become the biological foundation to the "non-racial" outlook that has characterized the work of Ashley Montagu from that time hence.[16] A cline is simply the gradient in the response of a trait to the graded intensity of the selective force that controls its appearance, and, as Huxley clearly indicated, it was just a further consequence of looking at the nature of biological variation from a thoroughly Darwinian perspective along with an understanding of the way in which genetics contributes to the physical development and appearance of a given organism.

Of course, speaking from the basis of the purely theoretical in the absence of supporting data is never as compelling as it is when one can actually point to the assembled evidence of continent-wide distributions of this or that. This is always the case when a new theoretical position is first proposed. Not only is the stance still not crystal clear in the minds of the proposers, but, in the absence of illustrative examples, it can often strike the reader as just so much empty verbiage. This was largely the situation when the first edition of *Man's Most Dangerous Myth* appeared in print. Still, the social message concerning the misapplication of the concept of "race" to the human scene was so compelling that the book went through three editions before biologists began to make the first tentative steps towards catching up with the biological theory on which the critique was established.

By 1949, it was clear that the geographic distribution of the common leopard frog in the eastern part of North America from Canada to the Gulf of Mexico was best portrayed in terms of gradients of adaptive characters.[17] Subsequently, it was realized that the attempt to depict variation in terms of "subspecies" or "races" in creatures as diverse as butterflies,[18] the North American marten,[19] and the zebras of Africa[20] were doomed to failure as biologically indefensible. It was the growing perception that cases such as this represent the norm for the biological world that led to the realization that the presumed existence of units such as "subspecies"—or "races" in the human realm—derived more from the traditions of medieval theology than from an assessment of how the biological world is actually put together. The demonstration that such a concept does more harm than good in the everyday business of trying to make sense out of variation in ordinary biological species was first articulated by E. O. Wilson, the Harvard entomologist later to become famous for his promotion of *Sociobiology*.[21]

Ashley Montagu, of course, had long since documented the harm that could be done in the name of "race" as it was applied to the human world. Biological anthropologists in the field had begun to collect data that, from the perspective of traditionalists, showed a disconcertingly non-racial kind of distribution. Obviously, human beings have done a lot of moving about during the last 10,000 years, particularly those whose numbers have expanded as a result of the adoption of an agricultural way of life. Still, it has been possible to test the distribution of genetically controlled traits over large, continuously occupied areas, and it has become clear that these distributions can only be understood after the concept of "race" is dropped. The late Joseph Birdsell plotted gene distributions in aboriginal Australia, and showed that the genes for given traits changed in frequency from one part of the continent to another with relatively little regard for what the genes for other traits were doing.[22] Finally, late in the 1950s, the first major effort was made to trace the distribution of an inherited human trait—in this case, the form of the hemoglobin responsible for sickle-cell anemia—according to what could be reconstructed of population history in relation to the relevant selective force—malaria in this instance—that influenced the prevalence of the trait. This yielded a picture in which the frequency of the sickle-cell gene was determined solely by the intensity of the forces of selection and not at all by locality as such.[23]

The theoretical implications dawned upon the author of this study—Frank B. Livingstone—and led him to create his famous aphorism, "There are no races, there are only clines."[24] This, of course, fit in perfectly with the stance defended twenty years earlier by Ashley Montagu, and, hardly surprisingly, Montagu quickly solicited Frank Livingstone's presentation as a centerpiece for a collection of essays by those who were adopting clinal thinking as the appropriate way to go about dealing with the nature of human biological variation. This was published under the title *The Concept of Race*, which appeared in 1964, the same year as the fourth edition of *Man's Most Dangerous Myth*.[25]

I remember the era well. I had been a student when Joe Birdsell's study of Australian gene frequencies had been published, and, steeped in the standard racialist assumptions of the time, I recall being baffled by the seemingly senseless gene distributions he had plotted. Then as it became clear that variation in frogs, butterflies, pine martens, and human beings was characterized by trait gradients that crossed each other in completely independent fashion, it became evident that those gradients were responding to the distribution of separate and unrelated gradients of selective forces—in the fashion of human hemoglobins responding to the distribution of malaria—and the whole non-racial nature of biological variation came into focus for me for the first time. The biological justification for Ashley Montagu's denunciation of race as *Man's Most Dangerous Myth* was patently obvious, and I was honored to be included as one of the contributors to his 1964 volume, *The Concept of Race.*[26]

A decade earlier, the Supreme Court had ruled that schools that were "racially" segregated were inherently unequal.[27] By 1964, Title VII of the Civil Rights Act had belatedly prohibited employers from engaging in discrimination based on "race," color, religion, sex, or national origin, although there has been a continuing reluctance to accept this prohibition.[28] Even at that moment, the candidate for United States Senator in Texas offered his opposition to the Civil Rights Act as one of his qualifications for being elected. Subsequently the perception that he was indeed opposed to eliminating the results of the legacy of unequal treatment for minorities was sufficient to boost his aspiration for the office of President of the United States, although it was not enough to earn him re-election. That figure was the one-term President, George Bush.[29]

But 1964 was a third of a century ago. The "brave new world" that we hoped was dawning arrived in largely stillborn fashion. To be sure, the pursuit of genocide in the name of "race" is universally regarded as completely indefensible, but that should have been as much a foregone conclusion as was the realization emerging from the American Civil War a century earlier that perceptions of "race" were no justification for treating people as property—i.e., that the institution of slavery was incompatible with a recognition of human status. However, even an enlarged and reinforced fifth edition of *Man's Most Dangerous Myth* in 1974, over three decades after the appearance of the first, failed to affect the entrenched public assumption that the artificial American situation with population segments recently derived from three widely separate and locally circumscribed portions of the globe, juxtaposed and assigned different social status initially by force of arms, is a proper model from which to generalize about the nature of human variation in the world as a whole.

What happened instead was a kind of intellectual stasis or even backsliding. This seems to have been a recurring centennial phenomenon in America. Right after the ringing ideals phrased in the Declaration of Independence and the United States Constitution, the promise inherent in those words was denied to those who displayed evidence of African ancestry. Then after Abraham Lincoln signed the Emancipation Proclamation in 1863 and lost his life soon thereafter, the first Civil Rights Act in 1866 was passed over the veto of his successor, Andrew Johnson. Over the succeeding thirty years, the scope of those rights was whittled down in case after case until, in Plessy *v.* Ferguson in 1896, the Supreme Court ruled that there was no federal remedy for private discrimination.[30] In effect, this allowed the reinstitution of what amounted to slavery in everything except the name.[31] There things remained until the Court's decisions were reversed in 1954, and explicit civil rights legislation was enacted in 1966.

As was true for each previous instance of official attempts to undo the effects of the racism of the past, the most recent effort has been met with the same kind of maneuverings to preserve the privileges of those who have benefited from the long-lasting traditions of unequal conditions accorded to those who are perceived as belonging to different "races." Prominent among these are the ponderous attempts to "prove" that the lower average IQ scores achieved by Americans of African origin have nothing to do with the ubiquitous conditions of social deprivation under which they are born and raised.[32] The most notorious of these recent representatives of racism is *The Bell Curve* by the late psychologist Richard J. Herrnstein and the political scientist Charles Murray,[33] which has been called "a massive manifestation of genteel bigotry."[34] Other equally racist tracts are continuing to be produced where the basic nature of and circumstances surrounding human biological variation are distorted beyond recognition and old-fashioned "racial" prejudice emerges in all its traditional ugliness.[35]

As the end of the current millennium approaches and we contemplate the dawn of another, it is clear that entrenched and traditional attitudes towards "race" remain alive and well, continuing to make life miserable for millions of people. The time is obviously ripe for the administration of another dose of Dr. Montagu's medicine which is as topical and apt as it was when it was first formulated over half a century ago. Now in his tenth decade, the author remains as much on top of the situation as ever. All the points that had been made in earlier editions are polished and brought up to date, and the wholly new sixth chapter—"The Mythology of Race: For Whom the Bell Tolls"—is a crowning gem that can stand by itself. In effect it represents one of the most definitive rebuttals of that widely popular manifestation of American racism, *The Bell Curve,* mentioned above.[36] The very popularity of that work is a testimonial to the fact that "race" remains a powerful myth in the world of today. As much as anything else, that popularity is a measure of our need for an Ashley Montagu to help the public see the error of its ways.[37]

Several years ago, it was my honor to be able to present to him, on behalf of the American Association of Physical Anthropologists, the Charles Darwin Award for Lifetime Achievement. On that occasion, I declared, "It is no exaggeration to say that Ashley Montagu is the world's one and only free-lance physical anthropologist."[38] Just as he did in the dark days of World War II, now again in our hour of need he has sallied forth once more as our St. George to combat the continuing threat of what he has most aptly identified as *Man's Most Dangerous Myth: The Fallacy of Race*. We can only hope that, this time, the world will take his lesson to heart.

C. Loring Brace
Ann Arbor, Michigan
18 September 1996

Notes

1. *Mein Kampf*, by Adolf Hitler, originally published in Munich, 1925; translated by Ralph Manheim (Boston, Houghton Mifflin, 1943); Robert Cecil, *The Myth of the Master Race: Alfred Rosenberg and Nazi Ideology* (New York: Dodd, Mead, 1972).

2. Geoffrey G. Field, *Evangelist of Race: The Germanic Vision of Houston Stewart Chamberlain* (New York: Columbia University Press, 1981); Robert Kuttner, "Writers on the Grassy Knoll: A Reader's Guide," *New York Times Book Review*, 2 February 1992, 23–25; Richard Bessel, *Germany After the First World War* (Oxford: Clarendon Press, 1993); and see the continuity of the same views in the writings of that opponent of religious tolerance, Pat Robertson in *The New World Order* (New York: Word Publishing, 1991) and the assessment of its sources in "The Crackpot Factor," in his 'Abroad at Home,' column by Anthony Lewis, *New York Times*, 14 April 1995, p. A11, as they had been discussed in detail by Michael Lind, "Rev. Robertson's Grand International Conspiracy Theory," *The New York Review of Books* 42(3), 2 February 1995, 21–25; his "On Pat Robertson: His Defenders," *The New York Review of Books* 42(7), 20 April 1995, 67–68, and Jacob Heilbrunn, "On Pat Robertson: His Anti-Semitic Sources," in *The New York Review of Books* 42(7), 20 April 1995, 68–71.

3. Gerald Fleming, *Hitler and the Final Solution* (Berkeley: University of California Press, 1984); Irving Abrahamson, ed., *Against Silence: The Voice and Vision of Elie Wiesel*, 3 vols. (New York: Holocaust Library, 1986); Israel Gutman, editor-in-chief, *Encyclopedia of the Holocaust*, 4 vols. (New York: Macmillan, 1990); Christopher R. Browning, *The Path to Genocide: Essays on Launching the Final Solution* (New York: Cambridge University Press, 1993); Daniel Jonah Goldhagen, *Hitler's Willing Executioners: Ordinary Germans and the Holocaust* (New York: Alfred A. Knopf, 1996).

4. Ashley Montagu, *Man's Most Dangerous Myth* (New York: Columbia University Press, 1942).

5. The most recent reincarnation of this canard is in *The Evolution of Racism: Human Differences and the Use and Abuse of Science*, by Pat Shipman (New York: Simon and Schuster 1994), in which a discussion of the "evolution of racism" is conspicuous by its absence, and the abuse of science is on the part of the author and not the figures accused, Ashley Montagu being prominently included among the latter. For a documentation of the gaffes in Shipman's treatment, see my review in *The American Journal of Physical Anthropology* 96(2) (1995): 204–10.

6. F. Friedrich von Bernhardi, *Germany and the Next War* translated by Allen H. Powles (London: Longmans Green, 1911); A. Montagu, *Dangerous Myth*, 153.

7. Tsvetan Todorov "'Race,' Writing and Culture," in *"Race," Writing, and Difference* ed. Henry Louis Gates (Chicago: University of Chicago Press, 1985), 372.

8. Letter to Abbé Grégoire in 1809, in *Basic Writings of Thomas Jefferson*, ed. Philip S. Foner (New York: Halcyon House, 1950), 682.

9. Garry Wills, *Inventing America: Jefferson's Declaration of Independence* (Garden City, NY: Doubleday, 1978).

10. See Shipman *Evolution of Racism*, 190–91.

11. These matters are treated at length in *Biological Perspectives on Human Pigmentation*, by Ashley H. Robins (New York: Cambridge University Press, 1991).

12. William C. Boyd, *Genetics and the Races of Man, An Introduction to Modern Physical Anthropology* (Boston: Little, Brown and Company, 1950); Arthur E. Mourant, A. C. Kopec and K. Domaniewska-Sobczak, *Blood Groups and Disease: A Study of the Association of Diseases with Blood Groups and Other Polymorphisms* (New York: Oxford University Press, 1978).

13. Elsewhere I have urged the treatment of the distribution of inherited traits in terms of the history and distribution of the controlling selective forces as a general approach, see C. Loring Brace, "A Non-Racial Approach Toward the Understanding of Human Diversity," in *The Concept of Race*, ed. Ashley Montagu (New York: The Free Press of Glenco, 1964), 103–152, and C. Loring Brace "A Four-Letter Word Called "Race," chapter 7 in *Race and other Misadventures: Essays in Honor of Ashley Montagu in His Ninetieth Year,* eds. Larry T. Reynolds and Leonard Lieberman (Dix Hills, NY: General Hall Publishers, 1996) 106–41. Specific examples of how this can be applied are demonstrated in "Who Gave Whom Hemoglobin S: The Use of Restriction Site Haplotype Variation For the Interpretation of the Evolution of the (^{s}-globin gene," by Frank B. Livingstone, *American Journal of Human Biology* 1 (1989): 289–302; and "What Big Teeth You Had Grandma! Human Tooth Size, Past and Present," by C. Loring Brace, Shelley L. Smith, and Kevin D. Hunt, in *Advances in Dental Anthropology* eds. Marc A. Kelley and Clark S. Larsen (New York Wiley-Liss 1991), 33–57.

14. This had been done in the brilliant chapter, "The Concept of Race" in Lancelot Hogben's *Genetic Principles in Medicine and Social Science* (London: Williams and Norgate, 1931), 122–44.

15. *We Europeans: A Survey of "Racial" Problems,* by Alfred Cort Haddon and Julian S. Huxley (New York: Harper, 1936).

16. Julian Huxley, "Clines: An Auxiliary Taxonomic Principle," *Nature* 142 (1938): 219–20.

17. John A. Moore, "Geographic Variations of Adaptive Characters in *Rana pipiens* Schraber," *Evolution* 3(1)(1943): 1–23.

18. F. Martin Brown "Studies of Nearctic Coenonympha tullia," *Bulletin of the American Museum of Natural History* 105(4)(1955): 361–409; Nicholas W. Gillham "Geographical Variation and the Subspecies Concept in Butterflies," *Systematic Zoology* 5(3)(1956): 110–20.

19. Edwin M. Hagmeier, "Inapplicability of the Subspecies Concept to North American Marten," *Systematic Zoology* 7(1)(1958): 1–7.

20. R. E. Rau "Additions to the Revised list of Preserved Material of the Extinct Cape Colony Quagga and Notes on the Relationship and Distribution of Southern Plains Zebras," *Annals of the South African Museum* 77(2)(1978): 27–45.

21. E. O. Wilson and William L. Brown, Jr., "The Subspecies Concept and its Taxonomic Application," *Systematic Zoology* 2(3)(1953): 97–111; E. O. Wilson, *Sociobiology: The New Synthesis* (Cambridge: Belknap Press of Harvard University Press, 1975).

22. Joseph B. Birdsell, "Some Implications of the Genetical Concept of Race in Terms of Spatial Analysis," *Proceedings of The Cold Spring Harbor Symposia on Quantitative Biology* 15 (1951): 259–311.

23. Frank B. Livingstone, "Anthropological Implications of Sickle Cell Gene Distribution in West Africa," *The American Anthropologist* 30(3)(1958): 533–62.

24. Frank B. Livingstone, "On the Non-Existence of Human Races," *Current Anthropology* 3(3)(1962): 279.

25. Ashley Montagu, ed., *The Concept of Race* (New York: The Free Press of Glencoe, 1964).

26. C. Loring Brace, "A Non-Racial Approach Towards the Understanding of Human Diversity," in *The Concept of Race*, 103–52.

27. This was the landmark Brown *v.* Board of Education case, and it is treated in full in *From Brown to Bakke: The Supreme Court and School Integration, 1954–1978*, by Harvie Wilkinson III (New York: Oxford University Press, 1979); and in *The Burden of Brown: Thirty Years of School Desegregation*, by Raymond Wolters (Knoxville: University of Tennessee Press, 1984).

28. Kathleen Hall Jamieson, *Dirty Politics, Deception, Distraction, and Democracy* (New York: Oxford University Press, 1992).

29. While he did indeed continue to support the position that represented the survival of the traditions of "racial" discrimination, it was more a stance of window dressing than of genuine conviction. As one perceptive commentator noted, "The clothes have no emperor. There is no there there." In "No There There," by Anna Quindlan, in her column, "Public & Private," *New York Times,* 6 May 1992, A19.

30. "The Unhappy History of Civil Rights Legislation," by Eugene Gressman, in *Michigan Law Review* 50(8): 1323–58; and *Judicial Enigma: The First Justice Harlan*, by Tinsley E. Yarbrough, reviewed in, "The Great Dissenter," by William H. Chafe, *New York Times Book Review*, 28 May 1995, 14.

31. Gressman, "Unhappy History," 1324.

32. For instance, Arthur R. Jensen, "How Much Can We Boost IQ and Scholastic Achievement?" *Harvard Educational Review* 39(1)(1969): 1–123, in which the author implies that the answer to the question in his title is "none," and Arthur R. Jensen, *Bias in Mental Testing* (New York: The Free Press, 1980), in which he claims that there is no bias in mental tests themselves, but he then unwittingly provides a conclusive demonstration that there is a massive amount of bias among those who create them and assume that their results tell us anything about the average inherited capacities of the groups from which the testees are derived.

33. Richard J. Herrnstein and Charles Murray, *The Bell Curve: Intelligence and Class Structure in American Life* (New York: The Free Press, 1994). This work has provoked an enormous number of reviews and comments. So far, at least three collections have been assembled in book form: *The Bell Curve Wars: Race, Intelligence, and the Future,* ed. Steven Fraser (New York: Basic Books, 1995); *The Bell Curve Debate: History, Documents, Opinions,* eds. Russell Jacoby and Naomi Glauberman (New

York: Times Books, 1995); *Measured Lies: The Bell Curve Examined*, eds. Joe L. Kincheloe, Shirley R. Steinberg and Aaron D. Gresson III (New York: St. Martin's Press 1996). Two reviews deserve special attention. "Curveball" by Stephen Jay Gould, *New Yorker,* 28 November 1994, 139–49, has shown that the treatment of the massive data compilation assembled in *The Bell Curve* could practically serve as a textbook example of how to lie with statistics. And "The Tainted Sources of the Bell Curve" by Charles Lane, *New York Review of Books,* 1 December 1994, 14–19, documents the extent of the racist taint in the sources used by Herrnstein and Murray to support their preconceived stance.

34. C. Loring Brace, "Review of *The Bell Curve,*" *Current Anthropology* 37 (Supplement) (1996): S156-S161, S161.

35. For example, J. Philippe Rushton, *Race, Evolution, and Behavior: A Life History Perspective* (New Brunswick: Transaction Publishers, 1995). My own review of this, entitled "Racialism and Racist Agendas," appeared in *The American Anthropologist* 98(1)(1996): 36–37, and it concluded that, "Quite evidently, it is a manifestation of blatant bigotry" (p. 37). Other reviewers have used considerably stronger and less temperate language, for example, David P. Barash in *Animal Behaviour* 49(4)(1995): 1131–33.

36. The overwhelming consensus of the reviewers is that the work represents a continuation of the same attitudes that created and defended American slavery in the past. It does have its defenders, prominent among them being that product of the apartheid society of South Africa, J. Philippe Rushton, illustrated by his review in *Current Anthropology* 37 (Supplement): S168–S172.

37. In order to document and strengthen the position he has maintained for the last half century and more, I am currently in the process of preparing a work entitled *Race Is a Four-Letter Word*. It is dedicated to Ashley Montagu.

38. The text of that presentation is recorded in the "Proceedings of the Sixty-Third Meeting of the American Association of Physical Anthropologists in Denver, April, 1994," *American Journal of Physical Anthropology* 95(4): 456–57, and the quote is from page 456.

Preface to the Sixth Edition
by John H. Stanfield II

The other day I noticed something quite promising. While scanning over an application form I was surprised and impressed to find not only the usual *racial status* boxes but one called *"multiracial."* Even though the word racial perpetuated THE MYTH, at least the new box was a well overdue acknowledgment of the complexities of human identity. The *multiracial* box was also an indicator of how much the ethnic identity questioning that characterizes the 1990s as the temporal anteroom to the twenty-first century has finally begun to influence the red-tape aspects of public policy.

The materialization of the multiracial box on the application form certainly symbolizes why Ashley Montagu's *Man's Most Dangerous Myth* is not only still relevant over fifty years after its publication, but, more importantly, why it is that the text will become even more important as we cross the threshold into the next century. The next century, which is already here in so many ways, will be a time in which the traditional methods of drawing sociological distinctions among human beings will crumble. We see this already in the late twentieth century American and more global movements that have begun to radically redefine the status positions and official and subjective identities of historically marginized and excluded populations such as women, indigenous peoples, colonized people of color, homosexuals and lesbians and physically disabled persons. The breakdown and breakup of national and empire boundaries and the growing acknowledgment of transnational identities, kinship networks, and economic modes of production have made the already cumbersome issue of human status and identity issues even more cumbersome, complex, and paradoxical.

In the midst of these revolutionary movements of human place and consciousness are the efforts of many Americans and other global residents to call into question the racial definitions imposed on them through official state invented categories and social and cultural traditions and stereotypes. We have seen in the 1990s, for instance, a number of biographical accounts of Americans who have written about their multiethnicity which do not easily fit into neat racialized boxes. The emerging lobbying effort to include a multiracial status box on the 2000 United States Census is another example of the growing awareness of the limitations of singular racial boxes, which symbolize a mythology losing its relevance.

Montagu's *Man's Most Dangerous Myth* is an indispensable background text for anyone interested in the historical development and use of the fallacy of race in public policy-making and in social life. Though over the years several excellent books have been published on the fallacy of race, none surpasses *Man's Most Dangerous Myth* in intellectual brilliance and in level of comprehensive analysis. Even though some of the examples Montagu refers to date to earlier times, the spirit behind his bold articulations still holds.

It should be pointed out that Ashley Montagu in his usual thorough way gives credit to those who proceeded him and influenced his thinking about the fallacy of race. Indeed, the vast array of extensive endnotes that anchor the minute details of his arguments stand alone as a lasting significant contribution to the study of the fallacies of race thinking and acting. As much as Montagu gives exhaustive credit to others, he distinguishes himself from his intellectual predecessors in the depth of his analyses and the interdisciplinary creative insights he uses to discredit the dangerous myth of race in various disciplines such as genetics, physiology, psychology, anthropology, and sociology. It is Montagu's profound depth of inquiry into the intricacies of the fallacies of race thinking with such brilliant reconsideration and re-interpretations about what we know about the fallacies of race-thinking that makes Montagu's *Man's Most Dangerous Myth* a seminal piece of scholarship that has yet to be surpassed.

This book is a must read for anyone interested in the first comprehensive text in what is now called postmodern race theory. In more extensive interdisciplinary frameworks than found anywhere in the postmodern race theory literature, Montagu offers a social constructionist (socialization) approach to the study of the myth of race. It is an approach that is much more thorough and convincing than contemporary texts such as Stephen Gould's *The Mismeasure of Man* and Cornell West's *Race Matters*. Indeed, neither of those works, nor others published in the post-1970s, offer the depth that Montagu presents in his masterful work. This is especially the case when it comes to how Montagu grounds his socialization approach in a critique of genetic and biological folklore that is either ignored or watered down in post-1970s attempts at postmodern race theory. The depth and breadth of Montagu's historical discussions on the idea of race in biology, genetics, and in the social sciences is a synthetic review and critique missing in contemporary critical race theory. This is especially the case among cultural studies of racism published by scholars who may grasp the importance of socialization approaches to race study but who lack the biological and genetic sciences background necessary to critique biological and genetic folklore in their scholarship.

The recent responses to Richard Herrnstein's and Charles Murray's *The Bell Curve* by progressive cultural studies scholars demonstrates how much more work must be done to understand the wisdom of Ashley Montagu's *Man's Most Dangerous Myth*. As much as such scholars have fought a good fight against the alleged scientific claims of Herrnstein and Murray about the cognitive deficiencies of black people, they like the men they oppose assume that race is a real category. So, we have had reams of published studies debunking *The Bell Curve* through calling attention to research which puts blacks as a ethnic in a more favorable light.

If it were up to Montagu, adjectives such as black and white would no longer be used. Race as a myth is a distorting variable that convolutes and in other ways distracts attention from the variables that really matter in understanding how and why human beings think, act, and develop as they do. The extent to which race does exist, it is an experience, it is not phenotype real or imagined. This takes us back to the fact that race is social; that is, it is learned. If we can learn race, we can unlearn race. It means that people with different cultural backgrounds can under certain historically grounded social, economic, and political conditions be made to feel like a particular "race." The usual way that "race" feeling becomes sustained is through people being segregated geographically on institutional, community, societal, and world-system levels. It is possible, as Montagu so aptly points out in his discussion on whites captured by nineteenth-century Indians becoming Indians in identity, for people of different phenotypical characteristics to become members of a different "race" through socialization or re-socialization. We see this happening with Korean children growing up in predominantly black and Latino neighborhoods in Los Angeles who go off to college and find they have more in common with black and Latino than with Korean classmates. We see it with black suburban kids in predominantly white neighborhoods who find themselves identifying more with the political and cultural values and priorities of their affluent white playmates than with their ethnic brothers and sisters in the inner-city.

The growing mixed race movement in the United States and its increasing impact on U. S. Census policies and elsewhere are also indicators of how much race is a experience. More and more Americans are beginning to insist on being called more than one "race" and are maintaining their transnational identities publicly as well as privately. These movements remind us that singular racialized categories do nothing more than oversimplify the complexities of ethnicity and culture. When it comes to self-identity and how it becomes sustained and important in building institutions, communities, and societies, ethnic and cultural background, especially when it is multiethnic and multicultural, certainly matters more than a singular imposed identity called race. When we converge issues of age, regionalism, gender, religion, and class with ethnicity, culture, multiethnicity, and multiculturalism, we begin to understand how much singular race categorization is a dangerous myth that encourages derogatory prejudgements that drain human beings of their complexity while placing emphasis on irrelevant distinctions.

As much as there are cracks showing in the use of singular race categories to identify self and others in the United States, most American citizens and residents continue to be trapped in this irrelevant way of viewing human qualities and potential. By this point in American history, the emotional energy invested in race as a means to define and organize social life has been the major barrier to dispensing with the use of the term in everyday language. It is not because there is something biological or natural about race that prevents the dismantling of the term and its use to define self and others.

As the United States continues to become defined as a multiethnic society with transnational tentacles, it is going to become increasingly difficult to maintain race as a legitimate form of emotional investment. We reside in a nation-state and a world in which demographically non-white fertility is much higher than white fertility. Most of the people who control the wealth and power in the world are non-English speakers and non-whites. Most of the children born in the United States have parents who speak English as a second language. Even though the present anti-affirmative action movements in California and elsewhere may be picking up steam, the demographic, economic, and political changes occurring in this country and world are demanding that we become much more inter-culturally competent, and quickly. It is a matter of casting away race as an increasingly obsolete and dysfunctional way to distinguish human beings and make life decisions.

Even though it is true that the ethnic demographic transformation may not bear obvious fruit in terms of significant power shifts in American life for many years to come, the fact of the matter is, the wheels are already in motion. Those groups that are preaching racial exclusion from the left and right and among non-whites as well as whites will not help but be left behind in the dust of a nation-state in a global community struggling with the meaning of a society and world which is ethnically plural inside out.

As people continue to come out of their balkanized racialized shells as power arrangements continue to shift west to east; from Europe and America to Asia; and as significant regional and ecological pockets of the United States become significantly non-white, sensible men and women will begin to search for paradigms to decide the best ways to deracialize. It is in this way that Montagu's *Man's Most Dangerous Myth* will once again find itself in the middle of the action. While its first appearance met great resistance and scorn in a world still rigidly embracing notions of white supremacy, now it reappears in a time of searching for ways to get along in a time when the rules of traditional racial hierarchies simply no longer hold even a spoonful of water.

The profound depth of Montagu's statement on the mythology of race makes it a timeless contribution to intellectual history and for those interested in designing a socially just society and world. It was here before postmodern theorizing about race as social construction and will be here for many years to come after postmodern theorizing is a footnote in some future history of late twentieth-century western social thought. That is why we all need to pause and drink deeply from the wells of what this extraordinary scholar and magnificent human being has to tell us about what has been indeed the most dangerous myth invented by *Homo sapiens.*

John H. Stanfield II
Director, The Research Program on
Racial, Ethnic, and Immigration Studies
University of California at Davis

Introduction to the Sixth Edition

More than half a century has passed since this book was first published in 1942, and more than a generation has gone by since the fifth edition was published in 1974. In spite of those five new editions, each larger than the one before, the race problem, like a malady that will not go away, seems to have grown more troubling than ever. And yet, true as that may be on a quantitative basis, qualitatively the evidence indicates that there are many more people today than ever before who believe in the right of all Americans to life, liberty, and the pursuit of happiness. But racism, by action or inaction, constitutes the denial of that right, and in that sense there appear to be many more racists than ever before.

The purpose of the present, sixth edition is to make use of the scientifically established facts to show that the term "race" is a socially constructed artifact—that there is no such thing in reality as "race;" that the very word is racist; that the idea of "race," implying the existence of significant biologically determined mental differences rendering some populations inferior to others, is wholly false; and that the space between an idea and reality can be very great and misleading.

Speaking of "space," I have never before put what is wrong with the idea of "race" in the form of a formula. Let me do so here. What the formula shows, in simplified form, is what racists, and others who are not necessarily "conscious" racists, believe to be the three genetically inseparable links which constitute "race:" The first is the phenotype or physical appearance of the individual, the second is the intelligence of the individual, and the third is the ability of the group to which the individual belongs to achieve a high civilization. Together these three ideas constitute the concept of "race." This is the structure of the current conception of "race" to which most people subscribe. *Nothing could be more unsound, for there is no genetic linkage whatever between these three variables.* And that is what this book is designed to discuss and make clear.

As a student of anthropology, at University College and the London School of Economics, in the early 20s, I inherited the established view of "race" from my teachers and the books I read, to the effect that human populations were separable into different varieties in which the hierar-

31

chy of difference led from the most advanced to the most backward "races."

During the first half of the century, both English and American anthropologists, generally, continued to teach the nineteenth-century traditional view of "race," as if it were a demonstrable reality.[1] Indeed, the whole of anthropology seemed to stem from the concept of "race." Like everyone else, I took it for granted that such entities as were enshrined in terms like "lower races," "inferior races," "superannuated races," "backward races," "mongrel races," "mixed races," "primitive peoples," "savages," and the like, corresponded to actual realities. In fact one of my teachers, Sir Arthur Keith, held that racial antagonisms are deeply seated in the "primitive organization of the brain."[2] For that view there was no more evidence then than there is today, although it was implicit in the views of most anthropologists of the nineteenth and early twentieth centuries.

I can think of no better way of describing the intellectual atmosphere in which I lived and learned than to quote from the viewpoint of a great and unusually versatile scientist, Karl Pearson (1857–1936). Pearson was a professor of applied mathematics at University College (University of London) and a principal founder of modern statistics and biometry, as well as a proponent of eugenics and an intimate friend of Francis Galton, the founder of eugenics, of whom he wrote a magnificent biography.[3] Pearson became the first Galton Professor of National Eugenics at University College. A prolific author, at the age of 35 he published a brilliant book entitled *The Grammar of Science* in 1892.[4] This soon became a classic, and has been in print in several editions to this day and remains completely engrossing. Finally, it should be said that Pearson's great and enduring achievement was to make of the application of mathematical statistics a factor of utmost importance in many fields of scientific inquiry. And this, too, should be said: In spite of some eccentricities Pearson had a great and noble mind.[5]

As a young man Pearson was an active socialist and wrote much on politics and ethics, as well as folklore. As he grew older he became more conservative, and in the field of research on intelligence, in the name of statistics, as late as 1925 he was capable of committing the most egregious of follies.[6] Statistics and prejudices, whether declared or undeclared, do not go well together. In defense of Pearson, and before quoting the following passage from his *The Grammar of Science*, it should be pointed out that virtually every scientist writing during the nineteenth century was, like Pearson, caught in an inexorable web of racist beliefs. I have chosen Pearson's presentation of those beliefs as typical because he stated them so clearly, and because he spoke as a distinguished scientist. Yet in all fairness, it should be noted that there was generally no rancor involved in the views in Pearson's writings or those of his contemporaries. The trouble with nineteenth-century scientists was that they simply did not have available to them the research in genetics and anthropology of the first half of the twentieth century, facts that would have enabled them to deduce what was wrong with the customary arbitrary typological methods in the classification of the so-called "races of mankind." Addicted to their classificatory schemes, they saw them as confirming the "natural" stratification of the castes and classes of their own society. This was comforting because, among other things, it was powerfully reinforced by the ecclesiasticism of the day.[7]

I remember, as a small boy at school, singing with some feeling, the lovely hymn, *All Things Bright and Beautiful,* the final words of which put it all in a nutshell; although it was not until many years later that I understood what they meant.

> The rich man in his castle,
> The poor man at his gate,
> God made them high or lowly,
> And ordered their estate.
> —Cecil Frances Alexander 1818–1895

Such ideas were the common currency of the descendants of Calvinistic individualism, with its doctrine of the elect, and of the Puritans with their belief in wealth as an evidence of divine grace, and poverty as a proof of moral error.

After Darwin, many scientists were no longer comfortable with the idea of the divine ordering of nature, and felt that "natural selection" was a more efficient notion. Pearson was a firm believer in "natural selection," and his writings had a considerable influence well into the twentieth century, typifying the work and thinking of virtually every authority on the subject of "race." Here, then, are Pearson's views on "the races of mankind":

'The whole earth is mine, and no one shall rob me of any corner of it,' is the cry of civilized man. No nation can go its own way and deprive the rest of mankind of its soil and its mineral wealth, its labour-power and its culture—no nation can refuse to develop its mental or physical resources—without detriment to civilization at large in its struggle with organic and inorganic nature. It is not a matter of indifference to other nations that the intellect of any people shall lie fallow, or that any folk should not take its part in the labour of research. It cannot be indifferent to mankind as a whole whether the occupants of a country leave its fields untried and its natural resources undeveloped. It is a false view of human solidarity, a weak humanitarianism, which regrets that a capable and stalwart race of white men should replace a dark-skinned tribe which can neither utilize its land to the full benefit of mankind, nor contribute its quota to the common stock of human knowledge.[8]

This passage is followed by a footnote which reads: "This sentence must not be taken to justify a brutalizing destruction of human life. The anti-social effects of such a mode of accelerating the effects of the survival of the fittest may go far to destroy the preponderating fitness of the survivor. At the same time there is cause for human satisfaction in the replacement of the aborigines throughout America and Australia by white races of far higher civilization."

The best comment on this, I believe, was made at the time by one of Pearson's contemporaries in England, Alice James, the remarkable sister of William and Henry James, and like the latter permanently settled in England, who in February 1890 wrote in her diary of the English "profound ineradicable in the bone and sinew conviction that outlying regions are their preserves, that they alone of human races massacre savages out of pure virtue, it would ill-become an American to reflect upon the treatment of aboriginal races, but I never heard it suggested that our hideous dealings with the Indians was brotherly love masquerading under the guise of pure cussedness."[9]

Pearson's rigid application of the doctrine of the "survival of the fittest"—not Darwin's phrase, but Herbert Spencer's—and his "satisfaction in the replacement of the aborigines throughout America and Australia by white races of far higher civilization," may today make us shudder at its inhumanity and wrongheadedness, but in a very real sense the Victorian age was devastatingly inhuman. Pearson inherited a full share of its insensitivities. In his day the great divide was between the privileged and the poor or "the lower orders of society," as they were called, whose poverty and dreadful birth and mortality rates, were considered sins for which they were being punished.[10] It was therefore not difficult for thinkers like Pearson to apply such views to the extinction of the majority of the indigenous cultures not only of America, but of all the Americas, as well as to the aborigines of Australia and Tasmania, in which the extermination was virtually complete.

Reflecting upon the imminent extinction of the Tasmanian aborigines in 1836, the Reverend Thomas Atkins wrote, "Indeed, from a large induction of the facts, it seems to be a universal law in the Divine government, when savage tribes who live by hunting, fishing, and on the wild herbs, roots, and fruits of the earth, come into collision with civilized races of men . . . the savage tribes disappear before the progress of civilized races."[11]

And there we have it, the pietistic rationalization for the massacre and destruction of "savage tribes." It was clearly God's will, the divine dispensation, for were it not, He could hardly have permitted such a denouement.

And then there was Adolf Hitler, who said, "What good fortune for those in power that people do not think," who by utilizing the idolatry of "race" brought about the death and destruction of millions of innocent men, women, and children. During World War II approximately between fifteen and twenty million military personnel were killed in action, along with about twenty-five million civilians.[12]

It would take too long to tell the story of the manner in which, over the course of the years, and thanks to the work of many scientists in the biological and social sciences, I came to understand how wrong such beliefs as Pearson's were.

It was not so much through my biological and physical anthropological studies, as through my cultural anthropological ones that I began to comprehend what an important role culture—the way of life of a people—plays in producing the behavioral differences between societies. It gradually became clear to me that the most important setting of human evolution is the human social environment, and that the adaptive responses to the challenges of different environments can influence evolutionary changes through the media of mutation, natural selection, social selection, genetic drift, and hybridization. These views were first set out in *Science*, 6 June 1947,[13] by my friend Professor Theodosius Dobzhansky, a geneticist, and myself, a biosocial anthropologist. The paper, slightly revised for style, constitutes Chapter 5 of the present volume.

It was not until many years later that I found support for my conviction that everything a human being comes to know and do *as human being* has to be learned from other human beings, from the social environment.[14] Especially great support came from *The Social Construction of Reality: A Treatise in the Sociology of Knowledge* (1966) by sociologists Peter Berger and Thomas Luckmann.[15] What Berger and Luckmann showed is that everything that passes for knowledge in human society, particularly the "common sense knowledge" that constitutes the reality of everyday life, is socially determined. Following that demonstration, the authors proceeded to an equally convincing analysis of society as a dialectical process between objective and subjective reality.

In such a society one may readily understand how the unreal may often become more real than the real, a case in point being the idea of "race." In this connection one may recall Stephen Ullmann's remark, "Words certainly are the vehicles of our thoughts, but they may be far more than that: they may acquire an influence of their own, shaping and pre-determining our processes of thinking and our whole outlook."[16]

In pursuing the study of "race" my purpose has been not to prove or disprove anything, but to state the facts as they are; to identify error and faults; and, in the light of the evidence, to make the necessary corrections. Added to this one must, of course, discuss the significance of one's findings, conscious always that facts do not speak for themselves, but are often at the mercy of any juggler who chooses to play tricks with them, and above all bearing always in mind that falsification begins with language.

It was largely the distressing world in which I lived that sparked my interest in "race." The London of my childhood during World War I was characterized by an atmosphere of unbounded nationalistic belligerence, the shattering realities of death of loved ones, and the incomprehensibility of war. The postwar period was one of cynicism and depression. The feeling was of betrayal and abandonment, as if one had been emptied of all that one formerly believed to be the regularities of civilized life. But it was also a period of artificial gaiety, which gave one time furiously to think, among other things, about class differences, and pejorative nationalistic stereotypes. The latter, as through a glass darkly, caused me slowly to work my way toward some understanding that stereotypes and racism were inextricably related. World War II reinforced the suspicion that nationalism was but another form, even more dangerous, of racism. During what I came to see as the kleptomaniac period of imperialism, England had been engaged in expropriating other peoples' lands, usually by force and uninvited occupation, in either case the final effects, for the most part, were the same—the decimation of the indigenous peoples and the destruction of their cultures.

The gradual growth of my knowledge concerning the impact of civilized man upon so-called "primitive peoples," or "savages," validated by science and more than countenanced by the church, together with the arbitrariness and erroneousness upon which their views were based, led ultimately to the publication of the articles which together formed the first edition of *Man's Most Dangerous Myth: The Fallacy of Race* in 1942. To Julian Huxley, biologist, and Alfred Cort Haddon, physical and cultural anthropologist, I owed a great debt for the clarification of my thinking about "race" from the reading of their important and stimulating book, *We Europeans: A Survey of "Racial" Problems* (1936).[17] I owed a similar debt to Lancelot Hogben, for his chapter on "The Concept of Race," in his seminal book *Genetic Principles in Medicine and Social Science* (1931).[18] But before these books I had been greatly influenced by Franz Boas, cultural and physical anthropologist, whose writings on "race," beginning in the last decade of the nineteenth century, were made generally available in his book *The Mind of Primitive Man* (1911),[19] and subsequent editions, as well as in later books and articles on "race." Boas was one of those great scientists who never received a Nobel Prize. It would be difficult to think of anyone who was more worthy of that kind of recognition for his contribution to the understanding of the diversity and the cultural and physical development of humankind.

The first work I read on "race," began with a most unlikely title, *Christianity and the Race Problem*,[20] by J. H. Oldham, Secretary of the International Missionary Council, published by the Student Christian Movement, London, in May 1924. Highly informative, the book impressed me greatly for its humanity and reasonableness, while its Christianity was not in the least obtrusive. It is the kind of book that is worth rereading from time to time for the sheer pleasure of the author's fine mind. Beautifully written as it is, it remains one of the most quotable of books, and its influence stays with me to this day.

Now for some words concerning the sixth edition of *Man's Most Dangerous Myth: The Fallacy of Race.* It seems to me that the myth, the danger, and the fallacy remain, there are more people today who understand that racism is wrong, that there is no right way to do what is wrong, and that what is morally wrong cannot be politically right. But there are also more racists today than ever. This includes the morally apathetic as well as the active racists consisting largely of the generality of people, the least educated being the most racist. Today we are also faced with the new phenomenon of black leaders who, having learned from Hitler how well racism works, incite their people against "the enemy," "the Jews."

It is understandable in the light of the unspeakable wrongs that have been committed, and continue to be committed, against blacks, that many blacks should so easily fall victim to the demagoguery of unscrupulous leaders. Yet, it is sadly ironic to have to note that it has largely fallen to the lot of Jews to be the most earnest defenders of the rights of blacks, as well as the most active workers in the struggle to secure those rights. Jews have created foundations devoted exclusively to assist blacks to achieve their rights, and have helped in numerous other ways, in organizations or as individuals to break through the formidable wall of prejudice.

How can one forget that the friend and most active collaborator of the great black leader, W. B. Du Bois, in the founding of the National Association for the Advancement of Colored People, was an American Jew? Joel Spingarn, a charming personality who, at about this time, had resigned his professorship of comparative literature at Columbia University in protest against the wrongful dismissal of a colleague. Spingarn was a member of the Board and Chairman of the NAACP, and its most active speaker throughout the country, advancing the cause of the organization.[21] To list the foundations, funds, institutions, and benefactions created by Jews to improve the welfare of blacks would take a sizable volume.

The rise of anti-Semitism, the burning of dozens of black churches in the South, the growth of racist militias, various extremist movements, and innumerable hate groups, constitute a challenge to complacency, underscoring the urgency of understanding the nature of the "race problem." When that has been done, and more has been done than said, we may simultaneously proceed to the re-education of education, for what we have today that passes for education, is not education, but instruction, the technologization of education, a world in which we congratulate ourselves on making machines that think like human beings, mindless of the fact that for some time we have been creating human beings who think like machines. Until we understand that, and understand what needs to be done, we shall go on muddling through till we have exterminated ourselves, for we have become the most self-destructive species on this earth.

In 1920 H. G. Wells, in his magnificent work *The Outline of History,* remarked that "Human history becomes more and more a race between education and catastrophe."[22]

Since Wells wrote those words they have become even more apposite to our own times. I shall have more to say on that throughout this volume.

The unprincipled leaders of Serbia in 1991, in what has come to be known as the Yugoslav War, following the example of Hitler have, in the name of what they called "ethnic cleansing," committed the most unspeakable crimes against the Croat and Muslim populations of Bosnia and Herzegovina. Their "ethnic cleansing," which represented an extreme Nationalistic racism, permitted the Serbs to expel and massacre Croats and Muslims from Serb controlled areas, in the course of which they created some three million homeless refugees, all of them affected by the same vicious racism.

In November 1995 the Institute of Race Relations (London) published in its *European-Race Bulletin* a digest of reports on the rise of racism in thirty European countries.[23]

Clearly the demonology of "race," in its various forms, is very much with us elsewhere in the world, but no more so than in the United States. That being so it was thought that a new edition of *Man's Most Dangerous Myth* might be useful. Added to that, a number of anthropological friends felt that the book was of historic importance; and because a new generation of readers would relish savoring something of the flavor of the book that wrought some change in the thinking of anthropologists, as well as in the minds of various others, the call for a new edition seemed to be plausible. I have tried to bring the book up-to-date, and have retained most of the references which figured in the fifth edition. Some of them may appear to be out-of-date, but in fact very few, if any, of them are, for they refer to works which were built on solid ground. Bringing the book up-to-date meant casting a very wide net over the relevant literature, as the expanded bibliography will testify.

One of the great problems is that so much valuable research, discussion, debate, and works on "race" and "racism" exists—not by any means a surfeit, but in such numbers in quality so high and enlightening that it is quite impossible to read more than a fraction of them. So I take this opportunity to apologize to all those authors whose works I have been unable to read, and reference, much as I would have wished to. Time, alas, is the enemy and wounds us with its days. In any event I hope the bibliography, available in the unabridged edition, will be of use to the reader.

For the rest, the making of this new edition has been a great and refreshing, as well as a challenging adventure. I hope the reader may find the book so too.

Ashley Montagu
Princeton, New Jersey
September 1997

Notes

1. George W. Stocking, *Victorian Anthropology* (New York: The Free Press, 1987).

2. Arthur Keith, *Race and Nationality* (The Boyle Lecture, 1919), 17; Arthur Keith, *A New Theory of Human Evolution* (London: Watts, 1948).

3. Karl Pearson, *The Life, Letters and Labours of Francis Galton,* 3 vols in 4 (Cambridge: Cambridge University Press, 1914–1930).

4. Pearson, Karl, *The Grammar of Science* (London: Walter Scott, 1892), Final revised edition, (London: J. M. Dent, 1937).

5. Egon S. Pearson, *Karl Pearson: An Appreciation of Some Aspects of his Life and Work* (Cambridge: University Press, 1938).

6. Karl Pearson, and Margaret Moul, "The Problem of Alien Immigration into Great Britain, Illustrated by an Examination of Russian and Polish Children," *Annals of Eugenics,* vol. 1 (1925): 5–91, 126–7.

7. This was the period when Oxford and Cambridge were referred to as seminaries of the Church of England. It was not until 1871 that an Act of Parliament was passed abolishing the requirement to subscribe to any article or formulary of faith before reading for a degree.

8. Karl Pearson, *The Grammar of Science* (Everyman edition), 310.

9. Alice James, *The Diary of Alice James,* edited by Leon Edel (New York: Dodd, Mead, 1964), 88.

10. Patricia James, *Thomas Malthus: His Life and Times,* (London: Routledge & Kegan Paul, 1979), 130 sq.; [Joseph Townsend], *A Dissertation on the Poor Laws: By a Well-Wisher to Mankind* (London: C. Dilly, 1786). Reprinted with Foreword by Ashley Montagu. and Afterword by Clark Neuman (Berkeley: University of California Press, 1971).

11. Clive Turnbull, *Black War: The Extermination of the Tasmanian Aborigines* (Melbourne: F. W. Cheshire, 1948); Lyndall Ryan, *The Aboriginal Tasmanians* (Vancouver: University of British Columbia Press, 1953); H. Ling Roth, *The Aborigines of Tasmania* (Halifax, England, F. King & Sons, 1899); Alfred W. Crosby, Jr., *The Columbian Exchange: Biological and Cultural Consequences of 1492* (Westport, CT: Greenwood, 1972), Robert Hughes, *The Fatal Shore: The Epic of Australia's Founding*

(New York: Alfred A. Knopf, 1987); Alan Moorhead, *The Fatal Impact: An Account of the Invasion of the South Pacific* 1767–1840 (New York: Harper & Row, 1966); W. H. R. Rivers, ed., *Essays on the Depopulation of Melanesia* (Cambridge: Cambridge University Press, 1922); Lloyd Robson, *A History of Tasmania* (Melbourne: Oxford University Press, 1983); C. D. Rowley, *The Destruction of Aboriginal Society*, vol. 1 (Canberra: Australian National University Press, 1970); C. D. Rowley, *Outcasts in White Australia*, vol. 2 (Canberra: Australian National University Press, 1971); C. D. Rowley, *The Remote Aborigines*, vol. 3 (Canberra: Australian National University Press, 1971); Gary Witherspoon, *Language and Art in the Navajo Universe* (Ann Arbor: University of Michigan Press, 1977).

   12. Louis L. Snyder, *World War II*, Academic American Encyclopedia, vol. 29 (Danbury, CT 1996), 280.

   13. Theodosius Dobzhansky, and Ashley Montagu, "Natural Selection and the Mental Capacities of Mankind," *Science* 105 (1947): 587–90.

   14. Ashley Montagu, *The Direction of Human Development*, 2nd ed. (New York: Hawthorn Books, 1970); Geoffrey Cowley, "It's Time to Rethink Nature and Nurture," *Newsweek*, 27 March 1955, 52–53.

   15. Peter L. Berger, and Thomas Luckmann, *The Social Construction of Reality: A Treatise in the Sociology of Knowledge* (London: Penguin Press 1967).

   16. Stephen Ullmann, "The Prism of Language," *The Listener* (London), 22 July 1954, 131–132.

   17. Julian S. Huxley, and Alfred C. Haddon, *We Europeans: A Survey of "Racial" Problems* (New York: Harper & Bros. 1936).

   18. Lancelot Hogben, "The Concept of Race," in his book *Genetic Principles in Medicine and Social Science* (London: Williams & Norgate, 1931), 122–124.

   19. Franz Boas, *The Mind of Primitive Man* (New York: Macmillan, 1911, 1924, 1938); Franz Boas, *Race, Language and Culture* (Macmillan, 1940).

   20. J. H. Oldham, *Christianity and the Race Problem* (London: Student Christian Movement, 1925).

   21. David L. Lewis, *W. E. B. Du Bois: Biography of a Race* (New York: Henry Holt, 1993).

   22. H. G. Wells, *The Outline of History* (London: Newnes, 1920).

   23. Institute of Race Relations (London): *European Race Audit Bulletin No. 16*, November 1995.

1

The Origin of the Concept of Race

The idea of "race" represents one of the most dangerous myths of our time, and one of the most tragic. Myths are most effective and perilous when they remain unrecognized for what they are. Many of us are happy in the complacent belief that myths are what uncivilized people believe in, but of which we ourselves are completely free. We may realize that a myth is a faulty explanation leading to social delusion and error, but we do not necessarily realize that we ourselves share in the mythmaking faculty with all people of all times and places, or that each of us has his own store of myths derived from the traditional stock of the society in which we live, and are always in ready supply. In earlier days we believed in magic, possession, and exorcism; in good and evil supernatural powers; and until recently we believed in witchcraft. Today many of us believe in race. Race is the witchcraft, the demonology of our time, the means by which we exorcise imagined demoniacal powers among us. It is the contemporary myth, humankind's most dangerous myth, America's Original Sin.[1]

In our own time we have lived to see the myth of race openly adopted by governments as an expedient fiction. Myths perform the double function of serving both as models of and models for cultural attitudes and behavior. Thus myths reflect the beliefs and give sanction to the actions of society, while at the same time providing the forms upon which belief and conduct are molded. Built, as they are, into the structure of social relationships, racial myths often have a force which exceeds even that of reality itself, for such myths, in addition to the social encouragement they receive, draw upon both false biology and even worse theology for their sustenance. As Calas has said, myths are idealizations of social conditions, so that with regard to the matter of inequality, the main function of myths is to explain the origin of differences in ways that satisfy the needs of the group.[2] In short, the functional role of the myth is to provide a sanction for a course of action. Myths that account for social differences correspond to,

41

and often have the force of, legal fictions, while legalistic attempts to justify the status quo endow the myth with an aura of historical sanctity. As such, myths are almost impervious to rational thought, for it is the nature of myth to be elaborated, but never proved. Myths, therefore, are of great value since they make thinking, as a problem-solving exercise, unnecessary.

The monstrous myths that have captured the emotions of people and shackled their minds still afflict the minds of millions in so-called civilized societies. The ambiguities and uncritical use of our language give rise to ambiguities of their own and constitute the compost upon which myths proliferate and are sustained. In the reality of the mythologies which every society creates for itself, the unreal becomes more real than the real, ritual investing them with an importance that renders them sacred. Developing as they do, myths achieve an integrity, a validity, a power, which is quite impregnable to any attempted demonstration of the unreliability of their component parts. We realize that many people have different investments in their beliefs, that humans are governed more by emotion, custom, and precedent, than by logic and reason, that errors and illusions, serving some explanatory purpose, frequently become endemic myths shared in common in the world of unreason and political fantasy. Myths that at one time may have served a socially useful purpose may live on into a time when they have not only become useless, but thoroughly baneful, decayed, degraded, and degrading. As Paul Gaston has said, in his admirable book, *The New South Creed,*

> Myths are not polite euphemisms for falsehoods, but are combinations of images and symbols that reflect a people's way of perceiving truth. Organically related to a fundamental reality of life, they fuse the real and the imaginary into a blend that becomes a reality itself, a force in history.[3]

And as George Tindall put it, charged with values, aspirations, ideals and meanings,

> Myths may become the ground for either loyalty and defense on the one hand or hostility on the other. In such circumstances, a myth itself becomes one of the realities of history, significantly influencing the course of human action, for good or ill. There is, of course, always a danger that in ordering one's vision of reality, the myth may predetermine the categories of perception, rendering one blind to things that do not fit into the mental image.[4]

The function performed by myths is akin to that of religion, namely, the unification and intelligibility of experience. Racism often has its roots in religion, and like religion, can easily be accommodated to many diverse situations.[5]

The belief in race, as in Nazi Germany, became a secular religion whose myths recreated reality. The systematic murder of millions of human beings in the name of race was the final expression of the hideously brutal power of racial myths, of demonological mindedness.

The power of myths and their related ideologies lies not in their objective truth but in their being perceived as true. Of the myth of race it may be said that everyone seems to know, and is only too eager to tell. All but a few persons take it completely for granted that scientists have established the "facts" about race and have long ago satisfactorily recognized and classified the races of humankind. Scientists in the past did little to discourage this view, and, indeed, in most cases were even more wrongheaded than the layman on the subject. Exalted in their citadels of infallibility, scientists by their consensus gave security and comfort to those who believed in a hierarchy of races. Under such circumstances, it is not difficult to understand why so many people continue to believe that race is a reality, a fact, that some "races" are superior to others.

A scientific fact has been defined as a collective judgment of a specialized community. But the collective judgment of the specialized community of anthropologists during the nineteenth, and well into the twentieth, century was abysmally wrong concerning the "fact" of race. For this the scientists who subscribed to the concept of race cannot be faulted, for it was a product of a social environment which, through the distorting glass of prejudice, saw people divided by caste and class, and segregated by race. In a society that segregated people by caste and class, "race" was the term that categorized the most visibly distinguishable groups of people. As Lancelot Hogben, the eminent social biologist and early critic of the concept of race, remarked in 1932:

> Geneticists believe that anthropologists have decided what a race is. Ethnologists assume that their classifications embody principles which genetic science has proved to be correct. Politicians believe that their prejudices have the sanction of genetic laws and the findings of physical anthropology to sustain them.[6]

In reality, none of them had any grounds for such beliefs other than those which emanated prejudices.

In some nations, for example in Hitler's Third Reich, the myth of race also functioned as an ideology and continues to do so most prominently in such countries as South Africa, Australia, Brazil, and the United States of America, where it has come to be known as "the great divide."

An ideology is a prescriptive doctrine or system of belief that is not supported by rational argument, and flourishes in an environment of adverse political and social conditions. An ideology often originates with a charismatic leader or elite claiming exclusive authority as representing something like revealed truth; as such, an ideology may determine the lives and conduct of a whole population, providing its members with justifications, conviction, and moral fervor for their actions, regardless of the course of events.[7]

The myth of race refers not to the fact that physically distinguishable populations of humans exist, but rather to the belief that races are populations or peoples whose physical differences are innately linked with significant differences in mental capacities, and that these innate hierarchical differences are measurable by the cultural achievements of such populations, as well as by standardized intelligence (IQ) tests. This belief is thoroughly and dangerously unsound. It is the belief of racists and racism. Caught up in the vicious circle of prejudice, words become things, things become weapons—and the more weapons one has, the more convinced one is of the right to use them. But this is to anticipate.

It was as long ago as 1848 that John Stuart Mill wrote, in his *Principles of Political Economy*, "Of all the vulgar modes of escaping from the consideration of the effect of social and moral influences on the human mind, the most vulgar is that of attributing the diversities of conduct and character to inherent natural differences."[8] And even more forcibly, twenty-five years later in 1873, in his *Autobiography*, Mill wrote,

> I have long felt that the prevailing tendency to regard all the marked distinctions of human character as innate, and in the main indelible, and to ignore the irresistible proofs that by far the greater part of those differences, whether between individuals, races, or sexes, are such as not only might but naturally would be produced by differences in circumstances, is one of the chief hindrances to the rational treatment of great social questions, and one of the greatest stumbling blocks to the human improvement.[9]

Another political economist, Walter Bagehot, in 1869, similarly wrote: "When a philosopher cannot account for anything in any other manner, he boldly ascribes it to an occult quality in some race."[10]

Writing in 1915, Lord Bryce, author of *The American Commonwealth*, put the matter clearly: "No branches of historical inquiry," he wrote,

> have suffered more from fanciful speculation than those which relate to the origin and attributes of the races of mankind. The differentiation of these races began in prehistoric darkness, and the more obscure a subject is, so much the more fascinating. Hypotheses are tempting, because though it may be impossible to verify them, it is, in the paucity of data, almost equally impossible to refute them.[11]

Such views in the course of the years have had their effects, but nothing like the effect that the persisting myth of race has had upon the ignorant and the ill-educated. Taking it for granted that different populations could be classified into distinct groups—so-called "races"—anthropologists, on the basis of such differences as head shape, hair form, skin color, and similar traits drew up long lists of races. It was a game the classifiers played in all seriousness as if it were anything other than the postprandial indulgence it was, and the compilations of races that resulted numbered from half a dozen to two hundred.[12] Though taken seriously for a time were, these lists were ultimately a complete failure, primarily because they were based on a fundamental misconception of the nature and variability—and intractability—of the materials they attempted to put into some kind of order.

It was easy to see that an African black and a blonde Swede must have had a somewhat different biological history, and the difference in appearance considered sufficient to distinguish them as belonging to two different races. In biology a "race" has been customarily defined as a subdivision of a species that inherits physical characteristics distinguishing it from other populations of the species. By that definition then, do not "Blacks" and Swedes belong to different races? The answer, as we shall see, is that even in terms of the biological definition, they do not.

Is there a "black" race, or a Swedish race? There is not, any more than that there is a "white" race, a "yellow" race, or a "red" race. Both "black" and "Swede" are collective terms which lump together groups and individuals who differ from each other in physical and often in cultural traits. Furthermore, the variability in physical traits *within* any population is usually greater than it is *between* populations, while even more interesting and significant is the strikingly small number of gene differences between such populations, a fact evident in the gradational or climal variability which characterizes the populations of humankind.

For example, Richard Lewontin, professor of genetics at Harvard University, has carried out a most important investigation of genetic diversity in the human species. Taking the blood groups and various enzymatic traits for which the genetics is known, by means of a mathematical-genetic analysis Lewontin found that the mean proportion was 85.4 percent. The difference between populations within a race accounted for less than 8.3 percent, so that only 6.3 percent is accounted for by racial classification. Lewontin concludes,

> It is clear that our perception of relatively large differences between human races and subgroups, as compared to the variation within these groups, is indeed a biased perception and that, based on randomly chosen genetic differences, human races and populations are remarkably

similar to each other, with the largest part by far of human variation being accounted for by the differences between individuals.

Human racial classification is of no social value and is positively destructive of social and human relations. Since such racial classification is now seen to be of virtually no genetic or taxonomic significance either, no justification can be offered for its continuance.[13]

Such facts render the concept of race and the continuance of race classification erroneous and obsolescent—important subjects we shall discuss in detail. For such reasons, among others, modern biologists find that the use of the concept of race should be discontinued.[14]

The truth is that the "deceptively clear label," as Lucien Febvre called the concept of race,[15] obscures and renders divisible what is indivisible. This is not to say that there are no genetic or physical differences between various populations, but it is to say that they are by no means as large or significant as most scientists once supposed. Misleading simplifications embodied in word-labels, especially when they are given the respectability of long-usage and established authority, tend to be accepted uncritically, and do not constitute a substitution for critical examination and. We must constantly be on our guard against subscribing to a lexicon of unsound terms of which we elect ourselves the guardians, and make ourselves the prisoners of our own vocabularies.

In the biological sense there do, of course, exist distinctive human populations that exhibit an interesting variety of physical differences. These differences are superficial, and far fewer in number than the traits we have in common. It is well to remember that what makes us alike is very much more important than what makes us different. In a racist society which segregates people by race and divides them by class, in which exclusiveness is the unstated rule, it is not surprising that the classifiers would, often without being aware of it, bring their class-structured ways of thinking to the classifications of the "races of mankind." The consciousness of class and classificatory schemes were closely related. Embedded in this, of course was the tacit assumption that with the biological ranking there naturally went a socio-cultural grading, which combined with the physical ranking, from "high" to "low," or superiority to inferiority, enabled one to assign populations and individuals to their "proper" levels. "The higher races" were "superior," and "the lower races" were "inferior." In this way was established the basic axiom of physical anthropology, namely, the belief that distinctive human characteristics and abilities are determined by race, a view that was and is essentially racist. Since the meaning of a word is the action it produces, this was racism.

Racism is conduct based on the belief that physical and behavioral differences characterizing individual members of different groups or populations are determined by genetic, that is, innate factors, and that these differences enable one to rank each individual and group in the scale of humanity according to the attributed predefined values of those differences. The implication is that in such individuals and groups the genes that are supposed to determine their physical traits, such as skin color, hair form, head shape, and the like, are linked with the genes that determine the qualities and limits of their mental capacities or abilities, and that linked with these traits is the ability of the population or group to achieve a high level of civilization. Thus, three criteria are involved in the racist view: (1) physical traits, (2) mental capacities and abilities, and (3) the ability to achieve a high level of civilization. To put it briefly, the racist believes that physical characteristics, capacity, and creativity, are genetically related, fixed and unchangeable. He may never have formulated his belief in these words but in this own mind, however, vaguely this is what it amounted to.

This is the triad that constitutes the basic belief of the racist, and it is entirely unsound, for there is absolutely no genetic linkage between genes for physical traits, mental capacities, or civilization-building abilities. As we shall see, human beings are born everywhere with potentialities or capacities which must be stimulated and guided by learning if they are to become abilities. A capacity is a potentiality. An ability is a trained capacity. Allowing for individual differences existing in every population, the full range of abilities that has been developed in any society—given the same opportunities for development—is within the capability of every human population, for educability is the species trait of humanity. What human beings have learned to do in any culture, human beings can anywhere learn. We shall discuss these matters more fully in later pages.

Here it should be pointed out that the very word "race" is itself a racist term not simply because it represents a congeries of errors, or that it is a spurious "reality" with no objective existence, but in addition, and most importantly, because its baleful influence constitutes a threat to the very existence of humanity, much of which has already vanished as a direct result of racism. In a large number of cases it has led to wars and unjustifiable conquests, costing the lives of many millions, and the destruction of untold numbers together with their cultures in their own homelands. Such destructive conduct continues to the present day in North and South America, Australia, Africa, India, Sri Lanka, Ethiopia, the Middle East, the Philippines, in Poland, the Balkans, and the former USSR, now Russia and the independent republics of Eastern Europe and Northern Asia.

To summarize then, humankind may be regarded as comprising of a number of populations or peoples the members of which often differ physically and superficially from one another. These differences have come about as a result of the long isolation of such populations during which the physical differences have evolved. The cultural differences have come about as the result of differences in the history of experience to which each population has adaptively responded. Both the physical and the cultural differences are neither fixed nor permanent, but are subject to change. We see this occurring very rapidly when boundaries that formerly separated people are reduced and populations come into contact. In spite of occasional appearances to the contrary, humanity is moving toward unity without uniformity, toward the condition in which the differences that today separate humanity will be regarded as points of interest and value, not as excuses for fear and discrimination, but as no more important than the differences which separate the members of the same family.

The classificatory definition of humanity as *Homo sapiens,* properly interpreted, is appropriate because it gives quite accurate status to a unique class of creatures—human beings—characterized by an educability, a capacity for wisdom and intelligence approached by no other creature. These traits, *not* the external physical traits constitute the principal, the distinctive qualities, that make *Homo sapiens* human. When human beings are defined on the basis of the differences in physical traits we narrow the definition of their humanity. And that is, perhaps, the most telling criticism of the concept of race.

It is not that the classifiers of race were uninfluenced by their awareness of the cultural status of the groups they were classifying, ostensibly on the basis of their physical characters, for they could hardly have avoided introducing their prejudices when comparing the physical traits of "primitive" peoples with those of "civilized" peoples.

Even the term "civilized" has become a racist term because it has acquired the meaning that "civilized" people are superior, more advanced, than uncivilized peoples, that the "scale" of being is yet another racist term, for what it represents is a survival of a time when animals and humans were arranged on "the scale of nature" on the rungs of a ladder with the "higher" occupying the "highest," and the lower occupying the "lowest" position. All the peoples of Western Europe are arbitrarily bracketed with the same loosely-termed "Caucasoid major group," and the populational variability within this group simply represents small local differences arising from their circumscribed inbreeding or crossbreeding with members of adjacent populations. In Eastern Europe, among the Slavic-speaking peoples, the influence of "Mongoloid" admixture is to this day discernible in a number of them, even those far removed from the geographic habitat of the "Mongoloids." But this admixture does not make such Slavic-speaking peoples members of a distinct race. In Russia and in Poland, as in America, there are many different local types of men, but the majority of these belong to the white or "Caucasoid major group" of humans.

In Russia and Poland some are more or less obviously of Mongoloid origin, and in America some are clearly of black origin, but in both countries it is often difficult to say whether a person is of one major group or another. It is frequently just such difficulties as these that render it impossible to make the sort of racial classifications some anthropologists and others have attempted.[16] The fact is that all human beings are so much mixed with regard to origin that between different groups of individuals intergradation and "overlapping" of physical traits is the rule. It is for this reason, among others, that it is difficult to draw up more than a few hard and fast distinctions between even the most extreme types. As Huxley and Haddon have remarked,

> The essential reality of the existing situation . . . is not the hypothetical sub-species or races, but the mixed ethnic groups, which can never be genetically purified into their original components, or purged of the variability which they owe to past crossing. Most anthropological writings of the past and many of the present fail to take account of this fundamental fact.[17]

We may describe *ethnic group* here as follows: An ethnic group represents part of a population in process of undergoing genetic and socially, genetically unrelated, cultural differentiation, it is a group of individuals capable of hybridizing genetically and culturally with other groups to produce further genetic and cultural differentiation.

The classifiers of the races of mankind who have devised the various classificatory schemes during the past hundred years have mostly agreed in one respect—they have unexceptionally taken for granted the one thing which they were attempting to prove, namely, the existence of human races. Commencing with the assumption that "extreme" *types* of humankind, such as "Negro," "White," and "Mongol," could clearly be recognized as races, they proceeded to refine these grosser classifications by attempting to fit local groups of humans into similar racial schemes. Thus, to take a striking example, the late Professor Carleton Coon in his monumental two volumes *The Origin of Races* (1962) and *The Living Races of Man* (1965), created a large number of new European races and subraces upon the basis, principally, of slight differences in the physical traits of the head exhibited by different groups of Europeans, and this in spite of the fact that it has been repeatedly shown that the form of the head is not as constant a character as was at one time supposed.[18] It is true that some biologists have seen fit to create new subraces among lower animals on the basis of such single slight characters as differences in pigmentation of the hair on a part of the tail. Such a procedure would be perfectly justifiable if it were taxonomically helpful. Nor would it be necessary to stipulate that animals in other groups shall not exhibit this character, but one would have to insist that almost all members of one or both sexes of the new subrace shall exhibit it. No such requirement is fulfilled by the races and subraces that Coon created.[19] Coon simply assumed that within any group a certain numerical preponderance of heads of specified diameters and, let us say, noses of a certain form and individuals of a certain stature, are sufficient to justify the creation of a new race or "subrace." Few biologists would consider such a procedure justifiable, and there are few anthropologists who would. Yet this kind of overzealous taxonomy, which has its origin principally in the desire to force facts to fit preexisting theories, does not even require the sanction of facts to be put forward as such. In this sense the concept of race represents one of the worst examples we know of a viewpoint which from the outset begs the whole question. Anderson[20] has offered a practical example, which is quite typical of the way in which populations have in the past been classified by rule of thumb or authority in the most arbitrary manner. The Sami, a "Caucasoid" people, formerly referred to as Lapps, have for almost two centuries been forced into the mythical status of "Mongoloids," because in 1795, the father of physical anthropology, Johann Gottfried Blumenbach, said that they belonged to "the Mongolian variety."[21]

As Anderson remarks,

> In this day when scientists are entering precipitously into world council chambers, the history of Lapp racial classification reminds us anew that even venerable conclusions or the opinions of experts may be no more than scientific myths, perhaps useful in the development of ideas, but irresponsible bases for policy or administration.[22]

The very failure of ambitious anthropological attempts at classification strongly suggests that human populations do not, in fact, exist in anything like the embodiment the classifiers have given them. Indeed, all such attempts have been defeated by the intractability of the variability they sought to discipline.

For the purposes of convenience in referring to aggregates of humankind characterized by a relatively high frequency of distinctive physical traits, it has been the custom to refer to "Blacks," "Whites" or "Caucasoids," and "Mongoloids." These aggregates have been called "major groups," and in so calling them there has been no implication of a hierarchic difference in either physical or mental capacities. However, because the term "major" suggests some sort of superiority, it is better to use the term "extended," which rather more closely approaches the reality, for the extended groups are widely distributed and do not constitute an assemblage occupying a common territory. The populations that are part of the extended groups are best referred to as *ethnic groups*.[23]

The use of the term "extended group" is purely arbitrary and is merely calculated to indicate that the likenesses in certain traits exhibited by the members of some populations appear to link them in some respects more closely than to other populations. Nothing more is implied in the term than that.

Within the four extended groups of humans there exist many local types, but most of these local types are much mixed, so that only in a relatively small number of cases is it possible to distinguish distinctive local types or ethnic groups among them. Every honest attempt to discuss such types or ethnic groups within the larger parent groups or major groups deserves the fullest encouragement.

Truth will not be advanced by denying the existence of large population groups characterized, more or less, by distinctive inherited physical traits. Such physical differences are found in geographic and genetic populations of animals and plants in a state of nature, and in many varieties of domestic animals and cultivated plants. They are, to a certain extent, also found in the human species, but in a much more fluid condition, since human biological development and diversification has proceeded upon quite different lines from that of animals and plants. With the exception of the domesticated animals and plants, few if any other living forms have had a comparable history of migration and hybridization, and this is the fundamentally important fact to be remembered when comparisons are made between humans and other living forms. Not one of the "major groups" is unmixed, nor is any one of its ethnic groups pure; all are, indeed, much mixed and of exceedingly complex descent. Nor is there any scientific justification for overzealous or emotional claims that any one of them is in any way superior to another.

As Darwin put it a century ago,

> Although the existing races of man differ in many respects, as in color, hair, shape of skull, proportions of the body, &c., yet if their whole structure be taken into consideration they are found to resemble each other closely in a multitude of points. Many of these are of so unimportant or of so singular a nature, that it is extremely improbable that they should have been independently acquired by aboriginally distinct species or races. The same remark holds good with equal or greater force with respect to the numerous points of mental similarity between the most distinct races of man.[24]

The differences between the four extended groups of humans and between the ethnic groups they comprise merely represent a distribution of variations which, for reasons that may be fairly clearly understood, occur more frequently in one group than they do in another. We shall deal with these reasons later. Laughlin, who uses the term "race" as a synonym for population, points out that such populations are simply groups between which restricted gene flow has taken place.[25]

It has already been stated that in biological usage a race has been conceived as a subdivision of a species that inherits the physical characteristics serving to distinguish it from other populations of the species. In the genetic sense a race has been defined as a population that differs in the incidence of certain genes from other populations, one or more genes of which it is exchanging or is potentially capable of exchanging across whatever boundaries (usually geographical) that may separate them.[26] If we are asked whether in this sense there exist a fair number of ethnic groups in the human species, the answer is that there do. It is, however, more than questionable whether such a narrow definition of an ethnic group can be profitably employed in relation to humankind. Furthermore, this is not the sense in which racists and many race classifiers employ the term. For them race represents a unity of physical, mental, personality, and cultural traits which determines the behavior of the individuals inheriting this alleged interconnection. Nowhere was this false creed of the racist more exploited than in Nazi Germany from 1933 to 1945, with fatal consequences for millions of human beings.

The foundation upon which the Nazi view of humanity was based was the concept of race. Let us see, as a typical example, what a leading exponent of Nazi "race science," Dr. Lothar G. Tirala, had to say upon this subject. Writing in 1935, he begins by asserting that it is "a well-grounded view that it is highly probable that different human races originated independently of one another and that they evolved out of different species of ape-men. The so-called main races of mankind are not races, but species."[27] Far from being "well-grounded," this is a view which no biologist and no anthropologist with whom I am familiar would accept.[28] It was generally agreed then as it is today that all humans belong to the same species, that all were probably derived from the same ancestral stock, and that all share in a common heritage.

Dr. Tirala's principal argument was that "the voice of blood and race operates down to the last refinements of thought and exercises a decisive influence on the direction of thought." Hence, "race science" proves that there exist irreconcilable differences in soul, mind, and blood between the numerous races which German "race scientists" have recognized. And, of course, that the German, or "Aryan," race was "superior," the "master race." Precisely similar views were expounded by a well-known German anthropologist in a work published in 1951.[29]

As early as 1931 Ludwig Schemann, professor of physical anthropology at the University of Freiburg put the matter very simply when he wrote that "race defines a definite physical type which is common to a larger national and tribal circle of men, and maintains itself by hereditary descent . . . Race is the alpha and omega of the life of nations in its entirety."[30]

In an article, published in 1939, entitled "Race: A Basic Concept in Education," Alfred Baeumler, a leading Nazi "philosopher," clearly presented the racist conception of the individual. "History," he wrote,

> has shown, and daily shows anew, that man can be trained to be nothing that he is not genuinely, and from the beginning, in the depths of his being; against this law, neither precept, warning, punishment, nor any other environmental influence avails. Realism in the study of man does not lie in attributing evil tendencies to him, but in recognizing that all that man can do emerges in the last resort from himself, from his innate qualities.[31]

Herr Baeumler modestly describes this as thinking "Copernically" when most others so far as such matters are concerned are still thinking "Ptolemaically"—an unfortunate slip on the part of Herr Baeumler, in view of the fact that Copernicus belonged to an allegedly "subhuman race," for Copernicus was Polish.

In 1933 the professor of New Testament at the University of Tubingen, Gerhard Kittel, welcomed National Socialism as "a renewal movement based on a Christian moral foundation," an antidote to the decadence and immorality of the Weimar republic. In a public lecture he delivered on "The Jewish Question," Kittel defended Hitler's anti-Semitic legislation, on the ground, among other things, that the Scriptures themselves teach such rejection. By rejecting Christ the Jews had themselves incurred rejection.[32]

Divine sanction for "purity of race" was most forcefully expressed by Hitler's fanatical Christian supporters, the Deutsch Christen, who described race, nationality, and nation, as "orders of life given and entrusted to us by God." God's law required them to resist all admixture, "the danger of racial mixture and bastardization."

The Nazi view of race, in all its starkness, could not have been more succinctly described than in a thesis by Hans Puvogel in 1936. In his discussion of the precepts of the Nazi Party, Puvogel wrote,

> The guideline for German criminal law in the future is recognizing the idea of race, which is the basis of the National Socialist conception of life.
>
> An individual's worth in the community is measured by his racial personality. Only a racially valuable person has a right to exist within the community. Someone who is useless for the community because of his inferiority, or even harmful to it, is to be eliminated.[33]

There is a certain irony in the fact that in later years, under Hitler, Hans Puvogel became the Justice Minister of the State of Lower Saxony, and did not resign his post until March 1978, on the grounds that although he had "no Nazi past," he did not wish to embarrass West Germany's Christian Democratic Party.

A new twist was added to the idea of race by Señor Perón, the dictator of Argentina. On 12 October 1947, in a speech on the "Day of Race," he put Argentina right on the side of Torquemada. On that occasion he said:

> For us, race is not a biological concept. For us, it is something spiritual. It constitutes a sum of the imponderables that make us what we are and impel us to be what we should be, through our origin and through our destiny. It is that which dissuades us from falling into the imitation of other communities whose natures are foreign to us. For us, race constitutes our personal seal, indefinable and irrefutable.

Lest it be thought that these mystical and mythical conceptions of race are a peculiarity of the Germans, we may turn to what a Greek professor of anthropology, John Koumaris, wrote in a respected English anthropological journal in the year 1948.

> The Greek race has almost uniform physical characteristics, physical and psychical, inherited in its descendants, it has all the characteristics of the basic elements, which are all Greek and indigenous in spite of the variety of types. If the British, for instance, with their various nuclei, form one race,[34] the Greeks have a greater right to be so considered. This race is distinguished today by a kind of 'fluid constancy,' with its own soul and especially with its own variety, dating from prehistoric times. Races exist and will continue to exist; and each one defends itself. Because every infusion of new 'blood' is something different and because children of mixed parents belong to no race, the Greek race, as all others, has to preserve its own 'fluid constancy' by avoiding mixture with foreign elements.
>
> The Greek race was formed under the Acropolis Rock, and it is impossible for any other to keep the keys of the sacred rock, to which the Greek Soul is indissolubly linked.[35]

The racist views presented in the above sampling represent those held by untold numbers of every kind, and with varying degrees of virulence are to be encountered in almost every civilized land in the world.

In America discrimination against Blacks is of long standing. No American needs to be told that racism is scarcely moribund in the United States. He may, however, be surprised to learn that at the present day there are in the United States over one thousand organizations, more than one hundred of them on a national basis, whose declared purpose is the suppression of "foreigners." In addition there are a large number of hate groups that operate out of private homes and are secretly organized, and others that are actively violent and dangerous.[36]

In the legislatures of the United States there has been a long tradition of actively open and clandestine racist members. The truth is, of course, that racism is endemic in the United States, and affects every one of its institutions, including its churches, which have a shameful record in their failure to speak out against racism, even when their own ministers were actively promoting it.[37] The demonological mindedness of the average American remains a psychosis and an outrage, the social costs of which are beyond calculation.

American writers such as Lothrop Stoddard, Madison Grant, Henry Fairfield Osborn, Ruggles Gates, Henry Garrett, and Carleton Putnam have freely espoused racist views of the most reactionary kind. Osborn, in his preface to Madison Grant's widely read book, *The Passing of the Great Race* (1921), writes,

> Race has played a far larger part than either language or nationality in moulding the destinies of men; race implies heredity, and heredity implies all the moral, social, and intellectual characteristics and traits which are the springs of politics and government.[38]

By the simple device of identifying biological traits with cultural or social traits, Osborn was able to make "hereditary" the carrier and determinant of both. As Chorover has said of sociobiologists,

> When they attempt to 'explain' why people behave in a certain way, they do not generally examine the structure of their own society but rather make an effort to graft selected patterns of behavior onto a biological core. In this way the selected pattern can be made to appear as if it results not from modifiable social conditions but from fixed biological causes. The effect of such 'explanations', of course, is implicitly to justify a given form of behavior by locating its origins outside the social order.[39]

Endlessly shuffled and reshuffled, the typical statement of the racist position is that something called "race" is the prime determiner of all the important traits of body and soul, of character and personality, of human beings and nations. And it is further alleged that this thing called "race" is a fixed and unchangeable part of the germ plasm, which, transmitted from generation to generation, unfolds in each people as a characteristic expression of personality and culture.

The gallery of race concepts set out above has no basis in scientific or any other kind of demonstrable fact; these concepts are compounded of socially acquired muddy myth—the tragic myth of our era. Tragic, because it is believed and made the basis for action, in one way or another, by so many people in our time. It is principally this idea of race that is examined in the following pages.

The modern understanding of race owes its widespread diffusion mainly to the white man. Wherever he has gone he has carried it with him. The rise of racism as an endemic disorder is associated with slavery and the growing opposition to it, so that it is not until the second half of the eighteenth century that one begins to encounter its development. This is not to say that discrimination against persons or groups on the basis of skin color or difference did not exist in the ancient world. There is plenty of evidence that it did.[40] But it is to say that such views never became the officially established doctrine, upon any large scale, of any ancient society.

The ancient Egyptians considered foreigners to be rustic and uninitiated, and indeed, distinguished between themselves as "men" and Libyans or Asiatics or Africans. Not that foreigners were not human, but the Egyptian simply considered himself more human than others. However, as John A. Wilson makes clear,

> The Egyptian isolationist or nationalist feeling was a matter of geography and of manners rather than of racial theory and dogmatic xenophobia. 'The people' were those who lived in Egypt, without distinction of race or color. Once a foreigner came to reside in Egypt, learned to speak the language, and adopted Egyptian dress, he might finally be accepted as one of 'the people' and was no longer the object of superior ridicule.[41]

Libyans, Asiatics, Africans, foreigners of every kind, once they had become acculturated, could obtain Egyptian citizenship and achieve the highest positions. Indeed, they might rise to the most elevated position of all, that of the god-king who possessed the nation.[42]

Caste and class differences certainly were made the basis for discrimination in many societies, and in ancient Greece some attempt was even made to find a biological foundation for such discrimination, but this was of a limited nature and never gained general acceptance.[43] When, in the fourth century, the institution of slavery in Greece began increasingly to come under attack, it fell to Aristotle to develop the necessary theoretical bases upon which to justify its existence. His justification consists of nothing but the most ill-founded rationalizations, and shows Aristotle—as it does every man, when he rationalizes—at his weakest. The slave, Aristotle argued in the *Politics*, was but a partial man, lacking the governing element of the soul and therefore needed to be ruled by those possessing this element. In short, that some men were more fitted by nature to be slaves than others.[44]

Before Aristotle, Plato had deliberately proposed a piece of disingenuous fiction concerning the innate differences existing between men, calculated to convince the workers that there were people who by nature were better qualified to rule than they.[45] But this "Phoenician lie," as Plato called it, failed to germinate.[46] Most serious scholars are agreed that, with the exception of the lone Aristotle, while the Greeks affected to despise the barbarian, they did so on purely cultural grounds, never on biological ones.[47] The Greeks, indeed, as Isocrates (436–338 B.C.) put it, thought of Hellenism as a thing of the spirit rather than of race. "So far," he wrote, "has Athens distanced the rest of mankind in thought and in speech that her pupils have become the teachers of the rest of the world; and she has brought it about that the name 'Hellenes' is applied rather to those who share our culture than to those who share a common blood."[48] Menander (342–291 B.C.), the Attic poet and playwright, put the general feeling thus: "For me no man who is good is a foreigner. The same nature have we all, and it is character that makes men kin."

The Greeks, as also the Romans, were singularly free of anything resembling race prejudice.[49] The Roman view was succinctly put by Terrence (ca. 195–150 B.C.) the writer of comedies who had been a slave. Borrowing from Menander he wrote in a play *The Self Tormentor:* "I am a man: nothing human is alien to me." For the modern racist that sentiment takes the form of a complete turnabout, "I am a man: nothing alien is human to me."

A study of both ancient and recent cultures and literatures shows us that the conception that there are natural or biological races of humankind that differ from one another mentally as well as physically is an idea that was not developed until the latter part of the eighteenth century. In this connection, Lord Bryce, after surveying conditions in the ancient world, the Middle Ages, and modern times up to the French Revolution, arrived at the following conclusions, which he regarded as broadly true. The survey of the facts, he wrote,

> has shown us that down till the days of the French Revolution there had been very little in any country, or at any time, of self-conscious racial feeling . . . however much men of different races may have striven with one another, it was seldom any sense of racial opposition that caused their strife. They fought for land. They plundered one another. . . . But strong as patriotism and national feeling might be, they did not think of themselves in terms of ethnology, and in making war for every other sort of reason never made it for the sake of imposing their own type of civilization. . . . In none of such cases did the thought of racial distinctions come to the front.[50]

The justification and divine sanction for slavery appear with the very year of its European birth. Gomes Eannes de Azurara, in his *Chronicle of the Discovery and Conquest of Guinea* (1453), for example, after commenting on the "happy" condition of the kidnapped Africans, writes,

> And so their lot was not quite contrary to what it had been; since before they had lived in perdition of soul and body; of their souls, in that they were yet pagans, without the clearness and the light of holy faith; and of

their bodies, in that they lived like beasts, without any custom of reasonable beings—for they had no knowledge of bread or wine, and they were without the covering of clothes, or the lodgement of houses; and worse than all, through the great ignorance that was in them, in that they had no understanding of good, but only knew how to live in a bestial sloth.[51]

The black skin of the African was not only ugly, but was also the symbol of moral taint and turpitude. The African was the descendant of Ham, and thus accursed, and designed to be of service to his master, the white man.[52]

Christianity has much to answer for in the development of race prejudice. As Katherine George has pointed out, "Raw nature, 'fallen' nature, which for the Greek was disorder, is for the Christian even worse: it is sin." Far from eliminating the consciousness of class, caste, and other hierarchical divisions, Christianity, she writes, "collaborated with such hierarchies and more frequently than not strengthens instead of weakening them—though it did introduce the complicating idea of a possible restatement of human relations in the society of another world. The availability of salvation to all properly indoctrinated souls alike, despite bodily inequalities" is afforded by Christianity.[53] But does this lessen prejudice? It does not. On the contrary, it extols, as morally virtuous, conduct which is, by any means, designed to bring the pagan and the infidel into the arms of the Church. The justification for slavery then takes the form of the imposition of vassalage upon the savage for the good of his soul. The modern form of race prejudice is in the direct line of descent from this medieval Christian concept of the relation of Christians to their inferiors. In 1740 David Hume, the Scottish philosopher, wrote in his *Treatise on Human Nature:*

> I am apt to suspect all negroes, and in general all other species of men . . . to be naturally inferior to the white. . . . No ingenious manufactures amongst them, no arts, no sciences. . . . Such a uniform and constant difference could not happen, in so many countries and ages, if nature had not made an original distinction between these breeds of men. Not to mention our colonies, there are negro slaves dispersed all over Europe, of which none ever discovered any symptoms of ingenuity.[54]

It was a complacent assumption which Hume shared with many others. "No ingenious manufactures . . . no arts, no sciences." It was as simple as that. And if "symptoms of ingenuity" were occasionally exhibited, they were rare enough to prove the rule. If Hume had ever looked at an African woodcarving he would have called it primitive. Had he listened to the music the slaves had brought with them from Africa he would have branded it barbarous. Had he ever heard a West African Anansi story he would undoubtedly have held it to be childish. A critic has remarked upon the comforting relief afforded the conscience by Hume's speculative observation:

The Negroes were not beasts, but neither were they quite men. They added another link to the Great Chain of Being, strengthening it. They were designed to be subordinates, with faculties proper to their station. They were meant to hew and delve, and the gentleman and his lady need have no qualms as their voices floated in from the fields or up from the kitchen. The British public could go merrily ahead rattling the coins in a full pocket and relishing the taste of sugar. And as for those who had begun agitating on the Negroes' behalf, they could spare themselves the trouble. Were the slaves to be released and hoisted out of their rank, they would quickly drop back again to where they belonged. They simply lacked the innate abilities of the whites.[55]

It is not to be thought that ethnocentrism did not exist before the eighteenth century. It did. As Katherine George has said, "To be born into a culture has generally implied being supported by it, being upheld, as it were, on a pedestal, from which one might look down with varying degrees of disinterest or antagonism upon other, alien cultures."[56] The observer of alien cultures has tended to be prejudiced in favor of his own culture, and to view the alien and unfamiliar as barbaric and inferior. The Greeks divided the world into themselves and barbarians, but with a benevolence that has not been characteristic of later societies.

From the earliest times, the emotional attitude that one's own ethnic group, nation, or culture is superior to others, has been a concomitant of virtually every culture. Within any society, in earlier times, men might be persecuted or made the object of discrimination on the grounds of differences in religion, culture, politics, or class, but never on any biological grounds such as are implied in the idea of racial differences. In Europe during the Middle Ages and also during the Renaissance the Jews, for example, were singled out for discrimination and persecution, but this was always done on social, cultural, or religious grounds. The Jews, it was urged, had killed Christ; they were accused of murdering Christian children and using their blood for ritual purposes; they were infidels, anti-Christians, usurers; they were almost everything under the sun;[57] but whatever was held against them was never attributed to clearly defined biological reasons. The racial interpretation is a modern "discovery." That is the important point to grasp. The objection to any people on racial or biological grounds is virtually a purely modern innovation. That is the basic sense in which modern group antagonism differs from that which prevailed in earlier periods. It is perfectly true that in ancient Rome, as in ancient Greece and elsewhere, the suggestion was sometimes heard that other peoples were more stupid than they and that occasionally an attempt was made to link this difference with biological factors; but this idea, at no time clearly or forcefully expressed, seems, as we have already said, never to have taken root. On the other hand, in a stratified society based upon slavery, in which birth was operatively related to social status, it can readily be understood how the notion of the biological character of social classes, as of the persons comprising them, could have originated. Yet so far as the Western world is concerned anything remotely resembling such an idea was held by no more than a handful of Greek and Roman thinkers, and never for a moment extended beyond the boundaries of their own esoteric circles. In the year 1455 by papal decree approval was given for the subjugation of infidels by Christians. The net effect of this decree was the official sanction for the enslavement of Blacks, indigenous Americans, and other "infidels," for their benefit, of course: the salvation of their souls and their admission into God's Kingdom.

It was only among peoples who had themselves for centuries been emancipated from serfdom and slavery, but who themselves kept slaves, that the hereditary or biological conception of race differences was developed. What is of the greatest interest and importance for an understanding of this matter is that the concept developed as a direct result of the trade in slaves by European merchants. It is of even greater interest and importance to note that as long as the trade was taken for granted and no one raised a voice against it, or at least a voice that was heard, the slaves, though treated as chattels, were nonetheless conceded to be human in every sense but that of attainments. This may well be seen in the treatment accorded to slaves in Portugal and Spain, where many of them rose to high positions in church and state, as was the case in ancient Greece, Rome, and Arabia. Portugal, it should be remembered, initiated the African slave trade as early as the middle of the fifteenth century. A study of the documents of the English and American slave traders down to the eighteenth century also serves to show that these men held no other conception of their victims than that by virtue of their position as slaves, or potential slaves, they were socially their captors' caste inferiors. But that was not all, for many of these hardheaded, hardbitten men recorded their belief that their victims were often quite clearly their own mental equals and superior to many at home.[58] Similarly, almost all seventeenth-century observers agree in their high opinion of the abilities and intelligence of the American Indians.[59] All that they lacked was education and instruction, wrote Father Le Jeune more than three hundred years ago:

> I naturally compare our Savages with certain villagers, because both are usually without education; though our Peasants are superior in this regard; and yet I have not seen anyone thus far, of those who have come to this country, who does not confess and frankly admit that the Savages are more intelligent than our ordinary Peasants.[60]

Indeed, it was no less a person than the discoverer of America himself, Christopher Columbus who, in his famous letter to Ferdinand and Isabella announcing his discoveries, wrote, in March, 1493, of the great friendliness of the Indians and of their "excellent and acute understanding." Columbus described them as "a loving, uncovetous people, so docile in all things that there is no better people or better country . . . They loved their neighbors as themselves and they had the sweetest and gentlest way of speaking in the world, and always with a smile."[61]

Virtually everywhere the story is the same, the intruding, uninvited Europeans being made welcome by the trusting natives. So friendly were the natives at one place off the southeast coast of Africa where Vasco da Gama's ships first anchored, that the country was named by the Portuguese Terra da Boa Gente (Land of Good People).[62]

By the middle of the sixteenth century the Spaniards had decided that these same Indians were "lazy, filthy pagans, of bestial morals, no better than dogs, and fit only for slavery, in which state alone there might be some hope of instructing and converting them to Christianity." More than two centuries later, when voices began to make themselves heard against the inhuman traffic in slaves, and when these voices assumed the shape of influential men and organizations, that, on the defensive, the supporters of slavery were forced to look about them for reasons of a new kind to controvert the dangerous arguments of their opponents. The abolitionists argued that those who were enslaved were as good human beings as those who had enslaved them. To this, by way of reply, the champions of slavery could only attempt to show that the slaves were most certainly not as good as their masters. And in this highly charged emotional atmosphere there began the doleful recitation of the catalogue of differences which were alleged to prove the inferiority of the slave to his master.[63] When they had quoted at them the clear injunction from Exodus 21:16, "And he that stealeth a man, and selleth him, or if he be found in his hand, he shall surely be put to death," the proslavers could make reply, as the South still often does today, that the "Negro" was not a man, or by twisting meaning quote Scripture against Scripture, and the Bible as their authority for slavery.[64]

I have thus far only had in mind the literature published in England during the latter half of the eighteenth century. Much of this literature found its way to the American colonies, and after the successful conclusion of the War of Independence a certain amount of controversial literature was published in this country. In France and in Holland similar works were making their appearance. It is also well to remember that it was during this period that the conception of "the noble savage" was born in France and that the romantics were not slow to capitalize upon the new-found theme in such novels as Bernardin de Saint-Pierre's *Paul et Virginie* (1788).[65] In Germany, during this period, we have such distinguished thinkers as Kant,[66] Hardenberg, Herder, Goethe, and Novalis, not to mention many others, emphasizing the unity of humankind. Herder, in particular, foresaw the danger of those loose and prejudiced utterances of the defenders of the institution of slavery, and in a memorable passage of his remarkable book *Ideen zur Philosophie der Geschichte der Menschheit,* he writes:

> I could wish the distinctions between the human species, that have been made from a laudable zeal for discriminating science, not carried beyond due bounds. Some for instance have thought fit to employ the term races for four or five divisions, originally made in consequence of country or complexion: but I see no reason for this appellation. Race refers to a difference of origin, which in this case does not exist, or in each of these countries, and under each of these complexions, comprises the most different races. . . . In short, there are neither four or five races, nor exclusive varieties, on this Earth. Complexions run into each other: forms follow the genetic character: and upon the whole, all are at last but shades of the same great picture, extending through all ages, and over all parts of the Earth. They belong not, therefore, so properly to systematic natural history, as to the psysico-geographical history of man.[67]

This was written in 1784, and I have quoted from the English translation of 1803. That Herder was able to write so clearly and sensibly was, I suspect, principally due to the publication, in 1775, by a young countryman of his, of a work entitled *De generis humani varietate* (that is to say, "On the Natural Variety of Mankind"). In this work the author, Johann Friedrich Blumenbach (1752–1840), the founder of physical anthropology, who was in his twenty-third year, in his thesis for the M.D. degree, set out to classify the varieties of humankind and to show what significance was to be attached to the differences, physical and mental, which were supposed to exist between them. He insisted at the outset that no sharp distinctions could be made between peoples. Thus, he writes:

> Although there seems to be so great a difference between widely separate nations, that you might easily take the inhabitants of the Cape of Good Hope, the Greenlanders, and the Circassians for so many different species of man, yet when the matter is thoroughly considered, you see that all do so run into one another, and that one variety of mankind does so sensibly pass into the other, that you cannot mark out the limits between them. Very arbitrary indeed both in number and definition have been the varieties of mankind accepted by eminent men.[68]

A statement which stands with quite as great force today as when it was written nearly two centuries ago.

In the greatly enlarged and revised third edition of this work, published in 1795, Blumenbach concluded that "no variety of mankind exists, whether of color, countenance, or stature, etc., so singular as not to be connected with others of the same kind by such an imperceptible transition, that it is very clear they are all related, or only differ from each other in degree." Not only did Blumenbach make clear the essential unity of humankind, but he also clearly recognized and unequivocally stated the fact that all classifications of the so-called "varieties" of mankind are arbitrary. "Still," he remarked, "it will be found serviceable to the memory to have constituted certain classes into which the men of our planet may be divided."[69]

Almost echoing the words of Blumenbach, Emerson, writing of *English Traits* in 1856, observed that:

> The individuals at the extremes of divergence in one race of men are as unlike as the wolf to the lapdog. Yet each variety shades down imperceptibly into the next, and you cannot draw the line where a race begins or ends. . . . We must use the popular category as we do the Linnaean classification, for convenience, and not as exact and final.[70]

Yet with few exceptions most writers on the subject, with complete conviction, maintained their belief in the physical and mental inferiority of Blacks.[71]

The history of physical anthropology, after the middle of the nineteenth century, may be described in terms of the gradual inversion of this genetic approach to the problem of the variety of humankind. The investigation of causes steadily gave way to the description of effects, as if the classification of humankind into as distinctive groups as possible were the proper function of a science of physical anthropology. The Darwinian conception of evolution, understood as dealing with continuous materials which, without selection, would remain unchanged, led anthropologists to believe that taxonomic exercises in the classification of humankind, both living and extinct, would eventually succeed in elucidating the relationships of the various groups of humankind to one another. We now know, however, that the materials of evolution are not continuous, but discontinuous, and that these materials are particulate, independent genes, which are inherently variable and unstable. Thus, classifications based on the shifting sands of morphological characters and physique can be extremely misleading.[72] Just how misleading may be gathered from the fact that in nature there actually exist many groups of individuals in different phyla which are distinct species in every sense but the morphological one.[73] The converse also is true, that is, individuals of the same species may exhibit morphological differences which the taxonomist would be led to assign to different specific rank. Such classificatory efforts belong to the pre-Mendelian era.[74] Then, as now, the concept of the continuity of species and the existence of transitional forms was associated with a belief in missing links. The anthropologist conceived his task to be to discover these links so that when they were all joined together we should have a complete Great Chain of Being leading from the most "primitive" to the most "advanced" forms of humans.[75] In this manner was established a racial anthropology which sought to identify some of these links among existing peoples on the basis of the physical differences that averaged groups of them were supposed to exhibit. As Linton has remarked, "unfortunately, the early guesses on these points became dogmas which still have a strong influence on the thought of many workers in this field."[76]

It may be noted here that at the beginning of the nineteenth century Cuvier had clearly foreseen the danger of such arbitrary procedures, and in the preface to his *Le Regne animal* (Paris, 1817), he explained:

> It formed no part of my design to arrange the animated tribes according to gradations of relative superiority, nor do I conceive such a plan to be practical. I do not believe that the mammalia and the birds placed last are the most imperfect of their class; still less do I think that the last of the mammiferous tribes are superior to the foremost of the feathered race or that the last of the mollusca are more perfect than the first of the annelides or zoophytes. I do not believe this to be, even if we understand the vague term perfect in the sense of 'most completely organized.' I have considered my divisions only as a scale of resemblance between the individuals classed under them. It is impossible to deny that a kind of step downward from one species to another may occasionally be observed. But this is far from being general, and the pretended scale of life, founded on the erroneous application of some partial remarks to the immensity of organized nature, has proved essentially detrimental to the progress of natural history in modern times.[77]

Throughout Blumenbach's great work and the several editions that followed the author carefully examined and rebutted, point by point, many of the arguments that had been brought forward to prove the inequality of the varieties of man, and most convincingly showed that there was no good reason to believe anything other than that they were essentially equal. Thus the treatise, which is properly regarded as having laid the foundations of the science of physical anthropology, stood foursquare for the essential relative mental and physical equality of man. The writings which such works inspired were many and important.

For example, Blumenbach's pupil, the remarkable Alexander von Humboldt (1769–1859), wrote:

> Whilst we maintain the unity of the human species, we at the same time repel the depressing assumption of superior and inferior races of men.

There are nations more susceptible of cultivation, more highly civilized, more ennobled by mental cultivation than others—but none in themselves nobler than others. All are in like degree designed for freedom; a freedom which in the ruder conditions of society belongs only to the individual, but which in social states enjoying political institutions appertains as a right to the whole body of the community.

And then Alexander quotes his brother Wilhelm, who writes:

If we would indicate an idea which throughout the whole course of history has ever more and more widely extended its empire—or which more than any other testifies to the much contested and still more decidedly misunderstood perfectibility of the whole human race—it is that of establishing our common humanity—of striving to remove the barriers which prejudice and limited views of every kind have erected amongst men, and to treat all mankind without reference to religion, nation, or color, as one fraternity, one great community, fitted for the attainment of one object, the unrestrained development of the psychical powers. This is the ultimate and highest aim of society, identical with the direction implanted by nature in the mind of man towards the indefinite extension of his existence. He regards the earth in all its limits, and the heavens as far as his eye can scan their bright and starry depths, as inwardly his own, given to him as the objects of his contemplation, and as a field for the development of his energies ... the recognition of the bond of humanity becomes one of the noblest leading principles in the history of mankind.[78]

Wilhelm von Humboldt, the older brother of Alexander, declared himself even more emphatically in his extraordinary book on the Kawi language of Java. "All humans are one species," he wrote.

Different as men may be in size, color, bodily form, and facial features, their mental qualities are the same. Assertions to the contrary are refuted by abundant evidence. Were it not for the greed to profit from the traffic in Negro slaves, or for the ludicrous pride of color, it would never have been seriously claimed that it is otherwise.[79]

Such ideas were part of the revolutionary atmosphere of the time. During the first part of the nineteenth century, the reverberations of the French and American revolutions, the wars of liberation in Latin American, the series of revolutions in Europe that broke out in rapid succession in 1848, the growing reaction to the continuing problems ensuing from the Industrial Revolution, had raised many serious questions in the minds of thinking men and women. It was a time in which the human rights, freedom, fraternity, equality, and the pursuit of happiness, were seen to be within the power of ordinary people to accomplish.[80] It was a time—in

1809—when Wordsworth wrote, on the French Revolution, "Bliss was it in that dawn to be alive,/ But to be young was very heaven."

It was a time during which many gifted men and women found their voices, and among the many movements they initiated was the founding of antislavery societies and similar organizations. The activities of the abolitionists eventually impressed upon public opinion, and in 1807 Britain abolished the slave trade, and America did so a year later. In 1833 Britain outlawed slavery altogether, but slavery survived as an institution in America for almost sixty more years, and during that period the issue it presented kept the subject of race differences always at a high temperature. In America the differences in ways of life and the better social and economic conditions in the South compared with the North, produced a deep rift between the North and the South. On 4 February 1861 the South seceded from the Union, and on 12 April the new Confederation of Southern States hastened the Civil War by firing the first shot at Fort Sumter.

Slavery had been an abrasive issue between the North and South for almost half a century during the antebellum period. The South increasingly saw the unrelenting attacks upon this pillar of their society as intolerable; these attacks eventually could only be met by secession and force. The result was four years of the bloodiest and most destructive conflict in which over six hundred thousand men died, and every principle of humanity sacrificed, on both sides, to the evils of expediency and revenge.

It was not until 1 January 1863, two years after Fort Sumter, that Lincoln issued the Emancipation Proclamation, which declared all slaves living in the rebel states "henceforward and forever free." Lincoln at this time was a white supremacist, who initially viewed the war as the desperate, and on his part reluctant, means for preserving the Union. It was the pressure for abolition in the country and in Congress that led him to a more sympathetic view, a view which showed Americans, and the world, that the war was now being fought to end slavery. As one of the world's largest slave-holding republics, the Southerners began the war pledged to protect the rights of the slaveowners. Slavery, however, was by no means ended by the Proclamation; indeed, fugitive slaves were usually returned to their masters, and many of them were held by the Confederate forces throughout the Civil War. The formal end of slavery did not come about until the 13th Amendment to the Constitution was passed on 18 December 1865, eight months after the end of the war on 9 April 1865, and Lincoln's tragic death five days later.[81]

The Civil War was fought neither for the emancipation of the human spirit, nor for the civil rights of Blacks, for more than a hundred years later the emancipation of the human spirit remained unachieved, and while the civil rights of Blacks was now the law of the land, it was not a law that whites cared to observe. As Barbara Field has said, "the Civil War is not over, it is in the present, not in the past." The North may have won the war, but from the standpoint of white supremacy it was the South that won the peace. The story of the ignominious treatment of Blacks in the postbellum period is one of the most disgraceful in the history of America, and in spite of small gains, for many it is no better today than it was then. It is necessary to understand this if one is to comprehend the nature of the racism that has stood as a forceful barrier against the African American's right to "life, liberty, and the pursuit of happiness."

With the loss of the war and the ruthless assault upon its way of life, followed by the equally ruthless exploitation by Northern invaders who contributed to its further humiliation and impoverishment, the South had a ready scapegoat upon whom it could readily wreak its wrath, the "Negro." It was the "Negro" who was to blame for the war. And with that supreme rationalization, in the tradition of many that flourished in the antebellum period, it was clear that there would have been no war if there hadn't been any "Negroes." It is this feeling, in great part, that explains the peculiarly bitter antipathy toward the "Negro," and antipathy which continues to the present day, only slightly, if at all, modified.

Harry Ashmore, the distinguished journalist, who was born to and grew up in a white family in the first half of the twentieth century in Greenville, South Carolina, in his book *The Man in the Middle,* tells with appropriate irony what it was like to live in the socially stratified environment of a racist society. "People came in two clearly defined castes," he writes,

> those who wore faded blue overalls to work in the factories and fields and tended to be shiftless. There was another group, too, but it did not count for much—Negroes, who handled menial chores and performed personal services and were to be treated with tolerance and even affection, but were not exactly people. Negroes, I understood, were inextricably bound up in the Southern Way, but in that simple time they had not even risen to the status of a Problem.[82]

"Not exactly people." The mythology which supported such beliefs and conduct served as an ideological reinforcement of "the Southern Way." Anyone who questioned it was considered outside the pale, or worse.

And so it is in some Southern places it lingers on.

To return to the beginning. When we examine the scientific literature of the seventeenth century with a view to discovering what beliefs were held concerning the diversity of humans, we find it was universally believed that humankind comprised a single species and that it represented a unitary whole. With one or two heretical exceptions, it was the accepted belief that all the children of humankind were one, and that all had a common ancestry in Adam and Eve. Physical differences were, of course, known to exist between groups of humankind, but what was unfamiliar was the notion that the differences exhibited by such peoples represented anything fundamental. Such differences, it was believed, could all be explained as due to the action of differing climatic and similar physiographic factors. Humankind was essentially one. Questions concerning the variety of humankind occurred to few thinkers during the seventeenth century. This was not because the known varieties of humankind were so few that they suggested no problem requiring solution, but principally, it would seem, because the conception of the "superiority" or "inferiority" of races that followed the increasing exploitation of other peoples had not yet developed to the point of creating a "race problem." It was not until the economic relations between Europe and peoples of other remote countries had given rise to the necessity of defining their place in nature that attempts were made to deal with this question. Such endeavors naturally first appeared toward the end of the eighteenth century. It was only then that Samuel Johnson, in *The Vanity of Human Wishes,* could write:

> Let observation with extensive view
> Survey mankind, from China to Peru.

By the middle of the nineteenth century racism had become an important ideological weapon of nationalistic and imperialistic politics.[83] During the whole of the seventeenth century only five discussions relating to the varieties of humankind were published, and toward the end of the century Leibnitz, the great mathematician, summed up the prevailing view concerning the nature of the peoples of the earth when he wrote:

> I recollect reading somewhere, though I cannot find the passage, that a certain traveler had divided man into certain tribes, races, or classes. He made one special race of the Lapps and Samoyedes, another of the Chinese and their neighbors, another of the Caffres or Hottentots. In America, again, there is a marvelous difference between the Galibs, or Caribs, who are very brave and spirited, and those of Paraguay, who seem to be infants or in pupilage all their lives. That, however, is no reason why all men who inhabit the earth should not be of the same race, which has been altered by different climates, as we see that beasts and plants change their nature and improve or degenerate.[84]

The work which Leibnitz had in mind was a brief anonymous essay published in the *Journal des Sçavans* in April, 1684, and which remained almost completely unnoticed.[85] Race was definitely not yet in the air. It was not until 1749 that Buffon introduced the word "race," in its zoological connotation, into the scientific literature.[86]

It is commonly stated that Buffon classified man into six races.[87] Buffon, who was the enemy of all rigid classifications, did nothing of the sort. What he did was to provide an account of all the varieties of man known to him in a purely descriptive manner. This is how he begins: "In Lapland, and on the northern coasts of Tartary, we find a race of men of an uncouth figure, and small stature." And this is the type of Buffon's description. Here the word "race" is used for the first time in a scientific context, and it is quite clear, after reading Buffon, that he uses the word in no narrowly defined, but rather in a general, sense.[88] Since Buffon's works were widely read and were translated into many European languages, he must be held at least partially responsible for the diffusion of the idea of a natural separation of the races of humankind, though he himself does not appear to have had such an idea in mind.

With the voyages of discovery of Bougainville (1761–66), of Wallis-Carteret (1766), of Captain Cook (1768–79), and others in the eighteenth century, there were opened up to the view of Europe many new varieties of humans—people hitherto undreamed of who thickly populated the islands of the South Seas, of Melanesia, and the Antipodes. Soon the inhabitants of the most distant parts of the world began to be described, pictured, and some of their skulls and handiwork collected and placed in museums. Meanwhile, the African slave trade had increased to enormous proportions. During the eighteenth century the slave trade was regarded as sanctioned by the Bible and as fully consistent with the good life.[89] "For what could be more godly than to deliver poor Negroes from heathen darkness and the certainty of damnation, by carrying them to a land where they would receive the 'blessings of Christianity.'"[90] The institution of slavery was not without its critics almost from the day the first twenty Africans arrived at Jamestown in 1619.[91]

Curiously enough, the first recorded use of the phrase "Negro slave" occurs in a document issued 30 March 1660, the date of an act designed to encourage the importation of "Negroes" by the Dutch.[92] George Fox, the first Friend, had become convinced of the evil of slavery as early as 1671, but it was not until the Society of Friends had weathered the years of persecution to which they had themselves been exposed and overcome their own internal difficulties that they opened the campaigne on slavery. By 1714 Friends had commenced pamphleteering against slavery, using the doctrine of the Divine presence in every man as their main argument.[93] John Wesley, the founder of Methodism, had declared himself against slavery in 1743. In his *General Rules* he prohibited "the buying or selling the bodies and souls of men, women, and children, with an intention to enslave them." And in 1774, in his *Thoughts Upon Slavery*, he excoriated the barbarous and inferior white men who put the noble savage in fetters. "It is impossible," he wrote, "that it should ever be necessary for any reasonable creature to violate all the laws of Justice, Mercy, and Truth. No circumstances can make it necessary for a man to burst asunder all the ties of humanity."[94] Wesley was read religiously by his followers, his ideas nurturing an antislavery sentiment which was to grow in moral force as the confrontation with the mother country made more explicit the principles of freedom upon which the rights of man depend. The American Revolution was brought about by men who justly considered themselves oppressed, the victims of repeated injuries and usurpations, and of an absolute tyranny, which they were resolved to bring to an end. The principles fought for, and set out in the Declaration of Independence, clearly included Blacks. By 1780 the Pennsylvania legislature initiated steps toward the abolition of slavery in that State, and by 1804 the end of slavery was ensured above the Mason and Dixon line. By the vision of Thomas Jefferson and Congress the institution of slavery had been preempted for the Northwest.[95] In 1780 the Methodists formally decided to work for the emancipation of the slaves on the grounds that the institution was contrary to divine, human, and natural justice, a violation of the Golden Rule, and inconsistent with pure religion.[96]

In 1790 Cesar de l'Escale de Verone, writing on the Blacks of the French colonies, warned against the infusion "into the very heart of our country of that thick, heavy, impure, black, crafty blood so unworthy of that which flows in your veins, the reason of which has covered the whole earth and eclipsed all that was ever acquired by the Greeks and Romans."[97]

In 1837 Victor Courtet de l'Isle provided a quite original "proof" of the black's inferiority, and at the same time of the value of slavery, when he made the measure of a people's ability to govern and dominate, the enslavement of other races, declaring that Blacks were at the bottom of the scale of humanity, and their absolute inferiority demonstrated, because of the fact that "they have enslaved no foreign races; they have only enslaved one another."[98]

Toward the end of the eighteenth century, when the traffic in slaves was increasingly being opposed and challenged, the question of the status and relation of the varieties of humans became the subject of acrimonious debate. Long-term residents of lands in which Blacks were held in slavery published their beliefs concerning the mental and physical qualities of Blacks and the social arrangements they considered desirable between whites and Blacks. Thomas Jefferson, for example, had originally thought Blacks poor in mental endowment, but believed in their emancipation, with the qualification that when freed they were "to be removed beyond the reach of mixture."[99] But with increasing experience of Blacks, Jefferson later several times repudiated his earlier statements which he freely acknowledged to be prejudices. In 1791, in a letter to Benjamin Banneker, of

Maryland, the slave-born black inventor and mathematician,[100] praising the latter's almanac, Jefferson wrote,

> No body wishes more than I do to see such proofs as you exhibit, that nature has given to our black brethren, talents equal to those of the other colors of men, and that the appearance of a want of them is owing merely to the degraded condition of their existence, both in Africa and America. . . .[101]

In the same year, as Secretary of State, Jefferson appointed Banneker a member of the three-man commission to survey the site for the national capital. Some seventeen years later, in 1809, Jefferson wrote in a letter to Henri Gregoire,

> Be assured that no person living wishes more sincerely than I do to see a complete refutation of the doubts I have myself entertained and expressed on the grade of understanding allotted to them [Blacks] by nature, and to find that in this respect they are on a par with ourselves. My doubts were the result of personal observation on the limited sphere of my own State, where the opportunities for the development of their genius were not favorable, and those of exercising it still less so. I expressed them therefore with great hesitation; but whatever be their degree of talent is no measure of their rights.[102]

Two years later, in 1811, Leigh Hunt, commenting on Paul Cuffee, the son of slaves, who arrived in England in his own vessel entirely manned by Blacks, writes, "Nobody who pretends to sense or decency, thinks any longer, that a difference of color in human beings implies inequality of rights, or that because we find men ignorant we ought to make them wretched."[103]

Edward Long's remarks on the black man, whom he compared to an orangutan [the contemporary name for the chimpanzee], were written after a five-year residence in Jamaica, and first published in England in 1774,[104] and in 1788 reprinted in *The Columbian Magazine.* Mentally, wrote Long, Negroes were void of genius, destitute of moral sense, and incapable of making progress in civilization or science. As plantation slaves they do their work "perhaps not better than an orang-outang might, with a little pains, be brought to do."[105]

There were innumerable publications of a similar kind during this period, as there were countless others presenting the opposite viewpoint. Perhaps the most remarkable of the latter was the Reverend Samuel Stanhope Smith's book, *An Essay on the Courses of the Variety of Complexion and Figure in the Human Species,* first published in 1787 and greatly enlarged in a second edition in 1810.[106] Smith was a Presbyterian clergyman who became professor of moral philosophy in 1779 at the College of New Jersey (afterwards Princeton University), and in 1795 seventh president of the college. Smith wrote,

> If we compare together only those varieties of human nature by which the several sections of mankind differ most widely from one another, the difference is so great that, on the first view, it might very naturally lead to the conclusion that they must belong to distinct species. But, when we come to examine more particularly the intermediate grades which connect the extremes, and observe by what minute differences they approach, or recede from, one another; and when we observe further, that each of these minute gradations can be traced to obvious and natural causes, forming so many links, as it were, in the great chain connecting the extremes, we are ready to call in question our first impressions, and perceive the necessity of subjecting them to a new and more vigorous examination.[107]

After citing evidence for the unity of the human species, Smith concluded "that the denial of the unity of the human species tends to impair, if not entirely to destroy, the foundations of duty and morals, and, in a word, of the whole science of human nature."[108] Smith goes on to say, "It is a debt we owe to humanity to recognize our brethren in every class of men into which society is divided, and under every shade of complexion which diversifies their various tribes from the equator to the poles."[109]

In the discussion of the origins of modern racism it is necessary to recall that in America there was in existence a long tradition of antipathy toward the native "savages," the American Indian. Unable to "civilize" them, their dispossessors determined to destroy them.[110] Of the American Indians Benjamin Franklin wrote in his *Autobiography*, "And indeed, if it be the design of Providence to extirpate these savages in order to make room for the cultivators of the earth, it seems probable that rum may be the appointed means."[111]

When the issue of emancipation was at last settled, in 1833, for the English colonies, it was far from being so for those of France and Holland. It was not until 1848 that the French emancipated their slaves, and not until 1863 that the Dutch liberated theirs. During all these years the monstrous race legend was continually being reinforced by the advocates of slavery, so that when the matter was finally settled in favor of the freedom of the slaves, the race legend nonetheless persisted. It served to solace the hearts of the aggrieved supporters of slavery, while now, more than ever, they saw to it that the myths and legends which they had served to popularize would be perpetuated.

The idea of race was, in fact, the deliberate creation of an exploiting class seeking to maintain and defend its privileges against what was profitably regarded as an inferior social caste. Ever since the commencement of the slave trade there had been those who had attempted to justify their conduct in it by denying the slaves the status of humanity. Montesquieu with devastating irony nicely put the view of such traders with their consciences as well as their slaves: "It is impossible for us to suppose these creatures to be men, because, allowing them to be men, a suspicion would follow, that we ourselves are not Christians."[112] Conversely, since they conceived themselves to be Christians, it followed that the slaves could not be men. The notion does not appear to have occurred to them that since men are equal in the sight of their God they should also be equal in the sight of one another.[113]

More than two decades before the Civil War the most respected and influential Southern philosophers of slavery, Thomas R. Dew and William Harper[114] codified, as it were, and openly avowed and defended what Southern cotton planters had been thinking since the abolitionists had first challenged the "rights" upon which their economy was based. Dew and Harper were supported by the leading American physician-ethnologist, Josiah C. Nott,[115] of the University of New Orleans, who in his *Types of Mankind* [1854], formulated, together with his co-author George Gliddon, the principles of the natural inequality of man.

Like Dew, Harper attacked and repudiated the philosophy of equality of Thomas Jefferson. "Is it not palpably nearer the truth," he writes, "to say that no man was ever born free and that no two men were ever born equal? . . . Man is born to subjection. . . . The proclivity of natural man is to domineer or to be subservient." In the evolution of society each man or class of men comes to find his proper place and level, and the resulting differences are then codified and given a definite form and legalized by society. Laws are instituted to prevent outbreaks against this established order as well as to render the different classes contented and even ignorant—for "if there are sordid, servile, and laborious offices to be performed, is it not better that there should be sordid, servile, and laborious beings to perform them?" As William E. Dodd put it, "Society in the lower South was to be the realization unhindered of the social philosophy which began with the repudiation of the Declaration of Independence and ended with the explicit recognition of social inequality."[116]

Thomas Cooper characterized the rights of man as "a great deal of nonsense. Nothing can be more untrue; no human being ever was, now is, or ever will be born free." Man has no inalienable rights," wrote another Southerner, "not even those of life, liberty, and the pursuit of happiness. . . . Instead of that 'glittering generality' which might serve as a motto for the wildest anarchy, the truth is that men and races of men have certain natural capacities and duties, and the right to use the one and discharge the other."[117]

After 1840, denials and attacks upon the principles of the Declaration of Independence became a staple practice in the proslavery literature of the South. A learned legal proslavery authority, Thomas Cobb, writing in 1858, cited such evidence as the following in order to contest the notion that slavery is contrary to the law of nature, that all men are free, and at birth entitled by nature to no higher rights and privileges than another:

> The red ant will issue in regular battle array, to conquer and subjugate the black or negro ant . . . these negro slaves perform all the labor of the communities into which they are brought. . . . Upon this definition, therefore, of the law of nature, negro slavery would seem to be perfectly consistent with that law."[118]

If, argues Cobb, the black were by nature equal to the white, enslavement of the black would be wrong, for the law of nature imposes upon man in relation to his fellow man the obligation,

> so to shape his course as to attain the greatest happiness, and arrive at the greatest perfection of which his nature is susceptible. Consequently, whatever interferes with the attainment of this happiness and perfection does violence to the law of his nature, and whatever promotes and is consistent therewith is sanctioned by the law of his nature. In this view, natural rights depend entirely upon the nature of the possessor, not of the right.[119]

It is, therefore, a matter of the greatest ease for Cobb to show that the nature of the black man is such that his best interests and greatest happiness are secured by his enslavement to the white man.[120] The master is as necessary to the slave as the pilot is to the ship. By citing most of the leading authorities of the day Cobb has no difficulty in supporting his thesis. Cobb is transparently a man of great character, honesty, and worth. His learned book is written with dignity and sincerity—he is no ignorant rabble-rouser, nevertheless his book is a treasure house of most of the myths that have ever been uttered about the black. "In mental and moral development," says Cobb, "slavery, so far from retarding, has advanced the Negro race."[121] "Contact with the Caucasian is the only civiliser of the negro, and slavery the only condition on which that contact can be preserved."[122]

As Norlin has so well said, the slaveholding aristocracy of the South

> rationalized their freedom to exploit and enslave. Even before the Civil War broke out, they had persuaded themselves that the institution of slavery was divinely ordained; that it was good for master and equally good for slave, and therefore worthy to be extended beyond the states where it was sanctified by law. They felt themselves to be the heaven-appointed shepherds of their flocks, being better able to care for their black wards than those outsiders who proposed by the tyranny of legislation to set bounds to their freedom of thought and action.[123]

They would see to it, as one Virginian slaveholder wrote, that they continued to hold their property, "and for the right thereto, to be called in question by an unphilosophical set of political mountebanks, under the influence of supernatural agency or deceit, is insufferable."[124]

Some there were, like William Andrew Smith, Methodist minister and president of Randolph-Macon College, who, in the 1850s, argued that all men are really slaves, even such institutions as the family and democratic government contain elements of slavery. Hence, slavery could be identified in principle with good order in society.[125]

The slaveholder's representative rationalization for slavery was stated clearly when, in 1856, George Fitzhugh claimed that slavery combined three advantages: it fostered paternalistic and loving interdependence; it placed human conduct under adequate governmental controls; and it relied on a highly decentralized version of authority.[126] It is not quite true to suggest, as R. H. Tawney has done, that the one thing these political philosophers omitted to ask themselves was on what grounds the view could be sustained that inequalities in intelligence or biology justified the penalty of slavery. The fact is that they were asked and asked themselves this question ceaselessly, and they made answer, as Aristotle had done before them, that some men were born to be masters and others to be slaves. Like Aristotle, they deliberately invented a theory to justify social discrimination. As early as the year 1700, we find the Puritan judge John Saffin of Boston writing,

> To prove that all men have equal right to Liberty, and all outward comforts of this life . . . [is] to invert the Order that God hath set in the World, who hath Ordained different degrees and orders of men, some to be High and Honorable, some to be Low and Despicable; some to be Monarchs, Kings, Princes and Governors, Masters and Commanders, others to be Subjects and to be Commanded; Servants of sundry sorts and degrees, bound to obey; yea, some to be born Slaves, and so to remain during their lives, as hath been proved.[127]

From 1830 to 1860 vigilance committees were established throughout the South to punish anyone who in any way exhibited antislavery or pro-emancipation tendencies. Russel Nye has given an account of such cases in his book *Fettered Freedom*. Here are but two typical cases from the month of January 1850. Elijah Harris, an itinerant schoolteacher, from Dunbarton, New Hampshire, was arrested on a writ issued by the justice of the peace of Clinton, Barnwell District, South Carolina. He was arraigned before the local committee of safety, and convicted of carrying in his trunk an antislavery sermon by a New Hampshire minister. The committee shaved his head, tarred and feathered him, and gave him twelve hours to leave town.[128] Robert Esmond, a resident of Charleston, South Carolina, during the same month, was tarred and feathered on suspicion of teaching Negroes to read.[129]

For the slaveholders the strategic elaboration of erroneous notions which had long been held presented no great difficulty. In order to bolster their self-appointed rights the superior caste did not have far to seek for reasons that serve to justify its conduct. The deliberately maintained illiteracy and the alleged spiritual benightedness of the slaves supplied abundant material for elaboration on the theme of their essential inferiority. Their different physical appearance provided a convenient peg upon which to hang the argument that this represented the external sign of more profound ineradicable mental and moral inferiorities. It was an easily grasped mode of reasoning, and in this way the obvious difference in their social status, in caste status, was equated with their obviously different physical appearance, which, in turn, was taken to indicate a fundamental biological difference. Thus was a culturally produced difference in social status converted into a difference in biological status. What had once been a social difference was now transformed into a biological difference which would serve, it was expected, to justify and maintain the social difference.[130]

This was a most attractive idea to many members of a society in which the classes were markedly stratified, and it was an idea that had a special appeal for those who were beginning to take an active interest in the scientific study and classification of the races of humankind.[131] For the term "race," taken over from Buffon with all the emotional connotations that had been added to it, had by now become established. It was with this term as a tremendous handicap that most anthropologists of the nineteenth century embarked on their researches. The question they had begged was the one which required to be proved, namely, that mental and moral differences were associated with racial external physical differences. As Wundt once remarked in another connection, "in the seventeenth century God gave the laws of Nature; in the eighteenth century Nature did this herself; and in the nineteenth century individual scientists take care of that task."[132] And we may add that in the twentieth century the tasks determine for the scientists, and others, what the laws of nature shall be.

The allegedly scientific presentation of the case for slavery was produced by Josiah C. Nott, and published in 1854 under the title *Types of Mankind*. This 738-page volume, which enshrined most of the prejudices and pseudoscience of the day, was embellished with an essay contributed by Louis Agassiz, professor of zoology at Harvard, in which he identified himself with the pluralist position of the authors, and thus lent them and their views the prestige of his great authority as a scientist.[133] This work was not without some influence in the world, and all of it for the worse. Henry

Schoolcraft, the great authority on the American Indians wrote, in September, 1854, of this work,

> The types are . . . the fruits of the mountain that was in labor. From one end of the land to the other subscribers have been drummed up for this work, and when it came forth it is a patchwork of infidel papers . . . if this be all that America is to send back to Europe . . . it were better that the Aborigines had maintained their dark empire undisturbed.[134]

As an independent student of the evidence has put it:

> When between the years 1859 and 1870, anthropological societies were established successively in Paris, London, New York, Moscow, Florence, Berlin and Vienna, the attention of anthropologists was in the first place directed mainly to the statement and exploration of problems of racial divergence and distribution. The need for such a preliminary investigation was great. Popular opinion drew a rough but ready distinction between men of white, black, yellow and red color, vaguely supposed to be native to the continents of Europe, Africa, Asia and America respectively. Differences of average stature, of physiognomy, of growth and texture of hair were recognized; certain combinations of these characters were supposed to be typical of certain ultimate stocks. There was the self-satisfied view, influenced by an uncritical acceptance of the Biblical account of the Creation, Flood, dispersion of its survivors, selection of a favored race, which either alone or [together] conspicuously expressed divine purpose, that divergence from European standard[s] should ultimately be explained in terms of degradation.[135]

It was not principally the scientific student of the varieties of man who influenced European thought along these lines, but an aristocrat of the Second Empire, an amateur orientalist and professional diplomat, Count Joseph Arthur de Gobineau. Gobineau was a reactionary littérateur who rejected the principles of the French Revolution,[136] and looked upon the egalitarian philosophy of the Revolution as the hopelessly confused expression of a degraded rabble. If the founders of the First Republic had believed in the liberty, equality, and fraternity of mankind, this scion of the Second Empire would show that, on the contrary, a man was not bound to be free, that the idea of the brotherhood of man was a vain and empty dream, a repugnant dream which could never be realized because it was based upon a fallacious belief in the equality of man.[137] These views were fully set out by Gobineau in his four-volume work entitled *Essai sur l'inégalité des races humaines* (Paris, 1853–55). In 1856 an American translation of the first two volumes under the title *The Moral and Intellectual Diversity of Races* was published at Philadelphia. This was the work of H. Hotz, of

Montgomery, the pious Alabama proslavery propagandist. At the invitation of either Gobineau or Hotz, Josiah C. Nott, the proslavery anthropologist, contributed an anthropological appendix to the translation. Gobineau returned the compliment by subscribing to Nott and Gliddon's *Indigenous Races of the Earth,* which appeared in the following year, 1857, from the same publishing house which had issued the translation of the Essai. As Finot has pointed out, Gobineau never attempted to conceal or dissimulate the motives which led him to write the Essai. For him,

> It was only a matter of bringing his contributions to the great struggle against equality and the emancipation of the proletariat. Imbued with aristocratic ideas . . . he thought it useful to oppose to the democratic aspirations of his time a number of considerations on the existence of natural castes in humanity and their beneficial necessity.[138]

Ever since their publication Gobineau's works have enjoyed a considerable readership among reactionaries and demagogues of every kind. Among others they gave the composer Richard Wagner a "scientific" basis for his racist prejudices, fortifying him and encouraging him in the production of his virulent and influential racist writings.[139]

Some forty-five years later the views originally expressed in Gobineau's works were taken over lock, stock, and barrel by Wagner's son-in-law, Houston Stewart Chamberlain, and elaborated in his *Grundlagen des neunzehnten Jahrhunderts* (1899). The English translation, *The Foundation of the Nineteenth Century,* was published in 1910.[140]

John Oakesmith, in his book *Race & Nationality* (1919), arguably one of the best and most readable books ever written on the subject, brilliantly anatomized Chamberlain's monstrosity at some length. Here, briefly, is his characterization of it:

> We can have no hesitation in describing it as one of the most foolish books ever written. It is false in its theories; ludicrously inaccurate in its assertions; pompous and extravagant in its style; insolent to its critics and opponents. It is so dominated by a spirit of stormy rhetoric that it contradicts itself with passion at every turn. It asserts as dogmas fancies of whose futility the author would have been aware, had he consulted his Jew-baiting baby.[141] He frequently uses the term 'lie' and 'liar' of others while claiming that he is himself constitutionally incapable of lying. He can never quote an opponent without covering him with abuses: his critics are 'shallow, venal, ignorant, babblers, slavish souls sprung from the chaos of peoples.' He is a twentieth century exaggeration of the pompous and vapid bully[142] who used to lord it in the *Quarterly* [*The Edinburgh Quarterly Review*] of the early nineteenth; he is a street-corner preacher now assuming the toga of Roman oratory, and now the robes of Christian ceremony; but

he is a violent and vulgar charlatan all the time. We say, and say it deliberately, that he is the only author we have read to whose work Sydney
Smith's phrase, 'the crapulous eructations of a drunken cobbler,' could
appropriately be applied.

A judgement, I believe, that all impartial critics would share.[143]

It is not surprising that early in January 1923 Hitler, who was greatly influenced by Chamberlain's racist thinking, enjoyed a mutually gratifying
visit with his mentor at Bayreuth. Chamberlain was greatly taken with
Hitler, and the following day, in a mood of religious exaltation, wrote him a
long letter, telling his new found friend of his renewal of faith in the future
of the Fatherland which Hitler had inspired in him. "You have immense
achievements ahead of you . . . That Germany in its hour of greatest need
has given birth to a Hitler is proof of vitality. . . . May God protect you!"[144]
Thereafter whenever Chamberlain spoke or wrote of Hitler, it was with rev-
erence and affection. It proved to be of great propaganda value to the
Nazis in the development of their movement. When in January 1927
Chamberlain died, Alfred Rosenberg, the official Nazi philosopher,
praised him as the pioneer and founder of the German Future."[145]

Chamberlain's book enjoyed an enormous popularity in Germany.
Kaiser Wilhelm II, the principal architect of World War I, caller it "my fa-
vorite book," and distributed it widely among libraries, the military, the
nobility, his friends, and schools. Both Gobineau and Chamberlain's
works may be regarded as the spiritual progenitors of Hitler's *Mein Kampf.*
In this connection the works of John Oakesmith, written during World
War I, are of interest to all who, by forces similar to those which were operative then, have since been plunged into far more horrible wars. Oakesmith wrote:

> The essence of the racial theory, especially as exhibited by writers of the
> school of Houston Stewart Chamberlain, is profoundly immoral, as well as
> unnatural and irrational. It asserts that by virtue of belonging to a certain
> 'race,' every individual member of it possesses qualities which inevitably
> destine him to the realization of certain ends; in the case of the German
> the chief end being universal dominion, all other 'races' being endowed
> with qualities which as inevitably destine them to submission and slavery
> to German ideals and German masters. This essentially foolish and im-
> moral conception has been the root-cause of that diseased national ego-
> tism whose exhibition during the war [World War I] has been at once the
> scorn and the horror of the civilized world.[146]

From the commencement of the nineteenth century the Germans, in-
toxicated by their Faustian romanticism, have been especially prone to the
appeal of a magus who promises to exorcise the possessing evil spirits.[147]

Luther (1483–1546), to a large extent, had successfully destroyed the mythological element in Christianity for the Germans, and from 1517 onwards, when he posted the ninety-five articles on the door of the castle church at Wittenberg, to the advent of the Nazi Party, the Germans had been seeking for some new mythology wherewith to replace what they had lost. When Luther cleared the way for a more purely rational interpretation of the world, he failed to foresee that by withdrawing the experience of the mystical, the poetic, and metaphysical, and the dramatic, he was building for a time when the people would be glad to embrace a mythology whose barbarity would have appalled him. One may never deprive a people of its feeling of unity with the world, with nature, and with man without providing another set of such metaphysical beliefs—unless one is ready to brook disaster. We may recall the words of Ernest Renan, written in 1848:

> The serious thing is that we fail to perceive a means of providing humanity in the future with a catechism that will be acceptable henceforth, except on the condition of returning to a state of credulity. Hence, it is possible that the ruin of idealistic beliefs may be fated to follow hard upon the ruin of supernatural beliefs and that the real abasement of the morality of humanity will date from the day it has seen the reality of things. Chimeras have succeeded in obtaining from the good gorilla an astonishing moral effort; do away with the chimeras and part of the factitious energy they aroused will disappear.[148]

It is a fact worth remarking that throughout the nineteenth century hardly more than a handful of scientific voices were raised against the notion of a hierarchy of races. Anthropology, biology, psychology, medicine, and sociology became instruments for the "proof" of the inferiority of various races as compared with the white race. What H. G. Wells called "professional barbarity and braggart race-imperialism," played a major role in the rationalization justifying the disenfranchisement and segregation of "inferior races," and thus prepared the way for the maintenance of racial thinking and exploitation of "native" peoples, and the unspeakable atrocities of the nineteenth and twentieth centuries.[149]

After World War I the Germans found themselves particularly frustrated and alone. By providing them with a new mythology and making the Germans feel that they belonged to a "superior race," the "Herrenvolk," Hitler endowed them with a completely acceptable *Weltanschauung*. The fact that the Nazi race theories represented the most vicious mythology that had ever been perpetrated upon a people did not, as we know, prevent those myths from functioning as if they were perfectly true. "If one asks," as Bonger has done, whether these partisans are even partially successful in proving their thesis, then the answer must be a decided No. It is really no theory at all but a second-rate religion. Things are not proved but only alleged. It resembles the commonly witnessed phenomenon of persons who, quite without reason, fancy themselves (and often their families also) to be more exalted than others. But now it is carried out on a much larger scale, and with much greater detriment to society, since it affects wide-spread groups.[150]

What Hitler said about race is reported from a personal conversation by Hermann Rauschning. "I know perfectly well," Hitler said to Rauschning,

> just as well as all those tremendously clever intellectuals, that in the scientific sense there is no such thing as race. But you, as a farmer and cattle-breeder, cannot get your breeding successfully achieved without the conception of race. And I as a politician need a conception which enables the order which has hitherto existed on historic bases to be abolished and an entirely new and anti-historic order enforced and given an intellectual basis. . . . With the conception of race, National Socialism will carry its revolution abroad and recast the world.[151]

Similar statements were made by Hitler to his confidant Otto Wagener.[152] Lord Bryce, writing in 1915 during World War I, remarked:

> Whatever condemnation may be passed—and justly passed—upon reckless leaders and a ruthless caste that lives for and worships war, it is popular sentiment behind them, the exaggeration of racial vanity and national pretensions, that has been and is the real source of the mischief, for without such sentiments no caste could exert its baleful power. Such sentiments are not confined to any single nation, and they are even more widespread in the wealthier and more educated classes than in the humbler. As it is largely by the educated, by students and writers as well as by political leaders, that the mischief has been done, more or less everywhere, even if most conspicuously in one country, so it should be the function and the privilege of thinkers and writers as well as of practical men to enforce a broader, saner, and more sympathetic view of the world as a vast community, in which every race has much to give and much to receive, to point out that it is by the co-operation, unconscious but unceasing, by the reciprocal teaching and learning of the more gifted races, that all progress has been achieved. Perfection is obtained not by the ascendancy of any one form of excellence, but by the blending of what is best in many different forms.[153]

How much more true are these words today than when they were written. We all know only too well to what horrors the reckless "Führers" of the Axis nations and their ruthless conduct have led the world, and we have witnessed the exaggeration of racial vanity and national pretensions assuming the form of a national religion and serving as an incentive to the common people to follow wherever their "Führers" lead. We have seen the virus of the disease spread throughout the greater part of the civilized world in the form of racism, and in the United States we have heard the word race bandied about on radio and TV, on the screen, from the pulpit, in our houses of legislature, our Supreme Court, and used by demagogues in various mischievous ways. In the press, in books of all sorts, and in the magazines the same perverse looseness of usage is observable. Today, more than at any previous time in the history of man, it is urgently necessary to be clear as to what this term is and what it really means.

The fact is that the modern concept of race is a product of irrational emotional reasoning, and, as we have seen, from their inception racial questions have always been discussed in an emotional atmosphere. It might almost be called "the atmosphere of the scapegoat" or, possibly, "the atmosphere of frustration or fear of frustration." As a writer in the leading organ of British science, *Nature*, remarked:

> It is a matter of general experience that racial questions are rarely debated on their merits. In the discussion of the effects of inter-racial breeding among the different varieties of the human stock, the issue is commonly determined by prejudice masquerading as pride of race or political and economic considerations more or less veiled in arguments brought forward in support of a policy of segregation. No appeal is made to what should be the crucial factor, the verdict of science.[154]

And what is the verdict of science? It will be our purpose to make that verdict clear in the following pages. The members of the older school of anthropologists, some of whom are still with us, grappled with the problem of race unsuccessfully, and the great number of conflicting viewpoints they presented shows that they were, as a whole, never quite clear as to what was to be meant by the term. They were, indeed, something less than clear, if not altogether confused.[155] In the following chapter a brief attempt will be made to show how it came about that so many of the older anthropologists came to be confused upon the subject of race.

In using the term "anthropologist" in the succeeding chapter, I am mainly referring to the physical anthropologist as distinguished from the cultural or social anthropologist. Possibly because of their wider and more intimate acquaintance with a variety of different peoples, particularly in the more isolated parts of the world, cultural anthropologists have been somewhat more sound on the subject of race than have most physical anthropologists. Indeed, the physical anthropologist has virtually disappeared from the scene and been replaced by the biological anthropologist.

Notes

1. For excellent discussions of contemporary mythmaking and myths, see Barrows Dunham, *Man against Myth* (Boston: Little, Brown, 1947); Bergen Evans, *The Natural History of Nonsense* (New York: Alfred A. Knopf, 1964); Read Bain, "Man, the Myth-Maker," *Scientific Monthly* 65 (1947): 61–69; David Bidney, "The Concept of Myth and the Problem of Psychocultural Evolution," *American Anthropologist* 62 (1950): 16–26; D. H. Monro, "The Concept of Myth," *Sociological Review* 42 (1950): 115–32; Lewis S. Feuer, "Political Myths and Metaphysics," *Philosophy and Phenomenological Research* 15 (1955): 332–50; Harry A. Murray, ed., *Myth and Mythmaking* (New York: Braziller, 1960).

2. Nicholas Calas, "Myth and Initiation," *Chimera* 4 (1946): 21–24.

3. Paul M. Gaston, *The New South Creed: A Study in Modern Mythmaking* (New York: Alfred A. Knopf, 1970).

4. George M. Tindall, *The Ethnic Southerners* (Baton Rouge: Louisiana State University Press, 1976).

5. Alan Davies, *Infected Christianity: A Study of Modern Racism* (Kingston & Montreal: McGill Queen's University Press, 1988); Ervin Staub, *The Roots of Evil: The Origins of Genocide* (New York: Cambridge University Press, 1989); Michael Barkun, *Religion and the Racist Right: The Origins of the Christian Identity Movement* (Chapel Hill: University of North Carolina Press, 1994).

6. Lancelot Hogben, "The Concept of Race," in *Genetic Principles in Medicine and Social Science* (New York: Alfred A. Knopf, 1932), 122–44; see also L. Hogben, *Nature and Nurture* (New York: W. W. Norton, 1933).

7. Louis J. Halle, *The Ideological Imagination* (New York: Quadrangle Press, 1972). For an illuminating study of the causes of the ideological appeal of Naziism, see Peter H. Merkl, *Political Violence Under the Swaztika: 581 Early Nazis* (Princeton: Princeton University Press, 1975); Paul Massing, *Rehearsal for Destruction* (New York: Harper & Brothers, 1949); George L. Mosse, *Toward the Final Solution: A History of European Racism* (Madison: University of Wisconsin Press, 1985).

8. John Stuart Mill, *Principles of Political Economy* (London: Longmans, 1848).

9. John Stuart Mill, *Autobiography*.

10. Walter Bagehot, *Physics and Politics* (New York: Alfred A. Knopf), 3; Ashley Montagu, "The Language of Self-Deception," in *Language in America,* eds. Neil Postman, Charles Weingartner, and Terence P. Moran (New York: Pegasus, 1969), 82–95.

11. James Bryce, *Race Sentiment as a Factor in History* (London: University of London Press, 1915), 3.

12. As an example see A. C. Haddon's *The Races of Man* (Cambridge: Cambridge University Press, 1924). This was a book by a very noble man, a great scholar and founder of the anthropology department at Cambridge University. For a sympathetic biography of Haddon (1955–1940) see A. Hingston Quiggin, *Haddon the Head Hunter* (Cambridge: Cambridge University Press, 1942). Among many hundreds of scholarly articles and some twenty books, Haddon was the co-author with Julian Huxley of the admirable and influential *We Europeans: A Survey of "Racial" Problems* (New York: Harper & Bros., 1935).

13. Richard Lewontin, "The Apportionment of Human Diversity," in *Evolutionary Biology*, vol. 6, eds. T. Dobzhansky, M. K. Hecht, and W. C. Steere (New York: Appleton Century-Cotts, 1972), 396–97.

14. See Ashley Montagu, *An Introduction to Physical Anthropology*, 3rd ed. (Springfield, IL: Thomas. 1960); A. Montagu, "A Consideration of the Concept of Race," *Cold Spring Harbor Symposia on Quantitative Biology* 15 (1950): 315–36; A. Montagu, "The Concept of Race," *American Anthropologist* 64 (1962): 929–45; Livingstone, "On the Non-Existence of Human Races," *Current Anthropology* 3 (1962): 279–81; A. Montagu, ed., *The Concept of Race* (New York: Free Press, 1964).

15. Lucien Febvre, *A Geographical Introduction to History* (New York: Alfred A. Knopf, 1925).

16. For an anthropological example of this fractionating method of race-making see Carleton Coon, *The Races of Europe* (New York: Macmillan, 1939); also Stanley Garn, *Human Races* (Springfield, IL: Thomas, 1969).

17. Huxley and Haddon, *We Europeans*, 114. In order to avoid possible misunderstanding of this passage, it is desirable to point out that by the words "genetically purified into their original components" the authors are not referring to pre-existing "pure races," but to the earlier states of the ancestral groups entering into the formation of the mixed ethnic groups as we know them today.

18. Franz Boas, *Changes in Bodily Form of Descendants of Immigrants* (New York: Columbia University Press, 1912); Harry L. Shapiro, *Migration and Environment* (New York: Oxford University Press, 1939); Walter Dornfeldt, "Studien über Schädelform und Schadelveranderung von Berliner Ostjuden und ihren Kindern," *Zeitschrift für Morphologie und Anthropologie* 39 (1941): 290–372; Marcus S. Goldstein, *Demographic and Bodily Changes in Descendants of Mexican Immigrants* (Austin: Institute of Latin-American Studies, 1943); on the absurdity of classification by head shape, see Franz Weidenreich, "The Brachycephalization of Recent Mankind," *Southwestern Journal of Anthropology* 1 (1945): 1–54; Gabriel Lasker, "Migration and Physical Differentiation," *American Journal of Physical Anthropology*, n.s., 4 (1946): 273–300.

19. Coon, *Races of Europe*.

20. Robert T. Anderson, "Lapp Racial Classifications As Scientific Myths," *Anthropological Papers of the University of Alaska* 11 (1962): 15–31.

21. Blumenbach, *De Generis Varietate Humani Nativa* (London, 1865).

22. Anderson, "Lapp Racial Classifications," 29–30.

23. For a further discussion of the term "ethnic group" and why it is to be preferred to "race" see Appendix A of this volume.

24. Charles Darwin, *The Descent of Man*, Chap. 7 (London, Murray, 1871).

25. William S. Laughlin, "Race: A Population Concept," *Eugenics Quarterly* 13 (1966): 327.

26. Dobzhansky, "On Species and Races of Living and Fossil Man," *American Journal of Physical Anthropology*, n.s., 2 (1944): 251–65. For a criticism of this viewpoint, see Livingstone, "On the Non-Existence of Human Races."

27. Lothar G. Tirala, *Rasse, Geist, und Seele* (Munich: Lehman's Verlag, 1935).

28. A contrary view was, indeed, expressed by Dr. R. Ruggles Gates, who claimed that many of the races of man must be regarded as belonging to different species. Such claims were rendered possible by the utter disregard and com-

plete violation of the principles of zoological taxonomy and the accepted definition of a species, principles and definitions which represent the judgment of generations of scientists. For Gates's view see his "Phylogeny and Classification of Hominids and Anthropoids," *American Journal of Physical Anthropology*, n.s., 2 (1944): 279–92. As Franz Wiedenrich has said, "raising the differences between racial groups specific names is nothing but an attempt to exaggerate the dissimilarities by the application of a taxonomic trick," *Apes, Giants, and Man* (Chicago: University of Chicago Press, 1946), 2. For the designation of "races" of humankind as "species," see John R. Baker, *Race* (New York: Oxford University Press, 1974), 98.

29. Hans Weinert, *Der Geistige Aufstieg der Menschheit som Ursprung bis zur Gegenwart* (Stuttgart: Ferdinand Enke, 1951). For an interesting account of the Nazi application of the "methods" of "race science" in which the writer himself repeats many of the favored Nazi doctrines, see Tage Ellinger, "On the Breeding of Aryans," *Journal of Heredity* 33 (1942): 141–43. For replies to this article see Goldschmidt, "Anthropological Determination of 'Aryanism,'" *Journal of Heredity* 33 (1942): 215–16; and Ashley Montagu, "On the Breeding of 'Aryans,'" *Psychiatry* 4 (1943): 254–55. The term "Aryan" is frequently misused to describe a physical stock of languages which are spoken by a wide variety of ethnic groups. It has nothing whatever to do with physical characteristics.

30. Ludwig Schemann, *Die Rassenfrage im Schrifttum der Neuzeit* (Munich: Lehman's Verlag, 1931).

31. Alfred Baeumler, "Race: A Basic Concept in Education" (trans. from the original article in the *Internationale Zeitschrift für Erziehung* 8 [1939]), *World Education* 4 (1939): 506–9.

32. For an illuminating discussion of the role of German churchmen in the cause of what they called 'positive Christianity,' see James Bentley, "The Most Irresistable Temptation," *The Listener* (London), 16 November 1978, 635–37.

33. *The New York Times*, 15 March 1978, 3.

34. Which, of course, they do not.

35. John Koumaris, "On the Morphological Variety of Modern Greeks," *Man* 48 (1948): 126–7.

36. James Coates, *Armed and Dangerous* (New York: Hill & Wang, 1987); Arnold Forster and Benjamin Epstein, *The Trouble Makers* (Garden City, NY: Doubleday, 1952); Arnold Forster and Benjamin Epstein, *Danger on the Right* (New York: Random House, 1964); Donald A. Downs, *Nazis in Skokie* (Notre Dame: University of Notre Dame, 1985); Robert C. Liebman and Robert Wuthnow, *The New Christian Right* (New York: Aldine, 1983); Kevin Flynn and Gary Gerhardt, *The Silent Brotherhood* (New York: Free Press, 1989); Staub, *Roots of Evil;* Gary E. McCuen, *The Religious Right* (Hudson, WI: G. E. McCuen, 1989).

37. Davies, *Infected Christianity;* Forrest G. Wood, *The Arrogance of Faith: Christianity and Race in America from the Colonial Era to the Twentieth Century* (New York: Alfred A. Knopf, 1990).

38. Osborn, in Madison Grant, *The Passing of the Great Race*, 3rd ed. (New York: Scribner, 1919), vii.

39. Steven L. Chorover, *From Genesis to Genocide: The Meaning of Human Behavoir and the Power of Behavior Control* (Cambridge: MIT, 1979), 107.

40. Cedric Dover, "Antar for the Anthropologist," *The Eastern Anthropologist* 5 (1952): 165–69. Dover showed that the famous Bedouin warrior-poet of the sixth century was very conscious of the social disability of being a mulatto. See also Ibn Khaldun, the fourteenth-century Arab scholar, who quoted and criticized those who had appealed to biological factors as explanatory of Negro behavior. *The Muquaddimah* 1.1, trans. by F. Rosenthal (New York: Pantheon Books, 1958), 175–76; Ashley Montagu, *The Idea of Race* (Lincoln: University of Nebraska Press, 1965).

41. John Wilson, "Egypt," in *The Intellectual Adventure of Ancient Man*, eds. H. & H. A. Frankfort et al. (Chicago: University of Chicago Press, 1946), 33–34.

42. S. Davis, *Race-Relations in Ancient Egypt* (New York: Philisophical Library,1952); T. J. Haarhoff, *The Stranger at the Gate* (New York, Macmillan, 1948).

43. John Baldry, *The Unity of Mankind in Greek Thought* (New York: Cambridge University Press, 1947).

44. "By nature, too, some beings command, and others obey, for the sake of mutual safety; for a being endowed with discernment and forethought is by nature the superior and governor; whereas he who is merely able to execute by bodily labour is the inferior and natural slave." Aristotle, *Politics*, 1.2. To this Rousseau made an excellent reply. "Aristotle said," he writes, "that men were not naturally equal, but that some were born for slavery, and others for domination. Aristotle was right, but he took the effect for the cause. Nothing can be more certain than that every man born in slavery is born for slavery. Slaves lose everything in their chains, even the desire to escape from them; they love servitude as the companions of Ulysses loved their brutish condition. If then, there are slaves by nature, it is because there have been slaves against nature. Force made the first slaves, and their cowardice perpetuated them." Rousseau, *The Social Contract*, 1.2.

45. Plato, *The Republic*, 547a.

46. Robert Eisler, "Metallurgical Anthropology in Hesiod and Plato and the Date of a 'Poenician Lie,'" *Isis* 11 (1949): 108–12. On Plato see Karl R. Popper, *The Open Society and Its Enemies* (Princeton: Princeton University Press, 1950). It is not for nothing that during the nineteenth century Plato was considered an indispensable part of the education of a gentleman, that is to say, of a person who relied upon others to do the job of earning a living for him.

47. For discussions of this subject see E. E. Sikes, *The Anthropology of the Greeks* (London: Nutt, 1914),69–89; Robert Schlaifer, "Greek Theories of Slavery form Homer to Artisotle," *Harvard Studies in Classical Philology* 47 (1936): 165–204; F. M. Snowden, Jr., *Blacks in Antiquity* (Cambridge: Harvard University Press, 1970); W. L. Westermann, "The Slave Systems of Greek and Roman Antiquity," *Memoirs of the American Philosophical Society* 40 (1995): xi–180; W. L. Westermann "Slavery and the Elements of Freedom in Ancient Greece," *Quarterly Bulletin of the Polish Institute of Arts and Sciences in America* 1 (1943): 332–47.

48. Isocrates, *Panegyricus*, 4.50. Trans. By George Norlin, pp.xxiv, 149.

49. Aubrey Diller, *Race Mixture Among the Greeks Before Alexander,* Illinois Studies in Language and Literature, vol. 20 (Urbana, 1937); Hertz, *Race and Civilization* (London: Kegan Paul, 1928): 137 ff.; Martin P. Nilsson, "The Race Problem of the Roman Empire" in *Hereditas* 2 (1921): 370–90; Frederick G. Detweiler, "The Rise of Modern Race Antagonisms," *American Journal of Sociology* 38 (1932): 738–47;

Matthew Thomas McClure, "Greek Genius and Race Mixture," in *Studies in the History of Ideas* 3 (1935): 25–33; Haarhoff, *Stranger at the Gate;* Davis, *Race-Relations in Ancient Egypt;* A. N. Sherwin-White, *Racial Prejudice in Imperial Rome* (London and New York: Cambridge University Press, 1968); M. I. Finley, "Prejudice in the Ancient World," *The Listener* 79, 1968, 146–7; Baldry, *Unity of Mankind.*

50. Bryce, *Race Sentiment,* 25–26.

51. Gomes Eannes De Azura, *The Chronicle of the Discovery and Conquest of Guinea* 1 (1453) (London: Hakluyt Society, 1896), 84–85.

52. It was not God, but the drunken Noah, who cursed Canaan the son of Ham, whose descendants occupied Africa, to be a "servant of servants unto his brethren" (Gen. 9). This was clearly in contradiction to the Divine Mind as expressed by Jesus of Nazareth: "One is your Master and all ye are brethren."

53. Katherine George, "The Civilized West Looks at Primitive Africa: 1400–1800. A Study in Ethnocentrism," *Isis* 49 (1958): 66.

54. David Hume, *Treatise on Human Nature,* 1720.

55. Anonymous, "Black Girl's Search." *Times Literary Supplement* (London), 19 January 1967, 46.

56. George, "The Civilized West," 62–72.

57. For a fully documented, pitiless revelation of the history of Jew-hating from the idea stage to that of mass murder see Malcolm Hay, *Europe and the Jews* (Boston: Beacon Press, 1960). See also Joshua Trachtenberg, *The Devil and the Jews* (New York: Meridian Books, 1961).

58. Elizabeth Donnan, ed., *Documents Illustrative of the History of the Slave Trade to America,* 4 vols., (Washington, D.C.: Carnegie Institution, 1930, pub. 409); Eric Williams, *Capitalism and Slavery* (Chapel Hill: University of North Carolina Press, 1944).

59. A. Irving Hallowell, "Some Psychological Characteristics of the Northeastern Indians," in *Man in Northeastern North America,* Papers of the R. S. Peabody Foundation for Archaeology, vol. 3 (1946): 195–225; Lewis Hanke, *Aristotle and the American Indians* (Bloomington: Indiana University Press, 1959).

60. "Le June, Quebec and Hurons: 1640," *Jesuit Relations* 19 (1898): 39, quoted from Hallowell, "Psychological Characteristics," 200.

61. Richard A. Newhall, *The Columbus Letter* (Williamstown, MA: Chapin Library, Williams College, 1953), 8.

62. E. G. Ravenstein, ed., *A Journal of the First Voyage of Vasco de Gama,* 1497–1499 (London: Hakluyt, 1897), 17–18.

63. So far as I know, an historical study of this aspect of the subject has never been attempted. It would make a fascinating and highly desirable contribution to our better understanding of the period and of the antecedents of racism. For the early period see George H. Moore, *Notes on the History of Slavery in Massachusetts* (New York: Appleton, 1866). For the later period immediately preceding the Civil War there is the attractive little volume by William Dodd, *The Cotton Kingdom* (New Haven: Yale University Press, 1919). See also Lerone Bennett, Jr., *Before the Mayflower: A History of the Negro in America 1619–1962* (Chicago: Johnson Publishing, 1962); Eugene H. Berwanger, *The Frontier Against Slavery* (Urbana: University of Illinios Press, 1971); Robin Blackburn, *The Overthrow of Colonial Slavery, 1776–1848* (London and New York: Verso, 1988); John W. Blassingame, *The Slave Community*

(New York: Oxford University Press, 1979); Mary Cable, *Black Odyssey* (New York: Viking Press, 1971); David W. Cohen and Jack P. Greene, eds., *Neither Slave Nor Free* (Baltimore: John Hopkins University Press, 1972); Pete Daniel, *The Shadow of Slavery: Peonage in the South 1901–1969* (Urbana: University of Illinois Press, 1972); Basil Davidson, *Black Mother: The Years of the African Slave Trade* (Boston: Little, Brown, 1961); David Brian Davis, *The Problem of Slavery in Western Culture* (Ithaca: Cornell University Press, 1966); Carl N. Degler, *Neither Black Nor White: Slavery and Race Relations in Brazil and the United States* (New York: Macmillan, 1971); Martin Duberman, ed., *The Antislavery Vanguard* (Princeton: Princeton University Press, 1966); W. E. B. DuBois, *The Suppression of the African Slave-Trade to the United States of America 1638–1870* (Baton Rouge: Louisiana State University Press, 1969); Dwight L. Dumond, *Antislavery Origins of the Civil War in the United States* (Ann Arbor: University of Michigan Press, 1960); Robert F. Durden, *The Gray and the Black* (Baton Rouge: Louisiana State University Press, 1972); Stanley Elkins, *Slavery* (Chicago: University of Chicago Press, 1959); Stanley Feldstein, *Once a Slave: The Slaves' View of Slavery* (New York: Morrow, 1971); Betty Fladeland, *Men & Brothers* (Urbana: University of Illinios Press, 1972); Eric Foner, ed., *America's Black Past* (New York: Harper & Row, 1970); John Hope Franklin, *From Slavery to Freedom* (New York: Alfred A. Knopf, 1961); George M. Frederickson, *The Black Image in the White Mind* (New York: Harper & Row, 1971); L. Fuller, *The Crusade Against Slavery* (New York: Harper, 1960); Eugene D. Genovese, "The Slave South: An Interpretation," *Science & Society* 25 (1961): 320–37; Eugene D. Genovese, *The Political Economy of Slavery* (Middletown, CT: Wesleyan University Press, 1989); Eugene P. Genovese, *The World the Slaveholders Made* (New York: Pantheon Books, 1969); Thomas Gossett, *Race: The History of an Idea in America* (Dallas: Southern Methodist University Press, 1963); Douglas Grant, *The Fortunate Slave: An Illustration of African Slavery in the Eighteenth Century* (New York: Oxford University Press, 1968); Lorenzo J. Greene, *The Negro in Colonial New England* (New York: Atheneum, 1968); Herbert G. Gutman, *The Black Family in Slavery and Freedom, 1750–1925* (New York: Pantheon Books, 1976); Paul Jacob, Saul Landau, and Eve Pell, *To Serve the Devil*, 2 vols. (New York, Random House, 1971); Winthrop D. Jordan, *White over Black* (Chapel Hill: University of North Carolina, 1968); Herbert Klein, *Slavery in the Americas* (Chicago: University of Chicago Press, 1967); Aileen S. Kraditor, *Means and Ends in American Abolitionism* (New York: Pantheon, 1969); Lawrence Lader, *The Bold Brahmins* (New York: E. P. Dutton, 1961); Anne J. Lane, ed., *The Debate Over Slavery* (Urbana: University of Illinois Press, 1971); Leon F. Litwak, *Been in the Storm so Long: The Aftermath of Slavery* (New York; Alfred A. Knopf, 1979); John R. Lynch, *The Facts of Reconstruction* (Indianapolis: Bobbs-Merrill, 1970); Carelton Mabee, *Black Freedom: The Nonviolent Abolitionists from 1830 through the Civil War* (New York: Macmillan, 1970); Bernard Mandel, *Labor: Free and Slave* (New York: Associated Authors, 1955); Daniel P. Mannix, *Black Cargoes* (New York: Viking Press, 1962); Donald G. Mathews, *Slavery and Methodism* (Princeton: Princeton University Press, 1965); Howard McGary and Bill E. Lawson, *Between Slavery and Freedom* (Bloomington: Indiana University Press, 1992); Eric L. McKitrick, ed., *Slavery Defended: The Views of the Old South* (Englewood Cliffs, NJ: Prentice Hall, 1963); Melton A. McLaurin, *Celia: A Slave* (Athens: University of Georgia Press, 1991); Edgar J. McManus, *A History of Negro Slavery in New York* (Syracuse: Syracuse University Press, 1966); James M. McPherson, *The Struggle For*

Equality (Princeton: Princeton University Press, 1965). A bibliography on slavery in the Americas will be found in James M. McPherson et al. eds., *Blacks in America* (New York: Doubleday, 1971). See also August Meier and Elliot Rudwick, *From Plantation to Ghetto* (New York: Hill and Wang, 1966); Frederick Merck, *Slavery and the Annexation of Texas* (New York: Alfred A. Knopf, 1966); Randall M. Miller and John David Smith, eds., *Dictionary of African American Slavery* (Westport, CT: Greenwood Press, 1988); Wilbert E. Moore, *American Negro Slavery and Abolition* (New York: The Third Press, 1971); Michael Mullin, ed., *American Negro Slavery: A Documentary History* (Columbia: University of South Carolina Press, 1976); Charles H. Nichols, *Many Thousand Gone* (Leiden: Brill, 1963); Earl Ofari, *Let Your Motto Be Resistance* (Boston: Beacon Press, 1972); Ulrich B. Phillips, *American Negro Slavery* (Baton Rouge: Louisiana State University Press, 1966); James Pope–Hennessy, *Sins of the Fathers: A Study of the Atlantic Slave Traders: 1441–1807* (New York: Alfred A. Knopf); Benjamin A. Quarles, *Black Abolitionists* (New York: Oxford University Press, 1969); James A. Rawley, *Race and Politics: "Bleeding Kansas" and the Coming Civil War* (Philadelphia: Lippincott, 1969); J. Saunders Redding, *They Came in Chains* (Philadelphia: Lippincott, 1950); Donald E. Reynolds, *Editors Make War: Southern Newspapers in the Secession Crisis* (Nashville: Vanderbilt University Press, 1970); Leonard L. Richards, *Gentlemen of Property and Standing* (New York: Oxford University Press, 1970); David L. Robinson, *Slavery in the Structure of American Politics 1765–1820* (New York: Norton, 1979); Peter Rose, ed., *Old Memories, New Moods* (New York: Atherton, 1970); Peter Rose, ed., *Slavery and its Aftermath* (New York: Atherton, 1970); Willie L. Rose, ed., *A Documentary History of Slavery in North America* (New York: Oxford University Press, 1976); V. Freimarck Rosenthal and B. Rosenthal, eds., *Race and the American Romantics* (New York: Schoken, 1971); Clinton Rossiter, *The American Quest 1790–1860* (New York: Harcourt Brace Jovanovich, 1969); Louis Ruchames, *The Abolitionists: A Collection of Their Writings* (New York: Putnams, 1963); Louis Ruchames, ed., *Racial Thought in America* (Amherst: University of Massachussetts Press, 1969); A. G. Russell, *Colour, Race and Empire* (London: Gollancz, 1944); Lester B. Scherer, *Slavery and the Churches in Early America* (Grand Rapids: Eerdman's, 1975); Elbert B. Smith, *The Death of Slavery* (Chicago: University of Chicago Press, 1967); Kenneth Stampp, *The Peculiar Institution* (New York: Alfred A. Knopf, 1966); Robert S. Starobin, *Industrial Slavery in the Old South* (New York: Oxford University Press, 1970); James B. Stewart, *Holy Warriors: The Abolitionists and American Society* (New York: Hill & Wang, 1976); Charles S. Sydnor, *Slavery In Mississippi* (Gloucester, MA: P. Smith, 1965 [ca. 1933]); John L. Thomas, ed., *Slavery Attacked: The Abolitionist Crusade* (Inglewood Cliffs, NJ: Prentice Hall, 1965); Okon Edet Uya, *From Slavery to Public Service: Robert Smalls 1839–1915* (New York: Oxford University Press, 1971); Richard C. Wade, *Slavery in the Cities—The South 1810–1860* (New York: Oxford University Press, 1964); W. E. F. Ward, *The Royal Navy and the Slavers* (New York: Pantheon Books, 1969); Eric Williams, *Capitalism and Slavery* (Chapel Hill: University of North Carolina Press, 1944); Robin W. Winks, *The Blacks in Canada* (New Haven: Yale University Press, 1971); Harvey Wish, ed., *Ante–Bellum* (New York; Putnam's 1960); C. Vann Woodward, *American Counterpoint: Slavery and Racism in the North-South Dialogue* (Boston: Little, Brown, 1970); C. Vann Woodward, *The Strange Career of Jim Crow*, 2nd ed., (New York: Oxford University Press, 1966); Norman R. Yetman, *Voices From Slavery* (New York: Holt, Rinehart & Winston, 1970).

64. See, for example, Thomas R. R. Cobb, *An Inquiry into the Law of Negro Slavery in the United States of America* (Philadelphia: Johnson & Co., 1858).

65. For an account of the rise and development of the convention of the noble savage in French and, particularly, in English literature see Hoxie N. Fairchild, *The Noble Savage* (New York: Columbia University Press, 1928); see also Eva B. Dykes, *The Negro in English Romantic Thought* (Washington, D.C.: Associated Publishers, 1942).

66. Whose categorical imperative is seldom spelled out in our time. Here it is: "so act as to treat humanity, whether in thine own person or in that of another, in every case as an end withal, never as a means only."

67. Johann G. Von Herder, *Outlines of a Philosophy of the History of Man*, vol. 1, trans. by T. Churchill, (London: J. Johnson, 1803), 298. An attempt has been made to show that Herder was a racist; see Cedric Dover, "The Racial Philosophy of Johann Herder," *British Journal of Sociology* 3 (1952): 124–33.

68. Johann F. Blumenbach, *On the Natural Variety of Mankind*, trans. and ed. by Thomas Bendyshe in *The Anthropological Treatises of Johann Friedrich Blumenbach* (London: Anthropological Society, 1865), 98–99 ff.

69. Ibid., 100.

70. Ralph Waldo Emerson, "Race," in *English Traits* (Boston: Philips, Sampson & Co. 1856), 54.

71. Ibid., 62.

72. For a brilliant discussion of this subject see Lancelot Hogben, "The Concept of Race," in his *Genetic Principles in Medicine and Social Science* (New York: Alfred A. Knopf, 1931), 122–44. See also William C. Boyd, *Genetics and the Races of Man* (Boston: Little Brown, 1950); Lancelot Hogben, *Nature and Nurture* (New York: W. W. Norton, 1933).

73. W. H. Thorpe, "Biological Races in *Hyponemeuta Padella L.*," *Journal of the Linnaean Society (Zoölogy)* 36 (1928): 621; W. H. Thorpe, "Biological Races in Insects and Allied Groups," *Biological Reviews* 5 (1930): 177; W. H. Thorpe, "Ecology and the Future of Systematics," in *The New Systematics*, ed. Julian Huxley (Oxford: Clarendon Press, 1940), 358; Th. Dobzhansky and Carl Epling, *Contributions to the Genetics, Taxonomy, and Ecology of* Drosophila pseudoobscura *and Its Relatives*, Pub 554 (Washington, D.C.: Carnegie Institution, 1944).

74. For an admirable presentation of the new taxonomy see Ernst Mayr, *Systematics and the Origin of Species* (New York: Columbia University Press, 1970).

75. For a critical discussion of such terms as "advanced" and "primitive," see Ashley Montagu, "The Concept of 'Primitive' and Related Anthropological Terms: A Study in the Systematics of Confusion," in *The Concept of the Primitive*, ed. Ashley Montagu, (New York: Free Press, 1968), 148–68.

76. Ralph Linton, *The Study of Man* (New York: Appleton-Century, 1936), 22.

77. Georges Cuvier, *Le Regne Animal*, vol. 1 (Paris: Deterville, 1817), iv-vi.

78. Alexander von Humbolt, *Cosmos: A Sketch of a Physical Description of the Universe*, trans. from the German by E. C. Otté (London: Bohn: 1849), 368–69.

79. Wilhelm von Humboldt, *Über die Kawi-Sprach auf der Insel Java*, vol. 3 (Berlin: Königlichen Academie der Wissenschaften, 1836), 426.

80. David Brion Davis, *Revolutions: Reflections on American Equality and Foreign Liberation* (Cambridge: Harvard University Press, 1991).

81. Roger Bruns, ed., *Am I Not a Man and a Brother* (New York: Chelsea House, 1977); Robin Blackburn, *The Overthrow of Colonial Slavery: 1776–1848* (London: Verso, 1988; New York: Routledge, 1989); Terrence Brady and Evan Jones, *The Fight Against Slavery* (New York: W. W. Norton, 1977); Robert M. Cover, *Justice Accused: Antislavery and the Judicial Process* (New Haven: Yale University Press); Davis, *Reflections;* David Brion Davis, *Slavery and Human Progress* (New York: Oxford University Press, 1984); David Brion Davis, *The Problem of Slavery in Western Culture* (Ithaca: Cornell University Press, 1966); Morton L. Dillon, *Slavery Attacked: Southern Slaves and Their Allies, 1619–1865* (De Kalb: Northern Illinios University Press, 1990); Morton L. Dillon, *The Abolitionists* (De Kalb: Northern Illinois University Press, 1974); Duberman, ed., *The Antislavery Vanguard;* Louis Filler, *The Crusade Against Slavery: 1830–1860* (New York: Harper Bros., 1960); Eric Foner, *Reconstruction: America's Unfinished Revolution 1863–1877* (New York: Harper & Row, 1988); Eric Foner, ed., *America's Black Past;* John Hope Franklin, *From Slavery to Freedom: A History of Negro Americans* (New York: Alfred A. Knopf, 1961); George M. Frederickson, *The Arrogance of Race: Historical Perspectives on Slavery, Racism, and Social Inequality* (Middletown, CT: Wesleyan Univeristy Press, 1988); Frederickson, *Black Image;* Eugene Genovese, *The World The Slaveholders Made* (New York; Pantheon, 1969); Jack Greene and J. R. Pole, *Colonial British America* (Baltimore: Johns Hopkins University Press, 1984); J. Morgan Kouser and James M. McPherson, eds., *Region, Race, and Reconstruction* (New York: Oxford University Press, 1982); Duncan J. McLeod, *Slavery, Race and the American Revolution* (London, New York: Cambridge University Press, 1974); James M. McPherson, *The Abolitionist Legacy* (Princeton: Princeton University Press, 1975); James Oakes, *The Ruling Class: A History of American Slaveholders* (New York: Alfred A. Knopf, 1982); Orlando Patterson, *Slavery and Social Death* (Cambridge: Harvard University Press, 1982); Lewis Perry, *Radical Abolitionism* (Ithaca: Cornell University Press, 1973); James A. Rawley, *The Trans-Atlantic Slave Trade* (New York: Norton, 1981); Ruchames, ed., *Racial Thought;* Ruchames, *The Abolitionists;* Scherer, *Slavery and the Churches;* James B. Stewart, *Holy Warriors: The Abolitionists and American Slavery* (New York: Hill and Wang, 1976); Michael Tadman, *Speculators and Slaves* (Madison: University of Wisconsin Press, 1989); Larry E. Tise, *Proslavery: A History of the Defense of Slavery in America 1700–1840* (Athens: University of Georgia Press, 1988); Geoffrey Ward, Ric Burns and Ken Burns, *The Civil War* (New York: Alfred A. Knopf, 1990).

82. Harry Ashmore, *The Man in the Middle* (Columbia: University of Missouri Press: 1966), 24; H. Ashmore, *Hearts and Minds: The Anatomy of Racism from Roosevelt to Reagan* (New York: McGraw-Hill, 1982).

83. For a valuable discussion of this aspect of the subject, see Hannah Arendt, *The Origins of Totalitarianism* (New York: Harcourt Brace Jovanovich, 1951). "It is highly probable that the thinking in terms of race would have disappeared in due time together with other irresponsible opinions of the nineteenth century, if the 'scramble for Africa' and the new era of imperialism had not exposed Western humanity to new and shocking experiences. Imperialism would have necessitated the invention of racism as the only possible 'explanation' and excuse for its deeds, even if no race-thinking had ever existed in the civilized world," pp. 183–84. See also "Racism and Imperialism" in Richard Hofstadter, *Social Darwinism in American Thought, 1860–1915* (Philadelphia: University of Pennsylvania Press, 1944), 146–73;

Philip D. Curtin, "The Origin of the 'White Man's Burden,'" *The Listener* 66, 1961, 412–15; Christine Bolt, *Victorian Attitudes to Race* (London: Routledge & Kegan Paul, 1971); L. H. Gann and Peter Duignan, *Colonialism in Africa 1870–1960,* 3 vols. (London and New York: Cambridge University Press, 1969); Boris Gussman, *Out in the Mid-Day Sun* (New York: Oxford University Press, 1963); J. A. Hobson, *Imperialism: A Study* (London: Allen & Unwin, 1965); V. G. Kiernan, *The Lords of Human Kind* (Boston: Little, Brown, 1969); Philip Mason, *Patterns of Dominance* (New York, Oxford Univertisy Press, 1970); Louis Snyder, ed., *The Imperialism Reader* (Princeton: Van Nostrand, 1962).

84. Gottfried W. von Leibnitz, *Otium Hanoveriana; sive, Miscellanea* (Leipzig, 1718), 37.

85. [Bernier] "Nouvelle division de la Terre, par les différentes Especes ou races d'homme qui l'habitent, envoyée par un fameux Voyageur à Monsieur . . . à peu près en ces termes," *Journal des Sçavans,* 24 April, 1684, 85–89. In English translation this essay is reprinted in Bendyshe, "The History of Anthropology," in *Memoirs Read before the Anthropological Society of London,* I (1863–64): 360–64.

86. Georges Buffon, *Histoire naturelle, générale et particulière* (Paris, 1749), Natural History, General and Particular, trans. by William Smellie III, corrected by William Wood (London, 1812), 302 ff.

87. Ales Hrdlicka, for example, lists six varieties as purporting to be "Buffon's classification." See "The Races of Man" in *Scientific Aspects of the Race Problem,* ed. J. W. Corrigan (New York: Longmans, 1941), 174.

88. The word "race" is of obscure origin. In English many uses of the word are set out in the Oxford English Dictionary, but it is clear that it was already in use in the sixteenth century. In France, François Tant, in a book entitled *Thrésor de la langue française,* published in 1600, derived the word from the Latin *radix,* a root, and stated that "it aludes to the extraction of a man, of a dog, of a horse; as one says of good or bad race." See Paul Topinard, "La Notion de race en anthropologie," *Revue d'Anthropologie,* 2nd ser., 2 (1879): 590. Attempts have been made to derive the words from the Latin *ratio,* the Italian *razza* (fourteenth century), the Spanish and Portuguese raza, and even from the Arabic *ras.* See Cedric Dover, "Race," *Man,* art. 95 (1951): 1.

89. John Newton, captain of the slaver African in 1752, who afterwards aided Wilberforce in the campaign to abolish the trade, wrote, "During the time I was engaged in the slave trade I never had the least scruple as to its lawfulness." See Anne Holt, *Walking Together* (London: Allen & Ulwin, 1938), 155.

90. L. P. Jacks, *The Confessions of an Octogenarian* (London: Allen & Ulwin, 1942), 137–38.

91. Carl Bridenbaugh, *Jamestown 1544–1699* (New York: Oxford University Press, 1980); Stanley M. Elkins, *Slavery* (Chicago: University of Chicago Press, 1959), 38sq; Rose, ed., *Documentary History of Slavery in North America.*

92. Klein, *Slavery,* 45–46.

93. Mary Stoughton Locke, *Anti-Slavery in America From the Introduction of African Slaves to the Prohibition of the Slave Trade 1619–1808,* Gloucester, MA: P. Smith, 1965.

94. John Wesley, *Thoughts Upon Slavery* (London: n.p., n.d.), 35.

95. Dumond, *Anti-Slavery*.

96. Mathews, *Slavery and Methodism*.

97. Cesar de l'Escale De Verone, *Observations sur les Hommes Couleur des Colonies* (Paris, 1790).

98. Victor Courtet de l'Isle, *La Science Politique Fondee sur la Science de l'Homme*. (Paris, 1837).

99. Thomas Jefferson, *Notes on the State of Virginia,* in *The Complete Jefferson,* ed. Saul K. Padover, (New York: Tudor Publishing, 1943), 662. For by far the best study of Jefferson's views on Blacks and slavery see John C. Miller, *The Wolf By The Ears: Thomas Jefferson and Slavery* (New York: Free Press, 1977). See also the measured discussion of Jefferson's views in Dumas Malone's *Jefferson and His Time: The Sage of Monticello,* vol. 6 (Boston: Little, Brown, & Co., 1948), 316–27.

100. Silvio Bedini, *The Life of Benjamin Banneker* (New York: Schribner's Sons, 1972).

101. A facsimile of the original letter may be seen in Bedini, *Benjamin Banneker,* fig.17.

102. Thomas Jefferson, Letter of Henri Gregoire, 25 February 1809, in *Basic Writings of Thomas Jefferson,* ed. Philip Foner (New York: Halcyon, 1950), 682.

103. Leigh Hunt, "Negro Civilzation," *The Examiner,* 4 August 1811, No. 188.

104. Edward Long, *The History of Jamaica,* 3 vols. (London, 1774).

105. Edward Long, "Observations on thte Gradation in the Scale of Being Between the Human and the Brute Creation. Including Some Curious Particulars Respecting Negroes," *The Columbian Magazine or Monthly Miscellany* 2 (1788): 15.

106. Samuel S. Smith, *An Essay on the Causes of the Variety of Complexion and Figure in the Human Species,* reprint (Harvard University Press, 1965).

107. Ibid., 33.

108. Ibid.

109. Ibid., 34.

110. For an account of this aspect of the subject, see Roy H. Pearce, *The Savages of America,* revised (Baltimore: Johns Hopkins Press, 1965).

111. Albert H. Smyth, ed., *The Writings of Benjamin Franklin,* vol. 1 (New York: Macmillan 1907), 376. In passing, it may be noted that in 1760 Franklin was admitted to membership in the English Anti-Slavery Society, and that when he was eighty-one years old Franklin became the president of the Pennsylvania Abolition Society. Nevertheless, Franklin's own slaves were not freed until after his death.

112. Charles de Secondat Montesquieu, *The Spirit of the Laws,* book 15, chap. 5, trans. Thomas Nugent (New York: Hafner 1949).

113. Claudine Hunting, "The *Philosophes* and Black Slavery 1748–1765," *Journal of the History of Ideas* 39 (1978): 405–18.

114. Thomas Dew, *Review of the Debates in the Virginia Legislature of 1831–1832* (Richmond, VA: Randolph, 1832). Dew's discussion first appeared in pamphlet form in Richmond in May, 1832, and was widely noticed in the Southern press. See also William Harper, *A Memoir on Slavery* (Charleston: Burgess, 1838).

115. Josiah Nott, *Types of Mankind* (Philadelphia: Lippincott, 1854). In 1856 Nott contributed an appendix to Hotz's translation of Gobineau's *The Moral and Intellectual Diversity of Races,* in which he sought to provide the biological evidence for

the natural inequalities of the various branches of mankind. See Emmet B. Carmichael, "Josiah Clark Nott," *Bulletin of the History of Medicine* 22 (1948): 249–62.

116. Dodd, *Cotton Kingdom,* 146; see also chap. 3, "The Social Philosophy of the Cotton Planter."

117. Willliam S. Jenkins, *Pro-Slavery Thought in the Old South* (Chapel Hill: University of North Carolina Press, 1935), 125.

118. Cobb, *Inquiry,* 8–9.

119. Ibid., 16–17.

120. Ibid., 51.

121. Ibid., 49.

122. Ibid., 51.

123. George Norlin, *The Quest of American Life University of Colorado Studies,* Series B, Studies in the Humanities, vol. 2 (Boulder, 1945), ix.

124. Quoted from Herbert Apthekar, *Essays in the History of the American Negro* (New York: International Publishers, 1945), 139.

125. On Smith see Donald H. Meyer, *The American Moralists: Academic Moral Philosophy in the United States 1835–1880.* Unpublished Ph.D. dissertation, University of California, Berkeley, 1976, 34–366. Also Lewis Perry, *Radical Abolitionism* (Ithaca: Cornell University Press, 1973); Ann J. Lane, ed., *The Debate Over Slavery* (Urbana: University of Illinois Press, 1971).

126. George Fitzhugh, *Sociology for the South, or Failure of Free Society* (Richmond, VA: A. Morris, 1954.)

127. John Saffin, *A Brief and Candid Answer to a Late Printed Sheet, Entitled, The Selling of Joseph* (Boston, 1701). Quoted from Moore, *Notes on the History of Slavery,* 251. In our own time this doctrine has been even more efficiently preached by Protestant theologians of the Dutch Reformed Church of South Africa.

128. Russel Nye, *Fettered Freedom* (East Lansing: Michigan State College Press, 1949). For further reading, see *The National Anti-Slavery Standard,* 28 January 1850.

129. *The Anti-Slavery Bugle,* 12 January 1850.

130. It is of interest to note here that in what is undoubtedly the most important study of the problem of the American black that has ever been made, the author's independent analysis of the historical facts has led him to practically identical conclusions: "The biological ideology had to be utilized as an intellectual explanation of, and a moral apology for, slavery in a society which went out emphatically to invoke as its highest principles the ideas of the inalienable right of all men to freedom and equality of opportunity." Gunnar Myrdal, *An American Dilemma: The Negro Problem and Modern Democracy,* 2 vols. (New York: Harper, 1944), 83–89. "The correct observation that the Negro is inferior [i.e., socially inferior] was tied up to the correct belief that man belongs to the biological universe, and, by twisting logic, the incorrect deduction was made that the inferiority is biological in nature," ibid., 97. For a valuable discussion of the subject see John C. Greene, "The American Debate on the Negro's Place in Nature," *Journal of the History of Ideas* 15 (1954): 384–96.

131. We may refer, for example, to the case of the president of the Anthropological Society of London, Dr. James Hunt. On 17 November 1863, Dr. Hunt read a paper before the society entitled "The Negro's Place in Nature," in which he asserted the essential inferiority in every way of the Negro to the white man. "The Ne-

gro's Place in Nature," *Memoirs of the Anthropological Society* (London) 1 (1863), 1–64. This paper was discussed at the meeting in a very dignified manner by everyone but the egregious and insolent Dr. Hunt, who wound up his reply to his critics with the remark that "all he asked was that scientific evidence of this character should be met by scientific argument, and not by poetical clap-trap, or by gratuitous and worthless assumptions." *Anthropological Review* 1 (London, 1863): 391. The paper was the immediate cause of many acrimonious debates, and it was, of course, received with much applause by the proslavery party, especially in the United States. When, in 1869, Dr. Hunt died, a New York paper wrote that "Dr. Hunt, in his own clear knowledge and brave enthusiasm, was doing more for humanity, for the welfare of mankind, and for the glory of God, than all the philosophers, humanitarians, philanthropists, statesmen, and, we may say, bishops and clergy of England together." This last statement is taken from Alfred C. Haddon's *History of Anthropology* (London: Watts, 1934), 45.

132. Wilhelm Wundt, *Philosophische Studien,* vol. 3 (Leipzig: Englemann, 1883).

133. See Edward Lurie, "Louis Agassiz and the Races of Man," *Isis* 45 (1954): 227–42; William Stanton, *The Leopard's Spots: Scientific Attitudes Toward Race in America, 1815–59* (Chicago: University of Chicago Press, 1960); John S. Haller, Jr., *Outcasts From Evolution: Scientific Attitudes of Racial Inferiority* (Urbana: University of Illinois Press, 1971).

134. See C. L. Bachman, *John Bachman* (Charleston: Walker, Evans, and Coswell, 1888), 317.

135. T. S. Foster, *Travels and Settlements of Early Man* (London: Benn, 1929), 31.

136. For an account of Gobineau and a distillation of the essence of Gobineauism by an apostle of both Gobineau and Nietzsche, Dr. Oscar Levy, see Count Joseph A. de Gobineau, *The Renaissance,* trans. by Paul V. Cohn (London: Allen & Unwin, 1927). The introductory essay of some sixty pages by Dr. Levy is an amazing thing. See also Michael Biddiss, ed., *Gobineau: Selected Political Writings* (New York: Harper & Row, 1970).

137. Observe how, from the same motives, this reaction expresses itself in the more recent writings of one of the most confused of American racists, namely in Madison Grant's *The Passing of the Great Race.* He writes: "There exists to-day a widespread and fatuous belief in the power of environment, as well as of opportunity, to alter heredity, which arises from the dogma of the brotherhood of man, derived in turn from those loose thinkers of the French Revolution and their American mimics. Such beliefs have done much damage in the past, and if allowed to go uncontradicted, may do much more serious damage in the future" (p. 14).

138. Jean Finot, *Race Prejudice* (New York; Dutton, 1907), 7. For a brilliant analysis of Gobineau and his views see Ernst Cassirer, *The Myth of the State* (New Haven: Yale University Press, 1946), 225–47.

139. For a valuable account of these writings and their influence, see Leon Stein, *The Racial Thinking of Richard Wagner* (New York: Philosophical Library, 1950).

140. Houston Chamberlain, *Die Grundlagen des neunzehnten Jahrunderts* (1899), trans. by John Lees as *The Foundations of the Nineteenth Century* (London and New York: Lane, 1910).

141. This refers to Chamberlain's statement that "it frequently happens that children who have no conception of what 'Jew' means . . . begin to cry as soon as a genuine Jew or Jewess comes near them."

142. This is probably John Wilson (pseudonym Christopher North) whose lifelong friend wrote the works which Wilson passed off as his own. See Elsie Swann's *Christopher North* (Edinburgh: Oliver Boyd, 1934).

143. John Oakesmith, *Race and Nationality* (London: Heinemann, 1919), 58.

144. William L. Shirer, *The Rise and Fall of the Third Reich* (New York: Simon and Schuster, 1960).

145. For Chamberlain see Geoffrey E. Field's fascinating biography, *Evangelist of Race* (New York: Columbia University Press, 1981); for Chamberlain's letter see pp. 436–437.

146. Oaksmith, *Race and Nationality*, 50.

147. Mary Butler, *The Tyranny of Greece Over Germany* (Cambridge: Cambridge University Press, 1935); Leon Poliakov, *The Aryan Myth* (New York: Basic Books, 1974); Louis L. Snyder, *German Nationalism: The Tragedy of a People* (Harrisburg, PA: Stackpole 1952).

148. Ernest Renan, *The Future of Science* (London: Chapman and Hall, 1891), xviii. Almost a hundred years later we find Sigmund Freud writing, a little querously, "Because we destroy illusions, we are reproached with endangering ideas."

149. Michael D. Biddiss, ed., *Images of Race* (Leicester: Leicester University Press, 1979); William Stanton, *The Leopard's Spots: Scientific Attitudes Toward Race in America 1815–59* (Chicago: University of Chicago Press, 1960): Haller, *Outcasts From Evolution;* Ruchames, ed., *Racial Thought;* Nancy Stepan, *The Idea of Race in Science: Great Britain 1815–1800–1960* (New York: Anchor Books, 1982); Daniel Gasman, *The Scientific Origins of National Socialism* (New York: Basic Books, 1974); Elazar Bakan, *The Retreat of Scientific Racism* (Cambridge: Cambridge University Press 1991); Audrey Smedley, *Race in North America: Origin and Evolution of a World View* (Denver: Westview Press, 1993).

150. Willem A. Bonger, *Race and Crime* (New York: Columbia University Press, 1943), 11. On the invasion of Holland by the Nazis, Bonger became one of their first victims. For an admirable account of the rise of racism in Germany see Massing, *Rehearsal for Destruction.*

151. Hermann Rauschning, *The Voice of Destruction* (New York: Putnam, 1940) 232; George W. Stocking, Jr., *Victorian Anthropology* (New York: Free Press, 1987); Walter E. Houghton, *The Victorian Frame of Mind 1830–1870* (New Haven: Yale University Press, 1957).

152. Henry Turner Jr., ed., *Hitler: Memoirs of a Confidant* (New Haven: Yale University Press, 1985), 201–15.

153. James Viscount Bryce, *Race Sentiment as a Factor in History* (London: University of London Press, 1915), 31. For an excellent study of the "mischief" done by educated writers see Frederic E. Faverty, *Matthew Arnold the Ethnologist* (Evanston, IL: Northwestern University Press, 1951).

154. "Miscegenation in South Africa," *Nature* 3698 (1940): 357. The above remarks refer to the official report of the commissioners appointed by the Union of South Africa under the title Report of the Commission on Mixed Marriages in

South Africa (Pretoria, Government Printer, 1939). This document provides an interesting case study of "race" prejudice in action at a high governmental level. American precedents, laws, and decisions relating to intermarriage are heavily drawn upon. So was the way prepared for apartheid.

155. See the UNESCO Report *The Race Concept.* See also, Ashley Montagu, *Statement on Race,* revised (New York: Oxford University Press, 1972), and Appendix A of the unabridged edition of this volume.

2

The Fallaciousness of the Older Anthropological Conception of Race

At the famous 1860 meeting of the British Association for the Advancement of Science at Oxford, just a few months after the publication of Charles Darwin's *The Origin of Species,* the redoubtable young Thomas Henry Huxley scored a resounding victory over Bishop Wilberforce, who led the forces opposed to Darwin's new theory of evolution, and attempted to make a monkey of Huxley, whereupon the younger man rose to the occasion, turned the tables, and made a monkey out of the Bishop. It is told that when the Bishop of Worcester returned home he communicated the intelligence to his wife that the horrid Professor Huxley had stated that man was descended from the apes, whereupon the good lady exclaimed: "Descended from the apes! My dear, let us hope that it is not true. But if it is, let us pray that it will not become generally known."

More recently, the attempt to deprive the older generation of physical anthropologists of their belief in race was construed by its members as an affront akin to that which sought to deprive the Bishop's wife of her belief in the doctrine of special creation. Throughout the nineteenth century and well into the first half of the twentieth there was hardly a scientist who did not fully subscribe to the concept of race.[1] Indeed, the older anthropological conception of race and the belief in special creation have much in common, for race is, to large extent, the special creation of the physical anthropologist. Most physical anthropologists until recently took it for granted that race corresponded to some sort of physical reality in nature. Indeed, the concept of race was one of the fundamental ideas with which the physical anthropologist habitually worked. To question the validity of this basic concept upon which he was intellectually nurtured as if it were an axiom was something which never occurred to him. One doesn't question the axioms upon which one's science and one's activity in it are based—at least, not usually. One simply takes them for granted.

But in science, as in life, it is good practice to attach from time to time a question mark to the facts one takes most for granted, to question the fundamental postulates or facts which require no demonstration; for a fact as a postulate is largely the opinion of those who *should* know—and being human those who *should* know are sometimes fallible, and therefore liable to err. In science such questioning is important, because without it there is a very real danger that certain erroneous or arbitrary ideas, which may originally have been used merely as a convenience, may become so fortified by technicality and so dignified by time that their original infirmities may eventually be wholly concealed.

So it was with the older or classical anthropological conception of race. It was, indeed, nothing but a whited sepulcher, a conception which in the light of modern field and experimental genetics proved utterly erroneous and meaningless; "an absolutist system of metaphysical beliefs," as it has been called.[2] As such, it has been suggested that the term be dropped from the anthropological as well as from the popular vocabulary, for it is a tendentious term which has done an infinite amount of harm and no good at all.

The development of the anthropological conception of race may be traced from the scholastic naturalization of Aristotle's doctrine of the predicables of genus, species, difference, property, and accident. From the Middle Ages through the seventeenth century it may be followed to the early days of the Age of Enlightenment, when Linnaeus, in 1735, took over the concepts of class, genus, and species from the theologians to serve him as systematic tools.[3] As we have already seen, the term "race" was first introduced into the literature of natural history by Buffon in 1749. But Buffon did not use the term in a classificatory sense; this was left to Blumenbach (1752–1840) the founder of physical anthropology.[4]

As used by Blumenbach, the term "race" merely represented an extension of the Aristotelian conception of species; that is to say, it was a subdivision of a species. Like Buffon, Blumenbach recognized, as did Linnaeus, that all human beings belong to a single species and considered it merely convenient to distinguish between certain geographically localized groups of humankind. Thus, when with Blumenbach, in the late eighteenth century, the term assumed a classificatory value, it was understood that that value was purely arbitrary and no more than a simple convenience. It had no other meaning than that. The Aristotelian conception of species, the theological conception of special creation, and the natural history of the Age of Enlightenment, as represented particularly by Cuvier's brilliant conception of unity of type, namely, the idea was that animals can be grouped and classified upon the basis of assemblages of structural characters which, more or less, they posess in common. These three conceptions fitted together extremely well and yielded the idea of the fixity of species, an idea which, in spite of every indication to the contrary in the years which followed, was gradually extended to the typological concept of race, namely, that certain people or populations existed who were characterized by physical types that distinguished them from all other peoples or populations.

The Darwinian contribution showed that species were not so fixed as was formerly believed and that under the action of natural selection one species might give rise to another; that all animal forms might change in this way. It is, however, important to remember that Darwin conceived of evolution as a process involving continuous materials which, without the operation of natural selection, would remain unchanged. Hence, under the Darwinian conception of species it was still possible to think of species as relatively fixed and immutable, with the modification that under the slow action of natural selection they were capable of change. For the nineteenth-century physical anthropologist, therefore, it was possible to think of race or races, not as Blumenbach did in the eighteenth century, as an arbitrary convenience in classification, but as Cuvier did at the beginning of the nineteenth century for all animals, as groups which could be classified on the basis of the fact that they possessed an aggregate of common physical characters, and, as Darwin later postulated, as groups which varied only under conditions of natural selection, which otherwise remained unchanged.

This is essentially a scholastic conception of species with the one fundamental difference that a species is considered to be no longer fixed and immutable. As far as the older physical anthropological conception of race is concerned, a few anthropologists, still unaware of the significance of the findings of modern genetics, continued to think of race as the scholastics thought of species, as a knowable, even though mutable, fixed whole, the essence of which could be defined *per genus, species, propria, differentia, et accidens.* In fact, the physical anthropologist had simply taken over a crude eighteenth-century notion which was originally offered as a general term with no more than an arbitrary value—a convenient aid to the memory in discussing various groups of humankind—and, having erected an emmense terminology and methodology about it, deceived himself in the belief that he was dealing with an objective reality.[5]

Anthropologists failed in their vision because they neglected to subject to rigorous examination the presuppositions upon which their concept of race was based. With the exception of T. H. Huxley, Franz Boas, Julian Huxley, and Alexander and Wilhelm Humboldt, especially during the period of kleptomaniac imperialism of the nineteenth century, when good reasons had to be found to justify the conquest and exploitation of the "inferior races" one could hardly question what was so "clear" to everyone.

An illuminating reflection of a vanishing physical anthropological viewpoint occurs in an attractive book by a field student of physical anthropology. In explaining the object of her investigations, she wrote:

The purpose of these anthropometric measurements is the establishment of various physical types. The more generalized characteristics of any one locality can be determined, the resemblances to and differences from their near and remote neighbours, the ideal being to discover the various strains which are there combined. In anthropology there is as much information to be gathered from these physical measurements as from the study of social habits and customs.[6]

This represents a fair statement of the older anthropological viewpoint: "the purpose of these anthropometric measurements is the establishment of various physical types."

For more than a century physical anthropologists directed their attention principally toward the task of establishing criteria by means of which races of humankind might be defined—a diverting postprandial occupation in which by arbitrarily selecting the criteria one could nearly always make the races come out exactly as one thought they should. As Boyd wrote,

Those of the proposed criteria which were adopted are evidently those which were found to give 'reasonable results'—that is, they brought home the bacon; so that in cases where the anthropologist was convinced race differences ought to exist, these criteria proved that they did. Unobliging criteria that seemed to show no differences between races 'obviously' distinct, or which indicated differences within groups 'obviously' homogeneous, have been tactfully related to the scrap heap.[7]

In this observation we probably have the crux of the whole problem. Only those methods of race classification which indicated the "right sort" of race differences were encouraged and utilized.

Most physical anthropologists took completely for granted the one thing required to be proved, namely, that the concept of race corresponded to a reality that could actually be measured and verified and descriptively set out so that it could be seen to be a fact.[8] In short, they took for granted that the anthropological conception of race was verifiably true, and showed that in nature there exist groups of human beings comprising individuals each of whom possesses a certain typical aggregate of characters which individually and collectively serve to distinguish them from the individuals in all other groups.

Plainly stated, this is the conception of race that most physical anthropologists held and practically everyone else, even some geneticists, accepted. When, in the light of accumulating criticism in recent years, a growing number of physical anthropologists have admitted that the concept cannot be strictly applied in any systematic sense, they have thought to escape the consequences of such an admission by calling the term a "general" one and have proceeded to play the old game of blindman's bluff with a sublimity which is almost enviable. For it is not vouchsafed to everyone completely to appreciate the illusory grandeur of the doctrine here implied. The feeling of dissatisfaction with which the older physical anthropologists had viewed the many laborious attempts at classification of human groups had not, on the whole, succeeded in generating the disloyal suspicion that something was probably somewhere wrong. If there was a fault, it was generally supposed, it lay not with the anthropologist, but with the refractory material, with the human beings themselves who were the subject of classification, and who always varied so much that it was difficult to put them into the group where they were conceived properly to belong. This was distinctly a nuisance, but, happily, one which could be overcome by the simple expedient of "averaging"—the principal occupation of the self-appointed authorities on race.

Race: A Conceptual Omelet

The process of averaging the characters of a given group, of knocking the individuals together, giving them a good stirring, and then serving the resulting omelet as a race was essentially the anthropological process of race-making. It may have been good cooking, but it was not science, since it served to confuse rather than to clarify. When an omelet is done it has a fairly uniform character, though the ingredients which have entered into its making have been varied. So it was with the anthropological conception of race. It was an omelet that corresponded to nothing in nature: an indigestible dish conjured into being by an anthropological chef from a number of ingredients which were extremely varied in character. This omelet conception of race had no existence outside the statistical frying pan in which it had been reduced by the heat of the anthropological imagination; it was a meaningless concept because it is inapplicable to anything real. When anthropologists began to realize that the proper description of a group does not consist in the process of making an omelet of it, but in the analysis and description of the character of the variability of the elements entering into it—its ingredients—they discovered that the fault lay not with the materials but with the conceptual tool with which they had approached their study. *In passing, it is a good idea not to accept any concept until the presuppositions upon which it is based have been thoroughly examined.*

It is a sobering thought that as early as 1836, when the English were busily exterminating the Tasmanian aborigines, and elsewhere, the English anthropologist, James Cowles Prichard (1786–1848), in his book *Researches Into the Physical History of Man*, clearly pointed out the dangers of such thinking: "Races," he wrote, are properly successions of individuals propagated from any given stock; and the term should be used without any involved meaning that such a progeny or stock has always possessed a particular character. The real import of the term has often been overlooked, and the word race has been used as if it implied a distinction in the physical character of a whole series of individuals. By writers in anthropology who adopt this term, it is often tacitly assumed that such distinctions were primordial, and that their successive transmission has been unbroken. If such were the fact, a race so characterized would be a species in the strict sense of the word, and it ought to be so termed.[9]

There were a few others who saw this clearly, especially Franz Boas (1858–1942), the founder of anthropology in the United States, who, recalling his earliest days as a physical anthropologist in the 1890s wrote, "When I turned to the consideration of racial problems I was shocked by the formalism of the work. Nobody had tried to answer the questions why certain measurements were taken, why they were considered significant, whether they were subject to other influences."[10]

That many differences exist between different groups of human beings is obvious; but the older anthropological conception of these was erroneous, and the traditional anthropological approach to the study of their relationships was unscientific and pre-Mendelian.[11] Taxonomic exercises in the classification of assemblages of phenotypical, that is, observable traits produced in conjunction with the environment, will never succeed in elucidating the relationships of different groups of humankind to one another, for the simple reason that it is not assemblages of traits that undergo change in the formation of the individual and the group, but rather the single complex units, the genes, which are physiologically associated with those traits. One of the great persisting errors involved in the anthropological conception of race was due to the steady refusal to recognize this fact. The truth is that it is not possible to classify the various groups of humankind by means of the traits the older anthropologists customarily used, because those traits do not behave as complexes; they behave instead in a totally different manner: as the expression of many independent units, linked and unlinked, in interaction with the environment, that have entered into their formation.

The parallel in the history of biology is striking here, and was well illustrated by Dobzhansky, who, in his classic book *Genetics and the Origin of Species* wrote:

> Many studies on hybridization were made before Mendel, but they did not lead to the discovery of Mendel's laws. In retrospect, we see clearly where the mistake of Mendel's predecessors lay: they treated as units the complexes of characteristics of individuals, races, and species, and attempted to find rules governing the inheritance of such complexes. Mendel was first to understand that it was the inheritance of separate traits, and not complexes

of traits, which had to be studied. Some of the modern students of racial variability consistently repeat the mistakes of Mendel's predecessors.[12]

The materials of evolution are not represented by continuous aggregates of traits, but by discontinuous packages of chemicals, each of which is more or less independent in its action and may be only partially responsible for the genes, situated mostly within the chromosomes, structures with which many physical anthropologists were until recently scarcely on bowing acquaintance. The genes retain both their independence and their individual character more or less indefinitely, although probably they are all inherently variable, are known to jump around, are subject to many influences, and, in time, may undergo mutation. For these reasons any conception of race which operates as if inheritance were a matter of transmitting gross aggregates of traits is both erroneous and confusing. To quote Dobzhansky once more:

> The difficulty . . . is that . . . the concept is obviously outmoded and incapable of producing much insight into the causative factors at work in human populations. Although the genic basis of relatively few human traits is known, it seems that following up the distribution of these traits could tell us more about the 'races' than a great abundance of measurements.[13]

A typical example of the prevailing views at the time among physical anthropologists were those of Professor Earnest A. Hooton, Chairman of the Department of Anthropology at Harvard University, and the most amiable teacher of many later able anthropologists. In the Vanuxem Lectures delivered at Princeton University and published in 1940 by its press as *Why Men Behave Like Apes and Vice Versa,* Hooton averred that

> We must rid ourselves of the false prophets of cultural salvation and the witless preachers of human equality. The future of our species does not hang upon forms of government, economic adjustment, religious or social creeds, and purely environmental education. The future of man is dependent upon biology.

Such views were the expression of a physical anthropology unenlightened by a knowledge of genetics or evolutionary biology, pronouncements which led to the buttressing of a pseudoscientific eugenics and devastating governmental immigration policies.[14]

Evolution, Genes, and Race

The principal agencies of evolutionary change in humans are primarily gene variability and gene mutation. Evolutionary changes are brought

about through the rearrangements in the combination of genes in consequence of the operation of many secondary factors, physical and cultural,
and changes in the character of genes themselves. In order to appreciate
the meaning of the variety presented by humankind today it is indispensably necessary to understand the manner in which these agencies work.
Thus, in humans it is practically certain that some forms of hair and skin
color are due to mutation, while still other forms are due to various combinations of these mutant forms with one another, as also with nonmutant
forms. The rate of mutation for different genes in humans varies. It has
been calculated that the gene for normal clotting mutates, for example, to
the gene for hemophilia in one out of less than 10,000 males per generation. It is highly probable, for example, that such a mutation occurred in
the person of Queen Victoria's father, a fact which in the long run may perhaps constitute both his and her chief claim to fame.[15] The rate of mutation of the blood group genes, however, appears to be low. Mutation of
skin-color genes also is infrequent, while mutation of hair-form genes is
somewhat more frequent. If anthropologists are ever to understand how
the different groups of humankind came to possess such traits as distinguish the more geographically isolated of them, and those of the less isolated, more recently mixed, and therefore less distinguishable groups, it
should be obvious that they must cease making omelets of the very ingredients, the genes, which it should be our purpose to isolate and to map.
What must be studied are the frequencies with which such genes occur in
different groups of populations. The gene frequency method for the study
of the distribution of human genes is a simple one and has now been available for some time, as likewise has been the method for the study of genetic linkage in man.

If, roughly speaking, one gene be arbitrarily assigned to every component of the body, it should be fairly clear that as regards the structure of
man we are dealing with many thousands of genes. In the fruit fly
Drosophila melanogaster, in which there are four pairs of chromosomes, it has
been estimated that there are no less than 5,000 genes. Humans have 23
pairs of chromosomes, with one member of each pair being inherited from
each parent, the theoretical possible combinations between the 23 chromosomes of the male parent and those of the female parent in the production of sperm or ovum are 8,388,608, or 2 raised to the 23rd power. The
offspring produced by the parents can be genetically different by $7x10^{13}$,
or 70,000,000,000,000. It will be seen that the different combinations that a
46 chromosome system can take reach a stupendous figure. This is on a
purely numerical basis. Earlier and by totally different methods Spuhler arrived at the figure of about 34,000 genes in humans,[16] and Evans at an estimate of between 10,000 and 100,000 genes in humans.[17] Most sources currently agree on 100,000 genes. If we consider the newer concepts, which

recognize that the adult individual represents the end point in the interaction between all these genes, under the influence of the environments in which they have undergone development, the complexities become even greater.[18]

The morphological characters that anthropologists in the past have relied on for their racial classifications have been few indeed, involving a minute fraction of the great number of genes it would actually be necessary to consider in attempting to make any real—that is to say, genetically analytic—classification of humankind.

The reality is that within a region or over a geographical area populations grade into each other. Such gradation is called a *cline* (Gr. *klinein,* to incline, slope or bend), and refers to a measurable gradation of physical traits such as hair, color, body form, gene frequencies, and the like. In other words, it is a *process* of *direction* in which a trait varies. Also, interbreeding usually occurs at intergrading zones.

To sum up, the indictment against the older, or traditional, anthropological conception of race is that: (1) it was artificial, (2) it did not correspond to the facts, (3) it led to confusion and the perpetuation of error, and finally, (4) for all these reasons it was scientifically unsound, or rather, more accurately, that it was false and misleading. Based as it was on unexamined facts and unjustifiable generalizations, it were better that the term "race," corrupted as it is with so many deceptive and dangerous meanings, be dropped altogether from the vocabulary.

If it be agreed that the human species is one and that it consists of a group of populations which, more or less, adjoin each other geographically or ecologically and of which the neighboring ones intergrade or hybridize wherever they are in contact, or are potentially capable of doing so,[19] then it should be obvious that the task of the student interested in the character of these populations must be to study the frequency distribution of the genes which characterizes them—not misconceived and misconstrued entities.

In 1942 when this chapter was first written, I wrote that physical anthropologists must recognize that they have unwittingly played no small part in the creation of the myth of race, which in our time has assumed so dangerous a form. It is encouraging to be able to say that since the appearance of the first edition of this book in 1942 an increasing number of anthropologists have seen their responsibility clearly and the newer generation of students of humankind are taking active steps to exorcise the monster of race and deliver the thought and conduct of our species from its evil social consequences.[20]

In 1944 Dr. G. M. Morant, in delivering the address on physical anthropology at the centenary meeting of the Royal Anthropological Institute, made the important point clearly. "It seems to me," he said, that the time has come when anthropologists must fully recognize fundamental changes in their treatment of the problem of racial classification. The idea that a race is a group of people separated from all others because of the distinctive ancestry of its members is implied whenever a racial label is used, but in fact we have no knowledge of the existence of such populations today or in any past time. Gradations between any regional groups distinguished, and an absence of clear-cut divisions, are the universal rule. Our methods have never been fully adapted to deal with this situation.[21]

Notes

1. John Haller, Jr., *Outcasts From Evolution* (Urbana: Universtity of Illinois Press, 1971), 3 sq.

2. Gunnar Myrdal, *An American Dilemma: The Negro Problem and Modern Democracy* (New York: Harper & Bros., 1944), 116.

3. Linnaeus, *Systema naturae.*

4. Stephen Jay Gould, "The Geometer of Race," *Discover* 15 (1994): 64–69.

5. Franz Boas, "History and Science in Anthropology: a Reply," *American Anthropologist* 38 (1936): 137–51.

6. Charis Crockett, *The House in the Rain Forest* (Boston: Houghton Mifflin, 1942), 29.

7. William C. Boyd, *Genetics and the Races of Man* (Boston: Little, Brown, 1950), 195.

8. T. H. Huxley, in his essay, published in 1865, "On the Methods and Results of Ethnology" reprinted in *Man's Place in Nature and Other Anthropological Essays* (New York: Appleton & Co., 1890], refused to use the terms "stocks," "varieties," "races," or "species" in connection with man, "because each of these last well-known terms implies, on the part of its employer, a preconceived opinion touching one of those problems, the solution of which is the ultimate object of the science; and in regard to which, therefore, ethnologists are especially bound to keep their minds open and their judgments freely balanced."

9. James Cowles Prichard, *Researches Into the Physical History of Man,* 3rd ed. (London: Ballière, 1836), 359.

10. Franz Boas, "History and Science in Anthropology: A Reply," *American Anthropologist* 38 (1936): 140; also Franz Boas, *Race, Language and Culture* (New York: Macmillan, 1940).

11. Edmond Demolins, *Anglo-Saxon Superiority: To What is it Due,* 10th ed. (New York: R. F. Frenno, 1898).

12. Theodosius Dobzhansky, *Genetics and the Origin of Species* (New York: Columbia University Press, 1937), 62.

13. Ibid.

14. J.B.S. Haldane, *Heredity and Politics* (New York: Norton, 1938), 88; Michael R. Cummings, *Human Heredity: Principles and Issues* (St. Paul: West, 1991), 97.

15. For a clear exposition of the facts see William C. Boyd, *Genetics and the Races of Man* (Boston: Little, Brown, 1950); Curt Stern, *Principles of Human Genetics*

(San Francisco: Freeman, 1973); L. L. Cavalli-Sforza and W. P. Bodmer, *The Genetics of Human Populations* (San Francisco: Freemana, 1971); L. L. Cavalli-Sforza, Paolo Menozzi, and Albert Piazza, *The History and Geography of Human Genes* (Princeton: Princeton University Press, 1994); M. Levitan and A. Montagu, *Textbook of Human Genetics* (New York: Oxford University Press, 1971; 3rd ed. 1983); Daniel J. Kevles, *In the Name of Eugenics* (New York: Alfred A. Knopf, 1985); Mark H. Haller, *Eugenics: Hereditarian Attitudes in American Thought* (New Brunswick: Rutgers University Press, 1963); Donald K. Pickens, *Eugenics and the Progressives* (Nashville: Vanderbilt University Press, 1968); Hamilton Cravens, *The Triumph of Evolution: American Scientists and the Heredity-Environment Controversy 1900–1941* (Philadelphia: University of Pennsylvania Press, 1978); Kenneth Ludmerer, *Genetics and American Society* (Baltimore: Johns Hopkins University Press,1972), 1075; Audrey Smedley, *Race in North America* (Boulder: Westview Press, 1993); Richard C. Lewontin, Steven Rose, and Leon Kamin, *Not in Our Genes* (New York: Pantheon Books, 1984).

16. James N. Spuhler, "An Estimate of the Number of Genes in Man," *Science* 108 (1948): 279.

17. Robley D. Evans, "Quantitative Inferences Concerning the Genetic Effects of Radiation of Human Beings," *Science* 109 (1949): 299–304; W. F. Bodmer and L. L. Cavalli-Sforza, *Genetics, Evolution, and Man* (San Francisco: W. H. Freeman, 1976); Michael R. Cummings, *Human Heredity: Principles and Issues* (St. Paul, MN: West, 1991), 37.

18. See Ashley Montagu, *Statement on Race,* 2nd ed. (New York, Oxford University Press, 1972); Ernst Mayr, *Populations, Species, and Evolution,* (New York: Columbia University Press, 1970); Ernst Mayr, *The Growth of Biological Thought* (Cambridge: Harvard University Press, 1982); Ernst Mayr, *Systematics and the Origin of Species,* (New York: Columbia University Press, 1942), 154ff.

19. Ernst Mayr, "Speciation Phenomena in Birds," *Biological Symposia* 2 (1941): 66, and *Systematics,* 154 ff.; Ernst Mayr, *Animal Species and Evolution* (Cambridge: Harvard University Press, 1963).

20. Leonard Lieberman, Blaine W. Stevenson, and Larry T. Reynolds, "Race and Anthropology: A Core Concept Without Consensus." *Anthropology and Education Quarterly* 20 (1989): 67–73; Alice Littlefield, Leonard Lieberman, and Larry T. Reynolds "Redefining Race: The Potential Demise of a Concept in Physical Anthropology," *Current Anthropology* 23 (1982): 641–655; Frank B. Livingstone, "On the Non-Existence of Human Races," *Current Anthropology* 3 (1962), 279–281; C. Loring Brace and Ashley Montagu, *An Introduction to Biological Anthropology,* 2nd ed. (New York: Macmillan, 1977); Ashley Montagu, ed., *The Concept of Race,* (New York: Free Press, 1964); Ashley Montagu, *The Idea of Race* (Lincoln: University of Nebraska Press, 1965); Ashley Montagu, *An Introduction to Physical Anthropology* (Springfield, IL: C.C. Thomas, 1945, 2nd ed. 1951, 3rd ed. 1960); Joseph B. Birdsell, *Human Evolution: An Introduction to the New Physical Anthropology,* 2nd ed. (New York: Rand McNally, 1975); Elazar Barkan, *The Retreat of Scientific Racism,* (Cambridge: Cambridge University Press, 1991).

21. Geoffrey M. Morant, "The Future of Physical Anthropology," *Man* 44 (1944).

3

The Genetical Theory of Race

The traditional anthropological practice of describing the end effects of complex variations without attempting to consider the nature of the conditions responsible for them could never lead to any understanding of their real meaning. In order to understand the end effects with which the physical anthropologist of the past was so much concerned it is necessary to investigate the causes producing them, and this can only be done by studying the conditions under which they come into being, for it should be obvious that it is the conditions producing the end effects which must be regarded as their efficient causes.

Comparing numerous series of metrical and nonmetrical traits relating to different groups of humankind may produce some notion of their likenesses and differences or tell us something of the variability of their traits; this may be desirable, but no amount of detailed description and comparison will ever tell us how such groups came to be as we now find them, unless serious investigation is made to discover the causes involved in their production.

Such causes are at work before our eyes at the present time. In America and in many other parts of the world where members of different racial groups have met and cohabited, determinate sequences, if not the actual mechanism, of physical change may be studied. The discoveries of geneticists concerning the manner in which genetic changes are brought about in other organisms and what is known of human genetics render it perfectly clear that the genetic systems of all living things behave fundamentally according to the same laws. If this is true, it then becomes possible, for the first time in the history of humankind, to envisage the possibility of an evolution in genetical terms of the stages through which humans, as a variable species, must have passed in order to attain its present variety of form and also, in the same terms, to account for that variety.

The principles involved in the genetic approach to the study of the evolution of the variety of humankind cannot be discussed here fully, because such a discussion would demand a treatise in itself, and because such treatises already are available in great number.[1]

Here we have space only for a very condensed statement of the genetical theory of race. The conception of "ethnic group differences" proposed here is based upon the following fundamental postulates: (1) that the original ancestral population was genetically relatively heterogeneous; (2) that by migration away from this original ancestral group, individual families became dispersed; (3) that some of the groups thus dispersed became geographically isolated from one another and remained so isolated for a relatively significant period of time; (4) that upon all these isolated groups several of the following factors came into play as conditions leading to evolutionary change: (a) the random genetic drift or inherent variability of the genotypic materials of each member of the group, as compared to the parent population, and (b) physical change in the action of a gene associated, in a partial manner, with a particular trait, that is, gene mutation.

Genetic drift describes the fact that given a genetically heterogeneous or heterozygous group, spontaneous random fluctuations in gene frequencies will, especially in small populations, in the course of time, occur, so that such originally relatively homogeneous groups will come to exhibit certain differences from other isolated groups which started with a similar genetic equipment.

Mutation defines the condition in which a particular gene undergoes a permanent change of some sort, so that its physiological expression differs from that of the older form of the gene, and its action may express itself in the appearance of a new trait or new form of an old one. Mutations have almost certainly occurred independently in different human isolate groups, at different times and at different rates, and have affected different traits. Thus, for example, in one part of a population mutant dominant genes leading to the development of kinky hair may have appeared and have ultimately become scattered throughout the population, as among Blacks. We cannot, however, make a similar assumption for all or many of the traits which distinguish the various groups of humankind from one another. Skin color, for example, cannot be so simply explained, for the probabilities are high that even in early humans there were already in existence variations in skin color and also, incidentally, hair color.[2] Selection has undoubtedly played an important role here.

Up to this point we have seen that it is possible to start with a genetically heterogeneous population, from which independent groups have migrated and become isolated for a time from one another. By random variation in gene frequencies and the change in the action of genes themselves—disregarding for the moment the operation of such factors as selection of various sorts—new genetic combinations of traits have appeared in various groups, thus defining the differences existing between such groups. Such differences occur as gradients in each group and are called *clines*. In brief, random variation in gene frequency and the action of mutant genes are the primary agencies responsible for the production of physical differences between human groups. It has been estimated that some eighty mutations occur in every individual in a mating population. In fact, these constitute the basic processes in the evolution of all animal forms. But there are also other factors involved which, though secondary in the sense that they act upon the primary factors and influence their operation, are not less important in their effects than the primary factors. Indeed, these secondary factors, ecological, natural, social, and sexual selection, inbreeding, outbreeding, or hybridization, and so forth, have been unremitting in their action upon the primary factors, but the nature of that action has been highly variable. The action of these secondary factors does not require any discussion here; I wish here to emphasize principally that in the character of the action of the two primary factors, genetic drift and gene mutation, we have the clear demonstration that the variation of all human groups is a natural process that is constantly proceeding. The genetic and physical differences that characterize populations, the mislabeled races, merely represent an expression of the process of genetic change over a definite ecologic range. An ethnic group represents a dynamic, variable condition, characterized by potential for continuous change; populations become static and classifiable only when a taxonomically minded scientist arbitrarily fixes the process of change at his own temporal level.

In short, so-called races are populations that merely represent different kinds of temporary mixtures of genetic materials common to all humankind. As Shelley wrote,

> Man's yesterday may ne'er be like his morrow;
> Naught may endure but mutability.

Over a sufficient length of time, it is probable that all genes will mutate. Most mutations are known to be harmful, but useful mutations also occur, relative to ecology and timespan. The frequency with which various genes have undergone change or mutation in human populations is at present unknown, but when anthropologists address themselves to the task of solving the problem of gene variability in different human populations, important discoveries are to be expected. What is known is that in many cases and conditions it can be rapid.[3] The immediate task of the physical anthropologist interested in the origins of human diversity should be to investigate the problem presented by that diversity, not as a taxonomist but as a geneticist, since the diversity which is loosely termed race is a process which can be described accurately only in terms of the frequencies with which individual genes occur in groups representing adequate geographic isolates.

If between populations variability can best be described in terms of gene frequencies, then one of the most important tasks of the anthropologist must be the discovery of the roles played by the primary and secondary factors in producing that variability. The approach to the solution of this problem is twofold: first, through the analysis of the nature of the variability itself in localized groups; and, second, through the study of the effect of "ethnic" mixture among living peoples. Such studies as those of Boyd, Birdsell, and Garn, have already shown what can be achieved by means of the genetic approach.[4] As Dobzhansky pointed out, "the fundamental units of racial variability are populations and genes, not complexes of characters which connote in the popular mind a racial distinction."[5]

In humans the process of differentiation between populations is genetically best understood in terms of the frequency with which certain genes become differentiated in different groups derived from an originally somewhat heterogeneous species population and subsequently undergo independent development. We have already seen that the mechanisms involved in differentiating a single collective genotype into several separate genotypes, and the subsequent development of a variety of phenotypes within these genotypes, are primarily genetic drift or gene variability and gene mutation, and secondarily, the action of such factors as environment, natural, social, and sexual selection, inbreeding, outbreeding, and the like.

Perhaps the wisest thing ever said about the genetics of human variability is R. A. Fisher's admonition in one of the greatest scientific classics of the twentieth century, his *The Genetic Theory of Natural Selection* (1930), that

> While genetic knowledge is essential for the clarity it introduces into the subject, the causes of the evolutionary changes in progress can only be resolved by an appeal to sociological, and even historical facts. These should at least be sufficiently available to reveal the more powerful agencies at work in the modification of mankind.[6]

It is the failure of IQ testers to understand the powerful role that social factors play in the development of human behavior that renders their findings invalid. And the same is, of course, true of the arguments of racists generally.

Many of the physical differences existing between living human populations probably originally represent the end effects of small gene mutations fitting harmoniously into gene systems which remain relatively unaltered. Judging from the nature of their likenesses and differences, and from the effects of intermixture, the number of genes involved would appear to be relatively small, each being for the most part independent in its action. The processes involved are akin to those practiced in the production of domestic breeds of animals from wild types, in whom generic, specific, and population traits which, under natural condition, in the secular period of time concerned, would have remained stable, are rendered markedly unstable, as in our artificially produced varieties of cats, dogs, horses, and other domesticated animals. Considering the roles of mutation, inbreeding, crossbreeding, and selection in the evolution of other animals, the great geneticist Sewall Wright arrived at a judgment concerning the conditions for evolution based on the statistical consequences of Mendelian heredity which, allowing for the modifying effects of the secondary factors arising out of human social activities, may be applied to humans.

> The most general conclusion is that evolution depends on a certain balance among its factors. There must be gene mutation, but an excessive rate gives an array of freaks, not evolution; there must be selection, but too severe a process destroys the field of variability, and thus the basis for further advance; prevalence of local inbreeding within a species has extremely important evolutionary consequence, but too close inbreeding leads merely to extinction. A certain amount of crossbreeding is favorable, but not too much. In this dependence on balance the species is like a living organism. At all levels of organization life depends on the maintenance of a certain balance among its factors.
>
> More specifically, under biparental reproduction a very low rate of mutation balanced by moderate selection is enough to maintain a practically infinite field of possible gene combinations within the species. The field actually occupied is relatively small though sufficiently extensive that no two individuals have the same genetic constitution. The course of evolution through the general field is not controlled by direction of mutation and not directly by selection, except as conditions change, but by a trial and error mechanism consisting of a largely nonadaptive differentiation of local populations (due to inbreeding balanced by occasional crossbreeding) and a determination of longtime trend by intergroup selection. The splitting of species depends on the effects of more complete isolation, often made permanent by the accumulation of chromosome aberrations, usually of the balanced type. Studies of natural species indicate that the conditions for such an evolutionary process are often present.[7]

Precisely similar conditions have been operative in the evolution and diversification of humankind. The variety of traits exhibited by different ethnic groups almost certainly owe their being to the operation of the factors so well described by Wright. The common definition of race, however, is based on an arbitrary and superficial selection of traits, a statement which applies when the term is used by animal breeders as well as in connection with humans. As Kalmus has pointed out,

> Breeders of the old school rarely distinguish between the characters which are due to single gene differences and those which are due to many, and their use of the word race still remains rather vague. The term used by modern geneticists to take the place of race is strain, which has a more precise meaning; it is applied to forms which differ from the commonly found wild type by one or several precisely defined hereditary characters which usually breed true.[8]

Attempts have been made to define race as a group of individuals of whom an appreciable majority, taken at a particular time level, is characterized by the possession through a common heredity of a certain number of genes phenotypically (that is, on the basis of certain observable or measurable traits) selected as marking "physical" boundaries between them and other groups of individuals of the same species population not characterized by so high a degree of frequency of these particular genes.

This is, however, granting the common conception of race too much credit for either significance or intelligibility, for it should be obvious that such a definition represents a rather fatuous kind of abstraction, a form of extrapolation for which there can be little place in scientific thought. What, for instance, does "an appreciable majority" refer to? What are the traits which are to be exhibited by this "appreciable majority"? And upon what grounds are such traits to be considered as significantly defining a race? As Dobzhansky points out, "the geographical distributions of the separate genes composing a racial difference are very frequently independent."[9] Thus, blood group distributions are independent of skin color or cephalic index distributions, and so forth.

What aggregation, then, of gene likenesses and differences constitutes a race or ethnic group?

There is no point to an attempt at redefinition of the term "race," for that term is so embarrassed by unsound and inhumane meanings that its preservation would only defeat any hope of a better understanding of people than the term *ethnic group*. It is better to adopt the recommendation of Huxley and Haddon in their 1936 book *We Europeans* as well as by the UNESCO *Statement on Race* (1950) to replace the term "race" by the term *ethnic group* (see Appendix A in the unabridged edition).

In conformity with the genetic facts an ethnic group may be defined as a population in process of undergoing genetic and social differentiation; it is a group of individuals capable of hybridizing and intergrading with other such ethnic groups to produce further genetic recombination and differentiation.[10]

An example will perhaps help to clarify this definition. When American Blacks mate with other Blacks, their children more closely resemble other American Blacks, as well as Blacks elsewhere in the world, than they do American or other whites. This merely means that the offspring have drawn their genes from a local group in the population in which certain genes, say for skin color, were present that were not present in other local groups of the American population. The manner in which such genes are distributed within a population such as the United States is determined not so much by biological factors as by social ones. This may be illustrated by means of a homely example. Were the social barriers to intermixture be abrogated, the physical differences between Blacks and whites would eventually be completely eliminated. That this has not occurred to any great extent is due principally to the maintenance of social barriers opposed to such admixture. Such social and caste barriers tend to keep the stock with genes for black skin color separate from those who carry genes for lighter skin color. In this way such barriers act as isolating mechanisms akin to geographic isolating conditions, which have the same effect in maintaining the homogeneity of genetic characters within the isolated group.

It is clear, then, that the frequency distributions of one or more genes within a population that differ from those of other populations, for the most part, represent the effects of the action of different isolating agents upon a common stock of genetic materials. Such agencies as natural, social, and sexual selection result in the different gene frequencies among local groups and populations,result in gradational effect, and are called *clines*. Such, from the standpoint of the anthropologist, is an ethnic group.

It will be observed that such a definition emphasizes the fact that so-called racial differences simply represent more or less temporary or episodic expressions of variations in the relative frequencies of genes in different parts of the species population and rejects altogether the all-or-none conception of race as a static immutable process of fixed differences. It denies the unwarranted assumption that there exist any hard and fast genetic boundaries between any groups of humankind and proclaims the common genetic unity of all groups, a unity without uniformity. Such a conception of race cuts across all national, linguistic, religious, and cultural boundaries and thus asserts their essential interaction of social and genetic factors.

We may conclude with the words of the distinguished geneticist, Professor Albert Jacquard: "The geneticist has a definite answer if questioned about the content of the word 'race.' It is that in the case of the human species the term does not correspond to any objectively definable entity."[11]

Notes

1. L. L. Cavalli-Sforza, P. Menozzi, and A. Piazza, *The History and Geography of Human Genes* (Princeton: Princeton University Press, 1994); W. F. Bodmer and L. L. Cavalli-Sforza, *Genetics, Evolution, and Man* (San Francisco: Freeman, 1976); Max Levitan and Ashley Montagu, *Textbook of Human Genetics,* 3rd ed. (New York: Oxford University Press, 1988); G. Harrison et al., *Human Biology.* 2nd ed. (New York: Oxford University Press, 1977), Ashley Montagu, *Human Heredity* (New York: New American Library, 1963); Jonathan Marks, *Human Biodiversity: Genes, Race, and History* (Hawthorne: Aldine, 1994).

2. Among apes of the present day, for example, one encounters animals that are almost completely white skinned, other that are completely black or brown skinned; still others are mixed or differently colored, thus the face and hands and feet may be black and the remainder of the body white or brown. The hair on the crown of a young gorilla's head may contain almost every primary color that is to be found among humans today.

3. For mutation rates in humans, see Max Levitan and Ashley Montagu, *Textbook of Human Genetics,* 2nd ed. (New York: Oxford University Press, 1977). Mutations, it should be mentioned, do not direct development, but for the most part replenish the gene pool.

4. William C. Boyd, *Genetics and the Races of Man* (Boston: Little, Brown, 1950); Joseph B. Birdsell, "Some Implications of the Genetical Concept of Race in Terms of Spatial Analysis," *Cold Spring Harbor Symposia on Quantitative Biology* 15 (1950): 259–314; Joseph B. Birdsell, "The Problem of the Early Peopling of the Americas as Viewed from Asia," in *Papers on the Physical Anthropology of the American Indian,* ed. William S. Laughlin (New York: The Viking Fund, 1951), 1–68a; Carleton Coon, Stanley Garn, and Joseph B. Birdsell, *Races: a Study of the Problems of Race Formation in Man* (Springfield, IL: Thomas, 1950); Curt Stern, *Principles of Human Genetics* (San Francisco: Freeman, 1973); L. L. Cavalli-Sforza et al., *The History and Geography of Human Genes;* Marks, *Human Bioiversity;* Ashley Montagu, "Genetics and the Antiquity of Man in the Americas," *Man* 43 [nos. 103–124] 105: 131–35.

5. Th. Dobzhansky, *Genetics and the Origin of Species,* 3rd ed. (New York: Columbia University Press, 1951), 177; Th. Dobzhansky, *Mankind Evolving* (New Haven: Yale University Press, 1962); Richard Lewontin, *Human Diversity* (New York: H. Freeman, 1982); M. Levitan and A. Montagu, *Textbook of Human Genetics,* 3rd ed. (New York: Oxford University Press, 1988); Th. Dobzhansky, Francisco J. Ayala, G. Ledyard Stebbins, and James W. Valentine, *Evolution* (San Francisco: W. H. Freeman, 1977); Eviator Nevo, "Genetic Diversity and the Evolution of Life and Man, *Racism, Science and Pseudo Science* (Paris: UNESCO, 1981), 77–92; Albert Jacquard, "Science and Racism," *Racism, Science and Pseudo Science* (Paris: UNESCO, 1981), 15–49; Th. Dobzhansky, *Evolution, Genetics, and Man* (New York: Wiley & Sons, 1955); Steven Rose, ed., *Against Biological Determinism* (London: Allison & Busby, 1982).

6. Ronald A. Fisher, *The Genetical Theory of Natural Selection* (Oxford: Clarendon Press, 1930), 174. See also Games F. Crow, "Mechanisms and Trends in Human Evolution," in *Evolution and Man's Progress,* eds. Hudson Hoagland and Ralph W. Burhoe (New York; Columbia University Press, 1962), 6–21; Frank G. Livingstone

and James N. Spuhler, "Cultural Determinants in Natural Selection," *International Social Science Journal* 17 (1965): 118–20; Ashley Montagu, ed., *Culture and the Evolution of Man* (New York: Oxford University Press, 1962); George G. Simpson, "Behavior and Evolution," in Ann Roe and George G. Simpson *Behavior and Evolution* (New York: Yale University Press, 1958), 597–635; Frank G. Livingstone, "Anthropoligical Implications of Sickle Cell Gene Distribution in West Africa," *American Anthropologist* 60 (1958): 533–62.

7. Sewall Wright, "The Roles of Mutation, Inbreeding, Crossbreeding, and Selection in Evolution," *Proceedings of the Sixth International Congress of Genetics* 1 (Ithaca, New York, 1932), 356–66; Cavalli-Sforza et al., *The History and Geography of Human Genes.*

8. H. Kalmus, *Genetics* (London: Pelican Books, 1948), 46.

9. Dobzhansky, *Genetics,* 2nd ed., p. 77.

10. The conception of an ethnic group was clearly stated as early as 1844 by Alexander von Humboldt. He writes: "The distribution of mankind is . . . only a distribution into varieties, which are commonly designated by the somewhat indefinite term races. As in the vegetable kingdom, and in the natural history of birds and fishes, a classification into many small families is based on a surer foundation than where large sections are separated into a few but large divisions; so it also appears to me, that in the determination of races a preference should be given to the establishment of small families or nations. Whether we adopt the old classification of my master, Blumenbach . . . or that of Prichard . . . we fail to recognize any typical sharpness of definition, or any general or well established principle, in the division of these groups. The extremes of form and colour are certainly separated, but without regard to the races, which cannot be included in any of these classes." *Cosmos: A Sketch of a Physical Description of the Universe* (London, 1849), 365–66.

11. Albert Jacquard, "Science and Racism," in *Racism, Science, and Psuedo Science* (Paris: UNESCO, 1983), 15.

4

The Biological Facts

Concerning the origin of the living varieties of humans we can say little more than that there are many reasons for believing that a single stock gave rise to all of them. All humans belong to the same species and have the same remote ancestry. This is a conclusion to which all the relevant evidence of comparative anatomy, paleontology, serology, and genetics, points. On genetic grounds alone it is virtually impossible to conceive of the varieties of humankind as having originated separately as distinct lines from different anthropoid ancestors. Genetically the chances against such a process ever having occurred are, in terms of probability, of such an order as to render that suggestion inadmissible. On purely physical grounds it is, again, highly improbable that starting from different ancestral stocks the varieties of humans would have independently come to resemble one another as closely as they do. This is demanding too much from convergence.

In October, 1962, Professor Carleton S. Coon published a book entitled *The Origin of Races,* in which he attempted to trace the evolution of five races which he called Australoids, Mongoloids, Caucasoids, Capoids, and Congoids. The theory he presented is that

> At the beginning of our record, over half a million years ago, man was a single species, *Homo erectus,* perhaps already divided into five geographic races or subspecies, *Homo erectus* then evolved into *Homo sapiens* not once but five times, as each subspecies, living in its own territory, passed a critical threshold from a more brutal to a more *sapient* state.[1]

The reference to the "more brutal" state of the assumed five subspecies of *Homo erectus* as compared with their descendants of sapient state is capable of several meanings in such a context, and when juxtaposed to "sapient" perpetuates pejorative and odious comparisons which are out of place in scientific discussions, unless they can be justified. There are absolutely no grounds for believing that early humans were any more brutal,

121

even though morphologically and culturally "less" developed, than contemporary humans. It is a question whether early humans were, in fact, brutal at all.

The idea that five subspecies or geographic races of *H. erectus* (which refers to early humans of the pithecanthropine type), in isolation from one another, "evolved independently into *Homo sapiens* not once but five times," at different times and in different places, is a very dubious one. The theory simply doesn't square with the biological facts. Species and subspecies simply don't develop that way. The transmutation of one species into another is a gradual process, and the development of the subspecies reflects the biological history of the species as a whole. However few or many subspecies of *Homo erectus* there may have been, all of them, at one time or another, probably participated in the development of *sapiens* subspecies. Subspecies of one species do not usually become transformed into subspecies of another single species. On the contrary, independent subspecies of a single species, as incipient species, tend to speciate into different species.

If Coon had been right the living so-called races or subspecies of humans would present the most remarkable example of parallel or convergent evolution in the history of animated nature. The human species is a species because all its members have shared a more or less common biological history-making allowance for all the differences in that history which each population or so-called race, subspecies, or cline, has undergone. Coon implied that that history has been essentially and independently different for his five assumed races, and further implied that in isolation the genetic direction of *H. erectus* was predetermined—that each of the subspecies occupying their separate ecologic niches would inevitably have developed into *sapiens*. But the evolutionary process, even for humankind, the cultural creature, does not work that way, as is abundantly testified by the biological history of humanity itself. For had the subspecies of humankind developed in the kind of independent isolation Coon postulated, it would have exhibited, owing, among other things, to the inherent variability of the genetic constitution, far greater differences in their earlier and more recent forms than they in fact, have.

What is so remarkable about the varieties of humankind is their likenesses, not their differences. It would be putting too much of a strain upon, and demanding too much of, any theory to require it to make out a case for an independent or parallel and convergent evolution of varieties of any kind as like one another as are the miscalled "races" of humankind.

Were this all, Coon's theory could be written off as just another of those monumental flawed attempts that are made from time to time to unravel the tangled skein of humankind's biological history, and rejected on the ground of its improbability, were it not for the fact that the author of

The Origin of Races delivered himself, *ex cathedra*, of opinions as if they were facts, and these of a kind which are likely to be misunderstood by the unwary, or understood for what they are not, and misused by racists and others for their own nefarious purposes. Since its publication Coon's book has given aid and comfort to many academic racists and demagogues.

From the very first page of his book Coon made statements of the following kind: "Each major race had followed a pathway of its own through the labyrinth of time. Each had been molded in a different fashion to met the needs of different environments, and each had reached its own level on the evolutionary scale."[2] There can be no doubt about the meaning here: Each of the races occupies a different evolutionary level on the ladder of development, for that is what "evolutionary scale" means. That implied, of course, as we shall see, that some "races" stand higher in the scale of evolution than others. Indeed, this is exactly what Coon meant.

Coon regretted that "dead men can take no intelligence tests," thus revealing a rather misplaced faith in the value of intelligence tests, and an obvious failure to understand their worthlessness when applied cross-culturally or "racially." "However," he went on to say,

> It is a fair inference that fossil men now extinct were less gifted than their descendants who have larger brains, that the subspecies that crossed the evolutionary threshold into the category of *H. sapiens* the earliest have evolved most, and that the obvious correlation between the length of time a subspecies has been in the *sapiens* state and the levels of civilization attained by some of its populations may be related phenomena.[3]

This, again, reveals a rather naive faith in the value of brain size as a measure of mental capacity. Was Neanderthal man, with a mean cranial capacity of 1550 cc, brighter than contemporary humans with a mean cc of 1400? If not, then why should white men be any more gifted than many of their extinct ancestors with smaller brains than theirs? The statement that the subspecies which has been in the *sapiens* state longer than another—allowing for a moment that such a statement makes any sense at all—must therefore have evolved the most and have a correspondingly higher level of civilization is just the kind of thing that was being said by racist anthropologists a hundred years ago. Professor Coon is in the direct line of descent of Nott and Gliddon. Altogether apart from the fact that there are differences in biological rates of development, and that there is such a thing as "cultural" or "social time,"[4] facts which would alone be sufficient to dispose of Coon's "fair inference"(s), there is not the slightest ground for believing that any of the varieties of humankind attained the *sapiens* state either earlier or later than any other. Supposing one subspecies had arrived at the *sapiens* state later than any other, such a subspecies could very well, under favorable conditions, have far outdistanced the earlier subspecies in cultural development. The fact is that grandchildren have a way of sometimes outliving their grandparents! But this is all an argument *in vacuo.*

Since, according to Coon, "Congoids" (blacks) were the last of the subspecies of *H. erectus* to be transformed into *sapiens,*[5] the level of civilization attained by them is "explained"—they simply did not have as long a history as *sapiens,* as do Caucasoids, and, interestingly enough, nor have the so-called archaic Australoids (Australian aborigines, Papuans, Melanesians, Negritos, and the like), so it is not to be wondered at that we are as *we* are, and they are as *they* are. And if the reader desired to observe what one of the latest to be developed *sapientes* looked like, when compared with one of the earliest to be developed *sapiens* types, he had only to consult Plate 32, in which he would see the photographic reproduction of an Australian aboriginal woman above and of a Chinese scholar below. The captions read as follows: "The Alpha and Omega of *H. sapiens:* An Australian aboriginal woman with a cranial capacity of under 1,000 cc (Topsy a Tiwi); and a Chinese sage with a brain nearly twice that size (Dr. Li Chi, the renowned archaeologist and director of Academia Sinica)."

"Alpha and Omega," the first and the last, "Obviously," Topsy just growed, and is what she is, a poor benighted Australian aboriginal, primarily because she has a brain of under 1000 cc, and Dr. Li Chi is primarily what he is because he has a brain nearly twice as big. Of course, there are cultural differences, but the implication is clear: no matter what cultural advantages Topsy or any of her children had been afforded, neither she nor they could have achieved what Dr. Li Chi had achieved.

This seems to me a really shocking example of scientific illiteracy. Apart from the demonstrable biologistic fallacies involved in this sort of argument, does it really have to be re-proven again and again that brain size within the normal range of variation characteristic of the human species at the *sapiens* level, and characteristic of every human population, in which a brain size of 850 cc. in a perfectly normally intelligent European is occasionally encountered,[6] in a land area in which one may also encounter an Anatole France with a brain size no larger than Topsy's, has nothing whatever to do with mental capacity?[7] But then, according to Coon, the Australian aborigines "come closest of any living peoples, to the *erectus-sapiens* threshold."[8] So they ought to be "less gifted" than Caucasoids and the large-brained Mongoloids. And by the same token (though Coon omitted any reference to this), the large-brained Mongoloids, having larger brains, on the average, than Caucasoids, ought to be "more gifted" than the latter.

"The genetic basis for high intelligence," Coon announced, "has been acquired independently in different taxonomic categories of primates. There is no evidence that the most successful populations within several different human races have not also become bright independently."[9] In other words, different human "races" are likened to the different monkeys, orangutans, chimpanzees, and gorillas, and there is "no evidence" that just as these different "taxonomic categories of primates" had independently acquired their different mental capacities, that the different human "races" had not independently done likewise. It hardly needs to be pointed out that the "races" of humankind are not equatable with the "different taxonomic categories of primates," and that, in any event, the evolution of man's intelligence has proceeded upon very different lines from that of any other taxonomic category of primate. This is a subject to which we shall return in the next chapter.

Coon also found that "Human beings vary in temperament. It is a common observation among anthropologists who have worked in many parts of the world in intimate contact with people of different races that racial differences in temperament also exist and can be predicted."[10] This was news to many anthropologists, among whom it was the common observation that the more one gets to know "people of different races" the more fundamentally alike they appear to be beneath the surface of the superficial differences. It is the present belief of many anthropologists and others that this discovery constitutes one of the principal contributions made by anthropology to the understanding of the richness of human diversity.

African blacks—Coon's "Congoids"—would almost seem to have been specially created, according to Coon's reading of the evidence. "As far as we know now," he wrote, "the Congoid line started on the same evolutionary level as the Eurasiatic ones in the Early Middle Pleistocene and then stood still for half a million years, after which Negroes and Pygmies appeared as if out of nowhere."[11]

Of course, the joker in this particular pack lies in the "As far as we know now." And what we know now is precisely so unilluminatingly little relating to the physical evolution of blacks, that the half a million years of standing still, mentioned by Coon, represents nothing more than the reflection of the paucity of our knowledge concerning black physical evolution. Even the surface of the subject has not yet been scratched, for the materials which would enable us to reconstruct the barest outline of black evolution or, for that matter, that of any other ethnic group, are simply not available. In any event, "the top-drawer people" didn't originate in "the Dark Continent." "The Children of Light" originated elsewhere. "If Africa was the cradle of mankind," we are told, "it was only an indifferent kindergarten. Europe and Asia were our principal schools."[12] In other words, those who remained in Africa never developed as did those who went on to Europe and Asia. "Genes in a population," Coon held, are in equilibrium if the population is living a healthy life as a corporate entity. Racial intermixture can upset the genetic as well as the social equilibrium of a group, and so, newly introduced genes tend to disappear or to be reduced to a minimum percentage unless they possess a selective advantage over their local counterparts.[13]

The population genetics of these statements are entirely erroneous, in fact they are preposterous, and far from reflecting the facts, the truth is that under the ordinarily prevailing conditions newly introduced genes can establish themselves rapidly, especially within small breeding populations. As for racial intermixture upsetting the genetic equilibrium of a group, the evidence of everyday experience throughout the world and field investigations is entirely contrary to this statement.

Coon finally concluded that had it "been in the evolutionary scheme of things, and had it not been advantageous to each of the geographical races for it to retain, for the most part, the adaptive elements in its genetic *status quo*" we would all have been "homogenized" by now.[14]

It is a common practice of humans to identify their prejudices with the laws of nature. It would appear that Coon was guilty of the same error. In any event, he was not a reliable guide to "the evolutionary scheme of things." "The evolutionary scheme of things" is not some mystical process which has kept people apart from one another, from being "homogenized," to use Coon's exceedingly unpleasant word. The evolutionary process has no scheme, and it has not schemed to keep humans apart for adaptive or any other reasons. What has kept people apart has been physiographic and social barriers, principally the former, and this is why the so-called "geographical races" being separated by geography and similar barriers, have not been "homogenized."

Since the publication of Coon's anachronistic book the anthropological conception of "race" has pretty much yielded to genetic pressure. The future of what used to be called the study of "race" lies, in my view, largely in the direction of microevolutionary studies and population genetics. The older anthropological conception of "race" still occasionally lingers on, suggesting that in some cases it is perhaps beyond the reach both of scientific judgment and mortal malice. Insofar as the genetic approach to the subject is concerned, some anthropologists are, as it were, self-made men and only too obviously represent cases of unskilled labor. However, my feeling is that they should be praised for trying rather than blamed for failing. The new anthropology is on the right track. Garn and Coon have attempted to adapt the terms "geographic race," "local race," and "microgeographical race" for use in the human species. They define, for example, "a geographical race" as, "in its simplest terms, a collection of (race) populations having features in common, such as a high gene frequency for blood group B, and extending over a geographically definable area."[15]

In this definition I think we can see, in high relief as it were, what is wrong with the continuing use of the term "race." The term "geographical race" immediately delimits the group of populations embraced by it from others, as if the so-called geographical race were a biological entity "racially" distinct from others. Such a group of populations is not "racially" distinct, but differs from others in the frequencies of certain of its genes. It was suggested by the UNESCO group of geneticists and physical anthropologists that such a group of populations be called a "major group."[16] This suggestion was made precisely in order to avoid such difficulties as are inherent in the term "geographical race." Since Garn and Coon themselves admit that "geographical races are to a large extent collections of convenience, useful more for pedagogic purposes than as units for empirical investigation,"[17] it seems to me difficult to understand why they should have preferred this term to the one more closely fitting the situation, namely, "groups." It is a real question whether spurious precision, even for pedagogical purposes, or as an "as if" fiction, is to be preferred to a frank acknowledgment, in the terms we use, of the difficulties involved. Garn and Coon are quite alive to the problem, but it may be questioned whether it contributes to the student's clearer understanding of that problem to use terms which not only do not fit the conditions, but which serve to contribute to making the student's mind a dependable instrument of imprecision, especially in view of the fact that a more appropriate term is available.

The principle of "squatter's rights" apparently applies to words as well as to property. When people make a heavy investment in words they are inclined to treat them as property, and even to become enslaved by them, the prisoners of their own vocabularies. Stone walls may not a prison make, but technical terms sometimes do. This, I would suggest, is another good reason for self-examination with respect to the use of the term "race," and the recognition that definitions are obstinate.

Commenting on Garn's views on race, Dr. J. P. Garlick has remarked,

The use of 'race' as a taxonomic unit for man seems out of date, if not irrational. A hierarchy of geographical, local and microraces is proposed, with acknowledgments to Rensch and Dobzhansky. But the criteria for their definition are nowhere made clear, and in any case such a scheme could not do justice to the many independent fluctuations and frequency gradients shown by human polymorphic characters. Surely physical anthropology has outgrown such abstractions as 'Large Local Race.... Alpine the rounder-bodied, rounder-headed, predominantly darker peoples of the French mountains, across Switzerland, Austria, and to the shores of the Black Sea.'[18]

Garn and Coon do not define "local races" but say of them that they "can be identified, not so much by average differences, but by their nearly complete isolation." In that case, as Dahlberg[19] long ago suggested, why not call such populations "isolates"? However, today the proper term to describe such populations is *clines*, that is, populations characterized by gradient differences in the frequency of genes for physical traits as between one population and another.

Taxonomies and terms should be designed to fit the facts, and not the facts forced into the procrustean rack of pre-determined categories. If we are to have references, whether terminological or taxonomical, to existing or extinct populations of humankind, let the conditions as we find them determine the character of our terms or taxonomies, and not the other way round.

At present, no satisfactory classification of the varieties of humans has been devised, and it is greatly doubted whether such classification is possible in any manner resembling the procedure of the purely botanical or zoological taxonomist. The reason for this is that all human varieties are much more mixed than are plant or animal forms, hence there is a greater dispersion or scattering of traits, which has the effect of producing a considerable amount of intergrading between ethnic groups or varieties. The more or less great variability of all ethnic groups constitutes a genetic proof of their mixed character. From the biological standpoint the physical differences which exist between the varieties of humankind are so insignificant that when properly evaluated they can be described mainly in terms of a particular expression of an assortment of genes common to humankind as a whole. At most, human varieties probably differ from one another only in the distribution of a comparatively small number of genes, and at the phenotypic level by clinal differences. This one may say much more definitely of humans than one could say of the differences exhibited by any of our domesticated varieties of cats, dogs, or horses. There are numerous varieties of cats, dogs, and horses, many of which represent highly selected strains of animals which have been developed as more or less homogeneous strains and domesticated by humans. Humankind, too, is to some extent a self-domesticated species but, unlike our domestic animals, humans exhibit varieties that are much mixed and far from representing homogeneous breeds.

The range of variation in humans is considerably greater than that exhibited by any group of animals belonging to a comparatively homogeneous breed. All the evidence indicates that the differences between the so-called races to a large extent represent a random combination of variations derived from a common source, which, by inbreeding in isolated groups, have become scattered and more or less stabilized and hereditary in a large number of the members of such groups. Furthermore, the evidence suggests that such selection of variations as has occurred in different groups has been primarily restricted to physical traits. There is no evidence among the ethnic groups of humankind that any process of mental selection has ever been operative which has acted differentially upon them to produce different types of mind (see Chapter 5).

The conception of differential selection for mental qualities seems to be a peculiarly modern one, adapted to modern prejudices. The evolution of human mental capacities and traits is discussed in the next chapter. Humans have bred dogs for certain temperamental qualities useful in the hunt for many centuries. The Irish setter, for example, is almost always red-haired, but his red hair has no connection whatever with his temperamental qualities. The Irish setter has the same kind of temperament as the English setter, but the hair color of the English setter is white or black. The only difference between the white, the black, the white and black, and the red setters is in their coat color; there are no significant differences in their mental or temperamental qualities. No one ever asks whether there are mental and temperamental differences between white, black, or brown horses—such a question would seem rather silly. When, however, humans are involved, the prejudice of anyone who has ever made the statement that skin color is associated with mental capacity is accepted as gospel. For such an assumption there is about as much justification as there would be for the assumption that there exist substantial differences between different hair color varieties of setters. We know this to be false concerning setters only because we seem to have paid more unprejudiced attention to the mental qualities of dogs than we have to those of human beings. But those of us who have paid some attention to the character and form of the behavior of peoples belonging to different ethnic groups and to different cultures have satisfied ourselves by every scientific means at our disposal that significantly or innately determined mental differences between the ethnic groups have thus far not been demonstrable. It may be that some such differences do exist, but if they do they have so far successfully eluded every attempt to prove their existence. There is every reason to believe that such mental differences as we observe to exist between the different ethnic groups are due principally to factors of a cultural nature and are in no demonstrably significant manner inseparably related to biological factors. We shall presently refer to the nature of the mental differences alleged to exist between different ethnic groups.

Whether ethnic groups have a common origin or not is strictly a matter which need concern us little, in view of the fact that structurally and functionally, in spite of superficial differences, they are all so much alike. There are few physical traits which are limited to any particular ethnic group. Perhaps it is nearer the truth to say that different ethnic groups show higher frequencies in the possession of certain physical traits than others. Such differences in the distribution of the frequencies of physical traits in different human groups may mean that at some time in the past individuals of different heredity interbred, and in isolation continued to do so with the result that a new combination of traits became more or less evenly distributed throughout the group. In this way a new ethnic group was produced. The probability that such factors as isolation and hybridization have played a large part in the evolution of most human groups is suggested not only by what we know of human intermixtures today—particularly the American black—and the behavior of other animal groups, but also by the presence in all human beings of by far the most substantial majority of traits most frequently found in any one group. The fundamental genetic kinship of all the ethnic groups of this world would, therefore, seem to be clear.

Le Gros Clark, the distinguished anatomist and physical anthropologist of Oxford University, made the important point that

> From the purely anatomical point of view, there are already available certain elementary observations on the physical anthropology of race which, though well-known to anatomists, are not, I think, widely enough recognized by those who are concerned with the social problems of race. At first sight, the contrast in appearance between such extreme types of mankind as the 'Negroid,' 'Mongoloid' and 'Caucasoid' might suggest fundamental constitutional differences. In fact, however, a close anatomical study seems to show that the physical differences are confined to quite superficial traits. I may best emphasize this by saying that if the body of a black were to be deprived of all superficial features such as skin, hair, nose, and lips, I do not think that any anatomist could say for certain, in a isolated case, whether he was dealing with the body of a black or a European. Naturally, such a test, being limited to the rather crude evidence of gross anatomy, is not by itself to be taken as a final demonstration of the constitutional equivalence of one race with another. Nor does it take account of statistical differences of a relatively minor trait. But it does suggest very strongly indeed that the somatic differences of race may after all not be of a very fundamental nature.[20]

With respect to the nature of those physical traits in the frequency distribution of which various groups differ from one another, it needs to be said that not one can be classified as either "higher" or "lower," "superior" or "inferior," in the scale of development. Every normal physical trait must be appraised as equally valuable for the respective functions which it is called upon to perform. Whatever its origin; a black skin is undoubtedly a trait of adaptive value, for there is some evidence that it enables its possessor to withstand the effects of prolonged exposure to sunlight. It is known that under such conditions the black skin is less liable to sunburn and cancer than is the white.[21] Hence, for groups living in areas of intense sunlight black skin would, by the measure of natural selection, in general be superior to white skin.

By definition all members of the human species belong to the same classificatory and evolutionary rank, and the ethnic groups, for the most part, merely represent the expression of successful attempts at adaptation to the environment or habitat in which they have been isolated. It is not altogether an accident that we find dark skins associated with regions of high temperatures and intense sunlight and light skins associated with cooler climates and moderate degrees of sunlight. In this same connection, compare the habitat of the white bear with that of the black or brown bear; also, the frequency of black insects in deserts. Gloger's rule states the fact that melanin (black) pigmentation in mammals and birds increases in warm and humid regions, and lighter pigmentation increases in arid regions. Lukin finds that darkly pigmented races of insects are found in regions whose climate is humid, and lightly pigmented races of insects are found in regions with arid climates.[22] Black skin appears to represent a trait of adaptive value which in some groups followed upon the loss of the body covering of hair. Thus, most apes and monkeys that possess an abundant hairy coat have white skin beneath the hair. It might, therefore, be assumed that the skin of the earliest humans was probably white; but the opposite assumption may be equally true, that is, some groups of the earliest humans may have been black. In that case we would have to say, disregarding for the moment all other considerations, that white-skinned peoples have a reduced distribution of pigment in their skin merely because the shift from the birthplace of their ancestors, which there is good reason to believe was Africa south of the Sahara, to the cooler regions of Europe gradually resulted in a decrease in the distribution of pigment in their skin, so that in the course of time, by means of selection of genes for low pigmentation, this has become considerably reduced.[23] The pigmentary difference is not one of kind but of degree. The same chemical pigments are present in the skin of all humans (with the exception of albinos, who have no pigment at all), varying only in its diffusion throughout the body rather than in quality.

The principal pigment, melanin, is produced in pigment cells known as melanocytes, by a reaction between the amino acid tyrosine and oxygen. The enzyme tyrosinase in the melanocytes acts on tyrosine to produce and control the speed of production of melanin. Exposure to the ultraviolet rays of sunlight, for example, activates tyrosine to convert tyrosine into melanin. There are no differences in the number of melanocytes in the different ethnic groups. Differences in pigmentation in populations and in individuals, as also in different parts of the body, are due to differences in the dispersion and distribution of melanin particles in the melanocytes.

This is in part under genetic, and in part under environmental, control. To the present day, exposure to the intense sunlight will bring about the production of an increased amount of pigmentation in many whites, so that depending upon the degree of exposure the skin may turn dark—even black. This latter phenomenon will occur more readily in brunets than in blonds, simply because brunets possess a greater amount of the substances required for the production of pigment, whereas blonds possess them in much lower proportion.[24]

It should be obvious that black and white skins are, in their own ways, traits of physiological importance for the survival of the individual. In hot, humid climates those individuals would be most favored who possessed skins sufficiently dark to prevent heat loss at too rapid a rate, and thus avoid heat exhaustion. In cool climates in which the humidity is relatively low, those individuals would be at a advantage—that is, over a considerable period of time—who were characterized by a lesser amount of pigment in the skin. For the white skin, less abundantly supplied with sweat glands than the black, acts as a good insulator against heat and cold.

Albinos, individuals whose skin tissues are completely devoid of any pigment, suffer intensely when exposed to sunlight. Their pigmentless tissues are incapable of making the necessary adjustments to the rays of the sun; in other words, they have no adaptive mechanism to protect them from the effects of solar radiation. In so far as they lack such a mechanism they are biologically unadapted to meet efficiently the demands of their environment and to that extent they are adaptively inferior to those of their fellows who are so adapted. But there is no evidence of any associated mental inferiority in such cases. Blacks are much better adapted to meet the demands of the conditions of intense sunlight and high temperatures to which their ancestors were born than are whites,[25] just as whites are better adapted to meet the requirements of the cooler climates of their adopted homelands. Is the one therefore superior or inferior to the other? Is the white superior to the black because he has lost so much of his pigment? Because biologically his organism has not required its presence under the conditions in which he has lived? And is the black superior (or inferior) because he is the descendant of ancestors who were able to survive by virtue of the selective value of their darkly pigmented skins? Clearly, there can be no question here of either inferiority or superiority. Both black and white have survived because they and their ancestors possessed traits of adaptive value which, under the respective conditions of their differing environments, enabled them to survive. Traits of adaptive value, whatever form they may take, are usually desirable, because from the standpoint of the organism and of the group they enable it to survive under the unremitting action of the challenges of natural selection.

Is there any reason, then, for devaluing a person because of the color of his skin, that selfsame color which probably enabled the ancestral group that gave him birth to surmount the challenges of this world? Of course there is none, and there can be none from any possible point of view. The same is true of hair and eye color. But, as racists insist, it is not only the color of the skin which counts; what of the other differences, such as in hair, lips, or nose? These, surely, are all marks of inferiority? We may well ask: "Marks of inferiority in what sense? In the cultural or in the biological sense?" If the statement is made from the cultural point of view, there can be no argument, for what a community or person considers culturally satisfying in such connections is purely an arbitrary matter of taste, and concerning taste it is notorious there can be no disputing. Even blacks when educated in Western cultures, as in North America, owing to the cultural norms which are everywhere set before them as standards or values, frequently come to consider that straight hair and light skin are to be preferred to kinky hair and black skin.[26] But if the statement is made in the biological sense as meaning that such black physical traits are marks of biological inferiority, then it can be demonstrated that such a statement stands in complete contradiction to the facts.

The three traits in question, namely, tightly curled hair, thick lips, and general lack of body hair, are not marks of inferiority, but are, unequivocally, in the biological sense, examples of traits which have progressed further in development than have the same physical structures in whites. In these very traits the black is from the evolutionary standpoint more advanced than the white; that is, if we take as our criterion of advancement the fact of being furthest removed from such conditions as are exhibited by the existing anthropoid apes, such as the gorilla and chimpanzee. If racists would take the trouble to visit their local zoo and for a moment drop their air of superiority and take a dispassionate look at either one of these apes, they would find that the hair of these creatures is lank, that their lips are thin, and their bodies are profusely covered with hair. In these traits the white man stands nearer to the apes than does the black. Is the white, then, for this reason, to be judged inferior to the black? Surely not.

We do not know why the black's head hair, body hair, and lips have developed as they have or why whites have more nearly retained the primitive condition of these traits.[27] But we can be certain that biologically there is a good functional reason responsible in both cases, which in the system of values involved in biological judgments must be appraised as equally valuable for the respective functions which each is called upon to perform. It has been suggested that the broad nose of the black is adapted to meet the requirements of air breathed at relatively high temperatures, whereas the comparatively long, narrow nose of the white is adapted to breathing air at relatively low temperatures.[28] From the standpoint of aesthetics, a much stronger case could be made out for the black nose than for that of the white. The bone, cartilage, and soft tissue that juts out from the face of the white like a peninsula, with its stretched skin, which becomes shiny as soon as the sweat begins to break through its enlarged pores, is really something of an atrocity. At least, any ape would think so (as, indeed, the apes in *The Planet of the Apes* did). Let us try to imagine, for a moment, such an outgrowth from the middle of one's face. In such a case, we would regard this structure from our present aesthetic standards, as an unsightly abnormality. But were the nose growing out of the middle of one's forehead the usual thing, we would, of course, find it perfectly acceptable, and even a thing of beauty. Cultural habituation and social standards of beauty are all. We have all grown used to our noses and take them very much for granted.

All that one can say is that biologically the form of the black nose and the form of the white nose are each, in their own way, perfectly capable of performing the functions to which they appear to be equally well adapted in all environments. That being so, there can be no question of either superiority or inferiority. Whether such traits are due to adaptation, natural selection, social selection, or a combination of such factors is uncertain. What is certain is that such traits do enable individuals possessing them to meet the demand their environments have made upon them and those that were made on their ancestors.[29] They have adaptive value, and this may be said for most, possibly all, the normal characters of humankind.

There is one trait of the human body which has been cited more frequently than any other as a "proof" of the inferiority of blacks to whites. This is the size of the brain. The size or volume of the brain is usually estimated from the capacity of the brainpan of the skull in terms of cubic centimeters. The material available upon which to base a discussion of the value of the size of the brain as related to mental capacity is far from satisfactory. We do not possess sufficient series of thoroughly controlled measurements on numerically adequate samples taken upon the brains of skulls of different human groups; it is possible for anyone with the intention of proving a particular case to prove it in precisely the terms he desires. But upon the basis of the available facts the scientist can come to only one conclusion, and that is that since there is no demonstrable difference in the structure, gross or microscopic, of the brains of the members of different ethnic groups, and since the variability in the size of the brain is such that there is no demonstrable relationship between cultural and intellectual status and brain size, there is therefore no significance to be attached to brain size as a mark of cultural or intellectual development. Let us briefly consider the facts.

The cranial capacity of the Paleolithic Neanderthal was, on the average, 1,550 cc. What an extraordinary situation! So-called primitive Neanderthal man, who lived more than 50,000 years ago, had a larger brain than the average white man of today. Strange that this elementary fact has been so consistently overlooked. Are we to assume, then that Neanderthal man was culturally and intellectually superior to the average modern white man? Blacks are reported to have an average cranial capacity of 1,300 cc, 50 cc less than the white, whereas the modern white has a cranial capacity lower than that of the Neandertal by about 200 cc. Are we, then, to conclude that the modern white is intellectually four times as much or at least as much inferior to Neandertal man as the black is to the white? We believe not.

We know that Neandertal was hardly as highly developed culturally as the modern black or white. But that he possessed the same capacities for cultural and intellectual development as do modern humans seems highly probable. Neandertals were neither inferior nor superior to modern humans because of their larger brains—they were inferior culturally to modern humans for the simple reason that the opportunities for cultural and technological development open to them were not of the kind that have been open to us later peoples, but vastly more challenging, they responded admirably to meet all the needs of their time and place in the small bands with which they harmoniously lived. The Neandertal brain almost certainly was as good as that of modern humans, and had nothing whatever to do with the technologically undeveloped state of his culture.

The brain is essentially the organ that coordinates or integrates nervous activities, and to a large extent it performs that coordination or integration according to the educative pattern in which it is conditioned. That pattern is always culturally determined. Therefore, it depends to a considerable extent on the sort of cultural experience to which an individual has been exposed and caused to coordinate or integrate within his nervous system, whether he is capable of functioning at the necessary integrative level or not. The material bases of those structures which are eventually organized to function as *mind* are to a large extent inherited precisely as are all other structures of the body. This is an assumption, but it seems a perfectly legitimate one to make. The qualification "to a large extent" is introduced for the reason that in humans the nervous system continues to develop long after birth and is therefore appreciably influenced by the experience of the individual.[30] There is every reason to believe, as Edinger first pointed out, "that in certain parts of the nervous mechanism new connections can always be established through education."[31] And, as Ranson has put it, "the neurons which make up the nervous system of an adult man are therefore arranged in a system the larger outlines of which follow an hereditary pattern, but many of the details of which have been shaped by the experiences of the individual."[32]

It is evident that experience must play a considerable role in the development of the structure and functioning relations of the nervous system, and it is also clear that that aspect of the functioning of the body or nervous system which we know as *mind* is dependent upon the interaction of several factors; these are, primarily: the inherited, *incompletely developed,* structure of the nervous system; and the nature of the *external developing* influences. There can be little doubt that the material bases of mind are inherited in much the same manner as are the other structures of the body. While the organization of the structures of the body is appreciably influenced by external factors, the resulting effects appear to be incomparably fewer and less complex than are those capable of being produced through the organization of those nervous structures which functioned as mind.[33]

While it is possible—though it has never been demonstrated—that in different ethnic groups the nervous system differs in some of its structural details, it is certain that if such differences exist, they are of the most insignificant kind. Summarizing the findings of science, Professor W. E. Le Gros Clark, one of the most distinguished neuroanatomists and physical anthropologists of the day, is quite positive upon this point. He writes that "in spite of statements which have been made to the contrary, there is no macroscopic difference by which it is possible for the anatomist to distinguish the brain in single individuals of different races."[34] The measurable mental traits of different human groups strongly suggest that between such groups there exist no differences whatever that can be attributed to the nervous system alone. Furthermore, the mental differences that occur between human groups would appear to be much less considerable than those found to exist between individuals of the same group. In the light of our present knowledge, the evidence indicates that within the limits of normal, brain weight, cranial capacity, head size, or the gross structure and form of the brain, there is no relation of any kind to the qualities of the mind, as between individuals of the same or different ethnic groups.[35] As Professor C. Judson Herrick has remarked, "mental capacity cannot be measured in avoirdupois ounces on the scales." Nor is there any biologically determined association between certain ethnic group traits and certain kinds of mentality.[36]

Since mental functions are so largely dependent upon experience, upon cultural conditions, it is impossible to draw any inferences as to the equivalence or nonequivalence of mental potentialities as between ethnic groups or peoples among whom the cultural conditions are not strictly comparable. In short, no statement concerning the mentality of an individual or a group is of any value unless it is accompanied by a specification of the conditions of the cultural environment in which that mentality has developed. No discussion of "racial" mental traits can be countenanced which neglects full consideration of the associated cultural variables. For it is evident that it is precisely these cultural variables that play the most significant role in producing mental differences between groups. As I have already indicated, it is more than probable that genetically influenced mental differences do exist between *individuals* of the same and different ethnic groups, but there is absolutely no evidence that significant mental differences determined by any genetic factors exist between any two *ethnic groups*. It is, of course, possible that future researches may reveal that in some ethnic groups there exist differences in the frequency distribution of genes which exercise limiting effects upon some potentialities. It would, however, be very surprising if it were found that such differences were anything more than differences in the frequency with which such genes occur in such groups, genes which are common to all humankind. The evidence, as we know it, indicates that all human groups possess all the gene potentialities that all other human groups possess, but that there are differences, between groups, in the manner in which such gene potentialities are both distributed and environmentally conditioned. At the present time we know what amounts to absolutely nothing concerning the gene frequency distribution of such potentialities in any of the groups of humankind. It is quite possible that we never shall. In any event, the important point is this: While on theoretical grounds we may be interested in the gene frequency distribution of such potentialities in populations, we are in actual practice concerned with the expression of the potentialities of the individual. As human beings we are not, and should not, be concerned with groups, but with individual human beings, with persons. "Do not speak to me of mankind," said Goethe, "I know only men." We must judge each person on his own merits, and in making our judgments we must be careful not to attribute to genes what may be, and usually is, for the most part largely developmentally influenced by the environment in interaction with the genes.

Professor L. H. Snyder has summarized this view very clearly. He writes,

> Among the findings emerging from the study of population genetics is the conclusion that human populations differ one from the other almost entirely in the varying *proportions* of alleles of the various sets and not in the *kinds* of alleles they contain. The manifold combinations of traits which in turn derive from manifold combinations of genetic and environmental influences result in the almost infinitely diverse range of human individuality—a range which we are just beginning to comprehend.[37]

A range in which the ethnic groups of humankind are to be regarded as so many variations on a common theme. As we have already said, apparently it is principally, if not entirely, due to differences in cultural experience that individuals and groups differ from one another culturally, and it is for this reason that, where the cultural experience has appreciably differed, cultural achievement is an exceedingly poor measure of the mental value, genetically speaking, of an individual or of a group. For all practical purposes, therefore, and until further evidence to the contrary be forth-coming, we can safely take cultural achievement to represent the expression chiefly of cultural experience, not of biological potentiality.

As long ago as 1935, Professor Otto Klineberg, our then leading authority in the field of "racial" or ethnic psychology, after considering the evidence from every standpoint, offered the following important conclusion: "We may state with some degree of assurance that in all probability the range of inherited capacities in two different ethnic groups is just about identical."[38] Most authorities today thoroughly agree.

The environmental plasticity of mental traits is so great that when the evidence is all in, it will almost certainly show that the average differences between ethnic groups will be smaller than the amplitude of the differences to be found within each of the ethnic groups themselves. The brain does not secrete cultural or intellectual power in the same way that the liver secretes bile. One is not born with the ability to think brilliantly. Such an ability can be brought about only by exposure of the brain and nervous system to, and education in, the appropriate conditions.

Two thousand years before the birth of Christ the people of what is today England were living in an Early Bronze Age phase of cultural development. Long before this period the civilization of the Egyptians, as represented by the Old Kingdom (III–IV dynasties, 2780–2270 B.C.), had reached one of its most splendid periods. As a people the Egyptians had long been in contact with other peoples who had acted upon them as so many cross-cultural fertilizing agents, unlike the Britons who had been isolated from the main course of such contacts. Well might the Egyptians at this time have looked upon the Britons as a "primitive people."

Were the brains of the Britons in the Early Bronze Age made of such inferior stuff that they could only assume efficient qualities by an infusion of new genes? Clearly, genes and brain had nothing to do with the matter; on the other hand, the cultural stimulation which came to them increasingly after the Early Bronze Age, and particularly after the Iron Age, when Julius Caesar landed on their shores in 54 B.C., had everything to do with the development which eventually, in the fifteenth century, culminated in that great cultural efflorescence which has been called the Greece of the modern world.

Even so, it took the Britons some 1,500 years following the Roman Conquest to begin popping. Invasions and settlement by Scandinavians, Celts, Angles, Jutes, Saxons, and Normans, extending over a period of more than 1,000 years, following an occupation by the Romans of some 500 years, had produced very little effect. It would have been easy and even reasonable to conclude that the Britons were not an especially well-endowed people. Following such intensive and prolonged contacts with such highly civilized peoples, the Britons, after 1,500 years, had very little to show for it. And then, all of a sudden, it seemed, there was such an explosion of genius as the world had not witnessed since Periclean Athens. The pyrotechnical display of genius which illuminated the hitherto relatively empty English firmament, has brought light, and warmth, and joy to the whole of the literate world. Shakespeare, John Donne, Thomas Heywood, George Chapman, Ben Jonson, Thomas Dekker, Philip Massinger, Christopher Marlowe, Francis Bacon, Gilbert of Colchester, George Eliot, Jane Austen, the Brontës, as well as numerous other luminous spirits in the arts and sciences who followed in a continuous succession of new stellar births, would have been considered highly improbable by most of Britain's conquerors. These men and women were, of course, exceptional. They were men and women of genius. But it is customarily by the achievements of such individuals that we measure a society's or ethnic group's quality. Apparently certain specific conditions are necessary and must be present in every culture before the latent potentialities for achievement in each population can be expressed.

The English until very recently were the most notoriously unmusical people of our age. Yet in Elizabethan times they were among the most musical in Europe. What had happened? Had the "musical part" of the English brain atrophied? We can be certain that it had not. The cultural and economic development of the English had simply led in a direction away from such interests to other pursuits. Brain has nothing to do with the matter, culture everything. In short, it is culture which makes "brains"; not brains, culture. If this were not so, then the Amahosa of Africa, who have few cultural opportunities but more brains by size than whites, with 1490 cc as compared with 1400 cc for European males and 1350 cc for females, would be culturally and intellectually superior to whites, as would the Buriats, 1496 cc; the Iroquois, 1519 cc; the Eskimos, 1563 cc; and the Mongols, 1570 cc.[39] If we are to hold that blacks are mentally inferior to whites because their brains have, on the average, a volume of 50 cc less than that of whites, then by the same token we must hold that Amahosa, Eskimos, Mongols, and many other peoples are superior to whites. This we have reason to believe is untrue. There is no evidence that any people is either biologically or mentally superior or inferior to any other people in any way whatever. What we do know is that there exist considerable cultural differences between peoples and that these cultural differences are readily explained upon purely historical grounds, not upon any biological ones.

Differences in brain size have about as much relation to intelligence and cultural achievement as have differences in body size; that is to say, within the limits of normal variation absolutely none, either between groups of individuals or between individuals of the same group. In short, the concept of "race" which holds that the physical differences between peoples are reflections of underlying significant mental differences is an idea which, on the existing evidence, cannot be scientifically substantiated. It is, in fact, a myth and a delusion.

The average person in our society observes that certain other persons belonging to different ethnic groups possess physical and mental traits which differ from his own. He concludes that these physical and mental traits are somehow linked together, and these traits are inborn, and that they are immutable.[40] Vague notions about a unilinear evolution "from monkey to man" encourage him to believe that such "races" are "lower" in the "scale" of evolution than is the group to which he belongs; that there exists a natural hierarchy of "races." From such a starting point as "prehistoric man" he envisages a continuous progression upward, culminating in the final development of his own "race" or group. Between "prehistoric man" and himself stand, in an intermediate position, all the other peoples of humankind. "Race" is a definite entity to him, and all the intellectual supports for his conception of it are ready at hand. Newspapers, periodicals, books, radio, TV, publicists, politicians, and others tell him much the same story. The significance of "race" for him emotionally is, as we shall soon see, of considerable importance. Therefore, "race" exists. Such is the conception of "race" with which we have to reckon. We have seen that there are no scientific grounds whatever for such a belief.

Notes

1. Carleton Coon, *The Origin of Races* (New York: Alfred A. Knopf, 1962), 657.

2. Ibid., vii.

3. Ibid., ix–x.

4. Ashley Montagu, "Social Time: A Methodological and Functional Analysis," *American Journal of Sociology* 44 (1938): 282, 284.

5. Coon, *Origin of Races*, 655–56.

6. Bella Hechst, "Über einen Fall von Mikroencephalie ohne Geistigen Defekt," *Archiv für Psychiatrie und Nevenkrankheiten* 97 (1932), 64–76. See also G. C. Van Walsem, "Ueber das Gewicht des Schwersten bis jetzt Geschriebenen Gehirns," *Neurologisches Centrallblatt* (1899): 578–80.

7. Donald G. Paterson, *Physique and Intellect* (New York: Century, 1930), 80–123; P. Guillaume-Louis and Louis Dubreuil-Chambardel, "Le Cerveau d'Anatole France," *Bulletin de l'Academie de Medecine* (Paris) 98 (1927): 328–36.

8. Coon, *Origin of Races*, 427.

9. Ibid., 184.

10. Ibid., 116.

11. Ibid., 658.

12. Ibid., 656.

13. Ibid., 661.

14. Ibid., 662.

15. Stanley Garn and Carleton Coon, "On the Number of Races of Mankind," *American Anthropologist* 67 (1955): 997.

16. See Appendix A, *Ethnic Group and Race.*

17. Garn and Coon, *"On the Number of Races,"* 1,000.

18. J. P. Garlick, "Review of Human Races and Readings on Race by S. M. Garn," *Annals of Human Genetics* 25 (1961): 169–70.

19. Gunner Dahlberg, *Race, Reason, and Rubbish: A Primer of Race Biology* (New York: Columbia University Press, 1942).

20. W. E. Le Gros Clark, *Fitting Man to His Environment* (Newcastle-upon-Tyne: King's College, 1949), 19.

21. Harold Blum, "The Physiological Effects of Sunlight on Man," *Physiological Reviews* 25 (1945): 524; Harold Blum, "Does the Melanin Pigment of Human Skin Have Adaptive Value?" *Quarterly Review of Biology* 36 (1961): 50–63.

22. Th. Dobzhansky, "Rules of Geographic Variation," *Science,* 99 (1944): 137–28; Julian Huxley, ed., *The New Systematics* (New York: Oxford University Press, 1940): 213–14; Farrington Daniels Jr., "Man and Radiant Energy: Solar Radiation," in *Adaptation to the Environment,* eds. D. B. Dill et al. (Washington, D.C.: American Physiological Society, 1964): 969–87.

23. For a further speculative discussion of skin color see Carleton S. Coon, Stanley M. Garn, and Joseph Birdsell, *Races: A Study of the Problems of Race Formation in Man* (Springfield: Thomas, 1950), 51–55; and Blum, "Menlanin Pigment,"; M. L. Thomson, "Relative Efficiency of Pigment and Horny Layer Thickness in Protecting Skin of Europeans and Africans Against Solar Ultraviolet Radiation," *Journal of Physiology* 127 (1955): 236–46.

24. T. Edwards and S. Quimby Duntley, "The Pigments and Color of Living Human Skin," *American Journal of Anatomy* 65 (1939): 1–33. The darkening of white skin under sunlight has, of course, no effect on the genes for white skin. Any permanent change in skin color could only come about by the selection of genes for more pigmentation. See Thomas B. Fitzpatrick, M. Seiji, and David McGugan, "Melanin Pigmentation," *New England Journal of Medicine* 265 (1961): 328–32, 374–78, 430–34.

25. Julian H. Lewis, *The Biology of the Negro* (Chicago: University of Chicago Press, 1942), 94–6.

26. For the preferences of African Americans in these and other respects see Margaret Brenman, "Urban Lower-Class Negro Girls," *Psychiatry* 6 (1943): 311–12.

27. For some interesting conjectures see Coon, Garn, and Birdsell, *Races.*

28. Arthur Thompson and L. H. Dudley Buxton, "Man's Nasal Index in Relation to Certain Climatic Conditions," *Journal of the Royal Anthropological Institute of Great Britain and Ireland,* 52(1923): 92–122.

29. For an excellent discussion of this subject see Lewis, *Biology of the Negro,* 77–81; Paul T. Baker and J. S. Weiner, eds.), *The Biology of Human Adaptability* (Oxford: Clarendon Press, 1966); Emilio F. Moran, *Human Adaptability: An Introduction to Ecological Anthropology* (Belmont, CA: Wadsworth, 1979); Jane H. Underwood, *Human Variation and Human Microevolution* (Englewood Cliffs, NJ: Prentice-Hall, 1979); Valerius Geist, *Life Strategies, Human Evolution, Environmental Design: Toward a Biological Theory of Health* (New York: Springer Verlag, 1978).

30. Margaret A. Kennard and John F. Fulton, "Age and Reorganization of the Central Nervous System," *Journal of the Mount Sinai Hospital* 9 (1942): 594–606; E. Tobach, L. R. Aronson, and E. Shaw, eds., *The Biopsychology of Development* (New York: Academic Press, 1971).

31. Ludwig Edinger, *Vorlesungen über den Bau der nervüsen Zentralorgane des Menschen und der Tiere* (Leipzig: Vogel, 1911).

32. Marian Diamond, *Enriching Heredity: The Impact of Environment on the Anatomy of the Brain* (New York: Free Press, 1988); Paul Ranson, *The Anatomy of the Nervous System* (Philadelphia: Saunders, 1939), 41.

33. It should be clearly understood that while mind is an aspect of the functioning body it is also a great deal more than that, and that in man it is at least as much a product of culture as of genes. See Leslie A. White, *The Science of Culture* (New York: Farrar, Straus, 1949); Ernst Cassirer, *An Essay on Man* (New Haven: Yale University Press, 1944); Gilbert Ryle, *The Concept of Mind* (New York: Barnes and Noble, 1949); Peter Laslett, ed., *The Physical Basis of Mind* (New York: Macmillan, 1950); Asley Montagu, ed., *Culture and the Evolution of Man* (New York: Oxford University Press, 1962).

34. Le Gros Clark, *Fitting Man to His Environment*, p. 19; for a thoroughgoing discussion see Phillip V. Tobias, "Brain Size, Grey Matter and Race—Fact or Fiction?" *American Journal of Physical Anthropology* 32 (1970): 3–26; Phillip V. Tobias, *The Brain in Hominid Evolution* (New York: Columbia University Press, 1971); Samuil Blinkov and Il'ya M. Glezer, *The Human Brain in Figures and Tables* (New York: Basic Books, 1968).

35. On these matters see Karl Pearson, "Relationship of Intelligence to Size and Shape of the Head and Other Mental and Physical Characters," *Biometrika* 5 (1906): 105–46; Raymond Pearl, "On the Correlation between Intelligence and the Size of the Head," *Journal of Comparative Neurology and Psychology* 16 (1960): 189–99; K. Murdock and Louis R. Sullivan, "A Contribution to the Study of Mental and Physical Measurements in Normal Children," *American Physical Education Review* 28 (1923): 209–15, 278–88, 328; R. R. Reid and J. H. Mulligan, "Relation of Cranial Capacity to Intelligence," *Journal of the Royal Anthropological Institute of Great Britain and Ireland* 53 (1923): 322–32; Paterson, *Physique and Intellect* (1930); S. P. Pickering, "Correlation of Brain and Head Measurements and Relation of Brain Shape and Size to Shape and Size of the Head," *American Journal of Physical Anthropology* 15 (1931): 1–52; Gerhardt von Bonin, "On the Size of Man's Brain, as Indicated by Skull Capacity," *Journal of Comparative Neurology* 59 (1934): 1–28.

36. Steven Jay Gould, *The Mismeasure of Man* (New York: Norton,1981).

37. Lawrence H. Snyder, "The Genetic Approach to Human Individuality," *Science,* 108 (1948): 586.

38. Otto Klineberg, "Mental Testing of Racial and National Groups," in *Scientific Aspects of the Race Problem,* ed. J. W. Corrigan, (New York: Longmans, 1941), 284; see also Otto Klineberg, "Race Differences: The Present Position of the Problem," *International Social Science Bulletin* (UNESCO), 2 (1950), 460–66; Richard Bergland, *The Fabric of the Brain* (New York: Viking, 1986); Diamond, *Enriching Heredity;* Herbert L. Leff, *Experience, Environment, and Human Potentials* (New York: Oxford University Press, 1978); R. D. Lund, *Development and Plasticity of the Brain* (New York: Oxford University Press, 1978); Steven Rose, *The Conscious Brain* (New York: Alfred A.

Knopf, 1973); Tobias, *The Brain in Hominid Evolution;* Russell Tuttle, *The Functional and Evolutionary Biology of Primates* (Chicago/New York: Aldine, 1972).

39. For a list of cranial capacites in fossil and living man, as well as in fossil and living apes, see Ashley Montagu, *An Introduction to Physical Anthropology* (Springfield, IL: Thomas, 1960). 458–59.

40. "We are apt to construct ideal local types which are based on our everyday experience, abstracted from a combination of forms that are most frequently seen in a given locality, and we forget that there are numerous individuals for whom this description does not hold true." Franz Boas, "Race and Progress," *Science* 74 (1931): 1.

5

Natural Selection and the Mental Capacities of Humankind*

The biological heredity of humankind is transmitted by mechanisms similar to those encountered in other animals as well as in plants. Similarly, there is every reason to believe that the evolutionary factors which led up to the development of our species were of much the same nature as those which have been operative in the evolution of other forms of life. The evolutionary changes that occurred before the prehuman could become human, as well as those which supervened since the attainment of the human estate, can be described causally only in terms of mutation, selection, genetic drift, and hybridization—common processes throughout the living world. This reasoning, indisputable in the purely biological context, becomes a fallacy, however, when used, as it often has been, to justify narrow biologism in dealing with human development.

The specific human features of the evolutionary pattern of *Homo sapiens* cannot be ignored. Humankind is a unique product of evolution in that human beings, far more than any other creatures, have escaped from the bondage of the physical and biological into the integratively higher and more complex social environment. This remarkable development introduces a third dimension, a challenging new zone of adaptation, in addition to those of the external and internal environments—a dimension many biologists, in considering the evolution of humankind, have tended to neglect. The most important setting of human evolution is the human social environment. The human social environment can influence evolutionary changes only through the media of mutation,

---

*This chapter is based on the article originally written in collaboration with Theodosius Dobzhansky, and published in *Science* 105 (1947): 587–90, with the title "Natural Selection and the Mental Capacities of Mankind."

natural selection, social selection, genetic drift, and hybridization. There can be no genuine clarity in our understanding of humankind's biological nature until the role of the social factor in the development of the human species is understood.

In the words of R. A. Fisher, author of *The Genetical Theory of Natural Selection,* "For rational systems of evolution, that is, for theories which make at least the most familiar facts intelligible to the reason, we must turn to those that make progressive adaptation the driving force of the process."[1] It is evident that humankind, by means of its reasoning abilities, has achieved a mastery of the world's varying environments quite unprecedented in the history of organic evolution. The system of genes which has permitted the development of the specifically human mental capacities has thus become the foundation and the paramount influence in all subsequent evolution of the human stock. An animal becomes adapted to its environment by evolving certain genetically determined physical and behavioral traits; the adaptation of humans consists chiefly in developing their inventiveness, a quality to which their physical heredity predisposes them, and which their social heredity provides them with the means of realizing. To the degree to which this is so, humankind is unique. As far as physical responses to the world are concerned, humans are almost wholly emancipated from dependence upon inherited biological dispositions, uniquely improving upon the latter by the process of learning everything their social heredity (culture) makes available to them. The individual possesses much more efficient means of achieving immediate or long-term adaptation than the member of any other biological species, namely, through learned responses or novel inventions or improvisations.

In general, two types of biological adaptation in evolution can be distinguished. One is genetic specialization and genetically controlled fixity of traits. The second consists in the ability to respond to a given range of environmental situations by evolving traits favorable in these particular situations; this presupposes genetically controlled plasticity of traits. It is known, for example, that the composition of the blood which is most favorable for life at high altitudes is somewhat different from that which is characteristic at sea level. A species that ranges from sea level to high altitudes on a mountain range may become differentiated into several attitudinal varieties, each having a fixed blood composition favored by natural selection at the particular altitude at which it lives; or a genotype may be selected which permits an individual to respond to changes in the atmospheric pressure by determinate alterations in the composition of the blood. It should always be remembered that every aspect of our biology is at some level the product of the environment. The responses may be more or less rigidly fixed, so that approximately the same traits develop in all environments in which life is possible. On the other hand, the responses may differ in different environments. Fixity or plasticity of a trait is, therefore, genetically controlled.

The biological makeup of humans provides one with the *capacity* to learn, the emergence of the *ability* to make choices is largely shaped by the environment, by culture, the human-made part of the environment, the culture of which one is a member—the culture that is the work of many minds, and a more or less long history.

Whether the evolutionary adaptation in a given phyletic line will occur chiefly by way of genetic fixity or by was of genetically controlled plasticity of traits will depend on circumstances. In the first place, evolutionary changes are compounded of mutational steps, and consequently the kind of change that takes place is always determined by the composition of the store of mutational variability which happens to be available in the species populations. Secondly, fixity or plasticity of traits is controlled by natural selection. Having a trait fixed by heredity and hence appearing in the development of an individual regardless of environmental variations is, in general, of benefit to organisms whose milieu remains uniform and static except for rare and freakish deviations. Conversely, organisms inhabiting changeable environments benefit from having their traits plastic and modified by each recurrent configuration of environmental agents in a way most favorable for the carrier of the trait in question.

Comparative anatomy and embryology show that a fairly general trend in organic evolution seems to be from environmental dependence toward fixation of the basic features of the bodily structure and function. The appearance of these structural features in the embryonic development of higher organisms is, in general, more nearly autonomous and independent of the environment than in other forms. The development becomes "buffered" against environmental and genetic shocks. If, however, the mode of life of a species happens to be such that it is, of necessity, exposed to a wide range of environments, it becomes desirable to vary some structures and functions, in accordance with the circumstances that confront an individual or a strain at a given time and place. Genetic structures that permit adaptive plasticity of traits become, then, obviously advantageous for survival and so are fostered by natural selection.

The social environments that human beings have created everywhere are notable not only for their complexity but also for the rapid changes to which immediate adjustment is demanded. Adjustment occurs chiefly in the mental realm and has little or nothing to do with physical traits. In view of the fact that from the very beginning of human evolution the changes in the human environment have been not only rapid but diverse and manifold, genetic fixation of behavioral traits in humans would have been decidedly unfavorable for survival of the individual as well as of the species as a whole. Success of individuals in most human societies has depended and continues to depend upon their ability to rapidly evolve behavior patterns which fit them to the kaleidoscopic conditions they encounter. Individuals are best off if they submit to some, compromise with some, rebel against or avoid others, or escape from still other situations. Those who display a relatively greater fixity of response than their fellows suffer under most forms of human society and tend to fall by the way. Suppleness, plasticity, and, most important of all, ability to profit from experience and education are required. No other species is comparable to *Homo sapiens* in its capacity to acquire new behavior patterns and discard old ones in consequence of training. Considered socially as well as biologically, humankind's outstanding capacity is its educability. The survival value of this capacity is manifest, and therefore the possibility of its development through natural selection is evident. Natural selection on the human level favors gene complexes which enable their possessors to adjust their behavior to any condition in the light of previous experience. In short, it favors educability.

The replacement of fixity of behavior by genetically controlled plasticity is not a necessary consequence of all forms of social organization. Attempts to glorify insect societies as examples deserving emulation ignore the fact that the behavior of an individual among social insects is remarkable precisely because of the rigidity of its genetic fixation. The perfection of the organized societies of ants, termites, bees, and other insects is indeed wonderful, and the activities of their members may strike an observer forcefully by their objective purposefulness. The purposefulness is retained, however, only in environments in which the species normally lives. The ability of an ant to adjust its activities to situations not encountered in the normal habitats of its species is limited. On the other hand, social organizations on the human level are built on the principle that an individual is able to alter his or her behavior to fit any situation, whether previously experienced or new.

This difference between human and insect societies is not surprising. Adaptive plasticity of behavior can develop only on the basis of a vastly more complex nervous system than is sufficient for adaptive fixity. The genetic differences between human and insect societies furnish a striking illustration of the two types of evolutionary adaptations—those achieved through genetically controlled plasticity of behavioral traits and those attained through genetic specializations and fixation of behavior.

The genetically controlled plasticity of mental traits is, biologically speaking, the most typical and uniquely human characteristic. It is probable that the survival value of this characteristic in human evolution has been considerable for a long time, as measured in terms of human historical scales. Just when this characteristic first appeared is, of course, conjectural. Here it is of interest to note that the most marked phylogenetic trend in the evolution of humans has been the special development of the brain, and that the characteristic human plasticity of mental traits seems to be associated with the exceptionally large brain size. The brain, for example, of the Middle Pleistocene fossil forms of man was, grossly at least, scarcely distinguishable from that of modern man. The average Neandertaloid brain of the Upper Pleistocene was somewhat larger than that of modern man. More important than the evidence derived from brain size is the testimony of cultural development. The Middle Acheulian handiwork of Swanscombe man of three hundred thousand years ago, the Tayacian handiwork of Fontéchevade man of 160,000 years ago, and the beautiful Mousterian cultural artifacts associated with Neandertal man of 100,000 years ago, indicate the existence of minds of a high order of development.

The cultural evidence suggests that the essentially human organization of the mental capacities emerged early in human evolution. However that may be, the possession of the gene system, which conditions educability rather than behavioral fixity, is a common property of all living humans. In other words, educability is truly a species character of *Homo sapiens.* This does not mean, of course, that the evolutionary process has run its course and that natural selection has introduced no changes in the genetic structure of the human species since the attainment of human status. Nor is there any implication that no genetic variations in mental equipment exist at our own time level. On the contrary, it seems likely that with the attainment of human status the part of the human genetic system related to mental potentialities did not cease to be labile and subject to change.

This brings us face to face with the old problem of the likelihood that significant genetic differences in the mental capacities of the various ethnic groups exist. The physical and, even more, the social environments of people who live in different countries are quite diversified. Therefore, it has often been argued, natural selection would be expected to differentiate the human species into local groups or races differing in mental traits. Populations of different regions may differ in skin color, head shape, and other bodily characters. Why, then, should they be alike in mental traits?

As Kenneth Mather has put it,

Many non-European peoples, especially savages, have been regarded as genetically inferior because their level of social development was below that of the European, and this view has drawn strength from these people's obvious genetical departures from the European in colour and physical characteristics. The existence of one genetical difference makes it easier to impute another. The falsity of such an argument is self-evident. Since genes can recombine, their effects can be reassociated, so that differences in the genetic determinants of one character do not imply differences in the determinants of another.[2]

It will be through investigation rather than speculation that the problem of the possible existence of genetic differences in the mental make-up of human populations of different geographical origins will eventually be settled. Arguments based on analogies are precarious, especially where evolutionary patterns are concerned. If so-called human races differ in structural traits, it does not necessarily follow that they must also differ in mental ones. Ethnic group differences arise chiefly because of the differential action of natural selection on geographically separated populations. In the case of humans, however, the structural and mental traits are quite likely to be influenced by selection in different ways.

We are not directly concerned here with the problem of ethnic differentiation of structural traits. Suffice it to say that ethnic differences in such traits as the blood groups may conceivably have been brought about by genetic drift, that is, the random fixation of genes, in populations of limited effective size, as well as by selection. Other ethnic traits are genetically too complex and too consistently present in populations of some large territories to be accounted for by genetic drift alone.

In agreement with the views here expressed, George Gaylord Simpson, the distinguished paleontologist, wrote,

> There are biological reasons why significant racial differences in intelligence, which have not been found, would not be expected. In a polytypic species races adapt to differing local conditions but the species as a whole evolves adaptations advantageous to all its races, and spreading among them all under the influence of natural selection and by means of interbreeding. When human races were evolving, it is certain that increase in mental ability was advantageous to *all* of them in approximately equal degrees. For any one race to lag definitely behind another in overall genetic adaptation, the two would have to be genetically isolated over a very large number of generations. They would, in fact, have to become distinct species; but human races are all interlocking parts of just one species.[3]

Differences in skin color, hair form, nose shape, and so on, are almost certainly products of natural selection.[4] The lack of reliable knowledge of the adaptive significance of these traits is perhaps the greatest gap in our understanding of human evolutionary biology. Nevertheless, it is at least a plausible working hypothesis that these and similar traits have, or at any rate had in the past, differential survival value in the environments of different parts of the world. By contrast, the survival value of a higher development of mental capacities in humans is obvious. Furthermore, natural selection seemingly favors such a development everywhere. In the ordinary course of events in almost all societies those persons are likely to be favored who show wisdom, maturity of judgment, and ability to get along with people—qualities that may assume different forms in different cultures. Those are the qualities of the plastic personality, not a single trait but a general condition, and this is the condition which appears to have been at a premium in practically all human societies.

In human societies conditions have been neither rigid nor stable enough to permit the selective breeding of genetic types adapted to different statuses and forms of social organization. Such rigidity and stability do not prevail in any society. On the other hand, the outstanding fact about human societies is that they do change and do so more or less rapidly. The rate of change was possibly comparatively slow in earlier societies, as the rate of change in present-day indigenous societies may be when compared to the rate characterizing western societies. In any event, rapid changes in behavior are demanded of the person at all levels of social organization even when the society is at its most stable. Life at any level of social development in human societies is a pretty complex business, and it is met and handled most efficiently by those who exhibit the greatest capacity for adaptability, flexibility.

It is this very plasticity of their mental traits that confers upon humans the unique position which they occupy in the animal kingdom. Its acquisition freed humankind from the constraint of a limited range of biologically predetermined reactions. Humans became capable of acting in a more or less regulative manner upon their physical environment instead of being largely regulated by it. The process of natural selection in all climes and at all times has favored genotypes which permit greater and greater educability and plasticity of mental traits under the influence of the uniquely social environments to which humans have been continuously exposed.

As Muller has pointed out, "racial genetic differences . . . may well be insignificant in comparison with the individual ones, owing to the lack of any substantial difference in the manner of selection of most of these characters in the major part of the past history of the various human races." And, again, as Simpson has put it, "Human races all belong to the same species and have generally had enough interbreeding so that genetic progress, as distinct from local adaptation, could and evidently did spread through the entire species."[5] Finally, as Hiernaux has said,

If we . . . consider man's place in nature, what made him so successful on earth is his genetic capacity for culture. This major distinction is so essential for his survival in any environment that, in the light of current knowledge at least, all populations seem to be equal in this respect. Adaptation to local environment was and still is a paramount factor in the genesis of genetical or 'racial' differences between human populations, both these differences are minor and unessential compared with man's general physiological adaptability and his general capacity to find non-biological means of coping with the variations of his environment, including the new biological challenges which cultural evolution itself unceasingly generates.[6]

Whether or not we are reasonably justified in assuming that there has been little if any significant change in the mental potentialities of humans during the major part of their past history, this does seem to be reasonably clear—namely, that the effect of natural selection in humans has probably been to render genotypic differences in personality traits, in mental traits, in genetic potentialities, as between individuals and particularly as between ethnic groups or races, relatively unimportant compared to their phenotypic plasticity. The human genotype is such that it makes possible the development of the widest possible range of behavioral adjustments and adaptations. Instead of having genetically fixed responses as in other animal species, *Homo sapiens* is the only species that invents its own responses, and it is out of this unique ability to invent, to improvise, his responses that his cultures develop.

There is every good reason to believe that natural selection has been operative upon traits making for educability in much the same way from the earliest beginnings of man's history, and in all human groups, no matter how long isolated they may have been from one another. It should be obvious that under any and all forms of social organization, as David and Snyder put it,

> Flexibility of behavioral adjustment to different situations is likely to have had a selective advantage over any tendency toward stereotyped reactions. For it is difficult to conceive of any human social organization in which plasticity of response, as reflected by ability to profit from experience (that is, by intelligence) and by emotional and temperamental resilience, would not be at a premium and therefore favored by natural selection. It therefore seems highly improbable that any significant genetic differentiation in respect to particular response patterns, populations or races has occurred in the history of human evolution.[7]

And that is the conclusion of this chapter; or, to put it more positively, the evidence considered in this chapter points to the conclusion that in human evolution natural selection has placed, as it were, a high premium upon flexibility or educability, that it has done so nondifferentially, and that for these reasons it becomes highly probable that the mental capacities of humankind are everywhere pretty much of a muchness.[8] This does not mean that all humans have become exactly alike; such a statement would be demonstrably untrue. Human beings differ from one another in many traits, and there can be little doubt that mental traits are influenced by many genes, and that as long as this remains the case people will always differ from each other—more so within groups than between groups. What this statement does mean is that the selection pressures to which the human species has been subject since its origin has been nondifferential selection for educability, "i.e., for the capacity to modify one's behavior under the influence of experience and reasoning."[9] This seems to have had the effect of allowing for individual differences, of bringing all human groups up to pretty much the same mental level.

Finally, it is becoming increasingly clear that intelligence, from the genetic standpoint, is not so much a product of major genes, that is, of single genes producing a large effect, but rather of polygenes, that is of many genes each of which produces a small individual quantitative effect. This being the case it is highly improbable that differences in intelligence could have been brought about in the small, separated populations of humankind by genetic drift. This would require the assumption of so many correlated changes in positive-acting or negative-acting genes as to render such an effect quite out of the question.[10]

Let us then, always remember that from the very earliest beginnings of the arrival at the human estate the development of humanity has involved a feedback process between genotype and environment, the social environment, and the recreative organization of his experience and the world by the individual himself.[11]

Notes

1. R. A. Fisher, *The Genetical Theory of Natural Selection* (Clarendon Press: Oxford, 1930).

2. Kenneth Mather, *Human Diversity* (Edinburgh: Oliver and Boyd, 1964).

3. George Gaylord Simpson, *Biology and Man* (New York: Harcourt, Brace & World, 1966),104.

4. For suggestive treatment of this subject see Carleton Coon, Stanley M. Garn, and Joseph Birdsell, *Races, a Study of the Problems of Race Formation in Man* (Springfield, IL: Thomas). See also Th. Dobzhansky, *Mankind Evolving* (New Haven: Yale University Press, 1962); W. E. Howells, ed., *Ideas on Human Evolution* (Cambridge: Harvard University Press, 1962); Ashley Montagu, ed. *Culture and the Evolution of Man* (New York: Oxford University Press, 1962); James N. Spuhler, ed., *The Evolution of Man's Capacity for Culture* (Detroit: Wayne State University Press, 1959); Anne Roe and George G. Simpson, eds., *Behavior and Evolution* (New Haven: Yale University Press, 1958); Marshall Sahlins and Elmin R. Service, eds., *Evolution and Culture* (Ann Arbor: University of Michigan Press, 1960); Sherwood Washburn, ed., *Social Life of Early Man* (Chicago: Quadrangle Press, 1961); Ashley Montagu, *The Human Revolution* (New York: World Publishing, 1965); Ashley Montagu, ed., *Culture: Man's Adaptive Dimension* (New York: Oxford University Press, 1968); Th. Dobzhansky, *Genetic Diversity and Human Dignity* (New York: Basic Books, 1973); Jonathan Marks, *Human Biodiversity* (New York: Aldine de Gruyten, 1995); Weston La Barre, *The Human Animal* (Chicago: University of Chicago Press, 1954); E.

Moran, *Human Adaptability* (Belmont, CA: Wadsworth, 1979); P. T. Baker and J. S. Weiner eds., *The Biology of Human Adaptability* (Oxford: Clarendon Press, 1966).

5. George G. Simpson, "The Biological Nature of Man," *Science* 152 (1966), 474.

6. Jean Hiernaux, "Adaptation and Race," *Advancement of Science* (1967), 658–62.

7. Paul David and Lawrence Snyder, "Genetic Variability and Human Behavior," in *Social Psychology at the Crossroads,* eds. J. H. Rohrer and M. Sherif (New York: Harper, 1951), 71.

8. Th. Dobzhansky and A. Montagu, "Natural Selection and the Mental Capacities of Mankind," *Science* 105 (1947), 587–90.

9. Th. Dobzhansky, "The Genetic Nature of Differences among Men," in *Evolutionary Thought in America,* ed. S. Persons (New Haven: Yale University Press, 1962), 154.

10. J. L. Fuller, *Nature and Nurture: A Modern Synthesis* (New York: Doubleday, 1954), 27–28.

11. Richard Lewontin, Steven Rose, and Leon Kamin, *Not in Our Genes: Biology, Ideology, and Human Nature* (New York: Pantheon Books, 1984), 272–73.

6

The Mythology of Race,
or "For Whom the Bell Tolls"

Old myths never die. Nor do they fade away. Not, certainly, if they are related to "race" and its boon companion "IQ."

For millions of people the terms "race" and "IQ" seemingly possess a clear and well-defined meaning. This common usage implies the users' belief in a reality beyond question. When, on occasion, the suggestion is made that these terms constitute an amalgam of erroneous and stultifying ideas of the most damaging kind, the suggestion is apt to be received with blank incredulity or derision. Despite the fact that "race" and "IQ" correspond to no verifiable reality whatever, they have been made the basis for social and political agendas of the most heinous kind. The most recent example of this phenomenon is *The Bell Curve*, by Richard J. Herrnstein and Charles Murray.[1]

When Murray was seeking a publisher for *Losing Ground* (1984), he stated in his proposal that: "[A] huge number of well-meaning whites fear that they are closet racists, and this book tells them they are not. It's going to make them feel better about things they already think but do not know how to say."[2] This is surely a perfect description of *The Bell Curve*. Not only has *The Bell Curve* (which more than made up for the sales the earlier book failed to attain) told numbers of "well-meaning" whites that it is perfectly permissible for them to voice what they already thought about "race" and "intelligence" (if, indeed, they were not already doing so). It also assured such book buyers that their preexisting beliefs are "scientifically" sound and should therefore prevail in the policy-making arena.

Involved in the concept of "race" intrinsic to *The Bell Curve* is the assumption that first there *is* such a thing as "race," and second that what is so obvious and beyond question is that the physical differences which allegedly mark off the "races" from one another are inseparably linked with individual and group achievement. Some "races," it is held, from this point of view, are in all significant respects inferior to others. Hence, all that is

155

necessary to arrive at a proper estimate of an individual's abilities is to identify, usually by external appearance, his or her "racial" membership. This method will at once tell one the limits of that individual's capacities, what he or she is likely to be able to accomplish, and, furthermore, what his or her particular "race" will be able to achieve.

This "manifest reality"—in which physical appearance, individual ability, and group achievement are inseparably linked by heredity—is what is generally understood by "race." It is, in other words, the popular, or social, concept of "race."[3]

What is wrong with the social or racist view of "race" is that, among other things, there happens to be no genetic association or linkage between genes for physical appearance, individual behavior, and group achievement. Nevertheless, believers in the doctrine of "race" choose to take it for granted that such linkage exists.

As an exponent of the "race" doctrine, Murray is understandably sympathetic to the plight of whites who "fear they are closet racists" because social pressures presumably cause them to hide their views. And Murray is all the more sympathetic because he and Herrnstein actually engaged in such behavior before their book was published: "Some of the things we read to do this work, we literally hide when we're on planes and trains. We're furtively peering at this stuff."[4] What could they have been hiding?

"Surely the most curious of the sources he and Herrnstein consulted is *Mankind Quarterly* . . . ," observes Charles Lane. Cited in *The Bell Curve*'s bibliography, Lane points out, are no less than seventeen researchers who have contributed to this "notorious journal of 'racial history' founded, and funded, by men who believe in the genetic superiority of the white race." Five articles from the journal itself are also listed in *The Bell Curve*. One of Herrnstein and Murray's advisors is Richard Lynn, an associate editor of *Mankind Quarterly* (the authors list twenty-three of his works). The causes that *Mankind Quarterly*'s editors and contributors have supported range from apartheid in South Africa to "eugenically minded" attacks on school desegregation in this country. The journal has also published works by individuals who conducted research in Nazi Germany.[5] Another of *The Bell Curve*'s sources is Frank C. J. McGurk, who surfaced in the mid-1950s as a "scientific" opponent of school desegregation. He was also a leader of the International Association for the Advancement of Ethnology and Eugenics, whose executive committee "reflect[ed] an alliance between American segregationists and neo-Nazi elements abroad."[6]

The Bell Curve has been treated by its supporters as a ground-breaking work, but its authors essentially recycle the claims Jensen made in "How Much Can We Boost IQ Scores and Scholastic Achievement?" (1969) and other works. Herrnstein and Murray bestow high praise on their predecessor, who, they say, is "respected for his meticulous research."[7] The "meticulous research" in Jensen's 1969 monograph was linked to claims that created a media sensation in their time and returned biological determinism to center stage.

According to Jensen, it is "a not unreasonable hypothesis that genetic factors are strongly implicated in the average Negro-white intelligence difference."[8] But Jensen's hypothesis *is* unreasonable: it requires that one share his assumptions that the black-white scoring difference on IQ tests represents a black-white intelligence difference, and that 80 percent of the scoring difference is attributable to genetic differences.

In justifying his claims, Jensen made much of his heritability measures.[9] But the truth is that the so-called heritability coefficient is an especially undependable measure when applied to the human species. It has been criticized from its very inception by mathematical geneticists such as R. A. Fisher, as well as others. Fisher, one of the founders of modern statistics and mathematical and population genetics, referred to the coefficient of heritability "as one of those unfortunate short-cuts which have emerged in biometry for lack of a more thorough analysis of the data."[10] And David Layzer devastatingly showed that Jensen's 80/20 percent estimate belongs to numerology rather than science.[11]

Herrnstein and Murray also offer a heritability estimate. Without saying how they arrived at the estimate, they reduce Jensen's 80/20 to 60/40. One may safely assume that the reduction was made to lend their argument an aura of reasonableness, but the gaping difference between their percentages and Jensen's merely reveals once again the capriciousness of heritability estimates—that they are, as another critic observes, "little more than a hollow quantification."[12] This is hardly surprising, given that the genetic contribution to intelligence, let alone test scores, is unknown both for individuals and populations. Thus, even though Herrnstein and Murray's central argument treats a genetic component in test scores as established fact (e.g., "Recent studies have uncovered other salient facts about the way IQ scores depend on genes"), they also hedge on the genetic argument: "ethnic" differences in test scores "May well include some (*as yet unknown*) genetic component" (italics added).[13]

Herrnstein and Murray present no "theoretical" justification for the claim that different physical characteristics among "races" bespeak different mental characteristics. Perhaps the authors dispensed with this matter because of the attention that Jensen and other contemporary biological determinists had already devoted to it. Jensen, for instance, states that he held discussions with a number of geneticists; these discussions, he says, revealed rather consistent agreement on several points, including the following: "genetic differences are manifested in virtually every anatomical, physiological, and biochemical comparison one can make between representative samples of identifiable racial groups (Kuttner, 1967). There is no reason why the brain should be exempt from this generalization."[14] The first generalization is quite unsound, the second blatantly wrong.

Jensen's reference to Kuttner as his authority for the second statement is not supported by the latter's own paper which is restricted to a review of the biochemical differences between so-called races.[15] (Jensen's misconstruction of Kuttner's paper could hardly have displeased Kuttner, who is an arch-segregationist and a former associate editor of *Mankind Quarterly*.)[16] In any event, Jensen sees only differences between "racial" groups in virtually every anatomical, physiological, and biochemical trait, when in fact the likenesses in all these classes of traits are far greater than the differences. Differences in these areas of structure and function exist, but to argue that therefore differences must also exist for the genetic distribution of mental functioning among "races" is to call in the ambiguity of language to add to the confusion of thought.

Jensen sees no reason why the brain "should be exempt from the generalization" that genetic differences exist in virtually every organic trait between "races." But contrary to his conclusion, there is every reason why the brain should be exempt from this generalization. To begin with, by "brain" Jensen presumably means the neural circuitry which under the processes of socialization and their organization will function as mind. Since the brain is an organic structure, it can easily be slipped into Jensen's generalization and quite erroneously equated with "mind." Certainly the brain has undergone considerable evolutionary change, but the pressures of natural selection have not acted directly on it but indirectly through its functions, especially capacities for culturally-acquired functions. The complexity and size of the human brain represent the end-effects of the action of selection on the functions of human behavior in human environments. What has been under selective pressure is not the brain as an organ, *but the skill in using it and its competence in responding as a culturally adaptive organ.*

This aspect of the manner of humanity's unique mental evolution was fully dealt with by Dobzhansky and Montagu as long ago as 1947,[17] and may well be reemphasized here in the words of the distinguished paleontologist George Gaylord Simpson, who has explained in his book *Biology and Man* how it would have come about that from a biosocial viewpoint the mental abilities of humanity should everywhere have developed alike in response to the complex challenges of the environment. Simpson writes: "There are biological reasons why significant racial differences in intelligence, which have not been found, would not be expected. In a polytypic species races adapt to differing local conditions but the species as a whole evolves adaptations advantageous to all its races, and spreading among them all under the influence of natural selection and by means of interbreeding. When human races were evolving, it is certain that increase in the mental ability was advantageous to *all* of them. It would, then, have tended over the generations to spread among all of them in approximately equal degrees. For any one race to lag definitely behind another in overall genetic adaptation, the two would have to be genetically isolated over a very large number of generations. They would, in fact, have to become distinct species; but human races are all interlocking parts of just one species."[18]

To this may be added the words of two other biologists, Paul David and L. H. Snyder, when they wrote that

> "flexibility of behavioral adjustment to different situations is likely to have had a selective advantage over any tendency toward stereotyped reactions. For it is difficult to conceive of any human social organization in which plasticity of response, as reflected by ability to profit from experience (that is, by intelligence) and by emotional and temperamental resilience, would not be at a premium and therefore favored by natural selection. It therefore seems to us highly improbable that any significant genetic differentiation in respect to particular response patterns, populations or races has occurred in the history of human evolution."[19]

The anthropologists Sherwood L. Washburn and C. S. Lancaster state, "To assert the biological unity of mankind is to affirm the importance of the hunting way of life. It is to claim that however such conditions and customs may have varied locally, the main selection pressures that forged the species were the same."[20]

The foodgathering-hunting way of life was pursued by the human species the world over during the greater part of its evolutionary history. However, the importance of hunting in early human evolution has perhaps been overemphasized. A more likely view of the facts, but one which surely includes hunting within its purview, is expressed in the latest survey of evidence from a number of scholars. This evidence indicates that human beings are and always have been a species of generalists, whose adaptive advantage lies in their ability to exploit all facets of their environment.[21] This view gives women an equal or even greater role in the provisioning of the group, and thus the basis for sharing in the opportunities for the development of intelligence.

Professor Jensen also thinks it not unlikely that

> different environments and cultures could make differential genetically selective demands on various aspects of behavioral adaptability . . . Europeans and Africans have been evolving in widely separated areas and cultures for at least a thousand generations, under different conditions of selection which could have affected their gene pools for behavioral traits just as for physical characteristics."[22]

Here Jensen has confused two different phenomena; that is, he fails to distinguish between the environmental pressures of widely separated and diverse geographic areas upon the physical evolution of the human species, and the virtually identical cultural pressures upon the mental development of people living as adaptive generalists. Again contrary to Jensen, the challenges to humanity's problem-solving abilities were essentially of a social nature—and as of a very different order from those which eventually resulted in differences in skin color, hair texture, breadth of nose, and so on. While physical environments have varied considerably, humanity's cultural environments during the whole of its history, right up to the present period, have been fundamentally alike, namely, that of omnivorous generalists.[23] Thus, the important fact that Jensen fails to understand is that while the differences in the physical environments may have been extreme, the conditions of selection under which humanity's mental evolution occurred were everywhere alike.

Jensen's "scientific" theorizing about genetic differences in intelligence among "races" lent a seemingly sophisticated aura to the hereditarian argument, which had traditionally been advanced in manifestly crude ways. Once the argument was modernized, new twists could be added that might make hereditarians appear as objective, unbiased researchers. Jensen himself supplied such an addition or variation in 1973, when he alleged that East Asians are in all likelihood genetically superior in intelligence to whites.[24] Herrnstein and Murray followed suit.

That Herrnstein and Murray's decision to reiterate the Asian-superiority thesis was not prompted by the nature of the available data is apparent: "Only two studies sampled Asians in America, and they were inconclusive," states Margaret Cohn. Five other studies made comparisons between Asians in Asia and white Europeans or white Americans.

A scientist who is testing for the effect of genes independently of environment could not think of a worse study than one which compares groups in radically different cultures," Cohn notes, adding: "comparing Asians in Asia to whites in America is like comparing apples to oranges—not to mention the fact that IQ is to intelligence as apples are to zebras." Pointing to the reason why Herrnstein and Murray assert that Asians may well be the most intelligent "race," Cohn states: "Once they establish a super human or 'good' minority, then there can't be any racism in their research.[25]

Other researchers who preceded Herrnstein and Murray in promoting the Asian-superiority myth include Richard Lynn and J. Philippe Rushton. Rushton is notorious for his claim that a correspondence exists between brain size and "race" and penis size and "race"—with Asians at the top in the first category, whites slightly below, and blacks far below, and a reverse ranking in the second category. Herrnstein and Murray, defending Rushton against charges of "crackpot" and "bigot," assert that he has "strengthened the case for consistently ordered race differences . . ."[26]

By comparing the times in which each was published, one can see in yet another way that *The Bell Curve* is an extension of Jensen's monograph. Jensen's article appeared in the *Harvard Educational Review* not long after the civil rights movement had won major victories. His approach was, one might say, microcosmic: he attacked one new program, Head Start. In doing so, it was evident, he placed a range of other programs in jeopardy. By the time *The Bell Curve* was a work in progress, the social climate had so drastically changed that its authors could not only engage in a macrocosmic attack on educational and social programs, but feel confident that this would help make their book a best seller.

Among Herrstein's and Murray's many targets is Head Start, whose growth had long been severely curtailed. Using statistics generated during the years since Jensen's attack, the authors repeat the by now standard criticism of the program: Head Start, whose goal is to "boost IQ's," has failed. At first the children show significant scoring gains, but by the time they reach the third grade, the gains are "usually gone"; by the sixth, the scoring gains have "vanished from aggregate statistics."[27]

In other words, according to this argument, if the children's intelligence had actually been boosted, their IQ scores would not rise only to decline; the gains would be permanent. This interpretation fails to explain either the rise or fall in the children's scores. The scoring pattern is, in fact, inexplicable if IQ tests are regarded as measures of intelligence. But if the tests are recognized as instruments whose covert standard is school performance, the reason for the scoring pattern is evident: When the children's aggregate scores increased, it was because Head Start allowed them to acquire scholastic-type skills to which they would not otherwise have had access. But skills acquired in pre-school will not earn a child high marks in the third grade, let alone the sixth. When the children's scores declined, it was because their education had regressed; after leaving Head Start, they were relegated to the inferior schools provided for poor children, particularly black ones.

One might well contend that the logic of the initial increase in the children's scores called for upgrading their education after they left Head Start. But IQ tests serve to justify racial and class inequities in education, not to help eliminate them. If inferior, segregated schools had been deemed the problem, Head Start would have been seen as the first step in upgrading the children's education, not as a program designed to "boost IQs." Although it is now all but forgotten, the reason Head Start was given the objective of "increasing" the children's intelligence—which, it was held, had been stunted by their family environments—was so that they could go on to end the "cycle of poverty." So, by placing the blame for their poverty on poor people rather than on the society, the concept underlying Head Start also put the onus for deficient school performance on the children rather than on deficient schools.

Implicit in the Head Start concept is the assumption that individuals are mere products of their environment. But human development is determined neither by genes nor environment. Nor is the process of development, as a variant of these views holds, simply a matter of interaction between environment and genes. This process is instead the reorganization of that interaction by the developing organism. As R. C. Lewontin, Steve Rose, and Leon J. Kamin stress, it is not a question of

> organism and environment insulated from one another or unidirectionally affected, but of a constant and active interpenetration of the organism with its environment. Organisms do not merely receive a given environment but actively seek alternatives or change what they find."

While this applies to organisms in general, it applies prepotently to humans: "Humans above all are constantly and profoundly making over their environment in such a way that each generation is presented with quite novel sets of problems to explain and choices to make; we make out own history, though not in circumstances of our own choosing."[28]

The concept that humans are simply products of their environment and that mental processes develop in one kind of environment rather than another—thus overlooking that individuals are active agents in their own development who, in every environment, must explain problems and make choices—has long been influential, and is reflected in a variety of contemporary studies. For instance, the Coleman Report (1966) found that the quality of schooling has little effect on scholastic performance because the children's intelligence or cognitive abilities, as measured by IQ tests, is essentially set by the family environment at levels that vary with the family's race and socioeconomic status.[29] Despite criticism of the report on matters ranging from crude statistical methods to reliance on administrators' claims that schools for blacks were separate but equal, it has been used for three decades to justify the "savage inequalities" in education for African American and other minority children.[30] Jensen's monograph leaned heavily for its data on the environmentalist Coleman Report, and Herrnstein and Murray also use it to argue that equalizing education along racial and class lines is futile.

Among the justifications Herrnstein and Murray present for applying the genetic thesis to social matters is the following: Proceeding from the incontestable premise that environmentalists as well as hereditarians interpret the black-white scoring gap as an intelligence gap, the authors assert that even if it were discovered "tomorrow" that "the B/W difference in measured intelligence is entirely genetic in origin," they can think of "*no legitimate argument why any encounter between individual whites and blacks need be affected...*" (italics in the original).[31]

That no discovery will be made tomorrow or at any other time linking black-white differences in IQ scores to genes is beside the point (as is Herrnstein's and Murray's notion of what constitutes a "legitimate argument"). The *assumption* that such a difference exists is sufficient to affect behavior. Take Herrnstein and Murray's behavior: Although they admitted that the existence of a genetic component in the black-white scoring gap is "as yet unknown," they did not hesitate to use the genetic argument to influence public opinion and policy in the direction they wanted it to go.

Herrnstein and Murray, however, deny that the genetic argument affects policy making: "The *existence* of the difference [in black-white intelligence] has many intersections with policy issues. The *source* of the difference has none that we can think of, at least in the short term."[32] The qualifying phrase "at least in the short term" is the prelude to an argument ostensibly concerned with the uselessness of long-range environmentalist programs aimed at boosting IQs, but the real message is in the subtext, which signals the uselessness of allocating funds for pre-school or any other level of education for poor children, particularly if they are African American. This position is not exclusive to hereditarians but, as the Coleman Report attests, is also shared by conservative environmentalists.

But the phrase "at least in the short term" has other ramifications: it is a reminder of the long-term intersections between biological determinism and public policies and/or practices ranging from slavery, "eugenic" sterilization, and Nazi genocide to the Herrnstein-Murray vision of groups with low IQ scores being placed on reservations. The authors' amnesia regarding the fact that the genetic argument has historically served as the justification for the most brutal policies and practices is so appalling that it may easily distract attention from a point that calls for the most careful consideration: that the *assumption per se* of a black-white intelligence differential does indeed determine the outcome of a host of policy decisions, as well as innumerable individual encounters.

For instance Herrnstein and Murray—posing a supposedly hypothetical question—state that if employers were to use "ethnicity" as their hiring standard, they would do so because of a "difference in observed intelligence regardless of whether the difference is genetic."[33] It would be difficult indeed to argue that employers who reject African American applicants care whether the presumed black-white intelligence gap is the product of heredity or environment. It is the presumption of inferiority that justifies discriminatory hiring practices and, at the same time, inflames opposition to affirmative action—which was not designed to compensate for allegedly inferior intelligence but to combat centuries-old discrimination. The same principle applies to segregation and discrimination in every area, including the classroom, where IQ scores, not the way in which they are interpreted, determine a child's destiny. Thus, while the environmentalist interpretation of a supposed African-American intelligence deficit may sound benign, particularly when compared with the alternate interpretation, the *assumption of inferiority* is the opposite of benign.

The assumed black-white "difference in observed intelligence," which was first "observed" during slavery, has been "confirmed" by IQ tests for most of this century. Almost from the start, test use was joined by test criticism. An early critic was Walter Lippmann, the most brilliant journalistic and political commentator of his time. In a trenchant anatomy of IQ testing, he pointed to a fatal flaw: That intelligence testers had "no clear idea of what intelligence means."[34]

To answer this recurring charge, the testers have often asserted that "Intelligence is what the tests test."[35] Such a circular definition is hardly likely to advance our understanding of intelligence, although it can be interpreted as making a point, namely, that IQ tests don't measure intelligence, for the simple reason that no one knows what it is.

Still, it might be thought that the tests provide a rough estimate of certain problem-solving abilities. But abilities represent trained capacities, that is, skills, and therefore experience and learning enter substantially into their development. Since the tested ability/skill represents to a large extent the trained expression of a capacity of capacities, the "measurement" of the skill can tell us nothing about the original quality of the capacity.

Although the creators of IQ tests had no definition of intelligence, they nonetheless "knew" that school performance is a measure of intelligence and that different races and classes have superior or inferior intelligence. Because they constructed their tests of problems that call for scholastic-type skills and information and because quality of education varies along racial and class lines, their tests appeared to support their assumptions.

The early testers also "knew" that their tests measured "innate" intelligence, despite the fact that, even today, our knowledge of the genetics of intelligence is virtually non-existent. Intelligence is clearly a function of many genes in interaction not only with the environment but, as has been stressed, with the verdicts of the organism itself. The fact that we have no idea how many genes may be involved would not in itself constitute a sufficient impediment to the study of the genetics of intelligence were we able to separate the contribution made by the environment from the action of the organism itself toward influencing the expression of intelligence. But we are unable to do that, and the best authorities agree that it does not seem likely that we shall ever—even though "ever" is a long time—be able to make such a separation. But, to repeat the point that cannot be too often repeated, since genes never function in isolation, but always in interaction with the environment and the active organism, it does not appear likely that we shall ever be able to say to what extent intelligence is due on the one hand to genes and on the other to organismal and environmental factors.

It is quite clear that there are many unknowns involved in the development of intelligence, as for example, aspects of physiological, biochemical, neurological, neurohumoral, molecular, and social conditions—conditions which are never taken into account because they are unknown. All of which leads to the conclusion that those who tell us that IQ tests measure intelligence by that very statement make it evident that they simply do not understand the complexity of the problem. In claiming to have solved the problem and making recommendations based on specious evidence, they deceive both themselves and those who rely upon their judgment. They perceive cause and effect relations between variables such as test scores and assumed genetic or environmental determinants, when in fact no such cause and effect relations exits.

Given that they are alleged to measure what has not even been defined, it is not surprising that criticism of IQ tests has mounted over the years. The criticism, particularly of the tests' ethnocentric and class biases, reached a peak after Jensen published his 1969 article.[36] To defend the tests, Jensen published *Bias in Mental Testing* (1980);[37] his defense is reiterated in *The Bell Curve*. This defense maintains, accurately enough, that the tests are not biased according to the test makers' own criterion. By this criterion—a statistical one that has nothing to do with what test critics mean by bias—an IQ test is bias-free if it has "predictive validity," that is, if its prediction for the school performance of each tested group correlates to the same degree with the group's performance. Not only would the results of a test whose biases match those of the schools be expected to correlate with school performance, but the test makers "confirm" the predictive validity of IQ tests by "achievement" tests, which are constructed of the same kinds of items as the IQ tests.

Jensen, Herrnstein, and Murray also maintain that the tests are free of "cultural bias." To support this view, the trio relies on Frank McGurk's dissertation (1951).[38] According to Jensen, the work is a "pioneer doctoral study" that tests the "hypothesis that the poorer performance of blacks, as compared with that of whites, on most mental tests, is the result of cultural bias in the tests."[39] But rather than investigating a hypothesis regarding test bias, as Jensen claims, McGurk set out to uphold the hereditarian interpretation of IQ tests.

To "prove" that black-white scoring differentials do not result from test bias but from black-white genetic differentials in intelligence, McGurk constructed his study so that it would appear to rule out any other explanation.

He selected as his subjects 213 black-white pairs of high school seniors; the members of each pair, he claimed, had been matched for socioeconomic status, including education. His socioeconomic indices were probably adequate for making rather crude intra-group distinctions, but only a researcher who wanted to deny that racial discrimination affects socioeconomic status would use them for a black-white comparison.[40]

Take, for instance, McGurk's claim that the members of each black-white pair were matched for education. The students were drawn from seven different high schools in New Jersey and Pennsylvania, with the members of each pair said to have attended the same high school for four years. One hundred ninety-five pairs had reportedly been enrolled in the same school *districts* since first grade; however, the black and white members of a pair were not said to have been enrolled in the same *school*—a crucial distinction, since the schools the blacks attended would by no means have matched those the whites went to. That the black and white members of each pair would have arrived at high school with significant differences in preparation is further illustrated by the remaining eighteen pairs: The members of each attended grade school in entirely different areas.

The subjects of the study were tested on IQ items that had been rated from "least cultural" to "most cultural" by seventy-eight judges. Allowed to define "cultural" as each saw fit, the judges ranked items calling for vocabulary and/or information "most cultural," and those calling for scholastic-type skills "least cultural." (Of course, McGurk saw nothing untoward in convening a white panel to decide if items were biased against blacks.)[41] Because blacks did better on the "most cultural" than the "least cultural," McGurk reported that there was "no evidence" that "culturally weighted test material discriminates against the Negro."[42]

Thus, to support a predetermined conclusion, McGurk compared *black* averages on two *different* types of items. Had he made the appropriate comparison—namely, between black *and* white averages on the *same* type, he would, by his own comparative standard, have demonstrated that the culturally-loaded items *were* biased against blacks: Whites as well as blacks did better on them, but the white average was higher than the black one.

Perhaps, one might argue, McGurk should have said that the "most cultural" items were less biased against blacks because the black-white scoring gap was smaller than on the "least cultural" ones. But in terms of the IQ method, this is a meaningless distinction. On an IQ test, each type of item (vocabulary, analogy, and so forth) plays its part in bringing about a predetermined result. Although this means that the black average for each category must be lower than the white one, it does not mean that the racial scoring differential for each item contributes to the desired outcome (items that do not are dropped during a test's tryout period).[43] Thus McGurk, who supposedly aimed to discover if culturally-loaded items discriminate against blacks, was "investigating" a matter that the testers had resolved decades earlier. (Culturally-loaded items that discriminate against blacks could be replaced with culturally-loaded items that discriminate against whites, but this would of course reverse the desired results.) McGurk seems to have had at least two reasons for limiting his "investigation" of test bias to culturally-loaded items. By doing so, he dismissed even the possibility that other types of items could be biased. At the same time, by emphasizing that blacks did better on "most cultural" items, while passing over that fact that whites did too, his study seemed to support the hereditarian claim that the reason for the larger black-white scoring gap on the "least-cultural" (for instance, those involving mathematical problems) is that these items test an "innate" quality, that is, what hereditarians call "g," or "general intelligence." In reality, what these items test are skills that come with a quality education; the more difficult the problem, the higher quality of schooling required to deal with it. Thus these items, as well as the culturally loaded ones, reflect the inherent bias of a test whose measure is school performance.

McGurk's ambitious project had yet another object: to revive the hereditarian interpretation of the black-white scoring differential on the much-criticized World War I Army Mental Tests. To this end, he charged that the studies refuting this interpretation had used "extreme methods of selection." The reality is quite different: where the hereditarians claimed that the difference in the national black and white averages reflected a difference in "innate" intelligence, the refutations uncovered hidden scoring patterns that told another story.

An early refutation, which McGurk does not name, was published in 1924 by Horace Mann Bond.[44] Bond noted that if the tests were measures of "native and inherent ability," whites from Georgia should score as high as whites from Oregon. In ranking the whites from each state by their median score on the Alpha, the test for literates, he found an almost 50 percent difference between the white scores in the top- and bottom-ranked states. He also compared the whites' median score for each state with the state's rank according to the amount it spent per pupil, on teachers' salaries, and related indices. There was a strikingly high (almost 75 percent) correlation between the two sets of rankings, with southern states at the bottom for both test scores and education. Bond also compared black median scores from four northern states with white median scores from four southern ones; he found, for instance, that blacks from Illinois outranked whites from several southern states. The "boasted superiority of the white over the Negro stock does not seem so impressive when the Negroes of Illinois" outscored whites in "at least four Southern states," Bond observed.[45]

One of the studies that McGurk accuses of using "extreme methods of selection" is Ashley Montagu's (1945).[46] When Ashley Montagu found, two decades after the Bond study, that no additional black-white medians had been computed, he set out to calculate them for the remaining states. As it turned out, there were no statistics for blacks in twenty-five states, but he computed black and white Alpha medians for nineteen more states and the District of Columbia. The results showed that blacks from four northern states outscored whites from nine *southern* ones. Ohio blacks did better than whites from nine *northern* states.

The distribution of scores over the states, Ashley Montagu found, showed that for both African Americans and whites, "the deeper the South the lower the score":

> The depressed socio-economic state of the South as compared with the greater part of the rest of the United States is an unfortunate fact. It is, therefore, not surprising that both Negroes and whites in the South should do worse on the tests than their fellows in any other part of the Union; and, since conditions are invariably worse for Negroes than for whites, that the Negroes should do worse than the whites.[47]

The combined findings of the Ashley Montagu and Bond studies also point to an extension of this conclusion: that is, to a connection between the fact that, although northern states with better socioeconomic conditions spent more for educating whites than blacks, and the fact that the white median for each state was higher than its black counterpart.

Ashley Montagu also calculated medians for the Beta, the test for nonliterates, which showed a generally high correspondence with Alpha rankings. Comprehensive medians for the draftees who took the Alpha plus the Beta, an individual examination, or all three tests, also demonstrated that northern blacks did better than whites from many southern states. The explanation for the consonance between the Alpha and Beta medians may lie in the fact that in states with better socioeconomic conditions, nonliterate draftees would have had more opportunities to acquire information, both through broader experiences and more contact with literates, who would have formed a larger percentage of the population in those states.

Since the fact that northern blacks outscored southern whites could not be denied outright, it was hidden from a public that had been deluged with claims that the WWI scores were proof of African-American inferiority. Had the testers acknowledged that, by their own standards, northern blacks were more intelligent than southern whites, they would have shown simple fairness. But such a declaration, while no more nor less unscientific than the claim of white mental superiority, would of course have been heretical.

In addition to refuting present as well as past hereditarian interpretations, the state-by-state analyses of the WWI scores have other implications.

Certainly they counter the Coleman Report's claim that the quality of schooling has little effect on tests scores. They also counter other environmental interpretations, such as the one that attributes the black-white scoring gap to the "legacy of slavery." As the records left by the slaves (and in some cases by their masters) attest, devastating as it was, slavery did not stunt the slaves' cognitive processes. In most cases the black WWI draftees would have been the grandchildren, if not the children, of slaves. Northern blacks could not have outscored the southern whites had the legacy of slavery—the supposedly deleterious effects of racism and segregation on cognitive, or problem-solving, abilities—affected their aptitude for acquiring knowledge according to the opportunities available to them.

When the false claim that the legacy of slavery has arrested blacks' mental processes is rejected, it becomes possible to consider the actual psychological burdens this legacy places on African Americans. For example, black test takers are confronted with doing well on the very instruments used to "prove" their inferiority. These test takers, including the relatively small percentage with a quality education, are subject to what Claude Steele, a professor of social psychology, calls "stereotype vulnerability." This phenomenon, Steele has found, has an adverse effect on test scores. This is not, he stresses, because these students accept, consciously or unconsciously, the pervasive claim that they are inferior in intelligence, but that they must contend with it at the very moment they are under intense pressure to counter it. Steele also stresses that stereotype vulnerability is a "patient predator" that affects African Americans in every aspect of their academic life.[48]

Testing's crucial role in sustaining black stereotypes in white minds is in itself critical evidence that Jensen's 1969 article and *The Bell Curve* do not simply misuse worthwhile data, as has often been contended. The data flaunted by such as Jensen, Herrnstein, and Murray are provided by tests that "validate" the separation of children by "race." The statistical treatment of these data may at times be quite unexceptionable, but when unexceptional statistical methods are applied to the analysis of unsound data, based on assumptions that are equally unsound, one can only end up with conclusions that are thoroughly unsound. Such are the erroneous constructs of "race" and "IQ."

Notes

1. Richard J. Herrnstein and Charles Murray, *The Bell Curve: Intelligence and Class Structure in American Life* (New York: Free Press, 1994).

2. Quoted in Jason DeParle, "Daring Research or 'Social Science Pornography'?," *New York Times Magazine,* 9 October 1994, 50.

3. Ashley Montagu, ed., *The Concept of Race* (New York: Free Press, 1964).

4. Quoted in DeParle, "Daring Research or 'Social Science Pornography'?," 51.

5. Charles Lane, "The Tainted Sources of *The Bell Curve*," *New York Review of Books*, 1 December 1994, 14–19; 14.

6. William H. Tucker, *The Science and Politics of Racial Research* (Urbana: University of Illinois Press, 1994), 173. For more information on McGurk's opposition to school desegregation, see pp. 152–53, 168; for McGurk's connections to the International Association for the Advancement of Ethnology and Eugenics, see p. 249.

7. Herrstein and Murray, *The Bell Curve*, 13.

8. Arthur Jensen, "How Much Can We Boost IQ and Scholastic Achievement?," *Harvard Educational Review* 39 (Winter 1969): 1–123; 82.

9. Heritability is the proportion of the genetic to the total phenotypic variance. It is a group or population measure, and cannot be determined on an individual. For any particular trait in a specified population H (Heritability) is obtained by genetic variance divided by phenotypic variance, that is, in the present instance the observable trait yielded as the IQ score and called "intelligence," as $H = VG/VP$ or $VG + VE$ (VG = genetic variance; VP = phenotypic variance; VE = environmental variance). Genetic variance denotes the portion of the phenotypic variance which is caused by variation in the genetic constitution of the individuals in a population.

10. R. A. Fisher, "Limits to Intensive Production in Animals," *British Agriculture Bulletin* 4 (1951): 317–18.

11. David Layzer, "Science or Superstition? A Physical Scientist Looks at the IQ Controversy," in N. J. Block and Gerald Dworkin, *The IQ Controversy: Critical Readings* (New York: Pantheon, 1976): 194–241.

12. Vernon W. Stone, "The Interaction Component is Critical," *Harvard Educational Review* 39 (1969): 628–39, 629.

13. Herrnstein and Murray, *The Bell Curve*, 108, 312.

14. Jensen, "How Much Can We Boost IQ," 80.

15. Robert E. Kuttner, "Biochemical Anthropology," in *Race and Modern Science*, ed. Robert E. Kuttner (New York: Social Science Press, 1967), 197–222.

16. For more on Kuttner's views and activities, including his neo-Nazi connections, see Tucker, *Science and Politics of Racial Research*, 170–72, 173, 175, 178, 180, 182, 190, 257, 262, 263.

17. Theodosious Dobzhansky and Ashley Montagu, "Natural Selection and the Mental Capacities of Mankind," *Science* 105 (1947): 587–90.

18. George Gaylord Simpson, *Biology and Man* (New York: Harcourt, Brace, & World, 1969), 104.

19. Paul David and Laurence H. Snyder, "Genetic Variability and Human Behavior," in *Social Psychology at the Crossroads*, eds. John H. Rohrer and Muzafer Sherif (New York, Harper & Bros., 1951), 71.

20. Sherwood L. Washburn and C. S. Lancaster, "The Evolution of Hunting," in, *Man the Hunter*, eds. Richard B. Lee and Irven De Vore (Chicago: Aldine, 1968), 303.

21. Robert S. O. Harding and Geza Teleki, eds., *Omnivorous Primates* (New York: Columbia University Press, 1981); Tim Ingold et al., eds., *Hunters and Gatherers*, 2 vols. (Oxford: Berg, 1988).

22. Arthur R. Jensen, *Educability and Group Differences* (New York: Harper & Row, 1973), 24.

23. Richard B. Lee and Irven De Vore, eds., *Man the Hunter* (Chicago: Aldine Publishing Co., 1968); Elman R. Service, *The Hunters* (Englewood Cliffs, NJ: Prentice-Hall, 1966); Tim Ingold et al., eds., *Hunters and Gatherers*, 2 vols. (Oxford: Berg, 1988).

24. Jensen, *Educability and Group Differences*, 289–90.

25. Margaret Cohn, "The Truth About Asian Americans," in *The Bell Curve Debate: History, Documents, Opinions,* eds. Russell Jacoby and Naomi Glauberman (New York: Times Books, 1995), 239. The article first appeared as "About Asian Americans: False Flattery Gets Us Nowhere," *New York Newsday,* 28 October, 1994. For further analyses of the data related to the Asian-superiority myth, see Lane, "Tainted Sources," 17; and Barry Sautman, "Theories of East Asian Superiority," in *The Bell Curve Debate,* eds. Jacoby and Glauberman, 210–21.

26. Herrnstein and Murray, *The Bell Curve*, 642–43.

27. Ibid., 402–44.

28. R. C. Lewontin, Steve Rose, and Leon J. Kamin, *Not in Our Genes: Biology, Ideology, and Human Nature* (New York: Pantheon, 1984), 12, 13. This is a fundamental work that presents the whole matter of genes, environment, organism, and reality with clarity and authority. See also Peter L. Berger and Thomas Luckmann, *The Social Construction of Reality* (New York: Penguin, 1971).

29. James S. Coleman et al., *Equality of Educational Opportunity* (Washington, D.C.: U.S. Government Printing Office, 1966).

30. The reference is to Jonathan Kozol's *Death at an Early Age: The Destruction of the Hearts and Minds of Negro Children in the Boston Public Schools* (New York: Houghton Mifflin, 1967), a devastating critique of the flagrantly unequal education the school systems provide along racial and class lines.

31. Herrnstein and Murray, *The Bell Curve*, 642–43.

32. Ibid., 313.

33. Ibid.

34. Walter Lippmann, "The Mystery of the 'A' Men," in *The IQ Controversy: Critical Readings,* eds. N. J. Block and Gerald Dworkin, (New York: Pantheon, 1976), 9. The article, one of six on testing by Lippmann, was originally published in the *New Republic,* 1 November 1922. The other five articles, which also appeared in the New Republic, are: "The Mental Age of Americans," 25 October 1922; "Tests of Hereditary Intelligence," 22 November 1922; "The Future of the Tests," 29 November 1922. All the articles, together with the debate that followed between Lippmann and Lewis M. Terman, the hereditarian creator of the Stanford-Binet IQ test, as well as the replies by those criticized, are included in Block and Dworkin. It is a fundamental, and fair, presentation of the whole subject. See also John L. Rury, "Race, Region, and Education: An Analysis of the Black and White Scores on the 1917 Army Alpha Test," *Journal of Negro Education,* 57 [1] (1988): 51–65; Stephen J. Gould, *The Mismeasure of Man* (New York: Norton, 1981), 192–233

35. Edwin G. Boring, quoted in Richard J. Herrnstein, *I.Q. in the Meritocracy* (Boston: Atlantic Monthly Press/Little Brown, 1973), 107. Herrnstein provides a rather tortured justification for Boring's remark, which was first published in the *New Republic* in 1923.

36. See Ken Richardson, David Spears, and Martin Richards, eds., *Race, Culture, and Intelligence* (Baltimore: Penguin Books, 1972); Evelyn Sharp, *The IQ Cult* (New York: Coward, McCann & Geoghegan, 1972); Carl Senna, ed., *The Fallacy of the IQ* (New York: Third Press, 1973); John Garcia, "IQ: The Conspiracy," *Psychology Today* (September 1972), 40–43, 92–92; Peter Watson, ed., *Psychology and Race* (Chicago: Aldine, 1974); Robert L. Williams, "Scientific Racism and IQ: The Silent Mugging of the Black Community," *Psychology Today* (May 1974), 32–41, 101; Elaine and Harry Mensh, *The IQ Mythology: Class, Race, and Inequality* (Carbondale: Southern Illinois University Press, 1991).

37. Arthur R. Jensen, *Bias in Mental Testing* (New York: Free Press, 1980).

38. Frank C. J. McGurk, *Comparison of the Performance of Negro and White High School Seniors on Cultural and Noncultural Psychological Test Questions* (Washington, D.C.: Catholic University Press, 1951) (Microcard) 12 July 1996.

39. Jensen, *Bias in Mental Testing*, 524.

40. McGurk used a revised Sims Record Card for ranking the students according to socioeconomic status. They were matched by such criteria as parents' education, wage earner's occupation (the question assumes only one wage earner), personal bank account, amount of dental care, family's attendance at concerts, mother's membership in clubs, private music lessons, number of books and magazines in the home. To illustrate why black-white differences are hidden by such questions, take Occupation: even if a black and white wage earner were in the same general occupation, the white would in almost all cases have had a higher-paying position (McGurk further blurred economic distinctions by reducing Sims' five occupational categories to two). Moreover, even in those cases where black income would have matched white income, the blacks as a rule would have lived in different areas, with different schools and cultural institutions.

41. The subjects of the study are identified by "race," the judges (who included psychology and sociology professors, teachers, and graduate students) are not. Given that McGurk would have considered whites the "norm" group, it would not have occurred to him to identify the judges by race.

42. Frank C. J. McGurk, "On White and Negro Test Performance and Socioeconomic Factors," *Journal of Abnormal and Social Psychology* 48[3] (1952): 448–50; 450; Frank C. J. McGurk, "Socio-economic and Culturally-Weighted Test Scores of Negro Subjects," *Journal of Applied Psychology* 37[4] (1953): 276–77.

43. McGurk's test was a composite of items from three different IQ tests. Although the items would not have performed statistically in the same way as in their original contexts, they produced the results McGurk required because they retained their original biases.

44. Horace M. Bond, "What the Army 'Intelligence' Tests Measured," in Jacoby and Glauberman, eds., *The Bell Curve Debate*, 583–98. Originally published in the *Crisis,* July 1924.

45. Ibid., 597.

46. M. F. Ashley Montagu, "Intelligence of Northern Negroes and Southern Whites in the First World War," *American Journal of Psychology* 58 (April 1945): 161–88. See Appendix D of the unabridged edition of this book.

47. Ibid., 186. Clearly, McGurk constructed his study so it could be alleged that it countered Montagu's conclusion: Montagu's study, McGurk asserted, was

not an experimental project but one based on the author's knowledge of differences in North-South socioeconomic conditions. Since an almost needless amount of data is available to support what is common knowledge about North-South socioeconomic conditions of that period only an individual determined to uphold biological-determinist claims at any cost (in this case by means that included spurious iindices for comparing black and white socioeconomic status) would try to cast doubt on the validity of the North-South comparison in Montagu's study. See Elaine Mensh and Harry Mensh, *The IQ Mythology* (Carbondale: Southern Illinois University, 1991).

48. Claude Steele, quoted in Ethan Waters, "Claude Steele Has Scores to Settle," *New York Times Magazine,* 17 September, 1995, 44–47; 6. For instance, together with Joshua Aronson of the University of Texas, he conducted an experiment on two groups of black and white Stanford undergraduates that involved the most difficult verbal skills questions from the Graduate Record Exam. One group was told that the project's purpose was simply to research "psychological factors involved in solving verbal problems"; the other was told that the exam was "a genuine test of your verbal abilities and limitations" (ibid., 45). The blacks who thought they were merely being asked to solve problems performed as well as the whites (whose performance was the same in both situations). But the test performance of blacks who were told that their intellectual potential was being measured was significantly worse than that of the other test takers.

In Steele's experiment, when stereotype vulnerability was eliminated the black students' academic preparation allowed them to perform equally with the white ones on a test of scholastic performance. In real-life situations, most blacks come to the tests with unequal academic preparation, so stereotype vulnerability would not be *the* factor lowering their scores but an *added* one.

Clearly, stereotype vulnerability is the product of a vast array of racist pressures and practices in and out of the schools, all of which are legitimated by IQ and IQ-type tests. To put it another way, white stereotyping, with which blacks must constantly contend, is justified by spurious tests that assign greater mental worth to whites than to blacks.

7

Race and Society

No activity of man, whether it be the making of a book, the contraction of a muscle, the manufacture of a brick, or the expression of an idea, can be understood fully without a knowledge of the history of that activity in so far as it has been socially determined. For, obviously, any neglect to take into consideration the relations of the social framework can only lead to an incomplete and defective understanding of such events. The social construction of reality is created for us from the moment we are born, and as we grow and acquire the knowledge, "the common-sense knowledge" of everyday life, our perceptions are formed by the particular socialization process within which we have learned, been conditioned, to behave.

It should be clear that humankind develops in and through an environment that is social as well as physical. There is, perhaps, no subject and no event of which this is more conspicuously true than of that tendentious and reverberative word race. I say "event," because in a very real sense it would be preferable to speak of race as an "event," a thing, "for this is the process of reification, that is, the apprehension of a human phenomenon as if it were a thing."[1] Apart from the cells of a dead lexicographer's brain or the taxonomist's judgment, race in reality hardly ever functions as a word, but almost always as an event, an emotion, an experience, an action. In our society—and it is within the universe of our society that I am speaking—race is not merely a word which one utters but it is also an event that one experiences. The word itself merely represents a series of sounds which usually serve as a stimulus to set in motion a host of feelings and thoughts which, together, form an emotional experience; this generally, for most people, is what race is.

It is of the greatest importance that this fact be clearly understood, and in this chapter an attempt will be made, among other things, to inquire into the development of those psychological factors which tend to make this event possible. That such psychological factors exist is indisputably clear, but these factors are not so well known as they deserve to be.

"Race," in our society, is not a term that clearly and dispassionately defines certain real conditions which can be demonstrated to exist, but, as I have already said, the word acts more as a stimulus that touches off a series of emotional charges that usually bear as much relation to the facts as bees do to bonnets. Feelings and thoughts concerning such a concept as race are real enough, and so, it may be pointed out, are feelings and thoughts concerning the existence of unicorns, pixies, goblins, satyrs, ghosts, Jews, blacks, Catholics, and foreigners in general. Endowing a feeling or a thought about something with a name and thereby imputing to that something a real existence is one of the oldest diversions of humankind. Humans impose on nature the limitations of their own minds and identify their views with reality itself. Pixies, ghosts, satyrs, Aryans, and the popular conception of race represent real enough notions, but they have their origin in traditional stories, myths, or imagination.

Language especially seduces us into believing that every noun is a thing, and that things are enduring and permanent. Error, imagination, emotion, and rationalization are among the chief components of these notions. Facts, it should always be remembered, do not speak for themselves, but invariably through an interpreter. The word "fact" (*facere*) originally meant a thing made; we still make our own "facts," but fail to realize how much of ourselves we put into them or how much others have put into them. This is especially unfortunate in a century in which, as Ignazio Silone pointed out, words have been so much perverted from their natural purpose of putting man in touch with man as they are today.[2] The lesson necessary for all of us to understand and learn is that *the meaning of a word is the action it produces.* No matter if words and beliefs are false, if men define them as real, they will be real in their consequences.

Nothing, indeed, can be so real as the unreal. It is not here my purpose to show that concepts denoted by such a term as "ghost" or race do not, in the sense in which they are commonly used and understood, correspond to anything scientifically demonstrable as having a real existence. Madame de Staël once remarked, "I do not believe in ghosts, but I am afraid of them." Rationally convinced of the non-existence of ghosts, Madame de Staël nonetheless reacted irrationally and emotionally to the notion of ghosts for all the world as if they had a real existence. Most of us are familiar with such reactions. It is evident that in her early childhood Madame de Staël had been emotionally conditioned to believe in the existence of ghosts to such an extent that as an adult, in spite of the fact that she knew that such beliefs were quite irrational, she was quite unable to throw off the effects of that conditioning. That is what occurs, in most cases, with regard to race. Even though they may know it is nothing but a "ghost," most persons continue to be haunted by it. As Mussolini put it in his pre-racist days, "Race! It is a feeling, not a reality."[3]

Indeed, where matters of race are concerned feelings are likely to be involved. The fault, however, lies not so much in the emotional involvement, but in the refusal to recognize that involvement for what it is, and to exercise some measure of rational control over it.

There can be little doubt of the fact that in many parts of the world children are emotionally conditioned early to a belief in the existence of race differences.[4] In many parts of Europe, for example, where the larger number of troubles of state and person have traditionally been attributed to the Jews, such attributions can hardly have failed to escape the attention of most children. Indeed, they usually become aware quite early in their lives that hostility toward Jews is a socially sanctioned, even required, form of behavior. Such children would grow up to accept the existence of imputed race differences as real and would act upon such beliefs as if it were perfectly natural to do so. But just as Madame de Staël became rationally convinced that ghosts do not exist in spite of the acknowledged strength of the emotion attached to the idea, so, too, it is quite possible to produce a rational appreciation of the nature of their error among those who have been emotionally conditioned to accept the mythology of race as real. Indeed, nearly all of us have been to some extent so emotionally conditioned, yet many of us have been more or less able to emancipate ourselves from the effects of such conditioning by becoming acquainted with the facts relating to these matters. But with many others it cannot be as simple as that, for the roots of their prejudices go much deeper—as we shall soon see. But for those whose prejudices are more superficial an adequate discussion of the facts should suffice. Hence, one of the first requirements necessary for the production in the individual of an intelligent understanding of race problems must be the existence of a readily available body of adequately correlated scientific facts relating to every aspect of the race problem for use in the education or re-education of the individual. Moreover, these facts must be used, and they must be made available in a form for use. In this field science and knowledge are valueless unless they can be applied in a practical way to increase human happiness.

The dispassionate scientific collection and analysis of facts are activities of the first importance, but the end of such activities should not rest with their publication in learned journals. The ultimate purpose of these scientific activities must be recognized as having been defeated unless the most pertinent results are disseminated in such a manner as to increase the understanding of these matters in every human being, until correct understanding is translated into sound conduct.[5]

All who at present appear to be hopelessly confused upon the subject of race are not beyond redemption. Methods can be developed by means of which many persons who now superficially harbor myths and delusions concerning race may be reached and re-educated. Through the press, periodicals, popular lectures, books, film, radio, TV, school, the church, and many similar agencies, innumerable misguided persons can be reawakened to their true relation to their fellow humans. With respect to those who are more pervasively infected with the virus of racism, I am not so sure. But more important than these is the growing generation. Through the lower and upper grade schools the most significant work can be done in clarifying the minds of children concerning the facts relating to the fascinating variability of humankind and in educating them to think critically for themselves in the light of the evidence.[6] Let us teach geography, but instead of presenting the subject in a dry-as-dust manner, let us humanize its teaching and furnish its field with the living peoples who inhabit the earth.[7] Let us teach our children what we know about the peoples of the earth, and about their respective values for one another and for civilization as a whole. Let us emphasize their likenesses and create interest in the meaning of the differences, differences which enrich the common heritage of humanity and make the world the richly variegated experience it can be. Let us teach appreciation of the other person's point of view, the more so since, if it is unlike our own, it will require more sympathetic appreciation if it is to be understood.

Relations between other human beings and ourselves form the most important of all the experiences and situations of our lives. Nevertheless, in our society human beings are permitted to enter into such relations without being equipped with the most elementary understanding of what they mean.[8] No attempt is made to supply them with the facts relating to race as demonstrated by science. On the contrary, for the most part they are supplied with the kind of information that makes fertile ground for the development of race prejudices.[9]

Prejudices early acquired are notoriously difficult to eradicate. The child picks up attitudes long before he becomes familiar with the facts. What should be done is to see to it that, instead of such prejudices, the growing personalities in our schools are taught the facts which the anthropological and social sciences have made available. Our children should be taught that the physical features of people, however different, are all of equal value, and that readily understood they are of great interest and that the whole area of difference is an inexhaustibly exciting terrain to explore. Children are fascinated by the explanation of the nature and development of such differences. One of the great basic needs which the child strives to have satisfied is its curiosity, and nothing can be more gratifying than to have that need satisfied, and nothing can be more gratifying to the caregiver than to observe the resulting humanizing effect upon the child. To explain to a child that even the expression of the face, which is by many taken to be biologically determined, is not necessarily so, that facial expression, as well as bodily behavior, gestures, like the clothes one wears, are often strongly influenced by class or caste membership.[10] Children should be taught that there are never any grounds in the appearance of people for discrimination against them. For it should be obvious that, though some of us may not be particularly attracted to people who exhibit a certain type of physiognomy, the cause of our dislike lies not in their physiognomy but in the values, the culturally conditioned ideas, in our own minds which have taught us to react in this way to the perception of such physiognomies. The causes of such dislikes must be looked for in the cultural background of one's conditioning, not in the shape of the nose or the color of the skin of our neighbors. Physical differences are merely the pegs upon which culturally generated hostilities are made to hang, ending with the smug and empty conviction that a superior race is one that you look like and an inferior race is one that you don't look like. Here, then, is a most important field in which a great and valuable pioneer work remains to be done. Academic discussions alone will not carry us far. We must be willing to roll up our sleeves and set to work on this immense and pressingly important problem in human relations, until it is solved.[11]

Community projects for teaching sympathetic understanding of other peoples and ethnic groups have demonstrated to what an extent race prejudice can be handled. Treated like any other disease, race prejudice can be prevented where it has not yet become endemic and eliminated where it has. Each community should make itself responsible for ridding itself of a disease which makes for so much social wastage and distress. Each community should see to it that it thinks and acts, in its own cooperative interests, in the light of the soundest modern knowledge and the best human practice. Where there is a desire for just action it will be achieved, and where there is more than a hope of clarity, confusion will yield. Our communities often have departments of sanitation, departments of roadways, why not a department of human relations?

One of the first points to be grasped before much progress in this subject can be made is that, so far as human beings and as far as society and social development are concerned, race is not a biological problem at all; furthermore, that it does not even present any socially relevant biological problems. "Race" is a term for a problem created by special types of social conditions and by such types of social conditions alone. In terms of social relations so-called race problems are, in the modern world, essentially of the nature of caste problems.

Race and Caste

"Race," wrote Wyndham Lewis in his book *The Art of Being Ruled,* "is the queen of the 'classes.'"[12] We must recognize the fact that in our own society the "race problem" is essentially a problem of social relations and that it is, therefore, fundamentally a social problem, always in a political context. In the social context of America, to take an example with which we are all familiar, what is usually referred to as a race or racial group in reality often constitutes a caste. Thus, African Americans, Jews, Japanese Americans, and Native Americans are to varying degrees, and in different regions, treated very much, by the dominant white groups, as if they were members of specific castes, "untouchables."

A caste may be defined briefly as a specific, socially limited status group, or more fully as an hereditary and endogamous group, occupying a position of superior or inferior rank or social esteem in comparison with other such groups. The functions of the limiting factors of caste are, in effect, primarily to create barriers against sexual relations between members of the "superior" caste and those of the "inferior" castes and, secondarily, to regulate the social status, privileges, and social mobility of the members of the "inferior" castes. A class differs from a caste in that a greater degree of social mobility is, in all respects, permitted between the members of the upper and the lower social classes than is permitted between castes.

"The presence of caste is revealed by two crucial attitudes: (1) a sentiment against intermarriage; and (2) the practice of judging individuals on the basis of their group membership rather than their individual merits."[13] When we speak of the race problem in America, what we really mean is the caste system and the problems which that caste system creates in America.[14] To recognize this fact is to recognize and to effect a clarification and a change in conceptual approach to a problem upon which, perhaps more than any other in our time, clear thinking and accurate concepts are an urgent necessity.

Humphrey has suggested that "the term race should be discarded entirely in the cultural reference, and the more appropriate term caste employed in its stead."[15] This is a worthy suggestion. There can be no cultural races; there can only be cultural castes. But when Humphrey adds that "the term race should be retained in its biologic context as a taxonomic category for the delineation of types of mankind," we must, as the lawyers say, put in a demurrer, for the term "race," as we have seen, is embarrassed, and it is a question whether as a taxonomic category referring to humans it is not unrescuably compromised. Even geneticists today tend to avoid its use.

As Kalmus pointed out, "A very important term which was originally used in systematics is 'race.' Nowadays, however, its use is avoided as far as possible in genetics . . . The term used by modern geneticists to take the place of race is strain, which has a more precise meaning; it is applied to forms which differ from the commonly wild type by one or several precisely defined hereditary characters which usually breed true."[16] In a widely consulted dictionary of biology the term "race" was altogether omitted,[17] while in his 1951 authoritative work on evolution the author Carter made it quite clear that such terms as "'race,' 'variety,' and 'form' are used so loosely and in so many senses that it is advisable to avoid using them as infraspecific categories."[18]

Let us consider a little further what the meaning of this term "race," in the social sense, really is. In countries such as England, France, Germany, and Spain, in which class distinctions are well marked and there exist no significantly large ethnic groups other than the dominant national population, race prejudice is replaced by class prejudice. In fact, there is scarcely any difference between the two phenomena. Almost every condition encountered in the one is to be found in the other, even down to the imputed biological differences. In his beautiful novel, *Bread and Wine,* Ignazio Silone, writing of his native Abruzzi in Italy, describes the social identification of "class" with "race." He writes:

> Don Paolo was surprised to observe the role that mustaches, beards, and hair still played in differentiating the professional class from the peasants and the landlords. He realized also why the various classes were indicated in dialect by the word 'race'—the 'race' of husbandmen, the 'race' of 'artists' (artisans), the 'race' of landowners. The son of a petty landowner who studies, and therefore inevitably becomes a state or municipal employee, promptly tries to obliterate the fact that he comes of the 'race' of husbandmen by brushing his hair in the style of his new station.[19]

A similar phenomenon is encountered in Brazil, where straight, shiny hair and thin, pointed nose are often more important than skin color, and where there is also a saying, "The black man who is rich is white—the white man who is poor is black."[20]

In Brazil blacks make up at least half the nation, and it is the blacks who are the underclass. There is a myth which has long enjoyed support among some North Americans that Brazil enjoys a racial harmony which is unique in the Americas. This is not true. Brazil is not a racially harmonious society. Brazil discriminates against and subordinates its blacks and ensures that they will be kept in "their place" and live the fate of their class.[21]

Perhaps the best book, and the most readable, that has been written on Brazil's racial problems is Roger Bastide's *The African Religions of Brazil: Toward a Sociology of the Interpenetration of Civilizations* (1978). Here in his own words, is what Bastide says of race relations in Brazil:

> In a racial democracy the black is split. Split between rebellion against the white, who tends to reject him, and rebellion against himself, which intensifies his feeling of inferiority. Split between African militancy, and the desire to be assimilated, through miscegenation, into the great white mass. In the United States, the mulattos belong with the Negroes. In Brazil the mulatto escapes from the colored caste and turns against the blacks. It is he, not the white, who holds the deepest prejudices against his darkest brothers.[22]

The "annihilating prejudice" as Bastide calls it, is in many ways more complex than it is in the United States.

Almost everywhere the upper classes make much of "breeding," of "good family" or "birth" or "quality" or "ancestry," and will not, generally, marry out of their "class" or "quality."[23] To marry out of one's class is to lose "caste," or status not only socially but also, it is considered, biologically, for such a person's children can belong only to the class and caste of the "inferior" parent. There are, of course, many exceptions, but this is the general rule. This rule tends to be more strictly applied to women than to men. The upper-class male generally elevates the woman he chooses to marry to his own class; the lower-class male generally reduces his wife and children to his own class. In the Western world the biology and stratification of the classes are patrilineally determined; that is to say, they operate through, and in favor of, the male line. This is not the case where ethnic crossing is concerned, and it constitutes one of the few differences between the working of class and race prejudice. Thus, for example, should an upper-class white male marry a black female, the offspring will, in the United States at least, be relegated to the mother's caste, and not to that of the father.

The mechanism of this "caste" form of race prejudice is clearly seen at work in England. During the last several decades there has been an appreciable increase in the colored population in England, principally owing to the immigration of West and Asiatic Indians, and a concomitant appearance of race prejudice where formerly it was nonexistent. But as Banton[24] and others[25] have pointed out, the English form of race discrimination, is not really race prejudice, but an expression of the desire to avoid losing caste in one's own group by behaving as an equal to those who are for one reason or another regarded as of lower social status. Since "class" is largely determined by the people with whom one associates, and since a dark skin color, in England, is largely identified with formerly subject peoples, association with persons of color detracts from one's social standing. Banton in his study found that by far the majority of Britons felt sympathetically toward colored people, but the problem of caste bothered them. In a study of colonial students in London, Carey found that London landladies preferred white to colored lodgers mainly because of their fears about what other people might think. One boardinghouse landlady remarked: "Of course, I don't take blacks; I'm sorry for the darkies, that I am, but I know what the neighbors would say: 'Look at Mrs. So-and-So! She really has come down in the world.'"[26]

This kind of discrimination must be distinguished from race prejudice. It is not based on emotional or irrational prejudgments or on hostility, but represents a response to social situations, defined by considerations of social status. There can be little doubt that elsewhere in the world such factors enter into much that is called race prejudice. In the United States,

Westie has shown that the occupational status is a significant determinant of the response that whites make to a particular African American.[27] And as Liston Pope has put it, "The mill worker, with nobody else to 'look down on,' regards himself as eminently superior to the Negro. The colored man represents his last outpost against social oblivion."[28] A study, by Dr. William T. Liu, mainly of Catholics who had emigrated to Tallahassee, Florida, from other regions, principally the North, revealed that moral values, though important, did not decisively determine these persons' attitudes toward segregation. Residential stability and subjective identification with the Southern community seem to have been the critical factors.[29]

Blumer has drawn attention to the fact that the collective process through which a group position is formed, vis-à-vis other groups, is a potent factor in the genesis of race prejudice. "Race prejudice becomes entrenched and tenacious to the extent the prevailing social order is rooted in the sense of social position."[30] The process of group definition produces an abstract image of the subordinate groups, which spreads out far beyond the boundaries of contacts with individual members of such groups, and transcending any experience with them. The reaction or response to all members of such subordinate groups is not in terms of experience of them, but in terms of the abstract image of the group that has been built up of them, and into which they are made to fit.[31]

Among the strongest supporters of the view that the upper classes are not only socially but biologically superior to the lower classes are those who have themselves recently migrated from the lower into the ranks of the upper classes. Success in life is held to be not so much a matter of social opportunity as of biological quality. Such views are, of course, rationalizations, but once made they help to determine the attitudes not only of the upper but also of the lower classes. Indeed, as Polanyi has pointed out, the poorer classes of England a century ago were the detribalized, degraded natives of their time.[32] And, as Johnson has stated, the arguments used to justify the practice of child serfdom in England were identical with those used to justify the slave trade.[33]

It should be fairly evident that in societies in which there is an extreme division of the population into classes whose interests are necessarily opposed and in which the means of earning a living, the economic system, is organized upon an unequal or extremely competitive basis, there will be abundant opportunities for class or race antagonisms. This is a matter with which we shall deal in the next chapter.

The point I wish to bring out here is that race prejudice is merely a special case of class prejudice, a prejudice that will be developed, under certain conditions, where different ethnic groups are thrown together in significant numbers.[34] In the absence of such conditions—or in the absence of a variety of ethnic groups the prejudices of the upper classes against all members of the lower classes and their conduct toward the members of such classes will, in almost every respect, take the form usually associated with race prejudice. Wherever classes exist there exists class prejudice. In socially stratified class societies the shift from class prejudice to race prejudice is easily achieved and, in fact, amounts to little more than a change of names, for the race against which prejudice is now especially directed is but another class or caste, even though it may be regarded as something substantially different.

Race and class prejudices are simply particular kinds of the group phenomenon of which national prejudices, religious prejudices, sex prejudices, and the like are similar kinds. As MacCrone points out,

> We must not think of race prejudices as if they were a unique kind of group or social attitude; instead we must think of them in their proper context as simply one of a class of group or cultural phenomena, all of which are dependent upon the same kind of conditions, display the same basic characteristics, and serve the same functions.[35]

In the case of the American black it is necessary to understand that the original difference in his status was one of caste, not of biology. It was only later that the allegedly biological differences were attached to the difference in caste. An African or American black would be enslaved by virtue of the fact that he or she was considered to belong to the infidel slave class, not biologically but socially. American Indians were not usually enslaved, because they had established themselves as a class that did not adapt itself to slavery. White men, however, could be bought and sold if they belonged to the class born to servitude, the lowest class. The status of the black could be recognized at once by the color of his skin, which was a great convenience, but nothing more than that. It was only afterward that the obvious physical differences were utilized to reinforce the strength of the arguments in favor of the necessity of continuing the depressed social status of the black.

Thus, in the case of peoples showing any physical differences distinguishing them from the dominant class or caste, the mechanism of exclusion works both ways: one may oppose such peoples on the ground of their social inferiority and one may oppose them on the basis of their biological inferiority, the physical differences being taken to signify the latter. One may then proceed to adopt the view that such peoples are socially inferior because they are physically or biologically inferior, and since the physical or biological difference was believed to be constant, the social difference would always remain so. In this way one could not only have one's cake but one could also cut it into thin slices and eat it too. Imperialism, itself a racist idea, extended this conception of human relations to all peoples.[36]

Looking back now at the history of the nineteenth century, it seems fairly clear that the drive to find differences in the races of humankind grew out of, among other things, the general social climate of the day. A natural stratification of the races mirrored the social stratification of the classes, and in the light of the baleful doctrine of "the survival of the fittest" sanctioned and justified the exploitation and oppression of both.

Most authorities at the present time entertain no doubts as to the meaninglessness of the older anthropological conception of race. They do not consider that any of the existing concepts of race correspond to any reality whatever; the general opinion is that these concepts are usually nothing but poor substitutes for thought. But they do consider that the persistence of the term and the concept has been responsible for much confused thinking and, what is worse, has rendered possible much confused and confusing action resulting in the most tragic consequences for millions of human beings. Race has, indeed, become a fratricidal word

> . . . And what if all-avenging Providence,
> Strong and retributive, should make us know
> The meaning of our words, force us to feel
> The desolation and the agony
> Of our fierce doings?
> —*S. T. Coleridge.*[37]

It is for these reasons, because the term, as it were, has been compromised, that a number of us, as biological and social anthropologists, have strongly urged that the term race be altogether dropped from the vocabulary. If we do no more than indicate our demotion of the term, this in itself will serve as a contribution to clear thinking, precisely as the banishment of the term "instinct" from psychological thought fifty years ago has had a most beneficial effect upon the development of the science of psychology. Not that there has been a loss of contact with what science means by "race," for many scientists are themselves far from clear as to what they mean when they use the term. In addition to that, some scientists who have concerned themselves with the problem have contributed to its confusion. "Verbal habits," remarked Ogden and Richards long ago, "overpower the sense of actuality even in the best of philosophers." And as Korzybski has stated,

> Because of the great semantic influence of the structure of language on the masses of mankind, leading, as it does, through lack of better understanding and evaluation to speculation on terms, it seems advisable to abandon completely terms which imply to the many the suggested elementalism, although these terms are used in a proper non-elementalistic way by the few.[38]

Huxley first suggested that "it would be highly desirable if we could banish the question-begging term 'race' from all discussions of human affairs and substitute the noncommittal phrase 'ethnic group.' That would be a first step toward rational consideration of the problem at issue."[39]

Since Huxley does not venture a definition of an "ethnic group," I shall offer one here: An ethnic group represents one of a number of populations, which grade into one another and together comprise the species *Homo sapiens,* but individually maintain their differences, physical and cultural, by means of isolating mechanisms such as geographic and social barriers. Such gradient differences will vary as the power of the geographic and social barriers vary. Where these barriers are of low power, or loose-jointed, as it were, neighboring ethnic groups will intergrade or hybridize with one another. Where these barriers are of high power, such ethnic groups will tend to remain more or less different from each other or replace each other geographically or ecologically.

From this definition or description of an ethnic group it will be seen that the problem of ethnic variation is in part a geographic problem involving the physical mobility of populations and the consequences resulting therefrom. Thus, the problem of ethnic variation falls definitely within the purview of the student of the social life of humankind.

The term ethnic is derived from the Greek *ethnos,* meaning a number of people living together, a company, a body of people. In the *Iliad,* Homer variously uses the word to mean a band of comrades a tribe, a group. Pindar uses it in the sense of a family a nation, a people.

One of the most important advantages of the term "ethnic group"[40] is that it eliminates all question-begging emphases on physical factors or differences and leaves that question completely open, while the emphasis is now shifted to the fact—though it is not restricted to it—that man is predominantly a cultural creature. The change in emphasis seems to me highly desirable. It does not exclude the consideration of the possible significance of physical traits, but it leaves the question of the latter open for further dispassionate analysis, omitting any suggestion that the physical traits are determined, fixed, or definable, or that they are in any way connected with mental or cultural traits. This is not to replace one term by another, but constitutes a significant shift in emphasis based on a fundamental difference in point of view. It is the point of view of the person who is desirous of taking a mature, responsible view of the words he uses and who is anxious to avoid the consequences of thinking in "fuzzy" terms.

If, then, we can eliminate the outmoded concept of race by presenting the advantages of the concept of "ethnic group," we shall have secured a real clarification and change in conceptual approach to a problem whose urgency requires no emphasis here. The sociologist will then be able to proceed with the study of the problem of caste, intra- and intersocially, with the clear consciousness of the fact that, as far as he is concerned, the problem is entirely a social problem and that for him, at any rate, it has no biological relevance whatever, but that, in so far as it is necessary for him to take cognizance of the biological evidence, the old concept of race has no more scientific justification for use in the field of human biology than it has in the field of human sociology.

Were we to pay attention to the realities of the situation in the cultural reference, the term race would be entirely discarded and the term "caste" would be employed in its stead; while the term race would, in popular parlance, be replaced by the term "ethnic group" in the biologic or social context with reference to humankind.

Notes

1. For an interesting discussion of the meaning of the word along these lines see S. I. Hayakawa, "Race and Words," *Common Sense* 12 (1934): 231–35; Reuven Bar-Levan, *Thinking in the Shadow of Feelings*, (New York: Simon & Schuster, 1988); Peter L. Berger and Thomas Luckmann, *The Social Construction of Reality* (New York: Penguin, 1971); J. Dan Rothwell, *Telling It Like It Isn't* (Englewood Cliffs, NJ: Prentice-Hall, 1982).

2. Ignazio Silone, *Bread and Wine* (New York: Penguin Books, 1946), 158.

3. In the spring of 1932, during his conversations with Emil Ludwig, Mussolini declared: "Of course there are no pure races left; not even the Jews have kept their blood unmingled. Successful crossings have often promoted the energy and beauty of a nation. Race! It is a feeling, not a reality; ninety-five percent, at least, is a feeling. Nothing will ever make me believe that biologically pure races can be shown to exist today . . . No such doctrine will ever find wide acceptance here in Italy . . . National pride has no need of the delirium of race." Emil Ludwig, *Talks with Mussolini* (Boston: Little, Brown, 1933), 69–70. In 1939, under the influence of his Axis partner, Hitler, he completely reversed himself and introduced racist measures of great severity. See Martin Agronsky, "Racism in Italy," *Foreign Affairs* 17 (1939): 391–401.

4. On this subject see Bruno Lasker, *Race Attitudes in Children* (New York: Holt, 1929); Mary E. Goodman, *Race Awareness in Your Children* (Cambridge, MA: Addison Wesley Press, 1952); H. G. Trager and M. R. Yarrow, *They Learn What They Live* (New York: Harper); Kenneth Clark, *Prejudice and Your Child* (Boston: Beacon Press, 1955); McDonald, *Not By the Color of Their Skin* (New York: International Universities Press, 1970); Judith D. R. Porter, *Black Child, White Child* (Cambridge: Harvard University Press, 1971); Florence Halpern, *Survival: Black/White* (New York: Pergamon Press, 1973); Jean D. Grambs, *Group Processes in Intergroup Education* (New York: National Council of Christians and Jews, 1953); David L. Kirp, *Just Schools: The Idea of Racial Equality in American Education* (Berkeley: University of California Press, 1982); David Milner, *Children and Race* (Harmondsworth: Penguin, 1975); David Milner, *Children and Race, Ten Years On* (London: Ward Lock Educational, 1983).

5. This is a task which has been undertaken by UNESCO. See Ashley Montagu, *Statement on Race* (New York: Oxford University Press, 1972), 361–71.

6. Excellent volumes along these lines published for the Bureau for Intercultural Education by Harper & Brothers, New York, are the following: William E. Vickery and Stewart G. Cole, *Intercultural Education in American Schools* (New York: Harper, 1943); Hortense Powdermaker, *Probing Our Prejudices* (New York: Harper, 1944); Spencer Brown, *They See for Themselves* (New York: Harper, 1944); Theodore Brameld, *Minority Problems in the Public Schools* (New York: Harper: 1946); Ina C. Brown, *Race Relations in a Democracy* (New York: Harper, 1949); William Van Til, et al., *Democracy Demands It* (New York: Harper, 1947); H. G. Trager and M. R. Yarrow, *They Learn What They Live* (New York: Harper, 1952). See also Goodwin Watson, *Action for Unity* (New York: Harper, 1947); Curriculum Office, Philadelphia Public Schools, *Open-Mindedness Can Be Taught* (Philadelphia, 1946); Kenneth Clark, *Prejudice and Your Child* (Boston: Beacon Press, 1955); Lillian Smith, *Now Is the Time* (New York: Dell, 1955); John P. Dean and Alex Rosen, *A Manual of Intergroup Relations* (Chicago: University of Chicago Press, 1955); James Martin and Frank R. Westie, "The Tolerant Personality," *American Sociological Review* 24 (1959): 521–28; Muzafer Sherif and Carolyn W. Sherif, *Groups in Harmony and Tension* (New York: Harper, 1953).

7. See, for example, the admirable book by Richard J. Russell and Fred B. Kniffen, *Culture Worlds* (New York: McMillan, 1951); Margaret Mead, *Peoples and Places* (Cleveland and New York: World Publishing Co., 1959); Ashley Montagu, *Man: His First Two Million Years* (New York: Columbia University Press,1969); Ashley Montagu, *The Science of Man* (New York: Odyssey Press, 1964); Ashley Montagu, *The Human Revolution* (New York: Bantam Books, 1965).

8. See Ashley Montagu, *On Being Human* (New York: Hawthorn Books, 1969); Ashley Montagu, *The Direction of Human Development* (New York: Hawthorn Books, 1970); Ashley Montagu, *Education and Human Relations* (New York: Grove Press, 1958); Ashley Montagu, *Growing Young* (Westport, CT: Bergin and Garvey, 1989).

9. See Emily V. Baker, "Do We Teach Racial Intolerance?" *Historical Outlook* 24 (1933): 86–89; Marian Radke and Helen Trager, "Children's Perceptions of the Social Roles of Negroes and Whites," *Journal of Psychology* 29 (1950): 1–33.

10. Weston La Barre, "The Cultural Basis of Emotions and Gestures," *Journal of Personality*, 16 (1947), 49–68; Leo Silbermann and Betty Spice, *Colour and Class in Six Liverpool Schools* (Liverpool: University of Liverpool Press, 1951).

11. See note 6, this chapter; also Helen P. Mudgett, *Democracy for All* (Minneapolis: General Extension Division, University of Minnesota, 1945). See also *Teaching Biologist* 9 (1939): 17–47.

12. Wyndam Lewis, *The Art of Being Ruled* (New York: Harper Bros., 1926), 234.

13. John H. Cooley, Robert R. Angell, and Julliard Carr, *Introductory Sociology* (New York: Schribner's Sons), 287. See Pitirim Sorokin, "What Is a Social Class?" *Journal of Legal and Political Sociology* 4 (1946): 15–28; Arthur Richmond, "Memories of South Africa," *The Listener* 60 (1958), 736—39.

14. The same is true for most other areas of the world. See: J. H. Hutton, *Caste in India* (New York: Cambridge Unversity Press, 1946); Ernest Beaglehole, "Race, Caste and Class," *Journal of the Polynesian Society,* 52 (1943): 1–11; Norman

Humphrey, "American Race and Caste," *Psychiatry* 4 (1941): 159–60; Ashley Montagu, "Race, Caste and Scientific Method," *Psychiatry* 4 (1941): 337–38; John Dollard, *Caste and Class in a Southern Town* (New Haven: Yale University Press, 1937); W. Lloyd Warner and Allison Davis, "A Comparative Study of American Caste," in E. T. Thompson, ed., *Race Relations and the Race Problem*, (Durham: Duke University Press, 1939): 219–45; Allison Davis, Burleigh Gardner, and Mary R. Gardner, *Deep South: A Social Anthropological Study of Caste and Class* (Chicago: University of Chicago Press, 1941); Liston Pope, *The Kingdom Beyond Caste* (New York: Friendship Press, 1967); Anthony de Rueck and Julie Knight, eds., *Caste and Race: Comparative Approaches* (New York: Little, Brown, 1967).

15. Humphrey, "American Race and Caste."

16. H. Kalmus, *Genetics* (London: Pelican Books, 1948) 45–46.

17. M. Abercombie, C. J. Hickman, and M. L. Johnson, *A Dictionary of Biology* (London and New York: Penguin Books, 1951).

18. G. S. Carter, *Animal Evolution: A Study of Recent Views of its Causes* (London: Sidgwick and Jackson; New York: Macmillan, 1951), 163. See also W. T. Calman, *The Classification of Animals* (New York: Wiley, 1949), 14; Cedric Dover, "The Classification of Man," *Current Science* 21 (1952): 209–13; Lionel Penrose, "Review of Dunn and Dobzhansky's Heredity, Race and Society," *Annals of Eugenics,* 17(1952): 252–53; J. P. Garlick, "Review," *Annals of Eugenics,* 25(1961): 169–70; P. A. Parsons, "Genetic Determination of Behavior (Mice and Men)," in *Genetics, Environment, and Behavior,* eds. Lee Ehrmann, Gilbert Omenn, and Ernst Caspari (New York: Academic Press, 1972), 4; L. L. Cavelli-Sforza, Paolo Menozzi and Albert Piazza, *The History and Geography of Human Genes* (Princeton: Princeton Unviversity Press, 1994); Jonathan Marks, *Human Biodiversity* (New York: Aldine, 1995).

19. Silone, *Bread and Wine,* 151.

20. Donald Pierson, *Negroes In Brazil,* (Chicago: University of Chicago Press, 1942); Charles Wagley, ed., *Race and Class in Rural Brazil.* (Paris: UNESCO, 1952).

21. Jeff H Lesser, "Brazil Pretends to Have no Race Problem," *The New York Times,* 10 Oct 1991, A26: Douglass G. Glasgow, "Brazil's Black Underclass: Almost Half a Nation," *The New York Times,* 30 November 1984, A30.

22. Roger Bastide, *The African Religions of Brazil: Toward a Sociology of the Interpenetration of Civilizations* (Baltimore: Johns Hopkins University Press, 1978), 307.

23. For some pithy remarks on this subject see Hogben, "Race and Prejudice," in his *Dangerous Thoughts* (New York: Norton, 1940), 45–58. "There is of course a parochial distinction between Rassenhygiene and its sister cult in Britain. In Germany the Jew is the scapegoat. In Britain the entire working class is the menace" (p. 51). To the same effect see R. H. Tawney, *Equality* (New York: Harcourt Brace, 1952).

24. Michael Banton, "Beware of Strangers!" *The Listener,* 3 April 1958, 565–67.

25. Kenneth Little, *Negroes in Britain* (London: Kegan Paul, 1948); Arthur Richmond, *The Colour Problem* (New York: Penguin Books, 1955); Michael Banton, *White and Coloured* (London: Cape, 1959); Maurice Freedman, ed., *A Minority in Britain* (Lonton: Valentine, Mitchell, 1955); Sydney Collins, *Coloured Minorities in Britain* (London: Lutterworth Press, 1957); Sydney Collins, "The Status of Coloured People in Britain," *Phylon* 18(1957): 82–87; Michael Banton, *Race Relations* (New York: Basic Books, 1967); John Rex, *Race, Colonialism and the City*

(London and Boston: Routledge & Kegan Paul, 1973). R. Moore, *Racism and Black Resistance in Britain* (London: Pluto Press, 1975); A. Dummet, *A Portrait of English Racism* (London: Penguin, 1973).

26. Alexander Timothy Carey, *Colonial Students* (London: Secker & Warburg, 1956). See especially Sheila Patterson, *Dark Strangers* (London: Tavistock, 1963).

27. Frank Westie, "Negro-White Status Differentials and Social Distance," *American Sociological Review* 17(1952): 550–58.

28. Liston Pope, *Millhands and Preachers* (New Haven: Yale University Press, 1942), 69.

29. William T. Liu, "The Community Reference System, Religiosity, and Race Attitudes," *Social Forces* 39 (1961): 324–28.

30. Herbert Blumer, "Race Prejudice as a Sense of Group Position," in *Race Relations,* eds. Jitsuichi Masuoka and Preston Valien, 217–27.

31. Angus Campbell, *White Attitudes Towards Black People* (Ann Arbor: Institute for Social Research, 1971); Bert T. King and Elliott McGinnies, eds., *Attitudes, Conflict and Social Change* (New York: Academic Press, 1972); George Frederickson, *The Black Image in the White Mind* (New York: Harper & Row, 1971); Morris Dees, with Steve Fiffer, *A Season for Justice: The Life and Times of Civil Rights Lawyer Morris Dees* (New York: Scribner's Sons, 1991).

32. Karl Polanyi, *The Great Transformation* (New York: Rinehart, 1944), 290.

33. Charles S. Johnson, "Race Relations and Social Change," in Thompson, ed., *Race Relations and the Race Problem,* 274.

34. For an account of the absence of race problems among ethnic groups of the same population see John Gillin, "'Race' Relations without Conflict: A Guatemalan Town," *American Journal of Sociology* 53 (1948): 337–43; Robert Redfield, "Culture Contact without Conflict," *American Anthropologist* 41(1939): 514–17; Robert Redfield, "Race and Class in Yucatan," in *Cooperation in Research* (Washington, D.C.: Carnegie Institution of Washington, 1938), 511–32.

35. I. D. MacCrone, *Group Conflicts and Race Prejudice* (London: Oxford University Press, 1937), 7.

36. B. Ashcroft, G. Griffiths, and H. Tiffin, eds., *The Post-Colonial Studies Reader* (London and New York: Routledge, 1995); E. Barker *National Character,* 4th ed. (London: Meuthen, 1948); Philip D. Curtin, "The Origins of the 'White Man's Burden,'" *The Listener* 66 (1961): 412–15; L. Greenfield, *Nationalism* (Cambridge: Harvard University Press, 1992); B. Gussman, *Out in the Mid-day Sun* (New York: Oxford University Press, 1963); J. A. Hobson, *Imperialism: A Study,* 2nd ed.(London: Allen & Unwin, 1965); R. A. Huttenback, *Racism and Empire* (Ithaca: Cornell University Press, 1976); M. Ignatieff, *Blood and Belonging: Journeys into the New Nationalism* (New York: Viking, 1993); O. Mannoni, *Prospero and Caliban: The Psychology of Colonization* (New York: Praeger, 1956); J. Rex, *Race, Colonialism, and the City* (London & Boston: Routledge & Kegan Paul, 1971); L. L. Snyder, *Encyclopedia of Nationalism* (New York: Paragon House, 1990); Louis L. Snyder, *The Imperialism Reader* (Princeton: Von Nostrand, 1964); T. Todorov, *On Human Diversity: Nationalism, Racism, and Exoticism in French Thought* (Cambridge: Harvard University Press, 1993); Ernest Gellner, *Conditions of Liberty: Civil Society and its Rivals* (New York: Penguin Press, 1994); Ernest Gellner, *Nations and Nationalism* (Ithaca: Cornell University Press, 1983).

37. From "Fears in Solitude," 1798.

38. Alfred Korzybski, *Science and Sanity,* 2nd ed. (Lancaster: Science Press, 1941), 31.

39. Julian Huxley, "The Concept of Race," in *Man Stands Alone* (New York: Harper, 1941), 126.

40. E. E. Sikes, *The Anthropology of the Greeks* (London: Nutt, 1914); R. R. Marret, ed., *Anthropology and the Classics* (Oxford: Clarendon Press, 1908); Joseph B. Gittler, ed., *Social Thought Among the Early Greeks* (Athens: University of Georgia Press, 1941); Louis Gernet, *The Anthropology of Ancient Greece* (Baltimore: Johns Hopkins University Press, 1981); John L. Myres, *Who Were the Greeks?* (Berkeley: University of California Press, 1930).

8

Biological and Social Factors

The problem of the origin and development of different physical types is as artificial and unreal a problem as is the study of race, for neither types nor races are anything more than abstractions which are believed and are treated as if they had a real existence, when in fact the only reality is the artificial construction of the terms and the meanings that have been given to them. It should be clearly understood that the meaning of a word is the action it produces. Because loaded words are capable of exploding with disastrous effects it is extremely important that we teach children to develop the habit of questioning every word for its meaning. We must be especially careful about the terms we use, for unsound terms like "race" and the systematics of race and human "types" lead directly to the systematic "extermination" of millions of human beings. It is necessary to be particularly cautious about so-called scientific and technical terms.

Goethe, in his play *Faust*, makes Mephistopheles say, "Where an idea is wanting a word can always be found to take its place, and a whole system of philosophy built thereon." The reign of such words may be long or short, but whatever their duration, their damage can be considerable.

The study of human variability is a fascinating one, and is part of the larger problem of discovering how we all come to be the way we are; that, too, is a social problem, and only arbitrarily, and in a limited technical sense, is it a biological problem. Humans are outstandingly the one animal species in which "biological" development has, from the earliest times, been substantially influenced by the operation of social factors—and this, ever increasingly, continues to be the case. The biological development of humans cannot be considered apart from their social development, for humans are, more or less, domesticated, self-domesticated, animals.[1]

Domestication is a social or cultural process by means of which biological changes are produced in animals. Such changes, to some extent, represent the socially preferred expression of genetic rearrangements of traits common to all humans. The chief agencies in the production of such changes are social, but the scientific study of such social agencies has only just begun. Thus far, the emphasis has for the most part been upon the biological aspect of such changes, while there has been an almost complete failure to recognize the role that social influences may have played in their development.[2]

The biological aspects of the subject are important, but only in so far as they render possible an understanding of the physiological and genetic mechanisms underlying the actual process of change. R. A. Fisher has remarked:

> While genetic knowledge is essential for the clarity it introduces into the subject, the causes of the evolutionary changes in progress can only be resolved by an appeal to sociological, and even historical facts. These should at least be sufficiently available to reveal the more powerful agencies at work in the modification of mankind."[3]

When the mechanism of these physiological and genetic changes is understood, it is then fully realized that "race" is a term that refers to a process representing a series of genetically active temporary or episodic conditions, always in process of change. It then becomes clear that the stage at which one catches this process depends upon the segment of time which one arbitrarily delimits from the space-time continuum in which the process is occurring. Neither races of men nor races of lower animals are immutable; they seem to become so, but then only conceptually, when an anthropologist or a taxonomist follows the traditional practice of pinning his specimens down for study and classification. It is erroneous to conceive of any animal group, particularly human groups, as static and immutable. It is an error to do so in the case of humans in particular, because the facts of prehistory and those of more recent times indicate the flexibility and variability of which humankind is capable. In this process social factors play a considerable role. Upon recognizing this fact we must further recognize that in our own society the problem of race is essentially a problem of caste and class relations and that it is, of course, fundamentally a social problem.

In our own society, explanations of the race problem have been offered in terms of economic forces, social stratification, biological differences, or all three. Such explanations have never been altogether convincing. The causes motivating human behavior are complex, and human behavior is hardly ever to be explained in terms of single processes, which in themselves are complicated enough, such as the economic, the biological, or the purely social. In all cases, in order to understand the nature of any event it is necessary to discover and to relate all the conditions entering into its production. In other words, what is required is a specification of all the necessary conditions which together then form the sufficient cause of the event into whose nature we are inquiring.

While it may be true, for instance, that certain conditions arising out of our present economic organization of society are responsible for maintaining and exacerbating the "problem of race," it is by no means certain that a reorganization of our economic system would automatically result in a solution of that problem, although it is probable that it would help. It is quite conceivable that race problems may exist under ideal economic conditions. These problems, indeed, are far from simple, and it is therefore necessary to approach them by the use of such methods as are calculated to reduce them. It would obviously be an egregious error to approach the study of race from the standpoint of the economic determinant alone, precisely as it would be an error to approach the study from the viewpoint solely of biology or of sociology.

This brings us to what I consider to be an extremely important methodological aspect of the whole problem. It is the matter of the person who discusses the subject of race. Hitherto, practically anyone with the ability to develop a hoarse throat, with arrogance and effrontery in place of erudition, has been able to set himself up as an authority on race. We need only recall the names of Gobineau, Stoddard, Houston Stewart Chamberlain, Madison Grant, Adolf Hitler, and their like,[4] to discover that the principal equipment necessary to qualify one as an authority on race consists in a well-rounded ignorance, a considerable amount of viciousness, and an unshakable confidence. To listen to such "tangled oracles which ignorantly guide" is to suffer a positive increase in one's ignorance. With the passing of the above-mentioned individuals the nuisance is not abated, for there are always others ready to take their place.[5] In the universe of science the situation, though incomparably better, is not by any means—as we have already seen—all that could be desired. Until very recently little progress had been made in the scientific study of race. This had been chiefly due to the fact that the subject had been dealt with in a piecemeal manner and by specialists with an insufficient grasp of the complexities of the subject. Thus, psychologists failed to take into account the sociological and biological factors (if only to dismiss the latter as of no significance); while sociologists have in the past failed to give adequate consideration to the psychological and anthropological factors. Finally, and worst of all, the physical anthropologists restricted their studies almost entirely to the morphological aspects of the subject. The complexity of the problem is today recognized by most students, and thanks to the increasing volume and quality of their work, we today see that problem much more clearly than we did a generation ago. Nevertheless, we still need more students who will combine the best qualities of the psychologist, the sociologist, the biologist, and both the cultural and physical anthropologist.[6]

Racism as an ideological phenomenon has its origins and being in social and political forces. Its motivations are never the discovery of what *is*, of the *facts*, but of what, according to its proponents, ought to be. And what ought to be is determined by the political and social necessities of the moment. These will vary at different times and in different places, but in general these necessities are interpreted to mean that the differences which characterize various races determine a hierarchy of values. These values are always distinguished in terms of "superiority" and "inferiority." The recognition of these values then determines the manner in which the "superior" must conduct themselves in relation to the "inferior," and vice versa. The racist is not interested in the scientific facts, except to the extent to which, in some special form, they may serve his purposes. Because he is not interested in the facts, but in an ideology, it is quite impossible to demonstrate the fallacy of his views to the racist. Any attempt to reason with racists on the basis of the facts is rather more than a waste of time. Anyone who has had experience of these persons will know how unspeakably vicious they can be. The whole history of racism testifies to that fact.

Let us recall the ringing words of William Lloyd Garrison, "With reasonable men I will reason; with humane men I will plead; but to tyrants I will give no quarter, nor waste arguments where they will certainly be lost."

As Manning Nash has pointed out, the skeletal form of any racial ideology may be stated in six propositions: as (1) the attempt to flout natural law by man-made edicts about race relations, (2) the races differ in their capacities to embrace the complexities of civilization, (3) the level of cultural achievement of races indicates their relative innate capacities, (4) left on their own, inferior races tear down a cultural heritage, (5) the fight against racial equality is the fight for truth in the interests of all people, and (6) those who favor equality are undesirables.[7]

The scientist is put in the position of having to make available the facts, for the benefit of those who may wish to judge the evidence for themselves. But, again, it needs to be said that human rights are not dependent upon the facts of science or the assertions of racists or of any other kind of statement. Those rights rest squarely and firmly upon an ethical principle, the principle that by virtue of their humanity humans have the right to the fullest development of their capacities, to realize their potentialities, to fulfill themselves. No one or group has the right to stand in the way of another's development. Such conduct is evil. It is a social evil, and it is only by social means that it will ever be eradicated. Race, it should always be remembered, is an abstraction, an arbitrary label of a human grouping culturally defined in a given society. Race prejudice is a system of reciprocal relations of stereotyping, discrimination, and segregation existing between human groupings that are considered as races.

Since, as I have already pointed out, facts do not speak for themselves, but are at the mercy of whoever chooses to give them a meaning, it is obviously of the first importance that the meaning which they shall receive be given them by those who have made themselves thoroughly acquainted with the facts. As Henry A. Wallace said:

> For the combating of 'racism' before it sinks its poison fangs deep in our body politic, the scientist has both a special motive and a special responsibility. His motive comes from the fact that when personal liberty disappears scientific liberty also disappears. His responsibility comes from the fact that only he can give the people the truth. Only he can clean out the falsities which have been masquerading under the name of science in our colleges, our high schools and our public prints. Only he can show how groundless are the claims that one race, one nation, or one class has any God-given right to rule.[8]

In the modern world, racial problems, as I have already said, are essentially social problems. But no student of human society can ever hope to assist in the solution of these problems without acquiring an adequate understanding of what the biologist, the psychologist, and the psychoanalyst can alone supply, namely, an appreciation of the nature of the fundamental facts of physical and mental development as well as their pathological materialization. Obviously, what we need is more human ecologists, liaison officers between the sciences of humankind.[9]

The Economic Factor and the Factor of Social Stratification

Our society is a socially stratified one, and social stratification in our society is determined principally by the manner in which our society is economically structured. It is usually possible to migrate from one social stratum or class to another only by means of the economic process. By the acquisition of economic power one rises in the social hierarchy; by the loss of economic power one falls. Groups and persons who are denied effective participation in the economic process clearly cannot rise above the lower social strata, while the only way to exclude groups and persons who have not been denied an effective participation in the economic process from rising and maintaining their places socially is to erect barriers against them, to deprive them, in various ways, of their economic rights. We need hardly go farther back than our own time for the evidence with which to prove the truth of this statement. In those parts of Europe under Nazi domination in World War II such barriers were deliberately created in the form of a mythological racial dogma which was imposed upon whole peoples—a dogma which, in operation as a barrier, deprived all those who were not mythical "Aryans" of the right to earn a living and to keep even the little they had. No more telling or painful example than this could be cited of the blatant economic motivation underlying the creation and practice of this mythology, which leads so effectively to the social and economic disfranchisement of powerless groups.

In the United States there are several ready examples that may be cited as illustrating the relationship between the economic factor and the presence of racial barriers. Along the Pacific coast, where the Japanese and Chinese constituted an appreciable competitive group, there was considerable race prejudice against them. With the increase in the number of Filipinos entering the United States within recent years, despite the heroic resistance of their compatriots against the Japanese in the Philippines during World War II and their loyalty to the United States, racial prejudices were rapidly transferred to them.[10] Along the Atlantic coast, where the numbers of these ethnic groups are comparatively small and they cannot possibly be conceived to constitute economic competitors, there has been relatively little prejudice against them, apart from that which was generated by war conditions. Similarly, in California, when Native Americans were numerous there was a great deal of prejudice against them. In the Midwest, where Native Americans are relatively few and under "control," there is little prejudice against them. In the East a trace of Native American ancestry has some prestige value, for Native Americans are so rare that they are almost worth their weight in genes. In areas such as the South, where the social status of the African American is changing and he emerges as an economic competitor, the prejudices against the large population of blacks constitute a serious problem. In the North, where the economic situation is much better, the African American has always enjoyed a greater degree of social and economic freedom, limited as that social and economic freedom has always been in this divided society. In England, when there were few representatives of either of these groups, there was little active prejudice against them. In localities, however, in which there exists a concentration of members of such ethnic groups, prejudices are easily generated.[11]

In the days when Englishmen went out to the "colonies" to govern the native people, they soon learned that the natives "threatened" their own interests and those of their own people, and reactively, frequently developed the usual racial prejudices. This lead to an exclusiveness and a capacity for making the local people feel second rate in their own land. This in turn produced that bitterness and loathing for their invaders that the stolid Englishman usually found unaccountable. Today, with the immigration into England of thousands of people, Englishmen no longer have to go abroad to develop race prejudice.

Sir Arthur Richmond, who as a young man was sent out to serve under Lord Milner in South Africa in 1901, recounts how without his being aware of it race prejudice crept up on him. He writes,

Before the Boer war no Kaffir had been allowed to walk on the side-walk in a town. He had to walk in the roadway. I had not particularly noticed that they always, women as well as men, walked in the middle of the road when, one day, a Kaffir came towards me striding along the side-walk of the principal street in Pretoria. Instantly I felt a surge of indignation. I had not before been conscious of any colour prejudice; I hardly knew of the rule forbidding the use of the side-walk to black men, yet subtly and unconsciously I had been infected with the accepted view that blacks must not be allowed any kind of equality with whites. I was horrified by my automatic reaction, and its immediate effect was to make me feel intense sympathy for the black man and to realize how conscious I had to be of the difficulties inherent in the relationship between the black man and the white.[12]

Lord Milner, under whom Richmond served, was, though he does not say so, a calamity. As the supreme British race patriot of the period, it was Milner's avowed intention to obliterate, by a ruthless and obdurate policy of Anglicization, all traces of national identity in the Afrikaner. It was the fanatical zeal of Milner in the holy cause of empire, which precipitated the Boer War, and led to the razing of farmsteads and crops, as well as the creation of the first concentration camps by the British. It was Milner's conduct which provided the impetus by which the then loosely-knit politically unsophisticated Afrikaners were welded into an acutely race-conscious fervently nationalistic people, whose supreme hatred was for the British, and whose increasing anxiety was the non-white population. It was this misguided British imperial policy that was directly responsible for the hideous practice of apartheid.[13]

Without in the least underestimating the important role economic factors play in the creation of race prejudice in Western society generally, it may be observed that there is no absolutely necessary or sufficient relationship between economic conditions and racial problems. Just as it is possible to conceive of difficult racial problems existing under ideal economic conditions, so it is quite possible to conceive of perfect ethnic relations and mutual appreciation under the most difficult economic conditions.

So far as the individual is concerned, race prejudice is by no means a necessary concomitant of economic anxieties. For example, Bettelheim and Janowitz in a study of a group of World War II veterans found that there were quite a number who, in spite of a doubtful economic future, were sufficiently well integrated to be able to control any hostilities they may have had without the need to discharge them upon some scapegoat.[14] These were men who were secure in their personalities, who had been given emotional security in their childhood. Fundamentally, the problem is one of personality structure—and whatever it is that may contribute to that structure is an essential part of the problem; it is of no use dealing with the one without the other. Economic conditions may, of course, produce substantive changes in the personality. When children are brought up in families in which the economic conditions are satisfactory, the children are likely to be emotionally more secure than in families in which the economic conditions have been poor. But whatever the economic conditions in the family, if the child is made to feel secure, he will not need to indulge in irrational discharges of hostility against the members of an outgroup. The problem, then, is fundamentally not one of economics, though improving economic conditions will help. The problem is really one of emotional integration and security, a problem of parent-child relationships, a problem of human relations.[15]

The fact is that in our own society the regrettable discovery has been made that by utilizing the physical and cultural differences existing between groups and individuals, it is relatively simple to disguise the motives and evade the consequences of one's own conduct by attributing existing and potential evils to the conduct of some other group or to utilize those differences for the most ignoble political purposes. In this way, by setting groups of people against one another, attention is diverted from the real sources of evil. The discovery is, in fact, an old one. As a device for moving people it is extremely well grounded in that it caters to a deep-seated tendency which many persons have acquired during their early conditioning to find a scapegoat outside themselves upon which to blame their troubles or release their aggressive, frustrated feelings. As long ago as the second century A.D., the early father Tertullian of pagan Rome was fully aware of the fact that the persecution of the Christian minority was merely being used as a device to divert the attention of the people from the real causes of corruption within the Roman state. Says Tertullian, "If the Tiber rose to the walls of the city, if the inundation of the Nile failed to give the fields enough water, if the heavens did not send rain, if an earthquake occurred, if famine threatened, if pestilence raged, the cry resounded: 'Throw the Christians to the lions!'" In this manner the Roman populace was provided, as later peoples have been, with a socially sanctioned outlet for their frustration. And that is the important point to grasp about the nature of race prejudice, namely, that it is a socially sanctioned and socially learned attitude. It is a ready-made and culturally accepted outlet for various forms of hostility and feelings of frustration. In the South, race hatred has long been kept alive and fanned to white heat at the instigation of unscrupulous industrialists and politicians, ever ready to capitalize on baseless popular superstitions, prejudices, and beliefs, because there is no issue more useful than race as a political platform for securing votes. Tell the poor whites, and others not so poor, that their status is due to, and continually threatened by, the competition of the blacks, and they will vote for anything to which such an issue is tied in promised favor of themselves.

Things have not changed much in more than half a century in the South, when in 1943 Thomas Sancton wrote:

> There are millions of white and black men in the South, and their children, on blighted farms and in the slums, who live a more bearable life because of what the Roosevelt administration made possible. But these are the poor and ignorant, and their race hate, kept alive for years just as Governor Dixon and the Alabama capitalists are keeping it alive now, makes them vulnerable. Of the millions of people whom the New Deal aided, the blacks cannot vote, and most of the whites who can have been poisoned by the belief that the President and Mrs. Roosevelt are trying to wipe out all racial barriers under the war emergency; the Dixons are now in the saddle; they seem to be able to foist upon the disfranchised masses anything they want to; and once more the white man's fear of the Negro has made it possible. It is no mystery why the South's congressman, elected by a small and privileged proportion of its population fight so hard to defeat an anti-poll-tax bill: and it is no mystery, come to think of it, why reactionary Northern members, their blood brothers, by one subterfuge and another let them get away with it.[16]

More than half a century later, things have changed somewhat for the better, but not nearly enough. The granting of statehood to the territories of Alaska and Hawaii had been opposed and blocked since 1916, largely by Southern Democrats who feared that the potentially incoming four Senate votes would bring about the advancement of civil rights. These territories are now full states within the Union. The fears of the Southern Democrats appear to have been groundless. In the November elections of 1966 racism won the ballot of a majority of white voters. The reaction against civil rights legislation and black demonstrations made the victory of Southern segregationists a foregone conclusion, and not without its considerable effect elsewhere throughout the land.[17]

The church in the South, which is largely Protestant, reflects the beliefs of its parishioners. Religion says no more to society than society says to itself. In the South, and in this the South is not alone, Jehovah is a tribal god. He serves the interests of the people. Hence, scripture is quoted in support of ideas, institutions, and practices, which to outsiders appear to be the very antithesis of Christianity.[18]

When we apply the measure of determining what people believe, by observing what they do—not by what they say, then Christianity has not only been one of the great failures of history, in not practicing what it preached, but has been a powerful source of racist propaganda. What is even worse, the church through its great power has failed to assume the leadership in speaking out against tyrants and demagogues wherever they may occur, and take active nonviolent measures where it ought. In The

Sermon on the Mount (Matthew 5–7), which sets forth the principles of the Christian ethic, the most important of these principles is "All things whatsoever ye would that men should do to you, do ye even so to them: for this is the law and the prophets." This also goes by the modern label, "The Golden Rule." A common phrasing is, "Do to others as you are done by." It was in the New Testament that the doctrine was developed that "the essential nature of God is love."[19]

Whether God is Love, or Love is God; or whether one should love others more than we love ourselves, the truth is that Christianity from the days of the early Church Fathers to the present day has been in the forefront of those institutions which created, maintained, and fanned the hatreds directed especially against the Jews. This is a subject which has been fully dealt with in many scholarly works, and in none of them, with a few individual exceptions, is there any evidence, of the Church ever having shown much love for Jews. However that may be, anyone who wishes to understand the origins of racism should read *The History of Anti-Semitism,* by Leon Poliakov; it is the most readable and scholarly work on the subject.[20]

A short work on the same subject is by Alan Davies, professor of religious studies at the University of Toronto entitled *Infected Christianity: A Study of Modern Racism.* In this admirable work focusing on five different Christs, the Germanic, Latin, Anglo-Saxon, Afrikaner, and black, Davies shows how the Christian church succumbed to the infection of racist ideas. He takes the reader through the steps which led from the myths of race and nation to become "sacred" myths and histories, and how infected Christianity in Germany and South Africa served to legitimate ruling racist elites. Davies traces the course of fascism to its roots in the religious, cultural, and intellectual history of western civilization and to its culmination in the formation of the European white supremacist Aryan myth. Racialized Christianity in this way became a powerful agency in the transmission of the virus of racism, the support of nationalist and imperialist ambitions, and the governmental control of "undesirable" elements.[21]

The Catholic Church has a long history of antisemitism. This has been dealt with admirably by Davies, who has shown how easy it was for the Church to adopt the language of racialism when it was expedient, or to remain silent when one might have expected it to speak out. There were always a number of popes, archbishops, bishops, priests, convents, and monasteries that failed to protest and to give shelter to their fellow human beings. Pope Pius XII, and the Vatican, found it expedient during the reign of Hitler to utter not a word.[22]

The Protestant press in the United States, from 1933 onwards, took note, if only in brief references and short new items, of what was happening to the Jews in Germany. At the end of the war in Europe its concern was chiefly what was happening to the churches in Germany. Robert Ross, professor of religious studies at the University of Minnesota, has discussed all this in his moving book *So It Was True: The American Protestant Press and the Nazi Persecution of the Jews.* Professor Ross concludes,

> The press reported far more extensively than has generally been thought to be the case. The accepted view is that the press had said little or nothing. Clearly, this was not true. It must be said, then, that American Protestant Christians did know, for, if the people read, the people knew. But the editors and writers of the American Protestant press tried to deal with the mass extermination of the Jews of Germany and Europe as if it were part of an ordered, stable, normal world of fact. In fact, it happened in a world gone mad. In the end, editors and writers seemed unable to cope with something as unreal, among them six million Jews in an organized, bureaucratic, planned extermination. They could report this madness, this unreality, but, beyond the reporting and even beyond the expressed shock and horror over the discovery of the death camps, there remains the awful pall that hangs over the entire episode in modern history.[23]

The crimes committed by the Nazis against the Jews and other peoples in civilized Europe between the years 1933 and 1945 tell us that civilization is a very fragile thing, so that when attacked by hordes of barbarians, its openness can seldom provide a successful defense against them.[24]

By the skillful use of the myth of race and the labeling of the Jews as the "super-State power," and "world danger," Hitler hypnotized a whole nation, and was able to conquer the greater part of Western Europe in the declared aim to conquer the world, for the glory of "a Reich that would endure a thousand years." And very well he might have, had it not been for several of his fatal blunders, and the massive forces the Allies were at last able to put into the field. Hence, the importance of civilization making racism a crime against humanity, while at the same time through education raising children as humane beings who will fully understand why racism is a crime necessitating prompt application of the law wherever bigotry raises its ugly head. Such a law of nations is long overdue.

When in 1933 Hitler came to power, antisemitism was transformed from a personal obsession and propaganda weapon into a national policy. With the cunning of a psychopath Hitler systematically manipulated the mass psyche of the German people to provide them with a scapegoat they happened to be more familiar with and ready to embrace as the cause of all their problems—the Jews as an affliction that had to be eradicated from the body politic. As Leon Wieseltier put it,

> Nothing could more bountifully satisfy the demonological needs of the day than antisemitism. It would be all things to all Germans—a 'scientific' theory of race, a metaphysics, a philosophy of history, an explanation of

the modern world, a theodocy and a plan for national regeneration. It accounted for what went wrong and showed how to make it right."[25]

It is not to the common people alone that we need to apply our remedies, but also to those who have enjoyed the advantages of what is customarily called "a good education." The latter is generally acquired at the best private schools and Ivy League colleges from which the expensively uneducated regularly emerge in influential numbers, without having learned anything at all about the most important of all the arts and sciences, the art and science of being a human being. And, of course, this is true of virtually all educational enterprises in the United States, and elsewhere. From our educational institutions, our children, our only hope for the future, have received no training whatever in the art and science of learning to live as if to live and love were one.[26]

Governments and government officials who could have rescued the fleeing victims of Hitler's genocidal wrath virtually everywhere failed to respond to their need. This was especially true of the fleeing victims who in their extremity were rejected by the United States and Britain, an attitude fairly summed up in the remark of one high ranking official of the Foreign Office in September 1944: "In my opinion a disproportionate amount of the time of this office is wasted on dealing with these wailing Jews . . ."[27]

"These wailing Jews . . ." The unconcern and insensitivity of these "cold fish" was shocking, but what was even worse was the chilling indifference, the utter heartlessness, and obstruction by high government officials who, on the basis of one pretext after another, even deceit, declined to grant asylum to those fleeing from Hitler's murderous pursuit. The world stood by even when, watching their movie screens, the viewers saw shiploads of victims turned away from every shore where they sought refuge. After all, they were only Jews. If this phenomenon is to be given a name, it should be "The Great Betrayal," not only of the betrayers, but also of their humanity.[28] Did any people, with the exception of the Danes, rise up and plead for the victims? The answer is a staggering "No!"

For many years it was the official policy of the USSR to harass its Jewish population and liquidate its intelligentsia. The communists continued this policy in an inhuman manner by the imprisonment and execution of hundreds of leading Jewish intellectuals, writers, painters, musicians, critics, and others. They were accused of being "rebels, agents of American Imperialism, nationalist bourgeois Zionists, and enemies of the USSR."[29] Bent on destroying the last remnants of Jewish culture the communist government actively encouraged antisemitism.[30]

Under Khruschev the terror was relaxed, but the basic policy remained in force. The thinly disguised antisemitism which was exhibited by the Communist representatives at the United Nations Security Council was clearly a policy fixed at the highest levels. With the advent of Mikhail Gorbachev in the 1980s and the move toward greater "democracy" or "glasnost," and the opening up of the media to calls for freedom and justice, there simultaneously appeared a virulent antisemitism, with the Jews being held responsible for everything that had gone wrong over the last seventy years. Again, as elsewhere, the Jews were accused of being Russia's most dangerous enemies. Writing in support of an article by Irina Ginsburg in The New York Times, entitled "We Russian Jews Fear For Our Lives" (5 May 1990), John and Carol Garrard, who visited Moscow several times in the 1980s and talked with many Russians, wrote

> There is an obvious parallel between Soviet society today and German society prior to the rise of Hitler. Here again is a weak democracy—really a democracy in its infancy—where the leadership has no popular support, including Mikhail Gorbachev, economic collapse seems imminent. Just as Germany went through the hyper-inflation of the 1920s, so Russians find their rubles growing increasingly worthless . . . In the midst of the growing corruption, Russians feel frustrated and angry. We listened in Moscow apartments to fears of famine in the countryside within the year, accompanied by street demonstrations and riots in Moscow itself. Such exasperation over the denigration of Russian culture during much of the Soviet period makes many Russians give in to the all-too-human desire to find a scapegoat. Inevitable, the old belief in the Jew as the source of the Russians' troubles has re-emerged."[31]

The Union of South Africa, which openly supported Hitler during World War II, is the only government in the world which for many years consistently defined itself as the embodiment of white supremacy, and adopted racism as an official ideology. This made race discrimination a dominant part of daily life. This institutionalized policy went by the Afrikaans name of "apartheid," which means "apartness." Apartheid was widely condemned by much of the civilized world, but to no effect. The United Nations repeatedly passed resolutions against it, but the government of South Africa left the Commonwealth rather than modify its racial policies. A small white population cruelly continued to protect its economic and social privileges against any incursions which might be made upon it by its African, Coloured, Asiatic, and Jewish populations. The percentage representation of the various groups of the South African population is as follows: Africans, 69.8; Whites, 17.4; Colored, 9.3; and Asiatics, 2.9. The Jews form only 4.0 percent of the *total* population, and they have from the first proved themselves loyal and able citizens of the Union.

What, then, is the reason for the prejudice against the Jews? Is it fear of economic competition? In view of their small representation this cannot be the whole story. The fact, again, is that, while they themselves do not constitute an economic problem, the prejudice against them is utilized and, indeed, inspired by politicians and other interested parties for economic purposes. In a sympathetic and penetrating study of the Union, Lewis Sowden returned an answer to the question

> Why prejudice against the Jews? Simply this, that South Africa, like most other countries, has its Jewish problem kept alive by politicians for purposes of personal or party aggrandizement. The Nationalists used it in 1930 to strengthen their hold on the country and to embarrass General Smuts's opposition. Their Quota Act [aimed against the Jews] had the full support of their own people and many sympathizers among the other parties. General Smuts's men could not effectively oppose it for fear of being accused as 'pro-Jewish,' fatal, of course, for any politician.[32]

In May 1948, the Nationalist Party of Dr. Malan was returned to power in South Africa on a straight racist ticket. "The election was mainly fought on the propaganda slogan: 'Vote for a White South Africa.' All the emphasis was on the 'Black Menace.'"[33] At a conference of Protestant theologians held early in 1954 in South Africa the question of apartheid as a policy of permanent political separation of blacks and whites was discussed. Is apartheid untrue to the teachings of Christ? The South African Anglican bishops replied, "No." The leaders of the Dutch Reformed Church, whose members have vast material and political interests at stake, answered that cooperation between blacks and whites was sinful. Equal rights for all men, it was held, is a perversion of true Christian doctrine. "It is a misinterpretation of Scripture and therefore a defiance of the will of God." "We know," stated these Reformed theologians,

> God the Creator in Scripture as Hammabdil, as the Maker of Separations. To create a cosmos God separated things; light from darkness,[34] waters above the firmament, dry land from the sea. From the very beginning it was the intention of the Lord that mankind should live in separate nations. In his awful self-conceit man wished to frustrate this intention. . . . Therefore attempts at unification, the equalitarian idea, and a revival of the Babylonian spirit.[35]

As for the Dutch Reformed Church, its position was made abundantly clear some years ago when, one Sunday morning, three blacks desired to attend the service at a prominent church in Johannesburg. Apprised of their intention, a phalanx of sextons, aligned at the head of the steps, was ready to bar their way, and barred they were. Whereupon one of the would-be worshippers inquired, "Is not this the House of God?" To which the leading sexton emphatically replied, "It is *not*. This is the Dutch Reformed Church of South Africa."

A year prior to this at a meeting of theologians Prime Minister Malan declared that "the color question is the greatest and most urgent matter on which the election must hinge," and in April 1953, Malan's Nationalist party received an overwhelming majority at the polls.[36]

In South Africa there is a serious land problem for "poor whites." Sachs states that

> About a quarter of the Afrikaner farmers do not own the land they work and there has set in among them the kind of spiritual degeneration described in Erskine Caldwell's *Tobacco Road*. Hitlerism gave them a new hope, as it did to the 'Lumpen' in the Berlin tenement houses. The slogan, 'The Jews are our misfortune,' proved an acceptable and satisfyingly simple explanation of their misery and want.[37]

In 1966 the Assembly of the United Nations voted to end South Africa's League of Nations mandate over Southwest Africa, now known as Namibia. But it was only after a long and heroic struggle for independence by the many peoples of this southwest portion of Africa that the South African Government reluctantly withdrew from what is now an independent Namibia.

During the time of apartheid the outcome of racism in South Africa seemed to be very unpromising. A typical expression of the feeling among many South Africans was that of Professor P. V. Pistorius of the University of Pretoria:

> We see our doom inevitably approaching, but we are powerless to avert it. And it is a doom of our own making. . . . He who creates a tribal god will perish by the tribal gods of others. He who worships his own group and regards even injustices as good if it is thought to be in the interest of his group, will perish by the injustices perpetrated by other groups.[38]

It has been said that rulers and ruling classes never voluntarily surrender their power and privileges. This is quite true. However, political events in South Africa in recent years provide a welcome exception to this rule. The rigid system of racial segregation designed to maintain white supremacy, "apartheid," was officially put into effect in 1948 and was inhumanly enforced in the most barbarous of ways.[39] But several remarkable events occured in 1989: a stroke suffered by the oppressive incumbent President Pieter Botha, his subsequent resignation, and the election of Mr. F. W. de Klerk as President of the Union of South Africa. Mr de Klerk was expected to continue the oppressive policies of his predecessors, but to everyone's astonishment he immediately embarked upon a course of change that led to the abolition of apartheid and the establishment of a democratic order in South Africa.

One of de Klerk's first acts was the unconditional release of Nelson Mandela after twenty-seven years of imprisonment, as well as the release of other political prisoners. In 1991 the Population Registration Act, which classified people by race at birth, was repealed. The Convention for a Democratic South Africa, a broad black-led coalition met, and formally began negotiations towards the creation of a new constitution extending political rights to all ethnic groups. In February 1992, following the loss by the National Party, under de Klerk's leadership, of an election in the Transvaal to the reactionary Conservative Party, de Klerk boldly called a nationwide referendum of whites to seek a mandate for his policies of social and political reform, together with the sharing of power with blacks. The result was a resounding 68.7 percent of the vote in favor of his program. In 1993 de Klerk abandoned the idea of power sharing; Mandela also agreed to the postponement until 1999 of an undiluted one-man-one-vote majority rule. This is but a small catalog of changes wrought by de Klerk. On 10 May 1994 Mandela became the first black president of South Africa, de Klerk sharing the presidency with Mandela. In 1993 Mandela and de Klerk were awarded the Nobel Prize for their joint efforts to bring peace and democracy to South Africa. We see, then, that one person with the right ideas seizing the opportunity can change the world, or at least a part of it.[40] One does not necessarily have to wait until "the wicked shall have ceased from troubling and the weary are at rest."

It has often been pointed out that under difficult economic conditions in a diverse population racism is likely to become exacerbated. For example, in a study of race relations between blacks and whites in Liverpool, England, Richmond has shown that under conditions of economic stress, the coincidence of the three factors, insecurity, visibility, and stereotype, will help to produce a predominating attitude of prejudice and hostility among the members of the "in-group" toward the members of the "out-group." The intensity of expression of this attitude will vary according to any changes in one or other of the three predisposing factors. The more highly visible the "out-group" the more derogatory are the stereotypes, or the greater the degree of insecurity felt among the members of the "in-group," the greater will be the tension.

During the October 1964 General Election in England the "white backlash" played a considerable role in unseating several Labour incumbents and in defeating a number of Labour candidates for office. An on-the-scene reporter wrote of the defeat of the Labour incumbent for Smethwick, an industrial suburb of Birmingham, "There is little doubt in the country that Mr. Gordon Walker had been defeated by the whispered slogan, 'If you want a nigger neighbour, vote Labour.'"[41]

In Perry Barr, an electoral district in Birmingham's inner ring, the Labour incumbent was defeated on the purely racial issue. In West

Bromwich, which borders on Birmingham, the Labour incumbent's majority was pared by nearly 8,000 votes, and in Bradford, Yorkshire, it was halved. Here 1,200 Pakistanis had taken over whole shifts in some of the woolen mills. Losses in Labour votes occurred wherever immigrants of color had established themselves as a permanent working force.[42]

In the March 1966 General Election, racism was given a decisive setback. Mr. Peter Griffiths, who unseated Labour's Patrick Gordon Walker in 1964 by exploiting the feeling against immigrants of color, was thoroughly repudiated by the electors. Throughout the Birmingham area candidates who campaigned on color or immigration or accepted support from the forces of bigotry were mowed down. It should be fairly evident that race prejudice is easily generated in the societies of the Western world, when those societies are socially and economically so structured as to be continually productive of frustrations in the individual, from childhood on; these, in turn, produce an aggressiveness, a hostility, for which the individual must find expression in some way. However, the aggressiveness for which the individual must secure release is not entirely produced by economic factors. It also should be clear that the frustrative situations called into being by economic and social factors, while producing some aggressiveness in the individual, do not in themselves and need not necessarily lead to race prejudice. That the aggressiveness produced by such factors may lead to race prejudice is largely to be explained by the fact that race prejudice constitutes a socially sanctioned and encouraged or socially directed means of releasing aggressiveness. The aggressiveness may in part be produced by socioeconomic factors, but the form of the response which that aggressiveness takes is not necessarily linked with such factors. Alternative responses are available, but race prejudice is among the easiest and the psychologically most satisfying.

Merton has effectively described the frustrative situation which exists in Western societies. He writes:

> It is only when a system of cultural values extols, virtually above all else, certain common symbols of success *for the population at large,* while its social structure rigorously restricts or completely eliminates access to approved modes of acquiring these symbols for a considerable part of the same population, that antisocial behavior ensues on a considerable scale. In other words, our egalitarian ideology denies by implication the existence of noncompeting groups and individuals in the pursuit of pecuniary success. The same body of success-symbols is held to be desirable for all. These goals are held to transcend class lines, not to be bound by them, yet the actual social organization is such that there exist class differentials in the accessibility of these common success-symbols. Frustration and thwarted aspiration lead to the search for avenues of escape from a culturally induced intolerable situation; or unrelieved ambition may eventuate

in illicit attempts to acquire the dominant values. The American stress on pecuniary success and ambitiousness for all thus invites exaggerated anxieties, hostilities, neuroses and antisocial behavior.[43]

The avenue of escape from such frustrative conditions is almost always the same, through aggressiveness. The object to which that aggressiveness may attach itself is culturally determined by what is rendered culturally available.[44] Race, from an objective point of view, represents a cultural misunderstanding of certain facts, but from the point of view of the psyche of the person (which is far from objective), it presents a most satisfactory solution of a particular problem, affording, as it does, both a convenient and a suitable release for aggressiveness. It should, however, be clearly understood that the misunderstanding is psychological or cultural in origin, not economic. The conception of race is a psychological or cultural artifact and does not in itself lead to race prejudice. What leads to race prejudice is the cultural manipulation of those psychophysical energies which, in most persons, overtly find expression in some form of hostility, no matter what the underlying motivation of that manipulation may be. Economic factors represent but one group of conditions—and these are of the greatest importance—by means of which such aggressiveness may be called forth under conditions and in situations in which it may be easily attached to race.[45]

Economic factors, in Western society, are certainly among the most important of the factors leading to situations in which race prejudice may be caused to develop. But their dependence upon cultural factors for the direction they can be made to give to individual aggressiveness is proved by the fact that the aggressiveness arising under those same economic conditions can also be directed toward the production of good-fellowship and mutual aid between different ethnic and social groups. Such fellowship and cooperation between different groups have been repeatedly witnessed in times of war, when, for example, an alien nation has become the socially sanctioned release-object for one's aggressiveness. In peacetime the repair of some natural disaster, affecting the lives of all, frequently produces the same effect, by providing a wholesome outlet for such aggressiveness. As Freud remarked in this connection,

> It is one of the few noble and gratifying spectacles that men can offer, when in the face of an elemental catastrophe they awake from their muddle and confusion, forget all their internal difficulties and animosities, and remember the great common task, the preservation of mankind against the supremacy of nature.[46]

The attack upon some social problem requiring solution is in every way a far more satisfactory outlet for aggression than an attack upon other human beings. Clearly, then, it is what is culturally offered as the most suitable object for the release of these aggressive tendencies that is the primarily important fact, the economic factors are only of secondary importance. As Dollard has put it, "Race prejudice seems, then, but a footnote to the wider consideration of the circumstances under which aggression may be expressed within a society."[47]

It is only under special kinds of conditions that worry, fear, and insecurity may be made to add up to race prejudice. Economic conditions are culturally utilizable, for good or for evil purposes, as each culture, or segment thereof, sees fit. If in some cultures the aggressiveness which arises under such conditions is made to discharge itself in hostile behavior toward some group, that can hardly be said to be due to economic conditions, but must clearly be held to be due to those factors which render possible the cultural manipulation of the situation to which such conditions give rise. In short, economic factors may provide some of the conditions in which race hostility may be generated but, unless those conditions are directed into channels leading to race hostility, there will be no race hostility, and the aggressiveness which must be released will have to find some other outlet. Under prosperous economic conditions, when the individual's feelings of security are at an optimum level, anxiety is not as likely to be aroused as under unfavorable economic conditions.

The history of prejudice against the Japanese in California affords a telling case study of the complexity of the factors involved. Here it would be an easy matter for the economic determinist to show that economic factors are chiefly responsible for that prejudice, but he would not be entirely correct. A study of the history of the prejudice against the Japanese in California proves that a large number of independent factors are involved. In the first place, Japanese immigration into California unfortunately coincided with the rise of Japan as a great power with territorial ambitions, hence Japanese immigrants came to be regarded as "the spearhead of Japanese invasion." Corrupt politicians, anxious to divert public attention from their own malpractices, and newspapers, supporting the latter or for their own particular purposes, have continually emphasized the danger that California might develop a race problem even worse than the color problem in the South. The continual emphasis on the inevitability of war with Japan, the fact that the Japanese present perceptible physical and cultural differences, their hard-won, but warmly resented, expansion into fields of commerce in which they have become "competitors" where whites formerly held the field exclusively, are important factors, among others, which together have been responsible for the development of race prejudice against the Japanese in California.[48]

The aggressive intentions of the Japanese government and fear of the development of another "color problem," two issues almost daily drummed into the ears of Californians, would alone have been sufficient to produce an acute case of race prejudice. Add to these the other factors already mentioned, and many others not mentioned, and it becomes clear that any explanation in terms of a single factor would do violence to the facts.

Many Californians disliked the Japanese, not because they constituted an economic threat but because they had been taught to believe that the Japanese were opposed to all that good Californians and good Americans stood for. This belief made it possible for the federal government to avail itself of racial discrimination as an instrument of national policy following the attack on Pearl Harbor. In February 1942 President Franklin D. Roosevelt signed Executive Order 9066 ordering the forcible removal from the area of the Western Defense Command of approximately 112,000 Japanese and Japanese Americans. 71,000 of these were American citizens. All were ruthlessly interned in concentration camps.[49] This was an act of naked racism. To this date not one single act of espionage, sabotage, or disloyalty has been traced to any person of Japanese descent either in Hawaii or on the mainland.[50] By this cruel, inhumane, and utterly illegal act, 112,000 men, women, and children were torn from their homes, schools, and employment, and imprisoned for more than four years, for the crime of race.

It is of interest to note that American citizens of German, Italian, Austrian, and Hungarian ancestry were subject to no restraints whatever. Can it be that it was due to their being racially indistinguishable from the rest of white America? In an article "Repay U.S. Japanese?" (*The New York Times,* 10 April 1983), protesting the government's belated intention to recompense the surviving prisoners of the concentration camp, John J. McCloy, an Assistant Secretary of War, who had played a leading role in persuading President Roosevelt to evacuate the Japanese American population justified the rounding up of everyone with common racial characteristics on the ground that "it was not feasible to carry out immediate personal evaluation . . ." and declared that it was the right thing to have done.

In spite of a sedulous search by many agencies, not a single act of disloyalty has ever been traced to a Japanese American, as such persons as Secretary of War Henry L. Stimson, Chief of the Federal Bureau of Investigation J. Edgar Hoover, and others have attested. Nevertheless a Public opinion survey conducted in 1946 revealed that two-thirds of the American public believed Japanese Americans had been guilty of such acts.[51]

Following the conclusion of World War II some Californians violently opposed the return of loyal American citizens of Japanese ancestry to their former homes in California. Scheming politicians declared that were they permitted to do so every Japanese seen on the streets would be killed, thus artfully inciting the public to riot and murder. What were the motives of these politicians? Obviously, what they have always been: to keep the race issue alive so that they might fully exploit it for their own and their friends' economic advantage. The California Alien Land Law which rendered Japanese Americans ineligible to own agricultural land and the California law barring Japanese from the fishing industry were clearly economically motivated, even though both were patently unconstitutional and in direct violation of the 14th Amendment, and in 1950 so declared by the Supreme Court of California, as "racism in one of its most malignant forms."[52]

An example of the little known many acts of mindless racism of the United States government is what happened to the peaceful Mongoloid inhabitants of the Aleutian Islands. Following the Japanese bombing of Dutch Harbor on the Aleutian Islands chain, in June 1942 all inhabitants of the Islands were forcibly removed from their villages to camps in southeastern Alaska. The two-year internment of these gentle people was described by Congressman Don Young as "a living nightmare." The "internment camps" were abandoned fish canneries and fishmeal plants, as was an abandoned gold mine in southeastern Alaska. Scores of people died from lack of proper shelter, poor sanitary conditions, and inadequate care. To this day there has been no adequate compensation paid to the survivors of the wrongs and massive losses suffered at the hands of the United States government.[53]

The details may vary where the members of different groups are involved and in different regions, but the general pattern of racism is the same wherever found and under whatever high-sounding name it may be disguised. Not one factor, but a complex of factors, is generally involved. Nevertheless, when this has been said and all the necessary conditions entering into the generation of race prejudice have been considered, it remains clear that economic conditions are among the most powerful. Our economic system, with all the frictions, frustrations, misery, and war which it brings, is a basic cause of racism and race situations. These, together, supply the motivation and a good deal of the aggressiveness expressed in race prejudice. Race prejudice is a socially sanctioned and socially channeled means of relieving aggressive tensions, because in our society there exist powerful groups of men who believe that in their own interest and in order to maintain their power or increase it they must maintain divisions between men. It is the domestic application of the formula "Divide and rule." What more simple than to produce such divisions between members of different ethnic groups within our society? They are "aliens," "foreigners," "the white man's burden," "the rising tide of color," "the yellow peril," "niggers," "the international Jew," "wops," "Greeks," "the lesser breeds without the law," and so on.[54]

In an economic organization of society which is frequently characterized by one crisis after another, with its attendant unemployment in the industries involved, the aggrieved part of the population is easily led to believe that if there were fewer people to be employed there would be employment and adequate wages for all. Race antagonism under such conditions is easily generated.

As Edward Reuter has put it,

> In the human as in the subhuman realm, the geographic distribution, the physical differences, the varying modes of life, and the mental traits and characteristics are, in large measure, the impersonally determined end results of the competitive struggle to live. Men live where they can secure the means of life, and they develop the physical, mental, and social characters that enable them to live in the area.[55]

One of the most serious "end results of the competitive struggle to live" in our society is race prejudice. It has been emphasized that the economic factor is not the sole condition involved in the causation of race antagonism; it is one of the conditions that facilitates the development of race prejudice, but it is not the only condition. It should, however, be quite clear that in our society the economic factor is a powerful condition in the causation of such antagonisms, a necessary condition without which—whatever we may be able to conceive to the contrary—such antagonisms would be much less likely to occur. Like good doctors, therefore, if we would prevent the disease we must eliminate or modify the principal condition or conditions that make it possible. In other words, we must attend to the conditions such as overpopulation and poverty of economic duress under which so many human beings are unjustly forced to live today.[56] By so doing we will have removed one of the most important breeding grounds in which the virus of race prejudice so readily grows; such other conditions as remain can then be dealt with efficiently. This is something to understand and to work for.

Notes

1. Upon this important subject see the following: Eduard Hahn, *Die Haustiere* (Leipzig: Dunckcker und Humbold, 1896); B. Klatt, "Mendelismus, Domestikation und Kraniologie," *Archiv für Anthropologie*, n.s., 18 (1921): 225–50; H. Friedenthal, "Die Sonderstellung des Menschen in der Natur," *Wege zum Wissen* 8 (1925); Eugen Fischer, "Rasse und Rassenentstehung beim Menschen," *Wege zum Wissen* 62 (1927): 1–137; Berthold Laufer, "Methods in the Study of Domestications," *Scientific Monthly* 25 (1927): 251–55; Melvile J. Herskovits, "Social Selection and the Formation of Human Types," *Human Biology* 1 (1929): 250–62; G. Renard, *Life and Work in Prehistoric Times* (New York: Alfred A. Knopf, 1929); Franz Boas, *The Mind of Primitive Man* (New York: Macmillan, 1938), 74–98; Franz Boas, ed., *General Anthropology* (Boston: Heath, 1938), 108; A. B. D. Fortuyn, "The Origin of Human

Races," *Science* 90 (1939): 352–53; Ashley Montagu, "The Socio-Biology of Man," *Scientific Monthly* 50 (1940): 483–90; J. B. S. Haldane, "The Argument from Animals to Men," in *Culture and the Evolution of Man,* ed. Ashley Montagu (New York: Oxford University Press, 1962), 65–83; Sherwood L. Washburn, ed., *Social Life of Early Man* (Chicago: Quadrangle Books, 1961); James Spuhler, ed., *The Evolution of Man's Capacity for Culture* (Detroit: Wayne State University Press, 1959); Melville J. Herskovitz, "Domestication," *Encyclopedia of the Social Sciences* 5 (1937): 206–8; Michael Banton, *Racial Theories* (New York: Cambridge University Press, 1987).

2. Montagu, "The Socio-Biology of Man"; Washburn, *Social Life.*

3. R. A. Fisher, *The Genetical Theory of Natural Selection* (Oxford: Clarendon Press, 1930), 174.

4. See Leo Lowenthal and Norbert Guterman, *Prophets of Deceit* (New York: Harper, 1949).

5. James Cook, *The Segregationists* (New York: Appleton-Century-Crofts, 1962); Benjamin Epstein and Arnold Forster, *The Troublemakers* (New York: Doubleday, 1952); B. Epstein and A. Forster, *The Radical Right* (New York: Random House, 1956); Neil McMillen, *The Citizens' Council: Organized Resistance to the Second Reconstruction, 1954–1964* (Urbana: University of Illinois Press, 1991); Gertrude Selznick and Stephen Steinberg, *The Tenacity of Prejudice* (New York: Harper & Row, 1969); A. Forster and B. Epstein, *Danger on the Right* (New York: Random House, 1964).

6. For an analysis of the problem of prejudice and discrimination, and a program of investigation and strategy, see Robert M. MacIver, *The More Perfect Union* (New York: Macmillan, 1948); also, Donald Young, "Techniques of Race Relations," *Proceedings of the American Philosophical Society* 91 (1947): 150–61; Gordon Allport, "Controlling Group Prejudice," *Annals,* American Academy of Political and Social Science (1946): 1–240, 244; Gordon Allport, *The Nature of Prejudice* (Cambridge, MA: Addison Wesley, 1953) and *Personality and the Social Encounter* (Boston: Beacon Press, 1960); Joseph B. Gittler, ed., *Understanding Minority Groups* (New York: Wiley, 1956); Philip Mason, *An Essay on Racial Tension* (London: Royal Institute of National Affairs, 1954); Arnold M. Rose, ed., *Race Prejudice and Discrimination* (New York: Alfred A. Knopf, 1951); Jacob Javits, *Discrimination–U.S.A.* (New York: Harcourt Brace, 1960); J. Masuoka and Preston Valien, eds., *Race Relations* (Chapel Hill: University of North Carolina Press, 1961); Irwin Katz and Patricia Gurin, eds., *Race and the Social Sciences* (New York: Basic Books, 1969).

7. Manning Nash, "Race and the Ideology of Race," *Current Anthropology* 3 (1962): 285–88; J. W. Vander Zanden, "The Ideology of White Supremacy," *Journal of the History of Ideas* 20 (1959): 385–402.

8. Henry Wallace, *The Genetic Basis for Democracy* (New York: American Committee for Democracy and Intellectual Freedom, 1939), 7. See also Henry Wallace, "Racial Theories and the Genetic Basis for Democracy," *Science* 89 (1939), 140–43.

9. A. Montagu, "A Cursory Examination of the Relations between Physical and Social Anthropology," *American Journal of Physical Anthropology,* 26 (1940): 41–61; A. Montagu, "Physical Anthropology and Anatomy," *American Journal of Physical Anthropology* 28 (1941): 261–71; John Gillin, ed., *For a Science of Social Man;* A. Montagu, *Man in Process* (Cleveland and New York: World Publishing. 1961); A. Montagu, *The Biosocial Nature of Man* (New York: Grove Press, 1956); Allan Mazur and Leon Robertson, *Biology and Social Behavior* (New York: Free Press, 1972).

10. "Unwanted Heroes," *New Republic* 106 (1942), 655; Carey McWilliams, *Brothers Under the Skin*, revised (Boston: Little, Brown, 1964). It is sad to have to record the fact that in the third week of September 1944, the Fourth Filipino Inter-Community convention held at New City, California, adopted as two of its objectives "the abolition of discriminatory legislation against Filipinos" and "permanent post-war exile of all Japanese from California" (reported in the *Pacific Citizen*, Salt Lake City, Utah, 23 September 1944, 3–4). The Filipinos apparently regarded the Japanese as serious economic competitors, and desired to eliminate their "competition" by this means. In a period of high feeling there was also the motive of jumping on the bandwagon of the most vocal California "patriots." In addition we may perceive here the mechanism of response to frustration of low status position in the scapegoating of another (even if temporarily) low status group. See Horace Miner, *Timbuctoo* (Princeton: Princeton University Press, 1953), 254.

11. Kenneth Little, *Negroes in Britain* (London: Kegan Paul, 1948); Michael Banton, *White and Coloured* (London: Cape, 1959); Anthony Richmond, "Racial Relations in England," *Midwest Journal* 3 (1951): 1–13; A. Richmond, *The Colour Problem* (New York: Penguin Books, 1955); Sheila Patterson, *Dark Strangers* (London: Tavistock, 1963).

12. Anthony Richmond, "Memories of South Africa," *The Listener* 60 (1958), 736–39.

13. Graham Greene, "African Chequerboard," *The Listener* 74 (1965), 421–22.

14. Bruno Bettelheim and Morris Janowitz, *Dynamics of Prejudice* (New York: Harper, 1950), 169–86.

15. Kenneth Clark, *Prejudice and Your Child* (Boston: Beacon, 1955); Ashley Montagu, *On Being Human* (New York: Hawthorn Books, 1969); A. Montagu, *The Direction of Human Development*, revised (New York: Hawthorn Books, 1970); Helen H. Davidson, *Personality and Economic Background* (New York: King's Crown Press, 1943); A. Montagu, *Growing Young*, 2nd ed. (Westport, CT: Bergen & Garvey, 1989); Report of the Joint Commission on Mental Health in Children: *Crisis in Child Mental Health: Challenge for the 1970's* (New York: Harper & Row, 1970); Charles V. Willie, Bernard M. Kramer, and Bertram S. Brown, eds., *Racism and Mental Health* (Pittsburgh: University of Pittsburgh Press, 1973); Mary E. Goodman, *Race Awareness in Young Children* (New York: Collier Books, 1964); Alice Miller, *For Your Own Good: Hidden Cruelty in Child-Rearing and the Roots of Violence* (New York: Farrar, Straus & Giroux, 1982); Jean S. Phinney and Mary J. Rotheram, *Children's Ethnic Socialization* (Thousand Oaks, CA: Sage Publications, 1987); David Milner, *Children and Race* (Thousand Oaks, CA: Sage Publications, 1965); Darlene P. Hopson and Derek S. Hopson, *Different and Wonderful: Raising Black Children in a Race-Conscious Society* (Englewood Cliffs, NJ: Prentice-Hall 1990).

16. Sancton, "Trouble in Dixie," *New Republic* 108 (1943), 51.

17. Paul Good, "Blue Notes From Dixie," *The Nation* 203 (196), 570–75.

18. Clyde L. Menschreck, "Religion in the South: Problems and Promise," in *The South in Perspective*, ed. Francis B. Simkins (Farmville, VA: Longwood College, 1959), 84–89; Harry S. Ashmore, *Hearts and Minds: The Anatomy of Racism From Roosevelt to Reagan* (New York: McGraw-Hill, 1982); Charles E. Wynes, ed., *Forgotten Voices: Dissenting Voices in an Age of Conformity* (Baton Rouge: Louisiana State University Press, 1967).

19. F. L. Cross and E. A. Livingstone, eds. *The Oxford Dictionary of the Christian Church,* 2nd ed. (New York, Oxford University Press).

20. Leon Poliakov, *The History of Anti-Semitism,* 4 vols. (New York: Vanguard Press, 1973–1983).

21. Alan Davies, *Infected Christianity: A Study of Modern Racism* (Kingston and Montreal: McGill-Queen's University Press, 1988).

22. Round Table Magazine, April 1954; David S. Wyman, *The Abandonment of the Jews: America and the Holocaust 1941–1945* (New York: Pantheon Books, 1984).

23. Robert W. Ross, *So It Was True: The American Protestant Press and The Nazi Persecution of the Jews* (Minneapolis: University of Minnesota Press, 1980), 300–301.

24. Hannah Arendt, *Eichman in Jerusalem* (New York: Viking Press, 1963); H. Arendt, *The Origins of Totalitarianism* (New York: Harcourt, Brace, 1951); Hans Askenasy, *Hitler's Secret* (Laguna Beach, Van Dyke Drive, 1984); David Barnow and Gerrold Van Der Stroom, eds., *The Diary of Anne Frank* Critical Edition (New York: Doubleday, 1989); Ruth Bondy, *Elder of the Jews* (New York: Grove Press, 1989); Lucy Dawidowicz, *The War Against the Jews* (New York: Holt, Reinhart and Winston, 1975); Lucy Dawidowicz, *The Holocaust and the Historians* (Cambridge: Harvard University Press, 1981); Terrence Des Pres, *The Survivor* (New York: Oxford University Press, 1976); Leonard Dinnerstein, *American and the Survivors of the Holocaust* (New York: Columbia University Press, 1982); Lucjan Dobroszycki, ed., *The Chronicle of the Lodz Ghetto 1841–1944* (New Haven: Yale University Press, 1984); Vaffa Elliach, *Hasidic Tales of the Holocaust* (New York: Oxford University Press, 1982); Helen Epstein, *Children of the Holocaust* (New York: Putnam, 1979); Richard J. Evans, *Hitler's Shadow: West German Historians and the Attempt to Escape From the Nazi Past* (New York: Pantheon Books, 1989); Helen Fein, *Accounting For Genocide* (New York: Free Press, 1979); Gerald Fleming, *Hitler and the Final Solution* (Berkeley: University of California Press, 1982); Martin Gilbert, *The Holocaust: A History of the Jews of Europe During the Second World War* (New York: Holt, Rinehart & Winston, 1986); Anton Gill, *The Journey Back From Hell* (New York: William Morrow, 1989); Leonard Gross, *The Last Jews of Berlin* (New York: Simon & Schuster, 1982); Peter Hayes, *Lessons and Legacies: The Meaning of the Holocaust in a Changing World* (Evanston, IL: Northwestern University Press, 1991); Raul Hilberg, *The Destruction of the European Jews,* 2nd ed. (New York: Holms & Meyer 1985); Jacob Katz, *From Prejudice to Destruction* (Cambridge: Harvard University Press, 1980); Hanna Krall, *Shielding the Flame* (New York: Henry Holt, 1986); Leo Kuper, *Genocide: Its Political Use in the Twentieth Century* (New Haven: Yale University Press, 1982); Leo Kuper, *The Prevention of Genocide* (New Haven: Yale University Press, 1981); Nora Levin, *The Holocaust* (New York: Crowell, 1968); Alfred D. Low, *Jews in the Eyes of the Germans: From the Enlightenment to Imperial Germany* (Philadelphia: Institute for the Study of Human Issues, 1979); Bert Mark, *Uprising in the Warsaw Ghetto* (New York: Schocken Books, 1975); Roger Maxwell and Heinrich Fraenkel, *The Incomparable Crime* (New York: Putnam, 1967); Judith Miller, *One, By One, By One: Facing the Holocaust* (New York: Simon & Schuster, 1990); Sarah Moskovitz, *Love Despite Hate: Child Survivors of the Holocaust and Their Adult Lives* (New York: Schocken Books, 1983); Benno Muller-Hill, *Murderous Science: Elimination by Scientific Selection of Jew, Gypsies, and Others, Germany 1953* (New York: Oxford University Press, 1988); Samuel Pisar, *Of Blood and Hope* (Boston: Little, Brown, 1980); Emanuel Ringelblum, *Notes From the Warsaw Ghetto* (New York:

McGraw-Hill, 1952); Alvin H. Rosenfeld, *A Double Dying: Reflections on Holocaust Literature* (Bloomington: University of Indiana Press, 1980); Alvin Rosenfeld and Irving Greenberg, eds., *Confronting the Holocaust: The Impact of Elie Wiesel* (Bloomington: University of Indiana Press, 1978); Michael Selzer, *Deliverance: The Last Days at Dachau* (Philadelphia: Lippincott, 1978); Jurgen Stroop, *The Stroop Report (The Official Nazi Report on the Destruction of the Warsaw Ghetto)* (New York: Pantheon Books, 1979); Rita Thalmann and Emanual Feinermann, *Crystal Night* (New York: Columbia University Press, 1971); Leonard Tusnet, *The Uses of Adversity* (South Brunswick: Thoman Yoseloff, 1966); Susan Zuccotti, *The Holocaust, the French, and the Jews* (New York; Basic Books, 1993).

25. Leon Wieseltier, "History and the Holocaust," *The Times Literary Supplement*, 25 February 1977, 220–221; see also Robert H. Abzug, *Inside the Vicious Heart* (New York: Oxford University Press, 1985); Omer Bartov, *Hitler's Army* (New York: Oxford University Press, 1992); Norbert Bromberg and Verna V. Small, *Hitler's Psychopathology* (New York: International Universities Press, 1983); Alan Bullock, *Hitler: A Study in Tyrany* (New York: Harper & Row, 1964); Robert Cecil, *The Myth of the Master Race: Alfred Rosenberg and Nazi Ideology* (New York: Dodd, Mead, 1972); Joan Coamy, *The Diaspora Story: The Epic of the Jewish People Among the Nations* (New York: Harper & Row, 1972); Charles B. Flood, *Hitler: The Path to Power* (Boston: Little, Brown, 1980); Karl Jaspers, *The Question of German Guilt* (New York: Dial Press, 1947); Sam Keen, *Faces of the Enemy* (New York: Harper & Row, 1986); Walter Laqueur, *The Terrible Secret: Suppression of the Truth About Hitler's Final Solution* (Boston: Little, Brown, 1980); Stein U. Larsen, Bernt Hagtvet, and Jan P. Myklebust, eds., *Who Were the Facists: Social Roots of European Fascism* (Bergen: Universitetsforlaget, 1980); Paul W. Massing, *Rehersal for Destruction: A Study of Political Anti-Semitism in Imperial Germany* (New York: Harper & Brothers, 1949); Paul R. Mendez-Flohr and Jehuda Reinharz, *The Jew in the Modern World: A Documentary History* (New York: Oxford University Press, 1980); Peter H. Merkl, *Political Violence Under the Swastika* (Princeton: Princeton University Press 1975); P. H. Merkl, *The Making of a Stormtrooper* (Princeton: Princeton University Press, 1980); Monty N. Penkower, *The Jews Were Expendable: Free World Diplomacy and the Holocaust* (Urbana: University of Illinois Press, 1984); William L. Shirer, *The Rise and Fall of the Third Reich: A History of Nazi Germany* (New York, 1960); Louis L. Snyder, *Encyclopedia of the Third Reich* (New York: McGraw-Hill, 1976); Hans Staudinger, *The Inner Nazi: A Critical Analysis of Mein Kampf* (Baton Rouge: Louisiana State University Press, 1981); Yavon Svoray and Nick Taylor, *In Hitler's Shadow* (New York: Doubleday, 1994); Peter Viereck, *Metapolitics: The Roots of the Nazi Mind* (New York: Capricorn Books, 1961); Benjamin Wilkomirski, *Fragments: Memories of a Wartime Childhood* (New York: Schocken Books, 1997).

26. Ashley Montagu, *On Being Human,* 2nd ed. (New York: Dutton, 1966); A. Montagu, *The Direction of Human Development,* 2nd ed. (New York: Hawthorn Books, 1970); M. A. R. Tuker, *Past and Future of Ethics* (London & New York: Oxford University Press, 1938). Tuker's book is certainly one of the most original and, probably, one of the best books of its kind ever written on the subject of human relations.

27. Bernard Wasserstein, *Britain and the Jews of Europe 1939–1945* (New York: Oxford University Press, 1979), 351; Leonard Dinnerstein, *America and the Survivors of the Holocaust* (New York: Columbia University Press, 1982); Martin Gilbert,

Auschwitz and the Allies (New York: Holt, Rinehart & Winston, 1981); Leo Gold-berger, *The Rescue of the Danish Jews: Moral Courage Under Stress* (New York: New York University Press, 1987); William R. Perl, *The Four Front War: From the Holocaust to the Promised Land* (New York: Crown, 1978). Perl's fascinating and revelatory book is one of the most important accounts of the connivance of the British and other governments to prevent the entrance of refugees in flight from Hitler into Palestine. See also David S. Wyman, *Paper Walls: America and the Refugee Crisis 1938–1941* (New York: Pantheon, 1968); D. S. Wyman, *Abandonment of the Jews* (New York: Pantheon, 1984); Yitzhak Zuckerman, *A Surplus of Memory: Chronicle of the Warsaw Uprising* (Berkeley: University of California Press, 1993). This is the story, told in his own words, of one of the great heroes of history.

28. Ashley Montagu, *The Humanization of Man* (New York: World Publishing, 1962); A. Montagu and Floyd Matson, *The Dehumanization of Man* (New York: Mc-Graw-Hill, 1983); A. Montagu, *On Being Human* (New York: Henry Schuman, 1950); Henry L. Feingold, *The Politics of Rescue* (New Brunswick: Rutgers University Press, 1970); Saul S. Friedman, *No Haven For the Oppressed* (Detroit: Wayne State University Press, 1973); Arthur D. Morse, *While Six Million Die: A Chronicle of American Apathy* (New York: Random House, 1967).

29. Robert Conquest, *The Great Terror* (New York: Viking, 1990); R. Conquest, *Stalin: Breaker of Nations* (New York: Viking, 1991).

30. Tibor Szamuely, "Jews in Russia: The Semi-Final Solution," *The Spectator,* 11 August 1969, 153–54.

31. John and Carol E. Garrard, "Glasnost Byproduct: Virulent Anti-Semitism," *The New York Times,* 27 May 1990; Irina Ginsburg, "We Russian Jews Fear for Our Lives," *The New York Times,* 5 May 1990.

32. Lewis Sowden, *The Union of South Africa* (New York: Doubleday, Doran, 1943), 216. See also John Burger, *The Black Man's Burden* (London: Gollancz, 1943); Russell, *Colour, Race and Empire* (London: Gollancz, 1944); Henry Gibbs, *Twilight in South Africa* (New York: Philosophical Library, 1950); Adamastor, *White Man Boss* (Boston: Beacon Press, 1951); Wulf Sachs, *Black Anger* (Boston: Little, Brown, 1947); "South Africa," *Time* 59 (1952), 32–38; "America and the Challenge of Africa," *Saturday Review* 36 (1953), 9–29; Patrick Van Rensburg, *Guilty Land: The History of Apartheid* (New York: Praeger, 1962); Muriel Horrell, *A Survey of Race Relations in South Africa* (Johannesburg: South African Institute of Race Relations, 1962); Norman Phillips, *The Tragedy of Apartheid* (New York: McKay, 1960); Peter Ritner, *The Death of Africa* (New York: MacMillan, 1960); Alfred Lowenstein, *Brutal Mandate* (New York: MacMillan, 1962); Leo Kuper, Hilstan Watts, and Ronald Davies, *Durban: A Study in Racial Ecology* (New York: Columbia University Press, 1958); T. Dunbar Moodie, *The Rise of Afrikanerdom* (Berkeley: University of California Press, 1975); Leonard Thompson and Jeffrey Butler, eds., *Change in Contemporary South Africa* (Berkeley & Los Angeles: University of California Press, 1975); Joseph Llelyveld, *Move Your Shadow* (New York: Basic Books, 1995).

33. T. C. Robertson, "Racism Comes to Power in South Africa," *Commentary* 6 (1948), 428; Herbert Adam, *Modernizing Racial Domination* (Berkeley: University of California Press, 1971); Douglas Brown, *Against The World* (New York: Doubleday, 1968); William A. Hance, ed., *Southern Africa and the United States* (New York; Columbia University Press, 1968); Jim Hoagland, *South Africa: Civilizations in Conflict*

(Boston: Houghton Mifflin, 1972); Trevor Huddleston, *Nought For Your Comfort* (New York: Doubleday, 1956); E. J. Kahn, Jr., *The Separated People* (New York: Ungar, 1967); Lowenstein, *Brutal Mandate;* Naboth Mokgatle, *The Autobiography of an Unknown South African* (Berkeley: University of California Press, 1971); Edward Roux, *Time Longer Than Rope: A History of the Black Man's Struggle for Freedom in Africa* (Madison: University of Wisconson Press, 1976); Benjamin Sacks, *South Africa: An Imperial Dilemma* (Albuquerque: University of New Mexico Press, 1967); Donald G. Mathews, *Law, Order and Liberty in South Africa* (Princeton: Princeton University Press, 1965); UNESCO, *Apartheid* (New York: Unipub., 1969); Pierre L. Van den Berghe, *South Africa: A Study in Conflict* (Middletown, CT: Wesleyan University Press, 1965); Albie Sachs, *Justice in South Africa* (Berkeley: University of California Press, 1973).

34. "Light from darkness," of course, means "white from black." See also Cross and Livingstone, eds., *Oxford Dictionary of the Christian Church.*

35. *Round Table Magazine,* April 1954.

36. Z. K. Matthews, "The Black Man's Outlook," *Saturday Review* 36 (2 May 1953) 13–14, 41–52; Alex La Guma, ed., *Apartheid: A Collection of Writings on South African Racism,* (New York: International Publishers, 1972); Robert W. Peterson, ed., *South Africa and Apartheid* (New York: Facts on File, 1975); UNESCO, *Apartheid: Its Affects on Education, Science, Culture, and Information,* 2nd ed. (New York: Unipub., 1972); William R. Frye, *In Whitest Africa: The Dynamics of Apartheid* (Englewood Cliffs, NJ: Prentice Hall; 1975); David Mermelstein, ed., *The Anti-Apartheid Reader: South Africa and the Struggle Against White Racist Rule* (New York: Grove Press, 1987); Nic Rhoodie, ed., *South African Dialogue: Contrasts in South African Thinking on Basic Race Issue* (Philadelphia: Westminster Press, 1972); John A. Marcum, *Education, Race, and Social Change in South Africa* (Berkeley: University of California Press, 1981); Leonard Thompson and Jeffery Butler, eds., *Change in Contemporary South Africa;* Leonard Thompson, *The Political Mythology of Apartheid* (New Haven: Yale University Press, 1985); Joseph Lelyveld, *Move Your Shadow: South Africa: Black and White* (New York: Time Books, 1985); Robert W. July, *A History of the African People,* 2nd ed. (New York: Charles Scribners, 1971); Robert Ross, *Cape of Torments: Slavery and Resistance in South Africa* (Boston: Routledge & Kegan Paul, 1983); Margo & Martin Russell, *Afrikaners of the Kalahari* (New York: Cambridge University Press, 1979); V. A. February, *Mind Your Colour: The Coloured Stereotype in South African Literature* (Boston: Kegan Paul, 1981).

37. Bernard Sachs, "South Africa: Life on a Volcano," *Commentary* 9 (1950), 536. For a full account of race problems in South Africa see Ellen Hellman and Leah Abrahams, *Handbook on Race Relations in South Africa* (London: Oxford University Press, 1949). See also John Laurence, *Seeds of Disaster* (London: Gollancz, 1968); Vincent Crapanzano, *Waiting: The Whites of South Africa* (New York: Random House, 1985).

38. Quoted in D. M. Paton, ed., *Church and Race in South Africa* (London: Student Christian Movement Press, 1958).

39. Stanley Meisler, "Our Stake in Apartheid," *The Nation* 201 (August 16, 1965), 71–73; B. Lapping, *Apartheid: A History* (London: Grafton, 1986); M. Meredith, *In the Name of Apartheid* (London: Hamilton, 1988); L. Thompson, *Political Mythology of Apartheid* (New Haven: Yale University Press, 1985); N. Worden, *Making of Modern South Africa* (Oxford and Cambridge MA: Blackwell, 1993).

40. Patti Waldmeir, *Anatomy of a Miracle: the End of Apartheid and the Birth of the New South Africa* (New York: W. W. Norton, 1997); Crocker, Chester A, *High Noon in Southern Africa: Making Peace in a Rough Neighborhood* (New York: W. W. Norton, 1992).

41. Lawrence Fellows, "Labourites Slate a Racial Inquiry," *New York Times* 17 October 1964, 9. "Tears streamed down the face of Mr. Gordon Walker last night when the election result was announced. 'This was the dirtiest election I ever fought,' he said."

42. Ibid. See also David Watt, "Colour and the Election," *The Spectator,* 28 August 1964, 261–62; Nicholas Deakin, *Colour and the British Electorate* (London: Pall Mall, 1965).

43. Robert K. Merton, "Social Structure and Anomie," *American Sociological Review* 3 (1938), 680. See also Edwaard McDill, "Anomie, Authoritarianism, Prejudice, and Socio-Economic Status: An Attempt at Clarification," *Social Forces* 39 (1961), 239–45.

44. For a development of the frustration-aggression hypothesis, see John Dollard et al., *Frustration and Aggression.* See also Leonard Berkowitz, *Aggression: A Social Psychological Analysis;* L. Berkowitz, ed., *Roots of Aggression* (New York: Atherton Press, 1969); E. F. M. Durbin and John Bowlby, *Personal Aggressiveness and War* (New York: Columbia University Press, 1939); Albert Bandura, *Aggression: A Social Learning Analysis* (Englewood Cliffs, NJ: Prentice-Hall, 1973).

45. Arthur Richmond, "Economic Insecurity and Stereotypes as Factors in Colour Prejudice," *Sociological Review,* 42 (1950), 147–70. See also Edward L. Ayers, *The Promise of the New South: Life After Reconstruction* (New York: Oxford University Press, 1991); Christopher Bagley and Gajendra K. Verma, *Racial Prejudice, the Individual and Society* (Lexington, MA: D.C. Heath, 1979); Rae Sherwood, *The Psychodynamics of Race* (Atlantic Highlands, NJ: Humanities Press, 1980); Gerald D. Berreman, *Social Inequality* (New York: Academic Press, 1978); T. A. Van Dijk, *Communicating Racism: Ethnic Prejudice in Thought and Race* (Thousand Oaks, CA: Sage Publications, 1987); Dorothy K. Newman, et al., Protest, Politics, and Prosperity (New York: Pantheon, 1978); Stephen Steinberg, *Turning Back: The Retreat from Racial Justice in American Thought and Policy* (Boston: Beacon Press, 1995); Richard L. Zweigenhaft and William Domhoff, *Blacks in the White Establishment* (New Haven, Yale University Press, 1991).

46. Sigmund Freud, *The Future of an Illusion* (London: Hogarth Press, 1928), 27.

47. John Dollard, "Hostility and Fear in Social Life," *Social Forces* 17 (1938), 15–26.

48. For an able analysis of the problem in California see McWilliams, *Brothers Under the Skin,* 147–75, and the same author's *Prejudice—the Japanese Americans: Symbols of Racial Intolerance* (Boston: Little, Brown, 1944); William Petersen, *Japanese Americans: Oppression and Success* (Washington, D.C.: Washington University Press, 1971).

49. For an objective account of conditions in these camps as experienced by internees see Mine Okubo, *Citizen 13660* (New York: Columbia University Press, 1925); Charles Kikuchi, *The Kikuchi Diary: Chronicle from an American Concentration Camp,* edited and with an introduction by David Modell (Urbana: University of

Illinois Press, 1992). The detailed story of the Japanese American evacuation is authoritatively told in Milton M. Grodzins' *Americans Betrayed* (Chicago: University of Chicago Press, 1949), and in Audrie Girdner and Anne Loftis, *The Great Betrayal* (New York: Macmillan, 1960). The socio-economic consequences are dealt with by Leonard Bloom and Ruth Riemer in their book *Removal and Return* (Berkeley: University of California Press, 1949); the social and psychological consequences by Dorothy Thomas and Richard S. Nishimoto, *The Spoilage* (Berkeley: University of California Press, 1946), George Jean Oishi, "The Anxiety of Being a Japanese American," *New York Times Magazine,* 28 April 1985, 54; and Alexander Leighton, *The Governing of Men* (Princeton: Princeton University Press,1945). For an account by four anthropologists who shared in the task of administering the camps see Edward Spicer et al., *Impounded People* (Tucson: University of Arizona Press, 1969).

50. In November 1946, the Privy Council of the government of England, the British Empire's highest court of appeals, upheld Canadian legislation forcing the deportation of citizens and resident aliens of Japanese ancestry. In short, the representatives of the British Empire ruled that a person's citizenship in one of its dominions may be revoked and that person exiled for no other reason than race. Against this may be set the achievement of the voters of Saskatchewan, Canada, who, on 1 May 1947, made it a punishable offense by law for anyone to infringe the right of any person "to obtain and retain employment; engage in business; own and occupy property; have access to public places, hotels, theaters, restaurants; to membership in professional and trade organizations; education and enrollment in schools and universities." Saskatchewan is the only Canadian province which has a Cooperative Commonwealth Federation government. Nevertheless the government of Canada made it very comfortable for Nazi war criminals to settle in Canada for the rest of their lives, with one deportation only, even though these murderers were receiving their pension checks regularly from the German government.

51. "Survey of the National Opinion Research Center of the University of Denver," *Pacific Citizen,* 21 (31 August 1946), 3.

52. For a full account see Frank F. Chuman, *The Bamboo People: The Law and Japanese Americans* (Del Mar, CA: Publishers Inc., 1976).

53. For further on this grim subject, see the comments of Senator Ted Stevens (R-Alaska) and Representative Don Young (R-Alaska), and editorial, "Aleuts WWII Tragedy," *Indian Affairs* 102, March 1981, 4.

54. See Michael Selzer, ed., *"Kike!"* (New York: World Publishing Co., 1972); Chang-Tsu Wu, *"Chink!"* (New York: World Publishing Co., 1972); Jay David and Elaine Crane, eds., *Living Black in White America* (New York: William Morrow, 1972); Norman Coombs, *The Black Experience in America* (New York: Twayne, 1972); William Brink and Louis Harris, *Black and White: A Study in U.S. Racial Attitudes Today* (New York: Simon & Schuster, 1967); H. Brett Melendy, *The Oriental Americans* (New York: Twayne, 1972); Leo Grebler, Joan Moore and Ralph Guzman, *The Mexican-American People* (New York: Macmillan, 1970); Matt S. Meier and Feliciano Rivera, *The Chicanos: A History of Mexican Americans* (New York: Hill & Wang, 1972); William Powell, *Tree of Hate: Propaganda and Prejudices Affecting United States Relations With the Hispanic World* (New York: Basic Books, 1971); Wayne Moquin and Charles van Doren, eds., *A Documentary History of the Mexican Americans* (New York: Praeger, 1973); Stan Steiner, *La Raza: The Mexican Americans* (New York: Harper & Row, 1970); William

G. Shade and Roy C. Herrenkohl, eds., *Seven on Black: Reflections on the Negro Experience in America* (Philadelphia: Lippincott, 1969).

55. Edward Reuter, "Competition and the Racial Division of Labor," in *Race Relations and the Race Problem*, ed. Edgar Thompson (Durham: Duke University Press, 1939), 49.

56. For a discussion of the facts and also for the necessary recommendations see Bruno Bettelheim and Morris Janowitz, *Dynamics of Prejudice* (New York: Harper, 1950), 174 et seq.; Robert M. MacIver, *The More Perfect Union* (New York: Macmillan, 1948); R. M. MacIver, ed., *Unity and Difference in American Life* (New York: Harper, 1947); Arnold Rose and Carolyn Rose, *America Divided* (New York: Alfred A. Knopf, 1948); David Spitz, *Patterns of Anti-Democratic Thought* (New York: Macmillan, 1949); Gerhart Saenger, *The Social Psychology of Prejudice* (New York: Harper, 1953); Andrew Lind, ed., *Race Relations in World Perspective* (Honolulu: University of Hawaii Press, 1955); Karl W. Bigelow, ed., *Cultural Groups and Human Relations* (New York: Columbia University Press, 1951); Muzafer Sherif and Carolyn Sherif, *Groups in Harmony and Tension* (New York: Harper, 1953); Stewart G. Cole and Mildred Wise Cole, *Minorities and the American Promise* (New York: Harper, 1953); Lillian Smith, *Now Is the Time* (New York: Viking, 1955); Philip Mason, *Common Sense About Race* (New York: Macmillan, 1961); Alfred J. Marrow, *Changing Patterns of Prejudice* (New York: Chilton, 1962); Melvin Conant, ed., *Race Issues on the World Scene* (Honolulu: University of Hawaii Press, 1955); George Abernethy, ed., *The Idea of Equality* (Richmond: John Knox Press, 1959); Paul Ramsey, *Christian Ethics and the Sit-In* (New York: Association Press, 1961); C. E. Silberman, *Crisis in Black and White* (New York: Random House, 1964); B. Brandt, ed., *Social Justice* (Englewood Cliffs, NJ: Prentice-Hall, 1962); Edward Budd, *Inequality and Poverty* (New York: W. W. Norton, 1966); Maurice Cranston, *Freedom* (New York: Basic Books, 1967); Frank Gell, *The Black Badge: Confessions of a Case Worker* (New York: Harper & Row, 1969); Alan Grimes, *Equality in America* (New York: Oxford University Press, 1964).

9

Psychological Factors

At this stage of our discussion I wish to focus attention on the general factor which is too frequently overlooked in discussions of the race problem. This is the factor of the normal psychological and psychophysical traits of the person—traits which are utilized in the generation of racial enmities and which have already been touched upon in the preceding chapter.

The one thing clear concerning racial hostility and prejudice is the ease with which persons are led to exhibit it. There are few persons in our society who have not, at one time or another, exhibited race prejudice. It would seem clear that most persons are capable of being brought to a state of mind in which they are glad of the opportunity of freely releasing their feelings against some group or person representing such a group. When society as a whole sanctions such provocations against any group, the free exercise of racial intolerance is enjoyed as a release for feelings that are ever ready to find expression. It is in the nature of such feelings—the nature of which we shall presently discuss—that they can be suitably directed against some person or particular group of persons, and it is for this reason that they can be so easily directed to the support and maintenance of race prejudices. People exhibit race prejudice because it affords them a means of easing certain tensions within themselves; because their tensions are reduced when they are most freely able to discharge those tensions. As far as the individual is concerned, the prejudice itself is unimportant, it merely provides the channel through which feelings are permitted necessary expression. Such feelings should, and for the sake of the health of the individual must, find expression. As I have already said, feelings will attach themselves to the most suitable object offered—whatever it may be. Such feelings are not feelings of race prejudice or any other kind of prejudice; and they are not inborn. On the contrary, such feelings are to a large extent generated during the early childhood development of almost every person. There can, however, be little doubt that the elementary forms of these affective states in their undifferentiated states are physiologically determined.[1] The manner in which such feelings are generated has been discussed in great detail by psychoanalysts and others.[2]

The aggressiveness that adults exhibit in the form of race prejudice would appear to have universally the same origin. That is to say, the aggressiveness, not the race hatred, has the same origin universally and that aggressiveness is merely arbitrarily directed, in some societies, against certain groups. Under other conditions, this same aggressiveness could be directed against numerous different objects, either real or imagined. The object against which aggressiveness is directed is determined by particular conditions, and these we shall later briefly consider. If in racial intolerance and prejudice a certain amount of aggressiveness is always displayed, we must ask and answer two questions: (1) where does this aggressiveness originate, and (2) why is it exhibited? Briefly, a considerable amount of the aggressiveness adults exhibit is originally produced during childhood by parents, nurses, teachers, or whoever else participates in the process of socializing the child. By depriving the infant, and later the child, of the many means of satisfaction which it seeks—the breast, the mother's body, uncontrolled freedom to excrete and to suck, the freedom to cry at will, to stay up late, to do the thousand-and-one things that are forbidden—expected satisfactions are thwarted and frustration upon frustration is piled up within the child. Such frustrations lead to resentment, to fear, to insecurity, to hostility, and to aggressiveness. In childhood this aggressiveness or resentment is displayed in "bad temper" and in general "naughtiness." Such conduct almost invariably results in further frustration—in punishment. At this stage of his development the child finds himself in a state of severe conflict. He must either control the expression of his aggressiveness or else suffer the punishment and loss of love which his aggressiveness provokes. Such conflicts are usually resolved by excluding the painful situation from consciousness and direct motor expression—in short, by the repression of one's aggressive energies. These are rarely completely repressed, but only in so far as they permit a resolution of the original conflict situation, and the further the original derivatives of what was primarily repressed become detached from the latter, the more freely do these energies gain access to consciousness and the more available for use do they become.[3] The evidence renders it overwhelmingly clear that these energies are never to any extent destroyed or exhausted. As a part of the functioning total organism, they must, in one way or another, find expression, and the ways in which they can find expression are innumerable. Race hatred and prejudice merely represent familiar patterns of the manner in which aggressiveness may later express itself.[4]

Fear of those who have frustrated one in childhood and anxiety concerning the outcome of the situation thus produced leads to the repression of aggression against the original frustrators and thereby to the conditioning of an emotional association between certain kinds of frustrative or fear situations and aggressive feelings. As a result of such conditioning, any object even remotely suggesting such fear or frustrative situations provokes the aggressive behavior with which such fears and frustrations have become associated.

The aggressiveness, more or less common to most human beings, is not a cause of race prejudice, but merely represents an expression, a motive force or affective energy that can be attached, among other things, to the notion that other groups or races are hateful and may thus serve to keep such ideas supplied with the emotional force necessary to keep them going. Under such conditions race becomes important, not as a biological description or ethnic classification but as a means of projecting an unconscious conflict.

Since the infliction of mental, and even physical, pain, as well as the frustration and depreciation of others, is involved in the process of race prejudice, and since much of the aggressiveness of the individual owes its existence to early experiences of a similar kind, it is perhaps not difficult to understand why it is that so many persons are so ready to participate in the exercise of race prejudice. By so doing they are able to find an object for their aggressiveness which most satisfactorily permits the free expression of it by means almost identically resembling those which in childhood were indulged in against them. In this way the individual is enabled, as an adult, to pay off—quite unconsciously—an old score of childhood frustration. The later appreciable frustrations suffered in adolescence and adult life naturally add to the store and complexity of aggressiveness, and require no discussion here. At this point reference should be made to such important psychological mechanisms as "displacement," which defines the process whereby aggression is displaced from one object to another, and "projection," the process of attributing to others feelings and impulses originating in ourselves which have been refused conscious recognition.

When the release of aggression toward certain objects or agents is socially interdicted or otherwise made difficult, as in the case of parents, teachers, or employers, aggressiveness may then be displaced toward some more accessible target. The government, blacks, Jews, Catholics, foreigners and the like, will conveniently serve as such targets, and where such displacement of aggression occurs the object of it becomes the scapegoat. Collective displacement of this sort is a well-known phenomenon. Both on the individual and on the group level, forbidden thoughts and aggressions are by such means turned into socially acceptable activities. Humans in search of a target readily utilize social tension for the displacement of personal tension.[5] Since the displacement occurs from what is forbidden to that which is not, it would be a psychologically sound procedure to make the socially acceptable in this case socially unacceptable in demonstrable form such as by legal fiat. For the displacers displace because they are, among other things, great respecters of authority, and will displace their aggression only where it is socially permissible. This analysis is fully supported by a number of clinical studies which were instituted in order to discover what kind of persons adopt and become active carriers of antisemitic ideas, why they so readily become "scapegoat-addicts," and what function, if any, antisemitism serves in their personality structure.[6] A group of approximately 100 state university students, 76 of them women, provided the material for this study. Subjects giving evidence of a high degree of antisemitism were classified as "high extremes," those showing the contrary tendency were classified as "low extremes," and those with in-between attitudes, as "intermediate."

The high extremes were conservative in their attitudes, automatically tending to support the status quo; they were generally Republicans, although they showed few signs of having developed an organized social-political outlook; and there was a tendency to hold their own ethnic or social group in high esteem, to keep it unmixed and pure, and to reject everything that differed from it. The fathers' income was higher than that of the fathers of the average intermediate or low-extreme subjects, and the high-extreme girls appeared to be well groomed, very different from that of the low-extreme girls (almost all subjects were members of the middle class). On the surface these antisemitic girls appeared composed and untroubled. They seemed to have little familiarity with their inner lives, but were characterized rather by a generally externalized orientation. They were sensitive to any encroachment from the outside. On the surface they showed an uncritical devotion and obedience to their parents, and to authority in general. They were mostly interested in social standing, and in making an appropriate marriage.

The low extremes, on all these points, contrasted strongly with the high extremes, being nondescript in appearance, less at ease socially, possessed of varied interests, quite willing to talk about themselves and their situations, and able to make critical appraisals of their parents.

Examination of the results of tests and interviews revealed the fact that the high extremes were markedly characterized by unconscious aggressive drives of a destructive nature, the repression of basic impulses, ambivalent attitudes of love and hate toward their parents, basic insecurity. Both sexes in the high-extreme group tended to be intellectually underproductive, somewhat lower in intelligence, and lacking in creative imagination. They were less interested in human beings as individuals, and tended to be more hypochondriacal.

"The analysis of the content of their responses suggests that the adoption of an aggressive attitude towards outgroups may stem from frustrations received (mainly at the hands of the mother-figure) in childhood"—frustrations which appeared to have produced definite inferiority feelings.

The rigidity with which the high-extreme girl adhered to her conventional values or stereotypes of behavior and the anxiety which she exhibited in the presence of opposite tendencies afforded the clue to the sources of her behavior. Insecurity was the condition with which such girls were struggling. "The fear of losing status is associated with the fear that they will be tempted to release their inhibited tendencies in the way they believe Jews and proletarians do." Anti-semitism thus helps them to maintain their identification with the middle class and to ward off anxiety.

"Thus," the authors of this enlightening study go on to say,

> it is not so much middle class values themselves that we would call into question, but rather the rigidity with which they are adhered to. And in the individual case this appears to be the result of the manner in which they have been put across. The mischief is done when those trends which are taboo according to the class standards become repressed, and hence, no longer susceptible to modification or control. This is most likely to happen when parents are too concerned and too insistent with respect to their positive aims for the child and too threatening and coercive with respect to the 'bad' things. The child is thus taught to view behavior in terms of black and white, 'good' and 'evil'; and the 'evil' is made to appear so terrible that he cannot think of it as something in himself which needs to be modified or controlled, but as something that exists in other 'bad' people and needs to be stamped out completely.[7]

Parent-child relationships clearly need to undergo a substantial change in the direction of greater understanding and sympathy on the part of parents, in the dropping of "either-or" attitudes, for disjunctive commands give rise to disjunctive personalities. As Frenkel-Brunswik and Sanford say, if the kind of repression which they have uncovered in their high-extreme girls, and its consequences, are to be prevented, "there must be less fear of impulses on the part of parents. The parental attitude toward children must be more tolerant and permissive. Parents must learn that 'bad' impulses can be modified and controlled and that it is of crucial importance to invite the child's participation in these processes."[8] Parents must learn how to give their children the maximum degree of security consonant with the ideal of a socially fully integrated personality. Parents must develop a greater interest in the significance of the whole socialization process. In this task teachers must play almost as large a part as parents.[9]

Ackerman and Jahoda have made available the results of a study calculated to reveal the dynamic basis of antisemitic attitudes in a number of persons who have experienced psychoanalytic therapy. The material was collected from some thirty accredited psychoanalysts, and the conclusions

230 MAN'S MOST DANGEROUS MYTH

both enlarge and confirm those of Frenkel-Brunswik and Sanford as well as those of other investigators.

Two extreme categories of anti-Semitic types were theoretically set up by the authors. The one is the antisemite whose attitude seems to be one of superficial conformity to the values, in this respect, of the dominant group; the other is the antisemite whose hostility derives from some definite disorder in his own personality structure to which his antisemitism has a specific relation. All the cases encountered fell between the two extremes, presenting both elements in varying proportions.

All these individuals suffered from anxiety. They were insecure in their group membership. They had a basic feeling of rejection by the world, a feeling of not belonging. They failed to form safe and secure personal attachments. They felt a continuous apprehension of injury to their integrity as individuals. They frequently suffered from an exaggerated sense of vulnerability. They did not seem able to derive support from their own identity as persons. Because of their insecurity, their confused and unstable image of themselves, they lacked direction and made erratic shifts in their group associations. Fundamentally they were weak, immature, passive, dependent, with the desire to control unrealized in the normal channels of constructive action. They endeavored to deny to consciousness the image of themselves as inferior and crippled.

> Overtly they have the urge to conform but unconsciously they resent the compulsory submission and react with destructive rebellion. At the unconscious level they have no hope of being able to repair their damaged identity as persons; basically they accept it as irreversible. However, this basic despair is concealed from consciousness, where they behave in exactly the opposite manner. The core of these character traits is the weak identity, the immaturity, the unconscious passivity, the intense sense of vulnerability to social injury—all of which are denied in consciousness where they are replaced by aggression.[10]

In relation to such a syndrome antisemitism plays a functionally well-defined role. It is a defense against self-hate, a displacement of the self-destroying trends of the character structure described. At the psychic level antisemitism assumes the function of a profound though irrational effort to restore the crippled self, and at the social level it constitutes a pattern producing secondary emotional gain. Were the antisemite to permit his internal conflict, between what he is unconsciously and what he thinks of himself as being consciously, to proceed to its logical conclusion, he would find the consequences unbearable. And so he escapes the dilemma by preoccupation with external events, thus achieving a spurious relief from tensions and the bogus satisfaction of being a member of a powerful, united group, an ingroup in whose program of action he can join. Nevertheless, the central conflict continues with unabated intensity.

To summarize: The prejudice pattern is created through the mobilization of the following series of mechanisms: *(a)* by denial of anxiety and substitution of aggression, *(b)* by an effort to reinforce affiliation with dominant social groups, *(c)* by the elaboration of a variety of reaction formations and compensatory emotional drives, and *(d)* by renunciation of parts of the person's image of self and the concomitant substitution of a borrowed identity. Associated with this there is a suppression and repression of anxiety-ridden impulses.

> Having submissively renounced parts of their own individuality they feel deep resentment against any one who does not do likewise. They demand that other people should conform to the same restrictions. The demand for conformity is thus a result of partial self-renunciation. The person who is forced to renounce his real self as the price of social acceptance is doubly sensitive to others who do not conform. Here lies the root of the excessive reaction to difference which characterizes our antisemitic patients. Every sign of nonconformity in another person is, as it were, an unwelcome reminder of the painful sacrifice that the prejudiced person has made by renouncing part of his self in the vain hope of achieving group identification. The fear of the 'different' is hence not in proportion to the extent of objective, measurable differences; rather it grows in proportion to the implied ego threat, in other words, to the degree to which the difference symbolizes the fruitless suppression of the self. All prejudiced people insist on conformity to the extent of trying to destroy the nonconformist. Since conformity denotes surrender of the individuality, a person who is 'different' symbolizes nonsurrender, and therefore, an individual who is strong, mature, independent, superior, able to stand up against others with his differences. The prejudiced person cannot bear the implied comparison. Because of the inherent weakness of his own self-image, the 'different' person represents a potential menace to his own integrity as an individual or whatever there is left of it. The inevitable response is to attack the menace, the person who symbolizes the difference.[11]

The elaborated and inconsistent picture of the stereotype Jew forms a perfect projective screen for the antisemite's irreconcilable impulses. The Jew is at once successful and low class; capitalist and communist; clannish, and an intruder into other people's society; highly moral, spiritual, and given to low forms of behavior such as greed, sharp business practices, and dirt; magically omnipotent and omniscient, and incredibly helpless and defenseless and therefore readily destroyed.

What any individual projects upon the Jew invariably represents unacceptable components of the self or components envied in others, at least unacceptable on the conscious level though unconsciously such attributes form an active part of the person's psychic drives.[12] Hence, the object which is consciously rejected, the Jew, may, at the unconscious level, be represented by a strong identification with him. This identification, because of the symbolic aspect of the Jew's weakness, his crippled, defenseless position, cannot be admitted, because to do so would be to endanger one's ego and social position. It is therefore denied and in its place there is substituted an identification with the attacker, in order to avoid being victimized and also to draw strength through identification. "Thus the Jew at one and the same time stands for the weakness or strength of the self; for conscience, for those parts of the person which blame and accuse the weakness of the self, and also for those primitive appetites and aggressions which must be denied as the price of social acceptance."[13]

It may be objected that inferences based on data obtained from patients who have been psychoanalytically treated cannot be justly applied to the analysis of the behavior of normal persons. To this objection several replies may be made. First, it is doubtful whether normal individuals are ever antisemitic in the disordered sense here described, and since a large proportion of persons give evidence of disordered character structure it is likely that the observations made and the conclusions drawn from them are valid for a great segment of the population of antisemites. Second, the inability to pay the fees of a psychotherapist is no mark of normality; and, third, in any event the study of the pathological is still one of the best ways of learning to understand the nature of the pathological, for antisemitism is a pathological disorder of individuals and of societies, carrying many pathogenic ideas.

Anti-Semitism is, of course, only one form of group prejudice, as is race prejudice in general.[14] Other kinds of group prejudice, such as religious prejudices, national prejudices, sex prejudices, class prejudices, and the like, as has already been pointed out, are merely special forms of the same general phenomenon of group prejudice. As soon as one becomes aware of group membership and identifies oneself with that group the ground is laid for the development of group prejudice in some particular form. The prejudice may be of the most benign kind and socially not make for the least disharmony. On the other hand, it may develop under certain conditions in so disoperatively strong a manner as to threaten the very existence of the society in which it appears. This happens to be the case in the United States as well as in some other lands. Awareness of this fact, together with our understanding of the psychodynamics of the development of such forms of behavior, suggests the immediate necessity of reconsidering our processes of socializing children in relation to the health of the social structure as a whole. Race prejudice is at its strongest where social maturity is at its weakest.

The teaching of the facts about race or race prejudice will not be adequate to solve the problem. The roots of prejudice are woven into the very psychic structure of the individual, and unless we attend to the soil from which they draw nourishment it will not help either the resulting plant or ourselves if we attempt to cure its sickness by lopping off the ailing leaves. The soil in which race prejudice grows is the social experience to which the developing individual is exposed, and it is to this that we must attend if we are ever to be delivered from the sickness which is race. As Bettelheim and Janowitz put it, "It seems reasonable to assume that as long as anxiety and insecurity persist as a root of intolerance, the effort to dispel stereotyped thinking or feelings of ethnic hostility by rational propaganda is at best a half-measure. On an individual level only greater personal integration combined with social and economic security seems to offer hope for better inter-ethnic relations."[15] These authors point out that on the social level a change of climate is necessary. Their subjects who accepted social controls and were more tolerant of other minorities were also less tolerant of the Black, because discrimination against blacks is more commonly condoned, both publicly and privately. They suggest, therefore, that this should lead, among other things, to additional efforts to change social practices in ways that will tangibly demonstrate that ethnic discrimination is contrary to the mores of society.

MacCrone, in a valuable study of the psychology and psychopathology of race prejudice in South Africa, has written that "the extra-individual conflicts between the two racial groups are but the intra-individual conflicts within the mind writ large, and until the latter are removed, reduced, or modified, they must continue to exercise their baleful influence upon the race relations and the race contacts of white and Black."[16]

It is these intra-individual conflicts, the psychological factor, the deep, early conditioned motive forces represented by the aggressiveness which is produced in so many human beings and is continually being augmented by the frustrations of adolescent and adult life, that must receive more attention than they have in the past. It is this aggressiveness that renders so easily possible the usual emotional and irrational development of race prejudice. A rational society must reckon with this, for since a certain amount of frustration is inevitable—and even desirable—in the development of the individual and a certain amount of aggressiveness is inevitably produced by some social controls, and by some is even considered a necessary part of the equipment of most human beings, the task of an intelligent society is clear.

At the adult levels society must provide outlets for individual aggressiveness that will benefit both to him or her, and by extension, society. Outlets for aggression which result in social friction and in the destruction of good relations between human beings must be avoided.

Frustrations in the early and subsequent development of the individual must be reduced to a minimum, and aggressiveness always directed toward ends of constructive value. But it is not through appeals to reason that the race problem will be solved, but by the provision of a healthy environment and a loving socialization of the child that will grow and develop into a warm, loving, human being. Indeed, as the writers of *The Authoritarian Personality* conclude, all that is really necessary is that children be genuinely loved and treated as human beings.[17] These are key words, the key to the solution of humanity's problems. But how are they to be made into living realities in a society so terribly disorganized as ours? How are we to learn to love in a cold climate, in which there is an absence of love behind the show of love? We shall attempt some answers in our final chapter.

The findings revealed in the studies of *The Authoritarian Personality* have been challenged as probably not applying to all classes of society. The subjects of that study were largely middle class. The findings and conclusions as a whole, however, have been supported by the independent studies of other investigators.[18]

A study by McCord, McCord, and Howard, based on interviews, in 1948, with 48 males aged 20 years of lower-class origin revealed that the apparently tolerant did not differ from the bigoted members of this small sample.[19] As Allport[20] and others have pointed out, not all prejudice is necessarily related to the personality as a whole, some prejudices are conformative or mildly ethnocentric. And as McDill has shown, in a study of 146 female and 120 male white non-Jewish adults in Nashville, Tennessee, anomie, the collapse of social stability, and authoritarian influences are equally important in accounting for intolerant attitudes toward minority groups.[21] The McCords and Howard incline to the belief that prejudice in the lower classes is based on a generally stereotyped culture, which is not related to specific personality needs or to unique familial environments. Prejudice in the lower classes appears to be the result of adult rather than childhood experiences, according to these investigators.

If this hypothesis is correct, and it would certainly appear to be so in many cases, then improvement in economic and educational opportunities and other social conditions would offer some hope of reducing the quantum of what we call bigotry.

Koenig and King, in a study of students on a coeducational campus in the Southwest, found that "Cognitively simple persons tend to overlook nuances and to classify experience into a few, inclusive categories. Unable to perceive the behaviors of others accurately, they project their own characteristics (including attitudes) onto others. This tendency is related to stereotyping and to intolerance or prejudice."[22] Such findings have been many times independently confirmed by other investigators.

Martin, in a study designed to determine whether some of the findings of *The Authoritarian Personality* would also obtain in a randomly selected adult sample drawn from a balanced urban community, Indianapolis, secured results which corroborated the California studies strikingly. The study involved visits to 668 households and preliminary interviews with 429 persons. The final study was reduced to 41 tolerant and 49 prejudiced individuals. Martin's well-described findings in the strongly prejudiced and strongly tolerant syndromes will be given here at some length.

In general, the strongly prejudiced person presents the following pattern or syndrome of traits and characteristics: he tends to be quite ethnocentric; he makes sharp distinctions between his in-groups and out-groups; he is a "social reductionist," in that his reference groups reflect an exclusive rather than an inclusive emphasis; he is unlikely to identify with "humanity," but prefers more exclusive levels of identification; he thrives on selective membership with himself on the "inside." Such an attitude provides a sustaining and compensating mechanism for psychological and social insecurity. Although typically obscure himself, he borrows prestige from his race, nation, whatever.

The prejudiced person tends to be suspicious, distrustful and extrapunitive. He attributes ulterior motives to blacks and other out-group members. The race problem is due to blacks, and if their lot is not to their liking then it is because they are at fault. He is afraid of contact with minority group members, and foresees dire consequences of intergroup interaction. Segregation is the political-social policy he urges and defends because he "knows" that blacks and whites cannot live peacefully together. He views the world as an arena of conflict, involving power struggles and competition among individuals and groups. Other people are not to be trusted in general, because everyone is seeking to maximize his own advantage at the expense of others. He prides himself on his "realism" and tends to regard "idealistic" people as naive and even dangerous, and he favors the "practical" over the "theoretical."

The strongly prejudiced person seeks certainty through the use of dichotomized absolutes. He does not think in relative terms; he keeps his fear of doubt repressed by the dogmatism he substitutes for it. He therefore views blacks and whites as being essentially and markedly different; a person is either good or evil, and a statement is either true or false.

The strongly prejudiced person favors obedience and submission to authority. This trait is congruent with his zeal for definiteness and his basic distrust of the impulses and motives of other people. He prefers order, discipline, and conformity in the social environment. He is likely to be conservative in his social attitudes and interests, and is often a vigorous supporter, at the verbal level, of conventional morality. He is moralistic, but distinctly unsentimental. Such a person evidently represses much and engages in considerable projection, particularly in connection with the matter of conventional moral norms and their violation.

The strongly prejudiced person also tends to be poorly endowed with imagination, humanitarianism, creativeness, and compassion. He tends to be fatalistic; he is pessimistic about the scientific study of human behavior. Superstition has a considerable appeal to him, as do the magical, the mystical, and the mysterious.

Compared with the tolerant type he tends to be more emotional and less rational, and he is more moralistic rather than ethical (in terms of the connotations of these two words). The strongly prejudiced individual is typically nonintellectual and frequently anti-intellectual; he is very often dogmatic in expression and angers easily when he meets with disagreement. He is likely to interpret intellectual disagreement as a personal affront.

In religion the bigot subscribes to the more fundamentalist, dogmatic, irrational, and authoritarian doctrines and beliefs. He is less likely to concur with ideals and values relating to brotherhood, basic humanity, and unselfish deeds. He is opposed to "modernism," and would appear to resent having to donate money to his religious group.

In terms of social characteristics, the prejudiced individual has less formal education, a lower occupational level, and perhaps a smaller circle of friends than the tolerant type, even though the latter may often have a lower income.

In general the very tolerant, or relatively unprejudiced individual presents the following pattern or syndrome of traits and characteristics: his tolerance tends to be general with respect to people; perhaps the only exception is his intolerance of persons who are bigoted. A conspicuous trait is his trust of other people. The tolerant individual is inclined to look for the best in people; he gives them the "benefit of the doubt." He tends to judge individuals as individuals, and rejects the practice of group stereotyping. He expects other people to be friendly, fair, and cooperative, and he is likely to suspend his judgment of others beyond the first impression.

The tolerant individual apparently feels reasonably secure, or at least he is not prone to exaggerate actual threats from other people. He may be neurotic but he is rarely paranoid. He is inclined to be rational, humanitarian, liberal in social attitudes, and intropunitive.

The tolerant individual is also characterized by a high degree of empathic ability, and is much more likely to be sympathetic and compassionate than the strongly prejudiced person. He is "sensitive" as distinct from being "tough"; he is opposed to cruelty, violence, and harsh discipline where the strongly prejudiced person would be likely to condone it. Whereas the bigoted male is often ultra-masculine (to the point of having almost no compassion), the tolerant male seemingly has no obsessive need to "prove" his masculinity, at least he is seldom "swaggering and arrogant" in his maleness.

The tolerant type is able to perceive variation accurately and realistically; thus he is less impelled to resort to stereotyping and dogmatism. He apparently realizes and recognizes that each individual is unique (though not radically different from other individuals), and that good and evil, shortness and tallness, darkness and lightness, stupidity and intelligence, are all relative concepts. He has no obsessive fear of being mistaken or wrong, he is willing to admit his own shortcomings and weaknesses.

The tolerant personality is not a highly rigid one. He is more likely to be witty and have a highly developed sense of humor than the bigot. For example, the tolerant person is capable of engaging in self-ridicule, whereas the image of a grim and rigidly serious expression is more plausibly associated with the bigot.

The tolerant individual is typically interested in and optimistic about the improvement of human society. He is likely to stress cooperation as against competition, conciliation rather than confrontation, in achieving human progress. He is often idealistic and utopian, and interested in intellectual matters. Likewise, the tolerant person values creative activities and is not so prone to stress the "practical" over the "theoretical." The tolerant type is much less of a "social reductionist." It is "humanity" that interests him. Being a member of an "exclusive" group has a weak appeal for him.

The unprejudiced person tends to be "kindhearted," if not "softhearted"; he is typically in sympathy with the underdog, and is not characterized by the "threat-competition orientation" so evident in highly intolerant people. This is readily observable in the religious values and beliefs of tolerance; there is an emphasis upon brotherhood, humanitarianism, charity, reason, and tolerance of personal deviation. Similarly, he is likely to be altruistic and somewhat sentimental, and be more appreciative of the aesthetic, as compared with the strongly prejudiced person.

Such a personality is more concerned with serving than leading; is likely to be relatively autonomous; does not have a strong need for dominance; is rarely ever obsessively conformist; and dislikes both subordination and superordination of any appreciable degree. He tends to view his social interaction and social relationships as possibilities for expression, mutual assistance, affective response, and so on, rather than as opportunities for exploitation and manipulation.

Socially speaking, the relatively unprejudiced person is almost certain to have more formal education than the highly intolerant person, and his occupational status is usually higher. Although it is not borne out by the reports of the subjects in this study, the investigators are of the opinion that the tolerant type usually experiences a childhood family environment characterized by an absence of harsh discipline and authoritarian parental control.

The child-rearing attitudes of the strongly prejudiced subjects certainly suggest that authoritarian discipline is actually applied by such parents, and one would assume that their offspring would show the effects of this conditioning in their intergroup attitudes. It is surmised that the tolerant individual would usually come from a more relaxed, secure, and lenient home environment, and would experience more affection and less rejection and hostility from parents than the highly intolerant individual.[23]

Race Prejudice and Classified Hostilities

Race prejudice in many cases may be regarded as one of a number of classified hostilities that are not a result of an immediate interpersonal relationship, but which arise out of the individual's need to fit his hostility into the dynamic framework of his personality structure, altogether apart from the presence of a direct and immediate stimulus situation.

In one very significant sense race prejudice arises from the individual's failure to make use of his own potentialities, particularly his powers to relate himself to other beings, to establish human ties. The failure to establish human ties on the basis of the integrity of the individuality of the self allows only one alternative—the adoption of attitudes which seek to justify to himself this failure. Race prejudice or the adoption of classified hostilities is one of the methods of trying to satisfy or complete the constellation of needs springing from this failure.

If the constellation of needs in itself arises from a failure to make use of one's powers to love, then there can be no satisfactory solution of the problem in any real sense. For the solution, as offered by rationalizing that there is no basis in reality to love, only succeeds in further stifling this potentiality.

Humans are born social beings who can reach their full development only through interaction with their fellows. The denial at any point of this social bond between humans brings with it disintegration. A major symptom of this denial is race prejudice. What is observed in this connection is not the failure to develop into that which the individual, the person, in the utmost sense, potentially is, but rather the failure to carry on the process of development. Race prejudice functions primarily as a barrier to the further development of the person, and ultimately a repudiation of humanity.

What is the alternative to holding such prejudices or rationalizations? What does it mean to the person to give up these rationalizations? In brief, what is the danger which the individual must face if he were to give up these prejudices? That there is a danger is apparent, otherwise people would not cling to ideas, however early formed and strongly held, that are demonstrably unsound.

All the evidence of research and inquiry indicates that the danger seems to lie in the fact that if rationalizations are perceived for what they are and abandoned, the individual faces the necessity of taking his own life seriously, and the essentiality of forming meaningful human relations on the basis of his personal integrity is challenged. He must give up the primary dependent ties. He is forced to see himself as an individual entity, and not as a part of another person either in the capacity of master or subject, ruler or ruled. He must be willing to bear the pain of isolation that is concomitant with mature independence.[24] He must recognize his actual position in the universe, feel his aloneness, and at the same time his power to overcome this through love on the basis of his own integrity.

The inability to give up the primary ties is crucial—the ties to the nurturing authority. Often people rationalize that they have given up what could be called their incestuous ties, when a closer examination will reveal that what they have done has been to transfer these ties to a more acceptable object. An interesting fact here is that when group affiliations are of this nature, that is, a source of power for the individual ("I am a member of this strong group"), we find that accompanying this group attachment is a complementary feeling of out-group hostility. That is to say, the stronger and more permanent the individual's attachment to the particular group, the stronger does his out-group hostility tend to be.

This particular consequence of group allegiances is one of the "services" the group performs for the person. If the group functions primarily as a transferred source of strength for the individual, a place of worship of power, this consequence will almost always follow. If, on the other hand, the group serves a cooperative function, if the individual on the basis of his integrity can lend support to efforts that cannot be accomplished on a personal basis, then the consequence of outgroup hostility is not a necessary result of such group relationships. It is evident that this problem can be manipulated in part by manipulation of the groups. In working with boys' clubs and children's groups, some of the hostility which is the side effect of in-group allegiance can be eliminated by reducing the strength of that allegiance. This can be done by making the groups less permanent and the membership more flexible.[25]

However, it is further clear that it is not the group as such which generates the out-group hostility, but rather the private and personal use to which the group is put by the persons constituting it. In a sense what develops is a vicious circle. If the group in some (usually disguised) way serves the person as a primary source of strength, a place where he can transplant his umbilical cord, where he can deny his individuality, then it becomes progressively necessary to develop the power of the group, but not his own strength. Since the group is a direct source of security, and since he cannot bear to have his security threatened, then progressively more and more effort must be supplied to this source of strength. But what happens is that the individual only more firmly binds himself to the nourishing mother. More and more it becomes clear to him that it is his position in the group that is of importance, and not his position in terms of his responsibility to himself. The greater the crippling of his own individualization, the greater the need to cripple it until at last we find men ready blindly to negate their own lives or even life in general in their efforts to protect and revere this source of strength.

The in-group has certain characteristics, too; it must be just that, an in-group. Its membership must be restricted and of relative permanency. For if its membership should be accessible to all (in actuality, not pretense), and if that goal were reached, this group could no longer serve as a source of strength. This kind of strength involves "power over" and there would no longer be any scapegoat to exercise this "power over."

In contrast to this vicious circle is the kind of group relationship where the effort is applied to achieving "power of"—power of thought, power of understanding, power of growth. The individual's relation to the group is one where his individuality is affirmed by his particular contribution to the group effort. Though the group here is also a source of power for the individual, it is a power that affirms life and his own identity. It is an affirmative strength that does not seek the negation of life itself, but rather the enhancement and growth of those conditions which lead to the fullest development of the individual's unique identity.[26]

The satisfactions yielded by and the epidemiology of hostility are interconnected phenomena. Thorne has investigated the epidemiology of hostility through family studies. He has shown that acute and chronic frustration-hostility states tend to be socially transmissible in epidemic form, because of the contagious, inescapable nature of the emotions involved. It is almost impossible to avoid the influence of a hateful person in one's environment, particularly when such a person can exercise great personal power to frustrate by control over money, work, family discipline, and the like. Such built-up hostilities have a contagious quality, and a tendency toward chain reactions. A further result of such hostilities is the building up of mutually suspicious paranoid attitudes.[27]

Attitudes of Mind

The problem of race in our society is social, and not biological in any but a vague technical tense.[28] Fairness toward other groups of persons or a person is a matter of simple human decency; and decency is an attitude of mind, for the most part culturally conditioned. Whether ethnic groups or castes are biologically equal is an utterly irrelevant consideration where fair-mindedness is concerned. In any event, it is not a matter of biological equality that is involved, but political and social equality. Whatever differences exist between peoples and however they may have been determined, the willingness to understand those differences and to act upon them sympathetically ought to increase in proportion to the magnitude of the differences believed to exist between ourselves and others. As Professor E. G. Conklin has so well put it:

> To the naturalist the differences between human races, subraces, and individuals are small indeed as compared with their manifold resemblances. Biology and the Bible agree that 'God hath made of one blood all nations of men.' Our common traits and origin and fate, our common hopes and fears, joys and sorrows, would call forth our common sympathy with all mankind, if it were not for the lessons of hate which have been cultivated and instilled by selfish and unscrupulous persons and social groups. These racial antagonisms are not the results of inexorable nature, nor of inherited instincts, but of deliberate education and cultivation.[29]

The plea for fairness in dealing with ethnic groups not our own is usually phrased in terms of "tolerance." But if we are to make progress in ethnic relations, it is desirable to recognize that tolerance is not good enough, for tolerance defines an attitude which constitutes a somewhat reluctant admission of the necessity of enduring that which we must bear, the presence of those whom we do not like. A New York high-school girl put the whole matter in a nutshell. "Tolerance," she said, "is when you put up with certain people but you don't like to have them around anyhow." That, it is to be feared, is the general nature of tolerance, the hand-washing indifference of the "superior" person who patronizingly condescends to ensure the co-existence of "inferior" beings on condition that they keep their "proper" distance. Tolerance is the attitude of mind of those who consider themselves not only different but superior. It implies an attitude toward different ethnic or minority groups, not of understanding, not of acceptance, not of recognition of human equality, but of recognition of differences which one must suffer—generally, not too gladly. We must be more than tolerant; we must be fair.

Tolerance is the best one can hope from bigots; fairness is the attitude of mind we look for in decent, humane people. By fairness, where ethnic relations are concerned, is meant the attitude of mind which takes it for granted, there being no actual evidence to the contrary, that for all their individual differences no human being is really superior to another by virtue of his group affiliation, and that, given the necessary opportunities, it is probable that the average person of any one group is capable of doing at least as well as the average individual of the culturally most advanced group. It is more than merely being willing to concede that the *others* are not inferior to us; it is readiness to accept the verdict that we are not superior to the *others*. One is not called upon to be magnanimous, still less is one called upon to condemn or condone, but one is called upon to attempt to be fair—to understand and then to act upon that understanding.[30] Until such an attitude of mind becomes part of the equipment of every individual, no amount of instruction in the facts concerning the biology of race will ever succeed in eliminating race prejudices.

Race prejudice is ultimately merely the effect of an inadequately developed personality—a personality that has failed to learn any of the simple fundamental facts concerning the nature of human nature and in the light of other human understanding to apply it not only to others, but also to oneself. A personality that has not achieved this is simply reacting to frustration by belaboring the object which it imagines has in some way been the cause of its frustration; it is a personality that is still projecting the blame on others for errors for which it alone is responsible. It is a personality that contrasts sharply with the mature personality which tries to understand and does not seek to wash its hands of its fellows by condemning or condoning their conduct and thus dismissing them from mind. The mature personality does not automatically resort to the infliction of punishment because it has been frustrated, but attempts to understand the cause of its frustration and then, in the light of that understanding, so to act that frustrations will not again be produced. He does not try to escape the exercise of understanding by emotionally letting off steam. He accepts responsibility for his own acts and is moved by the injustice of the acts of others to attempt to remedy the conditions which give rise to such conditions. He understands that no one's father is really bigger than anyone else's father, and that to act in a superior manner is merely an immature way of asserting one's desire to feel important, to feel that one amounts to something. He realizes that, on the other hand, the desire to feel that one belongs with all humankind and not above or below any group, to feel that one is of them and belongs with them, is the most satisfying and efficient way of living and thinking. He not only insists upon the right of everyone to be different, but rejoices in most of those differences and is not unsympathetically indifferent to those which he may dislike, that there are no strangers, only friends we have not yet met. He understands that if people are characterized by likenesses and differences, it is no argument against the likenesses to dwell on the differences, or that difference in any way implies inequality. He realizes that diversity is not only the salt of life but also the true basis of collective achievement, and he does everything in his power to further the purposes of that collective achievement.[31]

True culture has been defined as the ability to appreciate the other person. While this particular ability has many sources, it is generally derived from varied, sympathetic, and understanding contacts between people who differ from each other in several respects.[32]

If race prejudice is ever to be eliminated, society must assume the task of educating the individual—not so much in the facts of race as in the processes which lead to the development of a completely integrated healthy human being—one who is able to love, to work, to play, and to think critically. The solution here, as in so much else, lies in education; education for humanity first and with regard to the facts afterward. For of what use are facts unless they are intelligently understood and humanely used?

Suppose for a moment that significant differences did exist between different peoples which rendered one, in general, superior to the other; a reasonably developed human being would hardly consider such differences sufficient reason for withholding opportunities for social and cultural development from such groups. On the contrary, such a person would be the more anxious to provide them with such opportunities. Undeveloped personalities operate in the opposite manner and, creating most of the differences they condemn, proceed to intensify those differences by making it increasingly more difficult for the groups thus treated to avoid or overcome them.

Fromm writes:

> The implicit assumption underlying much reactionary thinking is that equality presupposes absence of difference between persons or social groups. Since obviously such differences exist with regard to practically everything that matters in life, their conclusion is that there can be no equality. When the liberals conversely are moved to deny the fact of great differences in mental and physical gifts and favorable or unfavorable accidental personality conditions, they only help their adversaries to appear right in the eyes of the common man. The concept of equality as it has developed in Judaeo-Christian and in modern progressive tradition means that all men are equal in such basic human capacities as those making for the enjoyment of freedom and happiness. It means, furthermore, that as a political consequence of this basic equality no man shall be made the means to the ends of another group. Each man is a universe for himself and is only his own purpose. His goal is the realization of his being, including those very peculiarities which are characteristic of him and which make him different from others. Thus, equality is the basis for the full development of difference, and it results in the development of individuality."[33]

It is or should be axiomatic that the natural inequality of endowment that exists between all human beings does not render equality of opportunity a contemptible principle. It is in our differences that our richness lies, that because you are different you are precious to me.[34]

There exist no really separative or divisive biological differences between ethnic groups; there are differences only between persons. In every group there will be found a large range of differences in the native endowment of its members, some individuals may be less capable than others in the realizable potentials of intelligence, in vigor, or in beauty. Such differences may, by some, be made the pretext for heaping contumely and humiliation upon those who are less fortunately endowed than their fellows; but it would be scarcely human to do so, and less than decent.

Furthermore, the common practice of attributing to individuals traits derived statistically from population studies is as deplorable as it is absurd. The individual is a unique entity and should never be regarded as someone describable as a statistical constant. The reverse practice is equally reprehensible, of attributing to a whole group or population traits, whether physical or psychological, that are seen in an individual.

The form of the mind and body are so dependent upon social conditions that when the latter are unequal for different groups, little or no inference can be drawn as to the mental and physical potentialities of these groups. As the great American anthropologist Alfred Louis Kroeber wrote many years ago, "Most ethnologists, at any rate, are convinced that the overwhelming mass of historical and miscalled racial facts that are now attributed to obscure organic causes or at most are in dispute, will ultimately be viewed by everyone as social and as best intelligible in their social relations."[35]

Race prejudice is a pigment of the imagination. It begins in the minds of men, but it doesn't end there. Until we have succeeded in producing emotionally secure, mature human beings, instead of emotionally insecure, immature human beings, until we have succeeded, by means of the appropriate educational methods,[36] in producing that cultivation of mind which renders nothing that is human alien to it, the race problem will never be completely solved. The means by which that problem may to some extent be ameliorated have already been indicated, and will be further discussed later. There is one more aspect of the psychology of race prejudice to which I should like to draw attention, that is, the process of rationalization, the process of finding reasons to justify emotionally held, essentially irrational beliefs, and the construction of one's "logic" to fit one's rationalizations.

We saw in Chapter 1 by what means race prejudice originally came into existence in the United States; that is, in large part as the stratagem by means of which the proslavery party attempted to overcome the arguments of the abolitionists that the slaves were men and brothers and should be free. The upholders of slavery avidly sought reasons with which to justify their interest in maintaining that institution, and they brought those reasons forward in force and from all sorts of sources, including the Bible. But no matter from what source they drew their arguments, they were nothing but the most patently fallacious.

Since race prejudice invariably rests on false premises, for the most part emotional in origin, it is not surprising to find that it is practically always rationalized. As Professor W. O. Brown pointed out:

> The rationalization is a moral defense. And the rationalizer is a moralist. The rationalization, in the nature of the case, secures the believer in his illusion of moral integrity. The morality of the rationalization is perhaps intensified by the fact that it represents an effort to make that which is frequently vicious, sordid, and inhumane rational, idealistic, and humane. The semi-awareness of the real nature of the attitude being rationalized intensifies the solemnity with which the rationalization is formulated. Securing moral values the rationalization naturally partakes of a moral quality. This fact explains, in part, perhaps, the deadly seriousness of the devotee of the rationalization. Its value lies in the fact that it removes the moral stigma attached to race prejudice, elevating this prejudice into a justified reaction.[37]

Practically every one of the arguments used by the racists to prove the inferiority of this or that race was not so long ago used by the antifeminists to prove the inferiority of that "lower race," the female of the species. In the case of these sexual prejudices one generation has suffered to show how completely unfounded they were.[38] It need not take longer to do the same for race prejudice. Since this subject provides an instructive and pertinently parallel case history, we shall devote the next chapter to its discussion.

The rationalization is not, of course, regarded as the expression of prejudice, but rather as an explanation of one's behavior—the reason for it. Few rationalizers are aware of the fact that their reasons are simply devices for concealing the real sources of their antipathies, many of which may be quite unconscious.[39] They fail to understand that thought is a means both of concealing and of revealing feelings and that a conviction in the rationality of one's conduct may signify little more than a supreme ability at self-deception. As Professor Brown remarks, "the rationalization is not regarded as cloaking antagonism, but is regarded as a serious interpretation of conduct. No good rationalizer believes that he is prejudiced." Hence, the stronger the reasons we hold for any belief the more advisable it is to inquire into the soundness of the supports upon which such beliefs rest. This is especially true when the beliefs are as strongly held as they are in connection with race prejudice. The prejudiced individual, constellating ahead of experience, is usually a conformist who worships institutions.

He cannot exist without his prejudices. He fashions an island of security for himself and clings to it. Any exceptions to his views or beliefs are regarded by him as nonrepresentative and dismissible, for they do not conform to his encrusted system of expectations. What is more, they make him uncomfortable and anxious. They must therefore be suppressed. As Oliver Wendell Holmes remarked, "The mind of a bigot may be compared to the pupil of the eye; the more light you pour on it the more it contracts."

When people have no moral justification for their beliefs or their conduct, they will invent them. Intelligence and humanity call for a tentative attitude, "for an attitude subject to change, 'good for this day only': prejudice is lack of plasticity. A tentative attitude decreases prejudice, for it replaces absolute with relative values... breadth of understanding decreases prejudice."[40] Seen through the filter of prejudice reality becomes distorted.

> Through the distorting glass of Prejudice
> All nature seems awry, and but its own
> Wide-warped creations straight; but Reason's eye
> Beholds in every line of nature—truth,
> Immortal truth, and sees a God in all.

Notes

1. Frank Fremont-Smith, "The Physiological Basis of Aggression," *Child Study* 15 (1938): 1–8, and "The Influence of Emotional Factors upon Physiological and Pathological Processes," *Bulletin of the New York Academy of Medicine* 15 (1939): 560–69; Hudson Jost, "Some Physiological Changes During Frustration," *Child Development* 12 (1941): 9–15; Melvin De Fleur and Frank R. Westie, "The Interpretation of Interracial Situations," *Social Forces* 38 (1959): 17–23, who found that autonomic physiological responses below the threshold of awareness indicated the degree of involvement; Roger N. Johnson, *Aggression in Man and Animals;* B. E. Eleftheriou and J. P. Scott, The *Physiology of Aggression and Defeat;* Richard E. Whalen, ed., *The Neurophysiology of Aggression* (New York: Plenum Press, 1974); Ashley Montagu, *The Nature of Human Aggression* (New York: Oxford University Press, 1976); Ashley Montagu, ed., *Learning Non-Aggression* (New York: Oxford University Press, 1978); Rae Sherwood, *The Psychodynamics of Race: Vicious and Benign Spirals* (Atlantic Highlands, NJ: Humanities Press, 1980); Peter Watson, ed., *Psychology and Race* (Chicago: Aldine, 1974); Morris Rosenberg and Ralph H. Turner, *Social Psychology: Sociological Perspectives* (New York: Basic Books, 1981).

2. Joel Kovel, *White Racism: A Psychohistory* (New York: Pantheon Books, 1970); Frank H. Tucker, *The White Conscience* (New York: Frederick Ungar, 1968); Gordon Allport, *The Nature of Prejudice* (Cambridge: Addison-Wesley, 1953); Isidore Pushkin and Thelma Veness, "The Development of Racial Awareness and Prejudice in Children," in *Psychology and Race,* ed. Peter Watson (Chicago: Aldine, 1974); Jean L. Briggs, "The Origins of Nonviolence: Aggression in Two Canadian Eskimo

Groups," in *The Psychoanalytic Study of Society,* vol. 6, eds. Warner Muensterberger and Aaron H. Esman (New York: International Universities Press, 1975), 134–203; Charles C. Hughes, *Eskimo Boyhood* (Lexington: University of Kentucky Press, 1974); Donald L. Horowitz, *Ethnic Groups in Conflict* (Berkeley: University of California Press, 1985); Christopher Bagley and Gajendra K. Verma, *Racial Prejudice: The Individual and Society* (Westmead, England: Saxon House, 1979); George B. de Huszar, ed., *Anatomy of Racial Intolerance* (New York: The H.W. Wilson Co., 1946); Hubert M. Blalock, Jr., *Toward a Theory of Minority Group Relations* (New York: John Wiley, 1967); Michel Barkun, *Religion and the Racist Right: The Origins of the Christian Identity Movement* (Chapel Hill: University of North Carolina Press, 1994); John L. Davidio and Samuel Gaertner, eds., *Prejudice, Discrimination, and Racism* (Orlando: Academic Press, 1986); V. Reynolds, Vincent S. E. Flager, and Ian Vine, *The Sociology of Ethnocentrism* (London: Croom Helm, 1987); Daniela Gioseffi, *On Prejudice: A Global Perspective* (New York: Anchor Books, 1993); Gustavus Myers, *History of Bigotry in the United States* (New York: Random House, 1943); Louis S. Snyder, *German Nationalism: The Tragedy of a People* (Harrisburg, PA: Stackpoole 1952).

3. T. W. Adorno et al., *The Authoritarian Personality* (New York: Harper, 1950).

4. For interesting treatments of this view see John Dollard et al., *Frustration and Aggression* (New York: Yale University Press, 1939); E. F. M. Durbin and John Bowlby, *Personal Aggressiveness and War* (New York: Columbia University Press, 1939); Lauretta Bender, *Aggression, Hostility, and Anxiety in Children* (Springfield, IL: Thomas); Lydia Jackson, *Aggression and Its Interpretation* (London: Metheun, 1954); Kurt Lewin, *Resolving Social Conflicts* (New York: Harper, 1948); Norman Maier, *Frustration* (Ann Arbor: University of Michigan Press, 1961); J. P. Scott, *Aggression* (Chicago: University of Chicago Press, 1958); Arnold Buss, *The Psychology of Aggression* (New York: Wiley, 1961); Leonard Berkowitz, *Aggression: A Social Psychological Analysis* (New York: McGraw Hill, 1962); Bruno Bettelheim and Morris Janowitz, *Social Change and Prejudice* (New York: Free Press, 1964); Hubert M. Blalock, Jr., *Toward a Theory of Minority-Group Relations* (New York: Capricorn Books, 1970); Donald L. Horowitz, *Ethnic Groups in Conflict* (Berkeley: University of California Press, 1985)); Alice Miller, *Prisoners of Childhood* (New York: Basic Books, 1981); Alice Miller, *For Your Own Good: Hidden Cruelty in Child-Rearing and the Roots of Violence* (New York: Farrar Straus, 1983); Alice Miller, *Thou Shalt Not Be Aware: Society's Betrayal of the Child* (New York: Farrar Straus, 1984); Alice Miller, *The Untouched Key* (New York: Doubleday, 1988); Ashley Montagu, *Nature of Human Aggression;* John E. Williams and J. Kenneth Morland, *Race, Color, and the Young Child* (Chapel Hill: University of North Carolina Press, 1976).

5. H. Hartmann, E. Kris, and M. Lowenstein, "Notes on the Theory of Aggression," *The Psychoanalytic Study of the Child* 3–4 (1949): 9–36.

6. Else Frenkel-Brunswik and R. Nevitt Sanford, "Some Personality Factors in Anti-Semitism," *Journal of Psychology* 20 (1945): 271–91.

7. Ibid., 289.

8. Ibid., 290. See also Bruno Bettelheim and Morris Janowitz, *Dynamics of Prejudice* (New York: Harper, 1950), 170, and Caleb Gattegno, *What We Owe Children* (New York: Avon Books, 1971).

9. See T. W. Adorno et al., *The Authoritarian Personality* (New York: Harper, 1950).

10. Nathan W. Ackerman and Marie Jahoda, "Toward a Dynamic Interpretation of Anti-Semitic Attitudes," *American Journal of Orthopsychiatry* 18 (1948): 168.

11. Ibid., 171.

12. N. Ackerman, and M. Jahoda, "Anti-Semitic Motivation in a Psychopathic Personality," *Psychoanalytic Review* 34 (1947): 76–101.

13. Ackerman and Jahoda, "Dynamic Interpretation" 173.

14. For the material on antisemitism see N. Ackerman and M. Jahoda, "The Dynamic Basis of Anti-Semitic Attitudes," *Psychoanalytic Quarterly* 17 (1948): 240–60; Detlev Peukert *Germany: Conformity, Opposition, and Racism in Everyday Life* (New Haven: Yale University Press, 1987); Nathan W. Ackerman and Marie Jahoda, *Anti-Semitism and Emotional Disorder* (New York: Harper, 1950); Adorno et al. *Authoritarian Personality;* Jean Amery, *At the Mind's Limits: Contemplations by a Survivor on Auschwitz and its Realities* (Bloomington: Indiana University Press, 1966); Hannah Arendt, *The Jew as Pariah: Jewish Identity and Politics in the Modern Age* (New York: Grove Press, 1978); Salo W. Baron, *The Russian Jew Under Tsars and Soviets* (New York: Macmillan, 1976); Ratner Baum, *The Holocaust and the German Elite* (London: Croom Heim, 1981); N. C. Belth, ed., *Patterns of Discrimination Against Jews* (New York: Anti-Defamation League of B'nai B'rith, 1958); Bettelheim and Janowitz, *Dynamics of Prejudice;* Morton Borden, *Jews, Turks, and Infidels* (Chapel Hill: University of North Carolina Press, 1984); Hamida Bosmajian, *Metaphors of Evil: Contemporary German Literature and the Shadow of Nazism* (Iowa City: University of Iowa Press, 1979); Randolph L. Braham, ed., *The Origins of the Holocaust: Christian Anti-Semitism,* (New York: Columbia University Press, 1986); Joel Carmichael, *The Satanizing of the Jews* (New York: Fromm International, 1989); Davidio and Gaertner, eds., *Prejudice, Discrimination, and Racism;* Alan Davies, *Infected Christianity: A Study of Modern Racism,* (Kingston & Montreal: McGill-Queen's University Press 1988); Alan Davies, ed., *Antisemitism and The Foundations of Christianity* (Mahwah, NJ: Paulist Press, 1979); de Huszar, *Racial Intolerance;* Leonard Dinnerstein, *America and the Survivors of the Holocaust* (New York: Columbia University Press, 1982); Leonard Dinnerstein, *Anti-Semitism in America* (New York: Oxford University Press 1994); Alan Edelstein, *An Unacknowledged Harmony—Philo-Semitism and the Survival of European Jewry* (Westport, CT: Greenwood Press, 1982); Todd M. Endelman, *The Jews of Georgian England 1714–1830: Tradition and Change in a Liberal Society* (Philadelphia: The Jewish Publication Society of America, 1979); Benjamin R. Epstein and Arnold Forster, *Some of My Best Friends . . .* (New York: Farrar, Straus, & Cudahy, 1962); Helen Fein, *Accounting for Genocide: National Responses and Jewish Victimization During the Holocaust* (New York: Free Press, 1979); Louis Finkelstein, ed., *The Jews: Their History, Culture, and Religion,* 2 vols. (New York: Harper, 1949); Saul Friediander, *Nazi Germany and the Jews, vol. 1: The Years of Persecution, 1933–1939* (New York: Harper-Collins, 1997); Otto Friedrich, *Before the Deluge: A Portrait of Berlin in the 1920's* (New York: Harper & Row, 1960); John G. Gager, *The Origins of Anti-Semitism: Attitudes Toward Judaism in Pagan and Christian Antiquity* (New York: Oxford University Press, 1983); Daniela Gioseffi, *On Prejudice: A Global Perspective* (New York: Anchor Books, 1993); Benjamin Ginsberg, *The Fatal Embrace: Jews and the State* (Chicago: University of Chicago Press, 1993); Bernard Glassman, *Anti-Semitic Stereotypes Without Jews: Images of the Jews in England 1290–1700* (Detroit: Wayne University Press, 1975); Michel Goldberg, *Namesake* (New Haven: Yale University Press, 1982); Daniel J. Goldhagen, *Hitler's*

Willing Executioners: Ordinary Germans and the Holocaust (New York: Alfred A. Knopf, 1996); Isacque Graeber and Steuart Britt, eds., *Jews in a Gentile World* (New York: Macmillan, 1942); Leonard Gross, *The Last Jews in Berlin* (New York: Simon & Schuster, 1982); Yisrael Gutman and Michael Berenbaum, *Anatomy of the Auschwitz Death Camp* (Bloomington: Indiana University Press, 1994); Ben Halpern, *The American Jew: A Zionist Analysis* (New York: Schocken Books, 1983); Malcolm Hay, *Europe and the Jews* (Boston: Beacon Press, 1960); Peter Hayes, *Lessons and Legacies: The Meaning of the Holocaust in a Changing World* (Evanston: Northwestern University Press, 1991); Celia S. Heller, *On the Edge of Destruction: Jews of Poland Between Two World Wars* (New York: Columbia University Press, 1977); Raul Hilberg, *The Destruction of the European Jews,* 2nd ed. (New York: Holmes & Meir, 1985); Isaac Jules Isaac, *The Teaching of Contempt* (New York: Holt, Rinehart and Winston, 1964); Jacob Katz, *From Prejudice to Destruction: Anti-Semitism 1700–1933* (Cambridge: Harvard University Press, 1980); Jonathan Kaufman, *A Hole in the Heart of the World: Being Jewish in Eastern Europe* (New York: Viking, 1997); Leo Kuper, *Genocide: Its Political Use in the Twentieth Century* (New Haven: Yale University Press, 1981); Primo Levi, *Moments of Reprieve* (New York: Summit Books, 1986); Primo Levi, *Survival in Auschwitz* (New York: Collier Books, 1961); Deborah E. Lipstadt, *Denying the Holocaust: The Growing Assault on Truth and Memory* (New York: Free Press, 1993); Sigmund Livingston, *Must Men Hate?* (New York: Harper, 1948); Leo Lowenthal and Norbert Guterman, *Prophets of Deceit* (New York: Harper, 1949); Roger Manwell and Heinrich Fraenkel, *The Incomparable Crime: Mass Extermination in the Twentieth Century: The Legacy of Guilt* (New York: Putnam's, 1967); Paul W. Massing, *Rehearsal for Destruction: A Study of Anti-Semitism in Imperial Germany* (New York: Harper, 1949); Edward C. McDonagh, "Status Levels of American Jews," *Sociology and Social Research* 32 (1948): 944–53; Carey McWilliams, *A Mask for Privilege* (Boston: Little, Brown, 1944); Paul R. Mendes-Flohr and Jehuda Reinharz, eds., *The Jew in the Modern World: A Documentary History* (New York: Oxford University Press, 1980); Donald E. Miller and Lorna Touryan Miller, *Survivors: An Oral History of the Armenian Genocide* (Berkeley and Los Angeles: University of California Press, 1993); Judith Miller, *One by One: Facing the Holocaust* (New York: Simon and Schuster, 1990); Montagu F. Modder, *The Jew in the Literature of England: To the End of the 19th Century* (Philadelphia: The Jewish Publication Society of America, 1939); Sarah Moskovitz, *Love Despite Hate: Child Survivors of The Holocaust and Their Adult Lives* (New York: Schocken Books, 1983); Filip Muller, *Eyewitness Auschwitz: Three Years in the Gas Chambers* (New York: Stein and Day, 1979); Myers, *Bigotry;* I. A. Newby, *Challenge to the Court: Social Scientists and the Defense of Segregation, 1954–1966* (Baton Rouge: Louisiana State University Press, 1969); James Parkes, *An Enemy of the People: Antisemitism* (New York: Pelican Books, 1946); James Parkes, *Anti-Semitism: A Concise World History* (Chicago: Quadrangle Books, 1969); James Parkes, *The Jewish Problem in the Modern World* (New York: Oxford University Press, 1946); Nathan Perlmutter and Ruth Perlmutter, *The Real Anti-Semitism in America* (New York: Arbor House, 1982); Detlev J. Peukert, *Inside Nazi Germany* (New Haven: Yale University Press, 1987); Reynolds, et al., *Sociology of Ethnocentrism;* Alvin Rosenfeld and Irving Greenberg, eds., *Confronting the Holocaust: The Impact of Elie Wiesel* (Bloomington: University of Indiana Press, 1978); Theodore I. Rubin, *Anti-Semitism: A Disease of the Mind* (New York: Continuum, 1990); Abram L. Sachar, *Sufferance is the Badge: The Jew in the Contemporary World* (New York: Alfred A. Knopf,

1939); Maurice Samuel, *The Great Hatred* (New York: Alfred A. Knopf, 1948); Jean P. Sartre, *Anti-Semite and Jew* (New York: Schocken Books, 1965), also see Sartre, "Portrait of the Anti-Semite," *Partisan Review*, 13 (1946): 163–78; Gertrude L. Selznick and Stephen Steinberg, *The Tenacity of Prejudice: Anti-Semitism in Contemporary America* (New York: Harper & Row, 1969); Jorge Semprun, *The Long Voyage* (New York: Penguin Books, 1997); Ernst Simmel, ed., *Anti-Semitism: A Social Disease* (New York: International Universities Press, 1946); Snyder, *German Nationalism;* Ervin Staub, *The Roots of Evil* (New York: 1989); Charles H. Stember, ed., *Jews in the Mind of America* (New York: Basic Books, 1966); Samuel Tenenbaum, *Why Men Hate* (New York: Jewish Book Guild of America, 1947); Joshua Trachtenberg, *The Devil and the Jews* (New York: Meridian Books, 1961); Pierre Vidal-Naquet, *Assassins of Memory: Essays on the Denial of the Holocaust* (New York: Columbia University Press, 1992); Stephen J. Whitfield, *Jews in American Life and Thought* (Hamden, CT: Shoestring Press, 1984); Elie Wiesel, *Night* (New York: Avon Books, 1960); Forrest G. Wood, *The Arrogance of Power: Christianity and Race in America from the Colonial Era to the Twentieth Century* (New York: Alfred A. Knopf, 1990); David S. Wyman, *The Abandonment of the Jews: America and the Holocaust 1941–1945* (New York: Pantheon, 1984); Susan Zuccotti, *The Holocaust, the French, and the Jews* (Basic Books, 1993); Susan Zuccotti, *The Italians and the Holocaust* (New York: Basic Books, 1987); Yitzhak Zuckerman ("Antek"), *A Surplus of Memory: Chronicle of the Warsaw Ghetto Uprising* (Berkeley: University of California Press, 1993).

15. Bruno Bettelheim and Morris Janowitz, "Prejudice," *Scientific American,* 183 (1950): 13.

16. I. D. MacCrone, *Race Attitudes in South Africa* (London: Oxford University Press, 1937), 310.

17. Adorno et al., *The Authoritarian Personality,* 975; Ashley Montagu, *The Direction of Human Development* (New York: Harper 1970); Ashley Montagu, *On Being Human,* 2nd ed. (New York Dutton, 1969); Ashley Montagu, *Growing Young,* 2nd ed. (Westport, CT: Bergin & Garvey, 1989); Ashley Montagu and Floyd Matson, *The Human Connection* (New York, McGraw-Hill, 1989).

18. D. B. Harris, H. G. Gough, and W. E. Martin, "Children's Ethnic Attitudes: II, Relationships to Parental Beliefs Concerning Child Training," *Child Development* 21 (1950): 169–81; Else Frenkel-Brunswik, "Patterns of Social and Cognitive Outlook in Children and Parents," *American Journal of Orthopsychiatry* 21 (1951): 543–58; Ackerman and Jahoda, *Anti-Semitism.*

19. William McCord, Jane McCord, and Alan Howard, "Early Familial Experiences and Bigotry," *American Sociological Review* 25 (1960): 717–22.

20. Allport, *Nature of Prejudice,* 395, 408.

21. Edward McDill, "Anomie, Authoritarianism, Prejudice, and Socio-Economic Status: An Attempt at Clarification," *Social Forces* 39 (1961): 239–45.

22. Frederick Koenig and Morton B. King, Jr., "Cognitive Simplicity and Prejudice," *Social Forces,* 40 (1962): 220–22.

23. James G. Martin, "Tolerant and Prejudiced Personality Syndromes," *Journal of Intergroup Relations* 2 (1961): 171–75.

24. For a penetrating discussion of this, see Dostoyevsky, *The Brothers Karamazov* 5.5.

25. Kurt Lewin, *Resolving Social Conflicts* (New York: Harper, 1948); Muzafer Sherif and Carolyn W. Sherif, *Groups in Harmony and Tension* (New York: Harper,

1953); Edward Spicer, ed., *Human Problems in Technological Change* (New York: Russell Sage Foundation, 1952); Chris Argyris, *Personality and Organization* (New York: Harper, 1957); Norman Maier, *Principles of Human Relations* (New York: Wiley, 1952); George E. Simpson and J. Milton Yinger, *Racial and Cultural Minorities*, 5th ed. (New York: Plenum Press, 1985); *Report of the Joint Commission on Mental Health of Children, Crisis in Child Mental Health: Challenge for the 70's* (New York: Harper & Row, 1970); Ruth H. Munroe, Robert L. Munroe, and Beatrice Whiting, eds., *Handbook of Cross-Cultural Development* (New York; Garland Press, 1981).

26. I have a feeling that I am not altogether the author of the words or ideas in this section on classified hostilities. My notes, made long ago, indicate no outside source. If I have used someone else's ideas or words without individual acknowledgment, I hope this brief note will serve both as explanation and apology.

27. Frederick E. Thorne, "The Attitudinal Pathoses," *Journal of Clinical Psychology* 5 (1949): 1–21; F. E. Thorne, "The Frustration-Anger-Hostility States: A New Diagnostic Classification," *Journal of Clinical Psychology* 9 (1953): 334–39. See also Arnold H. Buss, *The Psychology of Aggression* (New York: Wiley, 1961); Saul Siegal, "The Relationship of Hostility to Authoritarianism," *Journal of Abnormal and Social Psychology* 52 (1956): 368–72; Jack Hokanson, "The Effects of Guilt Arousal and Severity of Discipline on Adult Aggressive Behavior," *Journal of Clinical Psychology* 17 (1961): 29–32; Teun A. van Dijk, *Communicating Racism: Ethnic Prejudice in Thought and Talk* (Thousand Oaks, CA: Sage Publications, 1987); Ian D. Suttie, *The Origins of Love and Hate* (New York: Julian Press, 1966); Erich Fromm, *The Anatomy of Human Destructiveness* (New York: Holt, Rinehart & Winston, 1973); Floyd W. Matson, *The Broken Image: Man, Science and Society* (New York: Braziller, 1964), Ashley Montagu, *The Nature of Human Aggression* (New York: Oxford University Press, 1976.)

28. This statement has been interpreted to mean that race in the biological sense in man has no existence. Much more is meant here than that, namely that, in so far as social action is concerned, the biological facts about population differences do not constitute the social problem of race. It is the social attitude toward race that constitutes the problem. Frederick E. Thorne, "Epidemiological Studies of Chronic Frustration-Hostility-Aggression States," *American Journal of Psychiatry* 112 (1957): 717–21.

29. Edwin G. Conklin, "What Is Man?" *Rice Institute Pamphlet* 28 (1941): 163.

30. This is what Oscar Wilde meant when he said that "it is only by the cultivation of the habit of intellectual criticism that we shall be able to rise superior to race prejudices." "The True Function and Value of Criticism," *Nineteenth Century* 28 (1890): 123–47.

31. For a valuable discussion of this aspect of the subject see Henry A. Davidson, "The Anatomy of Prejudice," *Common Ground* 1 (1941): 3–12; and Julian Huxley, *Man Stands Alone* (New York: Harper); see also Henry A. Myers, *Are Men Equal?* (New York: Putnam, 1945)); David Thompson, *Equality* (London and New York: Cambridge University Press, 1949); Lyman Bryson et al., eds., *Aspects of Human Equality* (New York: Harper, 1956); R. H. Tawney, *Equality*, 4th ed. (London: Allen & Unwin, 1952); Michael Lewis, *The Culture of Inequality* (Amherst: University of Massachusetts Press, 1978); Christopher Jencks, *Inequality* (New York: Basic Books, 1972); William Ryan, *Blaming the Victim* (New York: Pantheon Books, 1971); William Ryan, *Equality* (New York: Pantheon Books, 1981); George L. Abernethy, *The Idea of Equality: An Anthology* (Richmond: John Knox Press, 1959); Donald M. Levine and

Mary Jo Bane, *The 'Inequality' Controversy: Schooling and Distributive Justice* (New York: Basic Books, 1975); Gerald D. Berreman, ed., *Social Inequality: Comparative and Developmental Approaches* (New York: Academic Press, 1981); Harvard Educational Review, *Equal Educational Opportunity* (Cambridge: 1969); Leonard Broom et al., *The Inheritance of Inequality* (London & Boston: Routledge & Kegan Paul, 1980); Ronald Dworkin, *A Matter of Principle* (Cambridge: Harvard University Press, 1985).

32.   Donald R. Taft, "Cultural Opportunities through Race Contacts," *Journal of Negro History* 14 (1929): 19; Robin M. Williams, Jr., *The Reduction of Intergroup Tensions* (New York: Social Sciences Research Council, 1947): 69–73; Kurt Lewin, *Resolving Social Conflicts* (New York: Harper, 1948); Bryson et al., eds., *Approaches to Group Understanding* (New York: Harper, 1947); Wallace Stegner, *One Nation* (Boston: Houghton Mifflin, 1945); Alfred Marrow, *Living Without Hate* (New York: Harper, 1951); Robert M. MacIver, ed., *Unity and Difference in American Life* (New York: Harper, 1947); Ernest F. Johnson, ed., *Foundations of Democracy* (New York: Harper, 1947); Oscar Handlin, *Race and Nationality in American Life* (Boston: Little, Brown, 1957); Leonard Bloom, *The Social Psychology of Race Relations* (Cambridge, MA: Schenckman, 1949); Ina C. Brown, *Understanding Race Relations* (Englewood Cliffs NJ: Prentice-Hall, 1973); David Loye, *The Healing of a Nation* (New York: W. W. Norton, 1971); Mary C. Waters, *Ethnic Options: Choosing Identities in America* (Berkeley: University of California Press, 1990).

33.   Erich Fromm, "Sex and Character," *Psychiatry* 11 (1943): 23.

34.   Albert Jacquard, *In Praise of the Difference: Genetics and Human Affairs* (New York: Columbia University Affairs, 1984); David Hawkins, *The Science and Ethics of Equality* (New York: Basic Books, 1977).

35.   Alfred Kroeber, "The Superorganic," *American Anthropologist* 19 (1917): 163–213.

36.   See Ashley Montagu, *On Being Human*, 2nd ed. (New York: Hawthorn Books, 1969); A. Montagu, *The Direction of Human Development*, revised (New York: Hawthorn Books, 1970); Hugh Miller, *The Community of Man* (New York: Macmillan, 1949); Lawrence K. Frank, *Nature and Human Nature* (New Brunswick: Rutgers University Press, 1951); Robert Ulich, *The Human Career* (New York: Harper, 1955); C. H. Waddington, *The Ethical Animal* (New York: Atheneum, 1960); Loren Eiseley, *The Firmament of Time* (New York: Atheneum, 1960); Gilbert Highet, *Man's Unconquerable Mind* (New York: Columbia University Press, 1954); Ashley Montagu, "Education, Humanity, and Technology," in *Advances in Telematics*, vol. 2, 1–15, ed. Jarice Hanson (Norwood, NJ: Ablex Publishing, 1994).

37.   W. O. Brown, "Rationalization of Race Prejudice," *International Journal of Ethics* 63 (1933): 305.

38.   Ashley Montagu, *The Natural Superiority of Women*, 3rd ed. (New York: Macmillan, 1974).

39.   Chester Alexander, "Antipathy and Social Behavior," *American Journal of Sociology* 51 (1946): 288–92.

40.   Wilson Wallis, "Some Phases of the Psychology of Prejudice," *Journal of Abnormal and Social Psychology* 24 (1930): 426.

10

Race and Culture

The questions are often asked: "Why is it that the cultures of different races differ so much from one another? Is this because race and culture are inseparable?" "Do differences in race have anything to do with the differences in cultural development as between the races?" The answer to these questions is really simple. Cultures differ from one another to the extent to which the history, the experience, of each of the interacting groups has differed. By "history," by "experience" we mean anything that a person or group of persons has undergone or lived, perceived, or sensed. No matter with what groups of humans we may be concerned, culture is in its broadest and fundamental sense not merely an aspect but a function of experience. Cultures are created by human beings. The definition of culture itself constitutes the answer to our question: culture is the humanmade part of the environment. It is human beings, not supernaturals or genes that create the ways in which they live. The way of life of a people is its culture. The visitor to an indigenous tribe who wrote of its manners and customs, "Customs beastly: manners none," was not likely to make much progress in the understanding of these matters. Race and culture do not appear to be in any way connected. As Klineberg has pointed out:

> The argument from the cultural contributions of a particular ethnic group to the inborn racial characteristics of that group falls down for many reasons: cultures may vary while race remains unchanged, the same culture may be found in groups of different race, what looks like a superior cultural contribution from one point of view may seem much less significant when another criterion is applied, etc. Studies of race mixture are similarly inconclusive, since individuals of mixed racial heredity cannot be shown to be different in their inborn psychological characteristics from those of 'pure' race. Finally, there is no evidence that some racial groups are biologically more 'primitive' or undeveloped than others.
>
> This does not mean that heredity plays no part in the determination of behavior. On the contrary, there is good evidence that 'individuals' and 'families' may be distinguished from others in terms of hereditary as well

as acquired characteristics. As regards large racial groups, however, there appears to be about the same range of hereditary capacities in one group as in another. The fact that differences in behavior between such groups obviously exist, is no proof that they exist because they are inborn.[1]

The reason the cultures of other ethnic groups are so often different from our own is that they have been exposed to experiences which differ as considerably from our own as do the cultures in question. If you or I, with our present genetic background, had been born and brought up among a group of Australian aborigines, we would be, culturally, behaviorally, Australian aborigines, though physically we would retain the appearance of our own background; although facial expression is likely to be strongly influenced by the unconcious influences of the aboriginal culture, even to the matter of gestures and gait. Experience is determined by the place and the culture in which groups and individuals live and have their being, and for this reason groups and persons belonging to different cultures will differ mentally from one another. Our physical structures would not have varied significantly, because they were for the most part genetically determined by our biological parents, but our physical expression would almost certainly have been modified, and our cultural equipment would be that of an Australian aboriginal. Why? Because culture is learned—and by "culture" is to be understood the way of life of a people; its ideas, sentiments, religious and secular beliefs, its language, tools and other material products, its institutions, customs, values, and ideals. Culture begins with socialization virtually at birth, if not before, with learning, and terminates only with death. Because culture is something that one acquires by experience, unlike one's physical appearance, which one acquires through the action, for the most part, of inherited genes, but which under the influence of socializing and culturalizing factors is subject to considerable modification. The culture of persons, as of groups, will differ according to the kinds of experience they have undergone. That socializing experience is *culturally, not biologically* transmitted.[2]

Illuminating in this connection is a study by Professor Erwin H. Ackerknecht, who has brought together the facts concerning white children who had been abducted from their parents by North American Indians during the eighteenth and nineteenth centuries. Professor Ackerknecht gives us the accounts of eight fairly well-recorded life histories of such children.

All these children were taken by the Indians when they were between the ages of four and nine years, with the exception of a girl who was taken in adolescence. All of them forgot their native culture, and even the girl who had been captured when she was 15 years of age became completely Indianized. In every case these "white Indians" resisted all attempts to persuade them to return to their white relatives and to the culture of their birth. As Ackerknecht says, the "white Indians" seemed to have found "a kind of unity of thought and action and a kind of social cohesion which deeply appealed to them, and which they did not find with the whites, especially not with the pioneers. There is no doubt that this fact largely contributed to their staying with the Indians."[3]

The remarkable fact about these "white Indians" is that they not only became completely Indianized culturally in the sense of manifesting purely Indian forms of social behavior, but they also developed all the physical powers of resistance said to be peculiar to Indians. Furthermore, most of them lived to be extremely old. Finally, all of them had acquired the facial expression and outward impassability characteristic of the Indian. Samuel Stanhope Smith was among the first, if not the first, to comment upon this fact. In 1810 he wrote,

> Another example of the power of society in forming the countenance is well known to all those who are acquainted with the savage tribes spread along the frontiers of these states. Among them you frequently meet with persons who have been taken captive in infancy from Anglo-American families, and grown up in the habits of savage life. These descendants of the fairest Europeans universally contract such a resemblance of the natives, in their countenance, and even in their complexion, as not to be easily distinguished from them; and afford a striking proof that the differences in physiognomy, between the Anglo-American, and the Indian depend principally on the state of society.[4]

Of many of these "white Indians" it is expressly recorded that, having been accustomed to Indian ways they could no longer sleep in a house or in a bed.[5]

Such facts should go a long way toward disproving the view that culture is something that will express itself in genetically determined form no matter what the environmental influences to which the person is exposed.

It should always be remembered that the organism does not inherit traits, but only genes, and that genes do not determine traits, but in interaction with the environment and the effects of its own idiosyncratic history, influence their physiological and behavioral development.[6]

The culture of different peoples, as of different individuals, is to a large extent a reflection of their past history or experience. This is a point worth more than laboring. If the cultural status of any variety of human is determined merely by its experience, then it is evident that by giving all people the opportunity to enjoy a common experience—supposing for the moment that this was desirable—all varieties would become culturally and mentally equal. That is, they would become equal in the sense that they would have benefited from exposure to the same kind of experience, the individual's own contribution to his or her development, always allowing, of course, for the idiosyncratic history of the individual, the fact that no two persons can ever be alike in their reception of and response to the same experience. There will always, fortunately, continue to exist great differences between persons.[7]

There can be little doubt that genetic differences in temperament and intellectual capacity exist between the individuals comprising every variety of human, no two individuals in this respect ever being alike; but it takes the stimulus of a common experience to bring them out and to render them comparable. It is because of differences in their history, in cultural experience, that individuals and groups differ from one another culturally, and it is for this reason that cultural achievement is an exceedingly poor measure of the cultural potentialities of a person or a group.[8]

This is not a novel idea. It was stated by the great French statesman and economist Robert Jacques Turgot (1727–1781) two centuries ago, when he wrote that "The human mind contains everywhere the germs of the same progress; but nature, partial in her gifts, has endowed certain minds with an abundance of talents which she has refused to others; circumstances develop these talents or relegate them to obscurity; and to the infinite variety of these circumstances is due the inequality in the progress of nations."[9]

For all practical purposes, and until further evidence to the contrary be forthcoming, we can safely take the culture of a people to be the expression principally of a particular history of cultural experience. Obviously, all learned activities are culturally, not biologically, determined, whether those activities are based upon physiological urges or traditional practices. The generalized needs which all human beings inherit in common continue to be present in all human beings in all cultures; but how these needs are permitted to express themselves and how they are satisfied is something determined by custom and tradition and varies not only in different cultures but within different groups within the same culture. For example, one of the fundamental needs which we all inherit is the need to eat. Different human groups, to whom the same foodstuffs may or may not be available; not only eat different foods but prepare them in different ways, and consume them, with or without implements, in various ways, usually established only by custom.

The potentiality for speech is biologically determined, but whether we speak, what we speak, and how we speak, is determined by what we hear in the culture in which we have been culturalized. Human beings everywhere experience, when they are tired, the desire to rest, to sit down, to lie down, or to sleep; but the manner in which they do all these things is culturally determined by the customs of the group in which they live. Many other instances will doubtless occur to the reader. The point to grasp here is that even our fundamental biological needs are more or less culturally controlled and regulated or culturalized and that their very form and expression, not to mention satisfactions, are molded according to the dictates of tradition. Culture, tradition, channels our biological processes.

In view of the immense number of different cultural influences that enter into the structure and functioning of different groups and the individuals composing them, it is surely the most gratuitous, as it is the most unscientific procedure to assert anything concerning assumed genetic conditions without first attempting to discover what part these cultural influences play in the production of what is predicated. Obviously, no statement concerning the mentality of a person is of any value without a specification of the conditions of the environment in which that mentality developed. The introduction of genes or heredity as the *deus ex machina* to account for cultural differences between people may be a convenient device for those who must do everything in their power, except study the actual facts, to find some sort of support for their prejudices, but it is a device which will hardly satisfy the requirements of an acceptable scientific method. Such devices must be accepted in a charitable spirit as the perverse efforts of some of our misguided fellows to maintain their own shaky feelings of superiority by depreciating the capacities of others. John Stuart Mill, more than a hundred years ago, in his *Principles of Political Economy* (1848), put the stamp upon this type of conduct. He wrote: "Of all the vulgar modes of escaping from the consideration of the effect of social and moral influence on the human mind, the most vulgar is that of attributing the diversities of conduct and character to inherent natural differences."[10] In his *Physics and Politics* (1869) Walter Bagehot said much the same thing: "When a philosopher cannot account for anything in any other manner, he boldly ascribes it to an occult quality in some race." While the number of people who do this sort of thing has greatly increased since the days of Mill and Bagehot, the number who realize the absurdity of such practices has also grown considerably, so that on this count there is no need to despair of the future. The situation often gets qualitatively better as it looks quantitatively worse. The facts now available concerning the peoples of the earth render it quite clear that they are all very definitely brothers under the skin.

It is, perhaps, too much to expect those who have been educated in the contrary belief to accept such a view; the least, therefore, that we can do is to provide the children in our schools with a straightforward account of the facts instead of filling their guiltless heads with the kinds of prejudice that we find distributed through so many of the books and so much of the teaching with which they are provided. Surely, a sympathetic understanding of people who behave "differently," look "differently," cannot help but broaden one's horizons and lead to better human relationships all around. Socially this is, of course, greatly to be desired, and in the United States a beginning has already been made in this direction in several cities. Such enterprises, however, must be multiplied several thousand times. Here, obviously, there is much work to be done.

But let us return to our main discussion, for though school children and others have frequently heard of physical relativity, few, if any, children, and hardly anyone else (apart from anthropologists), ever encounter the concept of "cultural relativity." From the standpoint of the well-being and happiness of humankind the latter is a vastly more important conception to grasp than the former.

Cultural relativity implies that all cultures must be evaluated in relation to their own history, and carefully, not by the arbitrary standard of any single culture such, for example, as our own. Judged in relation to its own history, each culture is seen as the resultant of the responses to the challenges which that history may or may not record. If those challenges have been limited in nature, so will the culture reflecting their effects. If the challenges have been many and complex in character, then the culture will reflect that complexity. Culture is essentially a relation that is the product of the interaction between several correlates—flexibility, formability sensitivity and experience, a biological being, who responds to the challenges of his environments, the other simply experience. If we agree that humankind is everywhere plastic, adaptable, and sensitive, then we can most satisfactorily account for the mental and cultural differences between the varieties of humans on the basis of different experiences. And this, when everything is taken into consideration, seems to be the principal explanation of the mental and cultural differences that exist between ethnic groups.

Let me give one or two examples of cultural relativity, as it were, in action. Five thousand years ago the ancestors of the present highly cultured peoples of Europe were "backward barbarians" settled in the wilds of Europe. The ancestors of the modern Englishman were living in a Stone Age phase of culture, being culturally not much more advanced than many peoples whom we today call primitive or non-literate. When in 54 B.C. Caesar conquered the Britons he found them to be in a Bronze Age phase of cultural development. Five thousand years ago Europe was inhabited by hordes of "barbarians," at a time when the kingdoms of Upper and Lower Egypt were at their height.[11] These have long since passed into history, but five thousand years ago and less the peoples of these great cultures could have looked upon the Europeans as barbarians who by nature were completely incapable of civilization—and hence better exterminated lest they pollute the "blood" of their superiors. Whatever sins the Europeans have since committed, they have at least shown that given a sufficient amount of time and experience they were capable of civilization to a degree not less than that to which the peoples of Egypt of the First and Second Dynasties (3200–2780 B.C.) attained.

It should be a sobering thought to learn that the great basic discoveries on which modern civilization rests—writing, and later the alphabet, the wheel, the astronomical calendar, metallurgy, and so on—were made in the Middle East, at a time when most of the peoples of Northwestern Europe were "backward barbarians."

Here we have an example of cultural relativity. If we use time as our frame of reference, we might ask: "Since the Egyptians have had a much longer time than we to develop culturally, why haven't they developed as far as we have?" Disregarding the dubious notion that any human group has enjoyed a longer time in which to develop than any other, the answer is that time is not a proper measure to apply to the development of culture or cultural events. Time is only a convenient framework from which to observe their development. Cultural changes that among some peoples it has taken centuries to produce are among other peoples often effected within a few years.[12]

The rate of cultural change is dependent upon many different factors, but the indispensable condition for the production of cultural change is the irritability produced by the stimulus of such new experiences; cultural change is exceedingly slow. Hence, if new experience is the chief determinant of cultural change, then the dimension by which we may most efficiently judge cultures is that of the history of the experience which has fallen to the lot of the cultures observed. In other words, to evaluate cultural events properly one must judge them by the measure of experience viewed through the framework of time.[13] We of the Western world have packed more experience into the past two thousand years than have the Australian aborigines, during their 60,000 years of continuous settlement of Australia.

Experience, or variety of cultural contacts, not time, is the all-important factor. It would obviously be wrong to expect an Australian aboriginal to behave like an Eton and Oxford graduate; but that is not to say that, with similar experience, he would not do at least as well at either institution. Until the very recent period the Australian aborigines were even more cut off from almost all cultural contact than the Britons were during the Upper Paleolithic and the Mesolithic. Britain was situated well within the periphery of the eddying streams of European cultural development— from Neolithic times onward. Britons experienced the influx of many different cultures, such as the Celtic, Scandanavian, Saxon and other cultures, and enjoyed the advantages of increasingly frequent and close contacts with the peoples of Europe. The fructifying influence of such contacts enabled them to acheive a comparatively appreciable measure of social development by the time Caesar landed on their shores. The Australian aborigines, on the other hand, had been almost completely isolated upon their continent for countless generations without such contacts with the cultures of other peoples; their culture is therefore quite different.

Race and culture are not inseparably connected. The basic biological needs and the potentialities for behavior associated with them probably do not vary significantly from one ethnic group to another. What varies is the social stimulation to which these needs and potentialities are exposed and subsequently organized. The diversity of cultures we encounter represent the adjustment different human groups have made to the experiences and the problems they have been called upon to meet and solve. As Haldane has put it,

> There are presumably differences in the median innate capacities of human groups for various forms of achievement. But the differences between members of a group are much greater than the differences between group medians. Hence, environment, and particularly tradition, are more important than innate differences between human cultures.[14]

Any judgments of value we may attempt to make between our own culture, whatever that may be, and that of other peoples will be invalid unless they are made in terms of history, of experience. Bearing this cardinal principle in mind, we shall be able to steer a clear course. It cannot be too strongly emphasized, as the distinguished historian Erich Kahler has said, that the

> historical evidence proves beyond doubt that the exact opposite of what the so-called race theory pretends is true; any desired advance in human evolution has been accomplished not by breeds that are pure either mentally or physically, not by any cultural inbreeding, but by intermixture, by mutual impregnation of different stocks and cultures.[15]

It is, indeed, from the mixtures of cultural traditions that many of the major triumphs of civilization have come. If the essential physical differences, then, between the varieties of humans are limited to superficial characters, such as color of skin, form of hair, and form of nose, and the cultural and mental differences are due merely to differences in experience, then from the social-biological standpoint all humans must be adjudged fundamentally equal; that is to say, equally good in a biological sense and in cultural potentiality.

All normal human beings are born as culturally undifferentiated organisms; they become culturally differentiated according to the social group into which they happen to be born. Some of the culturally differentiating media are neither so complex nor so advanced as others; the individuals developed within them will be culturally the products of their group. As individuals, they can no more be blamed or praised for belonging to their particular group than a fish can be either blamed or praised for belonging to its particular class in the vertebrate series. Culture, the culture of any group, is more or less determined by adventitious factors, which the group, as a group, has usually done little to bring about. Members of the more technologically advanced cultures have simply enjoyed the benefits of a broader experience and more varied contacts than members of the less technologically advanced cultures.[16] As Boas has said:

> The history of mankind proves that advances of culture depend upon the opportunities presented to a social group to learn from the experience of their neighbors. The discoveries of the group spread to others, and, the more varied the contacts, the greater are the opportunities to learn. The tribes of simplest culture are on the whole those that have been isolated for very long periods and hence could not profit from the cultural achievements of their neighbors.[17]

In short, history teaches us that there is no inherent tendency in any human group that distinguishes it from any other to develop from a state of "barbarism" to one of "high culture." It is only under certain culturally stimulating conditions, which are for the most part accidentally determined, that any group will ever progress to a state of technological advance, for human beings beyond all other creatures are gifted with the capacity to turn accidents into opportunities. In the absence of such conditions no human group will ever move beyond the state of culture determined by the totality of conditions operative upon it. That should be obvious.

With respect to the alleged unchangingness of human nature, which racists almost always proclaim, consider, for example, the case of the Greeks. In spite of a remarkable biological continuity with their ancestors of classical times,[18] the people of modern Greece have been unable to match the innumerable achievements in the arts and sciences of their ancestors more than two thousand years ago. To what, then, is due this striking difference between the Greeks of the fifth century before Christ and those of the twentieth century? A study of the tragic history of political anarchy, war, massacre, social disorganization, conquest, and oppression which has been the lot of the Greek people during the past two thousand years suggests the direction, at least, in which we should look for an answer.[19]

As Professor Wilder Penfield, one of the world's great neurologists, has written,

The brains of the Greek patricians who rose to such superiority of intellectual achievement during the golden age of Classical Greece were no different structurally from the brains of Greeks in the so-called dark ages that followed. The subsequent low level of intellectual output was the result of changing environment, and the disappearance of fair competition, freedom and public rewards for excellence.[20]

What were the Greeks in the second millennium B.C.? A few scattered peoples of peasant status. Who were the Romans in the sixth century B.C.? Some thousand farmers dispersed over the seven hills by the Tiber. What warrant was there for the promise they so richly realized subsequently in these Mediterranean lands? And yet from these lowly peasants came two of the most highly developed civilizations the world has known, the civilizations to which the western world owes so much it calls its own.

The seafaring Scandinavians of the Bronze Age were undoubtedly the ancestors of the modern Scandinavians, yet how different is the cultural behavior of the modern relatively sedentary Scandinavians from that of their raiding forebears!

The boisterous joy of life of the English of Elizabeth I's time and the lusty libertinism of the Restoration contrast sharply with the prudery of the Victorian Age. The Englishman's "nature" was different in the sixteenth century as compared with that in the seventeenth century, and still more different in the nineteenth century.[21]

With respect to the Germans it would be difficult to do better than cite the comments of an eighteenth-century Scotsman, William Guthrie, who wrote: "The Germans are brave, and when led by able generals, particularly by Italians, have often performed great deeds."[22] "Being led by able generals, particularly Italians" is a remark which in the light of later German-Italian military relations is quite too piquant, and should provide an interesting commentary in itself upon the mutability of human nature.

And what shall we say of the differences in cultural behavior of such biologically near kin as the New Mexican sedentary Pueblo and the nomadic Navaho Indians, or the behavior of those inhabitants of Mexican Indian villages that are completely Hispanicized? And what can have happened to the alleged "warlike nature" of the American Indians who today live at peace?[23]

Is the cultural behavior of the Island Japanese the same as it was a century and a half ago? Compare the great Polynesian maritime peoples with their descendants today in Hawaii and New Zealand. Biologically they are mostly the same people, but so far as the expression of their "nature" is concerned they are virtually completely Westernized.

What did white Americans achieve culturally or by way of invention up to the time of the War of Independence? Very little, indeed. "Who reads an

American novel?" asked Sidney Smith early in the nineteenth century. Who, indeed, if not the whole world? And who doesn't acclaim the inventiveness, the science, and the scholarship of Americans? Why, then, was it that Americans appeared to be so backward in comparison with Europeans? May not the fact that the conditions of life under which most Americans were forced to live by rulers primarily interested in exploiting the American colonies, have had something to do with this lack of achievement? The evidence points strongly in that direction.[24] The nature of Americans has changed with the changing conditions of life. The one thing characteristic of human nature is, surely, its changeability under changing conditions.

The outstanding characteristic of humans is the ability to make all the necessary changes within themselves to meet the demands of a changing environment. This trait, flexibility, plasticity, educability or adaptability, is the one which, in the human species as a whole, has had the greatest demands made upon it by natural selection. Survival of the human species and its progress has depended upon this ability of human nature to change in adaptation to changed conditions.

What most people take to be human nature is really second nature, a nature which has been acquired within the limits of the potentialities of being human within a specific culture. Human nature is a pattern of behavior, and this pattern of behavior is known to be capable of change not only from generation to generation but in the same individual within a single generation. As the second President of the United States, John Adams, wrote, "Education has made a greater difference between man and man than nature has made between man and brute."[25]

It has often been argued that racial enmities between people will disappear only when all physical racial differences between them have been obliterated. That is a fallacious argument for the simple reason that the real source of racial hostilities is not biological, but cultural. It would be equally erroneous to argue from this that such hostilities will therefore disappear only with the obliteration of all cultural differences between men.

The world would be immensely the poorer for such a cultural leveling, and such a process would not, in any event, bring about the desired effect. Perfection of human nature and achievements, it cannot be too often emphasized, is not obtained by the ascendancy of one form of excellence, but by the blending of what is best in many different forms; by harmonizing differences, not by rendering them more discordant. The deep peril and disease of our age is that the cultural differences that exist between ethnic groups tend to become attenuated too soon. In this attenuative process are often lost the unique virtues of a culture even before the dominant culture has grasped their meaning. And as often as this happens is humankind impoverished. As John Collier, a former commissioner of Indian Affairs, pointed out, the history of our species tells us that cultural diversity is the creative force in history. The ideal of a way of life which, in the Western world, the religion we call Christianity, for example, represents the blending of the elements of many different traditions. Hebrew monotheism and morality, Greek philosophy, Oriental mysticism, Roman law, all entered into its shaping. Christianity is only one of countless examples of the profound truth that cultural "diversity is the essential nurture of the spirit of man, the seed-bed of our human future. The cross-fertilization of contrasting cultures is the maker of our human power."[26]

Stressing superficial differences between people only helps to foster the illusion that there may be more fundamental differences behind them. What in truth and in justice requires to be done is to stress the fundamental kinship of humankind: to stress the likenesses which we all bear to one another, and to recognize the essential unity in all humankind in the very differences which individuals of all ethnic groups display. Unity neither implies nor necessitates uniformity. It is important that human beings shall be united, but not that they shall be uniform. We must learn to recognize the all-importance of our common humanity and the triviality of the things that divide us. The world must be re-established as a vast community in which every ethnic group is freely permitted to give as well as to receive. Such an ideal will never be achieved by the ignorant, the sinful, and the malicious stressing of differences, but by the broader, saner, and more humane sympathetic recognition of the fundamental likenesses, rejoicing in the significance of the differences, the preciousness, indeed of the differences, and, finally, by the utilization and interchange of the differences to strengthen each other in living a fuller, a more varied, a more gratifying, and a more peaceful life.

Notes

1. Otto Klineberg, "Race Differences: The Present Position of the Problem," *International Social Science Bulletin* (UNESCO) 2 (1950): 465.

2. Carl J. Warden, *The Emergence of Human Culture* (New York: Macmillan, 1936); Carl J. Warden, *The Evolution of Human Behavior* (New York: Macmillan, 1932); A. Irving Hallowell, *Culture and Experience* (Philadelphia: University of Pennsylvania Press, 1955); A. L. Kroeber, *The Nature of Culture* (Chicago: University of Chicago Press, 1952); Leslie L. White, *The Evolution of Culture* (New York: McGraw-Hill, 1949); Leslie L. White, *The Science of Culture* (New York: Farrar, Straus, & Co, 1949); Clyde Kluckhohn, *Culture and Behavior* (New York: Free Press, 1962); Clyde Kluckhohn, *Mirror For Man* (Tucson: University of Arizona Press, 1985); Ashley Montagu, *Man: His First Two Million Years* (New York: Columbia University Press, 1962); John Middleton, ed., *From Child to Adult* (New York: American Museum of Natural History, 1970); Andrew P. Vayda, ed., *Environment and Cultural Behavior* (New York: American Museum of Natural History, 1969); Robert Hunt, ed., *Personalities and Cul-*

tures (New York: American Museum of Natural History, 1967); Ashley Montagu, ed., *Culture: Man's Adaptive Dimension* (New York: Oxford University Press, 1968); Ashley Montagu, ed., *Culture and the Evolution of Man* (New York: Oxford University Press, 1970); George D. Spindler, ed., *Education and Culture: Anthropological Approaches* (New York: Holt, Rinehart & Winston, 1963); W. D. Hambly, *The Origins of Education Among Primitive People* (London: Macmillan, 1926); Michael Cole et al., eds., *The Cultural Context of Learning and Thinking* (New York: Basic Books, 1971).

3. Erwin Ackerknecht, "White Indians," *Bulletin of the History of Medicine* 15 (1944): 15–36, 34.

4. Samuel Smith, *An Essay on the Causes of the Variety of Complexion and Figure in the Human Species*, 2nd ed., (New Brunswick, NJ: Simpson, 1810), 171–72.

5. Howard H. Peckham, *Captured by Indians* (New Brunswick, NJ: Rutgers University Press, 1954); June Namais, *White Captives! Gender and Ethnicity on the American Frontier* (Chapel Hill: University of North Carolina Press, 1993).

6. For a discussion of the moral and international consequences of these facts see Barbara Wootton, *Testament for Social Science* (New York: Norton, 1951), 146–52.

7. Richard C. Lewontin, Steven Rose, and Leon J. Kamin, *Not In Our Genes* (New York: Pantheon, 1984).

8. For an illuminating exposition of cultural relativity see Ruth Benedict, *Patterns of Culture* (Boston: Houghton Mifflin, 1934).

9. Robert J. Turgot, *Tableaux Philosophique des Progrès Successifs de l'Esprit Humain*, in *Œuvres de Turgot*, ed. Gustave Schelle (Paris: Alcan), 214.

10. John Stuart Mill, *Principles of Political Economy* I (London: Longmans, 1848), 340.

11. It has been stated that Cicero had an extremely low opinion of the mental capacities of the Britons. Thus, he is alleged to have written in a letter to his friend Atticus, "Do not obtain your slaves from Britain, because they are so stupid and so utterly incapable of being taught that they are not fit to form part of the household of Athens." See Benedict, *Race: Science and Politics* (New York: Viking, 1943), 10. The truth is that Cicero made no such derogatory remark. What he wrote was " . . . there is not a scrap of silver in the island, nor any hope of booty except from slaves; but I don't fancy you will find any with literary or musical talent among them." Ep. ad Att. 4.16.13. Loeb Library, vol. 1, p. 324. Cicero was wrong. The talents were there, but it took some 1,500 years of development before they could find expression. This long period of cultural lag, in spite of the presence of the Romans in Britain for some four centuries is worth noting. It would be interesting to know who started the Cicero hare. It keeps recurring in the literature.

12. Pitirim A. Sorokin and Robert K. Merton, "Social Time: A Methodological and Functional Analysis," *American Journal of Sociology* 42 (1937), 615–29; P. Sorokin, *Sociocultural Causality, Space, Time* (Durham: Duke University Press, 1943) 158–225.

13. A. Montagu, "Social Time: A Methodological and Functional Analysis," *American Journal of Sociology* 44 (1938): 282–84.

14. J. B. S. Haldane, "The Argument from Animals to Men: An Examination of its Validity for Anthropology," *Journal of the Royal Anthropological Institute of Great Britain and Ireland* 36 (1956): 1–14.

15. Erich Kahler, *Man the Measure* (New York: Brazillier, 1943), 30.

16. It is of interest to note here that the eighteenth-century students of man, such as Ferguson, Reid, Hume, Stewart, and Adam Smith, solved the problem of the cultural diversity of man in much the same way. "They were struck with the vast differences in culture, as well as with accounts of men of different physical features, but, on the basis of their major presupposition that human nature is fundamentally the same, they solved the problem of differences in achievement by judging the different peoples to be at different stages of maturity." Gladys Bryson, *Man and Society* (Princeton: Princeton University Press, 1945), 53.

17. Franz Boas, "Racial Purity," *Asia* 40 (1940): 231–34.

18. See Chapter 10.

19. Georg Brandes, *Hellas: Travels in Greece*, translated by Jacob W. Hartmann (New York: Adelphi, 1926).

20. Wilder Penfield, "Letter to the Editor," *Perspectives in Biology and Medicine* 6 (1963): 540–41.

21. For some interesting comments bearing on these points see William D. Babington, *Fallacies of Race Theories* (London: Longmans, 1895), 235 ff.; also Geoffrey Gorer, "Some Notes on the British Character," *Horizon* 29 (1949–50): 369–79.

22. Quoted in Johann G. Kohl, *England, Wales, and Scotland* (London: Chapman & Hall, 1844), 79. It is necessary to add that Kohl did not quite approve these statements.

23. During the making of a film on location in Florida which required the firing by Indians at whites, the Seminole Indians who had been hired for the occasion balked on the ground that they had made a treaty with the United States that prohibited taking up arms against the white man. See *New Yorker* 27 (12 May 1951), 23.

24. For a good discussion of this subject see Mitchell Wilson, *American Science and Invention* (New York: Simon & Schuster, 1954).

25. Page Smith, *John Adams*, I (New York: Doubleday, 1963), 220.

26. John Collier, "The Creative Value of Cultural Diversity," *Trends & Tides* 2 (1946): 5–6.

11

Racism and Social Action

The reaction of scientists to the propaganda of those who sought to convince the world of the truth of racism has had an interesting history. At first the errors and spurious arguments of the racists were duly exposed by the simple appeal to the facts of science. Facts, after all—it was felt—speak for themselves. With the unfolding of the monstrous Nazi racist policy of extermination of the Jews in Europe, and mounting racial tensions in America, the very real seriousness of the problem at last broke in on many scientists, and as a result we have witnessed a considerable increase in the literature devoted to the examination of the causes of race tensions and prejudice, and the refutation of racist ideas and dogmas. By this means scientists have hoped to arrest, at least, the spread of the infection of racism. Ideally they would have liked to render immune those who stood in danger of acquiring it, and to relieve those of the pathogens with which they were infected.

The attempt has been a noble one, and it has enjoyed something of a success, but that success, in the face of a growing intensification of race feeling, has been a strictly limited one. Many persons and groups have, gratifyingly, been influenced to think and behave more intelligently with respect to race relations, but the population as a whole, in this country—not to mention other lands—has made little progress but has, instead, remained measurably race conscious. It has become evident that to make the truth readily available is not enough. Facts, it appears, do not speak for themselves, nor, it seems, are they necessarily understood when they do, and when they are understood it far from follows that they will be accepted and acted upon. These are by no means new discoveries, but the responses which they define have come to most workers in the field of race relations with something of the shock of new discovery; and this because the seriousness of the issues at stake has given so much greater force to the errors and perversions of thought and conduct of which so many persons and groups are guilty. The stereotypes, the absurd beliefs, the vulgar errors, and the unfortunate attitudes, when multiplied several million times actually add up to a tremendous social pathology. Western society, and our society in particular, is very sick indeed.

We have spent a fair amount of time inquiring into and investigating the causes of the social disease which is racism, and we have yet a great deal of work to do before we shall have brought such studies to completion. Investigations of this kind are invaluable and they must be encouraged to continue on an even larger scale than hitherto, but it should be quite obvious that investigation and the clearest analysis and description of causes will never succeed in curing the disease of racism. The better, however, we understand the causes of the disease the more efficiently it will be possible to prescribe the remedy for it. Hence, research into every aspect of the problem of prejudice and racism must continue on an ever-widening front. But it is now coming to be more and more widely understood that the prosecution of such researches and their publication in technical journals, periodicals, and books is not an end in itself, but a means to an end. The theoretical phase of the attack on racism has now reached the stage which renders it clear that not much more can be achieved by that means. What we now need is to enter upon the second, the applied, phase of the attack, in which, using our theoretical knowledge gained from the actual investigation of the necessary[1] conditions we embark upon the practical application of that knowledge.

We now know something of the nature of the causes of racism, and we know how spurious are the arguments that are used to support it, and of this we have heard a great deal. What we want to know now is what we can do about racism in a practical way in the form of social action in the attack upon this most critical of social problems.

One of the first things to be realized is that partial measures and measures which we know to have no more than a palliative effect are not going to accomplish very much. Education, full employment, and good housing will help, but they will not solve the race problem. Such measures are doomed to failure for the simple reason that race prejudice stems from sources which these remedies, for the most part, fail to reach. These sources are the internalized basic structures that determine the social functioning of the personality. The basic structures are those that are erected as the framework of the personality by the process of socialization; by the manner in which the socially undifferentiated human organism is turned into a socially differentiated human being. The basic personality structure of every human being is determined by the forms of social response that have been institutionalized in each society.

An analysis of the institutions determining such responses in American society makes it clear that in order to change any of those responses it will be necessary to change the character of some of our institutions. For example, perhaps the one value beyond all others which has become predominantly institutionalized in the United States is the value of success, success measured in terms of how many dollars a person possesses or how much he or she can "make" in a year, in a society in which *earning* a living has been turned into a *way* of living.

The emphasis is almost entirely upon material success in the open competitive market. Margaret Mead has discussed this trait of American culture at length in her book *And Keep Your Powder Dry*. The spirit of aggressive competition is inculcated in young Americans almost as soon as they are capable of understanding what is required of them. Many soon learn that their parents' love for them is conditional upon how they compare, measure up, with others; they must compete and be successful. The hunt for status and the impetus to obtain prestige by achievement of lots of dollars represents a very powerful drive indeed. All potential competing persons and groups, as a consequence of such a process of socialization, therefore come to be regarded as rivals, and inevitably they will be regarded with varying degrees of hostility and fear. The frustrations of infancy, childhood, adolescence, and adult life, which have been either wholly or partially repressed, find a very ready outlet in the sanctioned aggressiveness which the American competitive system of living encourages. Under such conditions racial prejudice and discrimination is inevitable, for in a society such as ours, in which there are distinctively recognized "in-groups" and "out-groups," that are regarded as in competition with each other hostility will always be directed toward the "out-group," since by its very presence it constitutes a threat to the security of the person whose personality is structured in terms of competition and the drive to succeed. In view of the fact that such persons spend a great part of their anxious lives in a state of actual or anticipated insecurity, it is not surprising that they should give their fears substantial form in the shape of some minority or ethnic—so-called racial—group, which may then serve as the object to which one may transfer or displace aggressions that have been directed to other frustrating objects, and thus serve as a convenient scapegoat.

The insecurities incident to life in highly industrialized societies continually produce frustrations, and race prejudices constitute a socially sanctioned outlet for the resulting accumulated aggressiveness. This in turn serves to explain the person's failure to himself and at the same time enables him to revenge himself upon the imagined cause of it.

As long as we maintain the kind of emphasis we do, in this country, upon competitive success, and as long as we continue to produce the kind of frustrations and insecurities that we do in infants, children, adolescents, and adults, active feelings of hostility towards members of "out-groups" will continue to plague our society no matter how well we succeed in restraining their expression by means of external constraints.

This is not to say that such external constraints are useless, they can, in fact, be of the first importance, and must be applied much more rigorously than any have yet been. But this *is* to say, that in order to eliminate the sickness of group hostility we must eliminate the conditions that give rise to it, and, as I have indicated, many of the most important conditions can be found in the character of some of our institutions.

In the first place, we must change our goal of success in terms of material achievement to one which will have as its goal the perfection of the human spirit, *humanitas*. We must change from the disoperative ideal of the American individualist, to the ideal of the cooperative citizen who is devoted to something other than himself—to his fellow men, and to the good of society. In other words, we must concentrate our energies on making *humane* beings out of humans. When we shall have achieved that we shall have solved not only the problem of group hostility but most of the social problems arising out of interpersonal relations. Obviously an ideal to be aimed at. But how is such an ideal to be practically achieved?

The answer is: By *social reform* and by *education,* and the two processes must proceed together, the development of one without the other will not be good enough. The person educated in certain values of behavior towards his fellows, must be given an opportunity to practice them. If the society in which he lives makes it difficult for him to do so, he will find himself at odds with far too many people for his conduct to make itself appreciably felt upon the masses, and if he makes any progress at all it will be slow, partial, and unsatisfying, and it is doubtful whether what little he may achieve at so great a cost will endure.

This is the lot of most would-be social reformers today. On the other hand, where conditions make it possible for the socially educated person to live life humanely and cooperatively, there can be little doubt of the great social progress that could be made within a single generation. If conditions could be made easier for the average person to cooperate in this way, even if, as in most cases, he or she would have to be directed by the imperatives of the law; we shall have made a very great advance in the right direction. And this brings me to the one great agency of social regulation which has thus far not been adequately utilized in the approach to the problem of group hostility. I mean the law. It has been said that one cannot legislate race prejudice out of existence. This may be true, but no more true than to say that one cannot legislate libel or slander out of existence.[2] The fact is that our laws of libel and slander exercise a most effective control over the publication, written or spoken, of malicious statements calculated to bring a person into group hostility of any kind based on race, religious, or ethnic prejudice. Race prejudice and race discrimination are not the same: Race prejudice is essentially an attitude of mind, but it does not always necessarily lead to race discrimination, though it usually does. Race discrimination is the active form of race prejudice as has been exhibited, for example, in exclusion laws against Jews, blacks, or others in educational institutions but more particularly as it functions in connection with business, housing, transportation, employment, voting, and so on. Race prejudice gives rise to race discrimination, and race discrimination serves to maintain and continually add fuel to race prejudice, and in this viciously circular manner to intensify and extend discriminative practices.

A law against group libel would obviously not necessarily affect the practice of race discrimination, while a law against race discrimination would not of itself eliminate race prejudice. The question arises whether both forms of group hostility should be approached, together or separately. This is ultimately a matter of strategy and the answer will vary for different areas. The strategy is a matter for those to determine who know their localities best. The case against group libel is clear: It should and must be enacted as a law by every State in the Union, at the same time, legislation should be passed against every form of discrimination on the basis of ethnic, religious or minority association. A concerted attack of this kind on group hostility will do more for the improvement of group relations than any other practical measures of which I can think. Coordinated with educational measures such a program will begin to produce results immediately.

Here, then, is something we can do in a practical way, here and now. We can not only begin thinking and working for State and Federal legislation against group hostility and discrimination, but the ground can be prepared for it, and local situations improved by working up sufficient interest to secure the passage of such legislation in one's own particular town.

With the establishment of a Federal Fair Employment Practice Commission, a first step was taken to deal with the problem of discrimination that still remains in our racist society, so that reinforcing our energies in this direction must be unflagging. As supplementary or perhaps as part of the task of securing this and allied legislation, we can, as has already been suggested, interest the proper people in our own particular localities in such legislation. But beyond all else it is legislation on a national scale that must be our objective.

With the passage of such anti-discriminatory legislation as FEPC the issue of group hostility, whether ethnic, religious or minority, would be squarely before the people. Let us then be prepared to meet the issue in the best possible manner, by paving the way now for the immediate passage of the bill making group libel a crime against society, a crime against the expressed ideal of this society: *"E pluribus unum,"* "out of the many one."

Education

From the viewpoint of the worker interested in the elimination of race prejudice, the early years of the developing person must receive far greater

attention than has traditionally been bestowed upon this capitally important period. The mind of the preschool child—the first five years—is to a
very large extent molded by its parents, particularly by the mother. Since
within the first five years of life the foundations of many later attitudes are
laid, and the antecedents of race prejudice can in most cases be clearly
traced to this early period of life, the knowledge of how to help the child
grow into a well-equilibrated cooperative human being must be put into
the hands of all who are involved in the process of socialization.

The growth of the pre-school movement in this country provides an
educational complement to education in the home, the potential importance of which cannot be overemphasized. It is through such schools that
parents can be reached and educated in the cooperative task of educating
their children. Because of the importance of the issues involved, the State
should provide a preschool experience at no cost to the parents, to accom-
modate the population of children between the ages of 2 and 5 years. In
this area of public instruction special emphasis should be placed upon the
parents' obligation to cooperate with the school. Parent-teacher relationships should be an integral part of the educational program, and the
school should be conducted as an integral part of the community, the
child being a member of a community as well as of a family.

In spite of some doubts that have been expressed concerning the benefits of compensatory education, intensive research has shown that compensatory education is remarkably efficient in raising, for what it is worth,
the IQ of underprivileged mothers as well as of children by as much as 30
points. These findings have been presented in two reports, one edited by
Dr. Sally Ryan, the other written by Professor Urie Bronfenbrenner. Together the two reports—the former containing eight different studies re-
counted by the investigators and the second presenting authoritative answers to the questions "Is Early Intervention Effective?"–constitute a
comprehensive rebuttal to those who prematurely claim the death of
Headstart and compensatory education programs. What these studies
show is that when one breaks through the walls of educational ghettos,
which reflect the surrounding ghettos of daily existence, and succeeds in
involving the parents in the education of their children (rather than acqui-
escing in the process of programming them to fail), it becomes possible to
transform the school into both an effective center of learning and a focus
for community activity and hope. In such schools, reading-score gains average 1.1 years—a full month above the national average; moreover, discipline is improved and vandalism is decreased. The program has been strikingly successful.[3]

It should be a prerequisite required of all teachers in such schools that
they shall be adequately trained in the guidance of young children in lay-
ing the foundations of good habits in interpersonal and intergroup rela-

tionships. Such teachers should come to the school in the full awareness of the structure and problems of their society and of the particular community in which they serve. Especially must they be aware of their particular function in assisting the child to avoid all those developments which are later easily turned into group hostility. More positively, teachers must help the child to a sense of security within the family and the community, and must help to lay the foundations of that feeling of fellowship with people of all kinds that is the true basis of cultural democracy. In this task the cooperation of the parents is indispensable, and parents can, in most cases, be made to see the advantages of such cooperation.

Before we proceed to consider some of the practical steps that can be taken in this area of the educational program, let us briefly consider some of the antecedents of race prejudice encountered in preschool children.

In the first place, most pre-school children do not show any developed form of race prejudice, they can and do show potentialities that may develop into socially destructive race attitudes, although these attitudes are not likely to materialize until later in life. They do, however, quite often show race discrimination. Such discrimination, as Ruth Horowitz has shown,[4] is frequently made in relation to racial self-identification. The differences discriminated mostly relate to skin color, language, clothes, customs such as eating differently or different foods, and absence on certain festivals.

The primary bases out of which group prejudices may easily grow if not properly handled are present in the predispositions found in all children. Among the fears, for example, that children exhibit, are the fear of being left alone, fear of a strange person—which is really the same thing as the fear of being left alone—and fear of the dark. These fears may become the bases for insecurities of various sorts and aggressive feelings towards members of other groups, unless they are properly handled and directed.

Crying when left alone as exhibited, for example, by infants of 3 or 4 months, when physical contact is reduced, is perhaps the first social fear. The child is a highly dependent being, and as it develops it draws its feeling of security from those persons upon whom it has learned to grow dependent. Unless this social development is properly handled the child will tend to feel "alone" and insecure in the presence of strangers, will be afraid, and will dislike the object of his or her fear. Hence, an unreasoned prejudice against persons of all "out-groups" may easily develop from this kind of development. Good early conditioning in interpersonal relationships, and the insurance of the maximum of security for the child are the two primary generalizations which can be made here concerning the manner in which such fears may be handled. More particularly, where fears arise in the child as the result of the observation of striking differences in other people, such occasions must be converted into as pleasantly conditioning ones as possible.

As Jersild and Holmes have shown,[5] pre-school children may not only be afraid of strangers, and cling to mother when seeing a stranger on the street, but they are often afraid of familiar people when they look temporarily different. Thus, one child may show extreme fright when seeing its mother with a thick layer of cold cream on her face; another child may show fear seeing its father without a beard. Anyone who has carefully observed young children in unfamiliar situations will have been struck by the extreme sense of insecurity, which they exhibit. The unfamiliar lacks the supportive quality of the familiar, and hence induces a feeling of insecurity.

Such situations should be anticipated, as far as possible, by such devices as picture books and accompanying stories designed to introduce the child to the unfamiliar in a friendly and interested spirit. The natural curiosity of the child should be fully exploited. When the child inquires whether a African American is black all over, and whether the color will rub off, correct conditioning at this time is a simple matter, and it should be of the first importance. The child should be given a sensible explanation of the facts as we know them, and afforded every opportunity to play with children of various ethnic backgrounds.

Improperly handled fear of the dark may bring about a generalized fear of whatever is dark. Hence, special attention should be paid to this aspect of the child's development.

Since the antecedents of race prejudice manifested by the child at the preschool level have their roots primarily in parent-child and adult-child relationships, and are very definitely not something that grow autochthonously from within the child itself, we must see to it, whenever possible, and principally through the medium of the school-parent relationships that the necessary equipment for directing these antecedents into the proper sympathetic channels is made available.

We stand in need of a reevaluation of the place of the schools in our society. If children are to be properly educated their parents must be, too. The development of parent-teacher associations all over the country represents a spontaneous recognition of this need. Parents and teachers must become even more fully aware of the need for cooperation between them. They can mutually be of the greatest help to one another in the process of socializing the child, and thus, between them, the principal contributors to a happy harmonious society.

Education for democratic living in a unified society should begin in the pre-school. The cultural, ethnic, and religious differences at that age level must be treated as of no less importance than at any other age. Such group differences should be made the basis for creating an understanding, enriching, and enduring interest in other persons not only as persons but as members of different groups. The differences should be utilized to interest and educate rather than to antagonize and prejudice. In this way the natural curiosity of the child will be constructively satisfied and the proper attitudes initiated. At the same time the essential likenesses must be fully stressed. Children must be made to feel unqualifiedly secure in the presence of what is too often left as the strange and unfamiliar. In this direction no pupils are so apt as the very young.[6]

The great curiosity which all small children exhibit can be creatively utilized in getting them accustomed to and interested in others. At the preschool level the foundations can thus effectively be laid of what may later be developed as the truly cultivated human perspective, understanding of and appreciation for the other person's point of view.[7]

By the calculated and judicious choice of toys, books, and dolls representing a good selection of the peoples which have entered into the formation of this nation, group games with emphasis on cooperation, fair play, and respect for others, and similar means, we can hope to achieve much good in the conditioning and preconditioning of good interpersonal attitudes and relations. But again it must be emphasized that at this age level as well as at those that follow, the parents must be persuaded to cooperate with the schools, otherwise the best laid plans of philosophers and teachers will go astray.

Notes

1. The term "necessary" is here used in its logical sense as an indispensable condition entering into the group of conditions which together determine a cause.

2. Let us remember that there were men in the seventeenth and eighteenth centuries who held that it would be impossible to legislate slavery out of existence.

3. Sally Ryan, ed., *A Report on Longitudinal Evaluations of Preschool Programs* (Department of Health, Education and Welfare Publication No. OHD 74-24 and No. OHD 74-25), 19; Urie Brofenbrenner, ed., *Influences on Human Development* (Hinsdale, IL: Dryden Press, 1972).

4. Horowitz, Ruth, "Racial Aspects of Self Identification in Nursery School Children," *Journal of Psychology* 1 (1939): 91–99.

5. A. T. Jersild and F. B. Holms, *Children's Fears, Child Development* Monograph 20 (New York: Teachers College, Columbia University, 1935).

6. Ashley Montagu, *Touching: The Human Significance of the Skin* 3rd ed. (New York: Harper & Row, 1986).

7. Ashley Montagu, *Growing Young*, 2 ed. (Westport, CT: Bergin & Garvey, 1989).

12

Intelligence, IQ, and Race

What is intelligence? Most people would answer: "Intelligence is what IQ tests measure." But as we shall see, despite the claims of their proponents, IQ tests do not measure intelligence.

The truth is, IQ tests cannot possibly measure intelligence because no one really knows what the *structure* of intelligence is. Without knowing this structure in considerable detail, we cannot even approximate a quantitative measure of it. What is quite clear, except to IQ testers, is that many conditions enter into the making of intelligence. Without taking these conditions into consideration, IQ tests are quite valueless in arriving at an understanding of what intelligence really is. Even worse than valueless, IQ tests often unjustifiably brand childred with the mark of inferiority, especially when what they need beyond all else is encouragement.

Since my days, in the early 1920s, as a student of Charles Spearman, the noted pyschologist, whose novel theory of the nature of intelligence[1] has been put to perfidious use in recent years, psychologists have tried hard to reach some consensus as to the nature and expression of intelligence. Nonetheless, the unraveling of the structure of intelligence remains largely unaccomplished.

The cumulative research of the last seventy years suggests that a good working hypothesis would be to regard intelligence as constituted of a large assembly of highly varied overlapping and adaptive abilities, rather than as a single faculty. Somewhat independent of its elusive structure, however, intelligence appears to be largely the summation and personal incorporation of the learning experiences of each individual.

As for the relation of the structure of the brain to the nature and level of intelligence, many scientific reputations have been compromised in the sinuous twists of the human brain when insupportable racial differences were claimed to have been found in weight, size, convolutions, and its other structures. These racial differences in structure were believed to be sufficient to account for racial differences in intelligence.

Unfortunately, claims to racial structural differences resulting in racial differences in intelligence continue. Yet, all such claims of the higher phrenology, as it has been called, have repeatedly been shown to be wholly unsound and have been thoroughly discredited over the last several decades. Quite simply, within the normal range of variation in brain morphology, there exists no demonstrable relation to intelligence.

Furthermore, the brain as an organ is vastly more than a physical structure. Indeed, it is the most complex and functionally educable system of structures within the body. Made up of trillions of neurons and associated entities in an amazingly complicated network of environmentally educable interconnections, as well as a remarkable hormonal secretary activity and chemistry which it manages on its own,[2] the brain is the domain of the learned part of the environment. As functioning *human beings*, everything we know and come to do, we have had to learn from others and from the environment.

The evidence drawn from many relevant researches is now overwhelming; *individual experiences* literally shape the developing brain and subsequent behavior.[3] The quality of those experiences is fundamentally important for the development of the problem-solving behavior we call intelligence or thinking: that is, the ability to make the appropriately successful *responses* rather than reactions to the challenges of the environment. Just as differences between the cultural developments of different societies can be explained by differences in the histories of their experiences, so may differences in intelligence between individuals be explained, for the most part, by the histories of their experiences. The parenthetic "for the most part" allows for whatever genetic factors may be involved.

The culture of IQ testing over the last 70 years has become so routinized, and its influence upon education so powerful, that what was once a by-product of education has become a determinant of education and of social action. Schools often tailor their curricula to so-called IQ tests. Accordingly, narrow skills are taught; with the consequent neglect of the natural abilities of each child.

An enormous number of influences enter into each individual's learning experiences. To properly assess intelligence, these learning experiences must be evaluated for the roles they have played in its formulation. Otherwise, IQ advocates will vainly continue their search in a dark room for a black cat that is not there, all the while stubbing their toes.

For example, what is never considered in IQ testing are such variables as: maternal stimulations, parental dispositions, parental education, socioeconomic status, prenatal and perinatal birth experiences, early childhood, schooling, and mental and physical health. Without a thorough investigation of these conditions, regardless of the innate predispositions of each individual, all tests of intelligence, and especially IQ tests, are worthless as measures of intelligence.

To understand the nature of intelligence, one needs to appreciate the transformation of a predisposition into an ability. A predisposition is inborn, whereas an ability is evoked from a trained predisposition. By learning, which is the increase in the strength of any act by repetition, a predisposition is trained and becomes an ability. Among the innate prenatal and perinatal undeveloped predispositions are the basic behavioral needs. In any test of intelligence it would be necessary, at the very least, to acknowledge that such needs exist. An understanding of the history and satisfaction of those needs is indispensably requisite to arrive at a relatively accurate estimate of an individual's intelligence.

A basic behavioral need is an urge or drive toward the satisfaction of that need. The thwarting of an expected satisfaction during childhood, especially the need for love, generally leads to serious disorders in physical and mental development. Additionally, the unfulfillment of expected satisfaction can lead to aggressive or dysfunctional behavior, sometimes called failure to thrive, and may even lead to death.[4] Satisfaction of the basic behavioral needs leads to healthy behavioral growth and development. Healthy growth and development includes the ability to love, to work, to play, and to think soundly.

Satisfaction of the basic behavioral needs is also requisite for the healthy growth and development of the body and mind.[5] The basic behavioral needs are love, which means not only to be loved but also to love others, curiosity, creativity, imagination, learning, explorativeness, experimental-mindedness, open-mindedness, speech, sound thinking, flexibility, joyfulness, play, laughter, weeping, work, song, and dance.[6] These basic behavioral needs have not been formally recognized as playing major roles in the development of intelligence, largely because the whole subject of the development of intelligence has been approached in too intellectualized a manner. Furthermore, to fail to consider the roles that religious, spiritual, and emotional influences may play in the development of intelligence is to neglect among the most dominant influences relating to the intellectual development of the individual.

It is a great error to approach the investigation of human intelligence and IQ testing as if every individual were a product of purely informational conditioning. Yet, intelligence testers repeatedly commit this egregious error and, thereby, simultaneously forfeit the most basic understanding of some of the critical influences on the shaping of intelligence.

Since the acronym "IQ" has entered the language as a scientific measure of intelligence, as if indeed it were a real thing, it has done a great deal of damage to untold numbers of human beings. Lured into a false belief of the estimate of their capacities, the victims of IQ tests have suffered a loss of self esteem and of confidence in their abilities. Too frequently these victims have also suffered a devastating hopelessness which has marred so many lives. The psychometricians of humankind involved in such pernicious activities have rarely exhibited the least concern for the victims of their labors, but have often claimed, as in the latest case by the authors of *The Bell Curve*,[7] that their findings are for the good of us all.

The reprehensible thing about these taxonomists of the mind is a cluster of traits they generally display which disqualifies them from having any valid opinion on the nature of intelligence, especially when that opinion affects blacks. These traits include but are not limited to: obvious bias; general insensitivity; close-mindedness; failure to consider the evidence opposing their views; citation of views favorable to their kinds of arguments, though such views have long been discredited; and, abysmal ignorance of biological and cultural anthropology. Worst of all, their ignorance of *genetics* is pronounced, evoking innumerable rejections of both their methods and their conclusions.

An elementary example from agriculture may help illuminate the mistake so often made by the mental taxonomists. If we were to take corn seed from one source and plant half of the seed in an enriched field and the other half in an impoverished field, we would see two types of variation in the heights of the individual plants. The variation in plant heights within each field could be explained by very small and essentially unimportant genetic differences in the seed. The differences in plant heights between the fields would be due almost entirely to differing soil conditions and not to genetic differences. Nonetheless, and consistent with the history of IQ testing, the taxonomists of the mind would see the differences in crop heights between the fields as genetic in origin, never considering the conditions under which the corn plants were raised.

Beginning in 1923 with Walter Lippmann's[8] devastating attacks on the works and findings of the leading IQ testers of World War I army recruits,[9] and continuing to the most recent of these criticisms on the flaws and failures of IQ testing, the denunciations have been unceasing. Outstanding among the more recent critiques are Stephen Jay Gould's *The Mismeasure of Man* (1981),[10] Professor Albert Jacquard's *In Praise of Difference* (1984),[11] and Elaine and Harry Mensh's *The IQ Mythology* (1991).[12] These three works were published long enough before *The Bell Curve* to have given its authors plenty of time to deal with such critiques of IQ tests and their consequences. Instead, they, and innumerable others, were ignored.

The authors of *The Bell Curve*, like so many of their predecessors, apparently were determinedly uninterested in pursuing a balanced course, a course that every genuine scientist follows as part of the normal procedure of checking the validity of his work. Professor William Tucker in his book, *The Science and Politics of Racial Research* (1994),[13] published just one month after the appearance of *The Bell Curve*, has shown pointedly and unequivocally that the authors of such works as *The Bell Curve* have not been interested in the facts or the most reasonable interpretation of their findings. Rather, he shows, such authors are most interested in the use of such devices as IQ tests to represent social and political inequality as the unavoidable and ineradicable consequences of natural differences. One wonders why these so-called scientists have never tried standing the argument on its head by considering the possibility that, far from being due to natural differences, the differences are largely due to social and political inequalities? And that race is a product of the social history of an individual or group, not of nature?

One also wonders why the extraordinary accomplishments of American blacks, who traveled from slaves to affirmative action status in little more than a century, are not highlighted by these so-called scientists? Why are events such as the practically inconceivable redrawing of voting districts and membership of blacks on the United States Supreme Court in a white-ruled society absent from their works?

And, incredibly, one wonders why these so-called scientists never seemed to have considered it functionally irresponsible to publish views in the name of science which have been repeatedly shown to be unsound and disastrous for millions of people. Why is it that in the face of the Holocaust, "ethnic cleansing," and the endemic social and political inequalities that exist in the United States between whites and blacks that these so-called scientists have persisted in perpetuating demonstrably unsound views as an explanation for those inequalities and the evils to which these views lead? Their arguments are circular and are demonstrably wrong.

Blindness is not the affliction from which these enemies of humanity suffer. Rather, they suffer from an attitude of mind, however acquired, which causes them to perceive members of another group as belonging to a different race and thereby as inferior. These members of different races are considered to be threats to the continued integrity and welfare of society. I have called this viewpoint "man's most dangerous myth."[14] Hitler, by organizing the murder of millions of Jews, gypsies, and other targeted victims in the name of race, proved in the deeds of many of his loyal followers that the belief in race is indeed man's most dangerous myth.[15] In America, the myth of race has been endemic for several centuries, and remains America's primary public health problem.[16] It is therefore hardly surprising that the tide of passion whipped up by American public figures and windy writers overflowed its banks and surfaced on foreign shores.

The ideas and writing of American scientists' and writers on race have been widely influential in contributing support and endorsement for the ideologies of foreign reactionary politicians and demagogues. This situation was the case most notably in Germany, whose leaders found in the racist works of Americans an encouragement for and a reinforcement of their extreme racist programs. Racism in Germany had been deeply entrenched long before the advent of Hitler and Nazism. With Germany's defeat in World War I and the forced acceptance of a humiliating peace treaty in 1919, followed by a catastrophic national depression, anarchy in the streets, and the pressing cry for an explanation, a target was needed upon whom to fix the blame. The populace was easily led to believe that Germany had lost the war because it had been betrayed; the famous "stab in the back," a convenient scapegoat for the massive frustration was readily available: the Jews.

As a matter of historical record, the first prominent victim of the racist nationalists was Walther Rathenau, Foreign Minister and a Jew, who had served his country nobly and with great ability during and after the war. Rathenau, a charming man who believed in conciliation rather than confrontation, was assassinated in June 1922.

In November 1923, the failure of Hitler's Munich *putsch* landed him in jail, where, during the five months he was ensconced, he wrote *Mein Kampf*. During this comfortable situation, often euphemistically called his "incarceration," he read an account of the passage of the United States Immigration Restriction Act of 1924. In *Mein Kampf*, he wrote of the Immigration Restriction Act with the greatest enthusiasm, saying that it would serve as a model for his program of racial purification. Not only that, having read the American Madison Grant's, *The Passing of the Great Race*,[17] the popular racist tract of its time which spoke of Jews with especial malevolence, Hitler, who called his deep-seated hatred of Jews "the granite-firm foundation" of his ideology, wrote Grant thanking him for writing the book, saying that it was his Bible.

Grant's book, published in 1916, was well written, very easy to read, widely reviewed, enlarged, and quickly reprinted. Grant was a New Yorker, a bachelor, and a socialite who traced his ancestry back to colonial America. He was the founder of the New York Zoological Society and of the Galton Society, an exclusive group with monthly meetings in The American Museum of Natural History. The Galton Society, as its name implies, was chiefly interested in eugenic issues. Grant was also a luminary of the American Eugenics Society and a vice-president of the Immigration Restriction League.

Grant's book spawned others in rapid succession, many of which were greeted with enthusiasm in Germany, especially by German anthropologists.[18] The German sociologist Stefan Kühl has shown in his graphically titled book, *The Nazi Connection: Eugenics, American Racism, and German National Socialism*, that not only did the German anthropologists welcome the contributions of American authors to the cause of National Socialism but were, in fact, in regular contact with many of them.

Some Americans actually served on the editorial boards of well-known German racist journals while others traveled to Germany to accept honorary degrees from Nazi-controlled German universities. Among such degree recipients were Henry Fairfield Osborn, President of The American Museum of Natural History and Harry Laughlin, the instigator and drafter of the U.S. Restrictive Immigration Act of 1924 and Assistant Director of the Eugenics Record Office.[19]

In 1916 Osborn wrote an adulatory preface for the first edition of *The Passing of the Great Race,* in which he stated the function of

> the modern eugenics movement in relation to patriotism, namely, the conservation and multiplication for our country of the best spiritual, moral, intellectual, and physical forces of heredity," and that "thus only will the integrity of our institutions be maintained in the future." Osborn concluded with the words, "If I were asked: What is the greatest danger which threatens the American republic today? I would certainly reply: The gradual dying out among our people of those hereditary traits through which the principles of our religious, political, and social foundations were laid down, and their insidious replacement by traits of less noble character.

In the German translation of Grant's book, the word for "insidious" in Osborn's preface is *hinterlistig,* meaning "crooked," "underhanded," and "stealthy." Try to imagine the impression that Osborn's words made upon Hitler. Unlike Osborn, who lacked the courage to name explicitly who these "insidious" creatures might be, Grant left no doubt in the reader's mind who they were. They were "the Slovak, the Italian, the Syrian and the Jew." "The man of the old stock," Grant wrote, "is being crowded out of many country districts by these foreigners just as he is to-day being literally driven off the streets of New York City by the swarms of Polish Jews . . . the Polish Jew, whose dwarf stature, peculiar mentality, and ruthless concentration on self-interest are being engrafted upon the stock of the nation."[20]

In December 1917, Osborn allowed his original preface to remain and added a completely new one for the 1918 enlarged new edition of Grant's book. With the then recent entry of the United States into World War I in mind, Osborn opened with the following ringing words: "History is repeating itself in America at the present time and incidentally is giving a convincing demonstration of the central thought in this volume, namely, that heredity and racial predisposition are stronger and more stable than environment and education." This portentous announcement was followed by an extended paean to "this strain of Anglo-Saxon life which has played so large a part in American history."[21]

To continue Osborn's history, it may seem ungracious to add the fact that in world history the American racist "strain of Anglo-Saxon" authors played a significant role in providing the Nazis, both before and during the Second World War, with support for a regime that was responsible for the monumental evil of the Holocaust and for the perpetation of many other genocides and acts of ruthlessness. It is estimated that those evils resulted in the deaths of more than fifty million human beings. The number of people indirectly subjected to unspeakable suffering was, of course, many times higher. All this was in the name of race.

It is generally held that anyone who cries "Fire!" in a crowded theater should be held responsible for the consequences of such conduct. The same rules should apply to anyone who, motivated by racism or callousness, publishes or utters inflammatory falsehoods concerning others. It should make no difference whether the perpetrators be individuals, groups, or populations; they should be held responsible for their conduct by law. More than 200 years of racial slander and libel are enough. The current use of IQ tests represents just such a continuing ethnic slander and libel by presenting demeaning falsehoods, regardless of the presence or absence of malicious intent. In the final analysis, what is involved is the matter of responsibility; that is, the welfare of human beings needs to be considered through the balancing of scientific responsibility by moral integrity and human concern.

It is important to understand that the whole concept of IQ is an arbitrary invention that has been given a spurious reality and an equally spurious quantification. In light of what is presently known and in fact has been known for quite some time, the persistent quantification of IQ is a travesty upon humanity, unleashed and maintained by irresponsible so-called scientists, for what are such scientists if they lack humanity?

Among the many weaknesses of IQ tests is that what they are said to measure—namely, intelligence—they do not in fact measure. For the most part IQ test results reflect the effects of socio-econimic background and schooling experience. What the test generally tells us is where a child stands in respect of his or her ability to respond to the test questions as compared with the performance of other children of similar chronologic age. Since, however, chronologic age is itself a poor index of developmental age, the value of the test even from the standpoint of its comparative value is more questionable than ever. IQ tests are, if anything, likely to be harmful to many children who happen to be slow developers who, when not condemned to a low IQ status, will catch up with and often outdistance the more rapid developers.

The future of humanity has its great diversity as its bedrock, not the categorization of humanity by IQ tests. It is in humanity's diversity that its greatest riches are stored, in the wonder of our individual differences seeking expression for the benefit of us all. We are born into a continuing social relationship. That relationship is the love shared between mother and child. The love is a bond and a relationship which is designed to grow and develop throughout our lives and by extension to the whole of humanity. Next to homicide, the greatest crime one can commit against others is to stand in the way of their development, to deprive them and society of the fulfillment of their unique individuality and their humanity.

The history of the concept of race is a truly dreadful one. From its beginning and by its very existence, the term has served to narrow the definition of humanity through the establishment of an hegemonic hierarchy of discrete entities. These entities, the so-called races, were primarily based on differences in physical traits. Such physical traits were soon linked with cultural and social differences, educability, and intelligence.

During the Victorian period, scientists were busily engaged in classifying the races of man, just as they had been classifying the races of animals. Books published as late as the latter half of the twentieth century still portrayed *typical* members of the races of mankind. The illustrations of the different races along with maps of their distributions were often attractively colored and, intended or not, served to reinforce two views of humankind. The first view was of an overall unity of humankind; and simultaneously, the second view confirmed the classifier's belief in the reality of "physical" races for all the world to see, and in the comforting uniformity of their beliefs they reigned supreme.

What the classifiers saw as they surveyed the peoples of the earth was a great deal of variability which, on the basis of the physical differences, they attempted to fit into the taxonomic pigeon-holes already available to them: *races*. In the pre-genetic age in which they lived and worked, the scientists of the day could hardly have done better than they did. Nonetheless, with the advent of genetics early in the twentieth century, it became quite clear where the classifiers had gone wrong; it was in treating populations as if they were composed of complexes of physical traits rather than of the distribution of the genes for the various traits they presented. When genetic explorations were done, it was found that the vast majority of genes for the various traits were shared by all the populations of humankind. In short, the genetic differences between human populations are very few. Furthermore, geneticists have found that the small extant differences are contributory to the welfare of us all, mentally as well as physically.

Classificatory ardor continued to the point of virtually excluding some peoples from the community of humankind and, like nationalism, succeeded in justifying enmity between nations.[22] Not only was the polarization of ethnicities between nations greatly facilitated by the idea of race, but race greatly justified and legitimized the stratifications of caste and class within nations. In Europe throughout the nineteenth century, especially during the kleptomaniac era of imperialism, slavery in America, and its offshoot called manifest destiny, it was customary to speak of higher and lower races. It is a mark of some progress that the use of these terms has been somewhat declining.

During the last 200 years, the work of anthropologists among the indigenous peoples of the earth incontrovertibly established the truth that if some groups of humanity are more advanced in some respects than others it is principally because the challenges of our highly technologized societies have been more complex. As such, more complex and challenging environments demand primarily different adaptive technologic inventions and social responses. Socially, the levels of complexity of a society, whether simple or complex, have everywhere elicited much the same kinds of responses by adapting to the requirements of the social pressures. In this way, intelligence, as measured by responses to the challenges of social and environmental pressures, does not seem hierarchically distributed but, instead, seems to be quite equally distributed among all of humankind.[23]

Every culture can be regarded as the historic result of a people's effort to adjust itself to its environment. Before the advent of the twentieth century, that environment was usually narrowly circumscribed. Today the boundaries which formerly divided people are crumbling before our eyes. Humankind is moving, in spite of occasional appearances to the contrary, toward greater understanding. This greater understanding means movement toward the condition whereby the differences that separate people today will be regarded as no more important than the differences that separate members of the same family. In a family, everyone, despite apparent differences, is ideally given the opportunity and encouragement to become a fully realized human being. Intra-family differences are not viewed as causes for suspicion, fear, discrimination, or pegs upon which to hang prejudices.

In 1920, H. G. Wells wrote in his *The Outline of History*, "Human history becomes more and more a race between education and catastrophe." Looking at the world that we have created since that time, it is clear that catastrophe has been winning out over education. Wells would have been appalled at what passes for education today. Wells thought of education as *humanitas*, the concern for and the involvement in humanity. What passes for education in our time is not education at all, but is, at best, instruction. Moreover, the instruction is all too often little more, and frequently less, than training in the traditional "three R's." Genuine education has been technologized by the technocrats of education to the point of being reduced to a handful of practical skills and routinized techniques.

Our love affair with technology, which was to have been our servant, has instead made willing servants of us.[24] We pride ourselves on having created machines that think much like human beings. What we have failed to understand is that, in the process, we have created human beings who think like machines. By any operative definition, that reductionism to cookbook skills and routine techniques is what, for the most part, we call education today.

The result is that we have turned our world into a technological disaster. We now have a citizenry that thinks in stereotypes and clichés, who have become the prisoners of their impoverished vocabularies. Having never been taught what thinking really is, we have "educated" a population into having little respect for those who do think.[25]

As Sir Joshua Reynolds put it, "Few have been taught to any purpose who have not been their own teachers." Thinking is a skill which can be taught as a searching and enchanting exercise which grows to be an immense and vitally important pleasure. Thinking can be taught in our schools, in all grades and at appropriately increasing levels of complexity. That teaching, however, does not appear to be one of the functions of today's educational institutions, for there we teach *what* to think, rather than *how* to think. The result has been catastrophic to the extent that we have become the most self-endangered species on this planet, composed as we are of so many ignorant minds and having the capacity to annihilate all life on Earth with the push of a few buttons.

We have a big challenge before us; namely, the complete revision of education and its replacement by a system that meets the basic needs of humanity. In the name of education our schools have become institutions for the promotion of illiteracy in the most important of all the areas: the art of being a warm, loving human being. Our educational system is largely responsible for producing a population of illiterates in a time when it has become imperative for each of us to care for others and think of the world not as full of strangers, but as full of friends we have not yet met.

To love our neighbors as we love ourselves is not enough. We must love others more than we love ourselves, for that is the true measure of love. In a world in which there is so much unloving love behind the show of love, it is necessary today more than ever before to understand that racism, in whatever form it may assume, represents and motivates the continuing dehumanizing loss of involvement in the welfare of our neighbors.

There is only one way to express a deeper truth or meaning than words themselves can do—by action! *The meaning of a word is the action it produces.* Think for a minute about the words *race* and *racism* and about the word *love*. For most people, what they do about these words is what they mean by them, and what they mean by them is, for the most part, thoroughly dehumanizing.

If we are ever to extricate ourselves from the slough of despond into which we have fallen, we must recognize that there is only one way; through education, education as love, the deep involvement in the welfare of others. It is only through learning to love that we find our own true identity. In giving love unconditionally, we fulfill ourselves and help others to do likewise.

When all is said and done, when all our scientific works have been published, when all our truths have been proven, we will not have made much more headway in dealing with racism than we have in the past unless we clearly understand the root cause and the cure of the disease which racism is. It is because scientists have shied away from the study of love that I have devoted so much attention to it. A scientist is one who believes in proof without certainty, while most other people believe in certainty without proof. Scientists are generally specialists who may have made invaluable contributions in their fields toward the better understanding of wider issues than those which they are not normally involved. They are not usually called upon to see the wood for the trees. Nonetheless, their contributions, when seen through the eyes of the thinking generalist, make the view of the wood highly rewarding.

It is largely through the anthropological investigations of the great and illuminating diversity of the peoples of the earth that we have come to understand the meaning of humanity. The remarkable discovery is of a common bond that unites us all in a kinship of wondrous variety and creativity, confirming the heart's profound feeling that every human is incomparable, unique, universal, and fundamentally alike in all the qualities that make us human. This discovery, cumulatively and repeatedly authenticated by anthropologists during the last seventy years, should encourage us to work in the belief that to the improvement of the environment, heredity offers no barrier. The news from both anthropology and genetics is truly heartening.

Finally, we need to appreciate that our genetic richness emanates directly from our diversity. As Saint-Exupery wrote in *A Letter to a Hostage*, "If I am different from you, I enrich rather than diminish you." That message contains a universal principle: you are precious to me because you are different, as I am to you.[26]

Notes

1. C. Spearman, *The Nature of Intelligence and the Principles of Cognition* (London & New York: Macmillan, 1922).

2. S. Rose, *The Conscious Brain* (New York: Knopf, 1973); S. Rose *Molecules and Minds* (Philadelphia: Open University Press, 1987); Marian C. Diamond, *Enriching Heredity: The Impact of the Environment on the Anatomy of the* Brain (New York: Free Press, 1988); J. Boddy, *Brain Systems and Psychological Concepts* (New York: Wiley, 1978).

3. Max Cynader, "Mechanisms of Brain Development and Their Role in Health and Well-Being," *Daedalus* 123 (4) (1995): 155–65.

4. Patton, R. G. & Gardner, L. I., *Growth Failure in Maternal Deprivation* (Springfield, IL: C. C. Thomas, 1963); G. F. Powell, Brasel, J. A., & Blizzard, R., "Emotional Deprivation and Growth Retardation, Simulating Idiopathic Hypopituitrism," *New England Journal of Medicine* 276 (1967): 1271–78; J. B. Reinhart & Drash, A. A., "Psychosocial Dwarfism: Environmentally Induced Recovery," *Psychosomatic Medicine*, 31 (1969) 165–72; A. Montagu, ed., *Culture and Human Development: Insights Into Growing Human* (Englewood Cliffs, NJ: Prentice-Hall, 1974).

5. R. H. Munroe, R. L. Munroe, & B. B. Whiting, eds., *Handbook of Cross-Cultural Human Development* (New York: Garland STM Press, 1981); A. Peiper, *Cerebral Function in Infancy and Childhood* (New York: Consultants Bureau, 1963).

6. Ashley Montagu, *Growing Young*, 2nd ed. (Westport, CT: Bergin & Garvey, 1989).

7. R. Herrnstein & C. Murray, *The Bell Curve* (New York: Free Press, 1994).

8. Walter A. Lippmann, "Future for the Tests," *New Republic*, 29 November 1922, 9–11; "The Mental Age of Americans," *New Republic*, 25 October 1922, 213–25; "Mr. Burt and the Intelligence Tests," *New Republic*, 2 May 1922, 263–64; "The Mystery of the 'A' Men," *New Republic*, 1 November 1922, 246–48; "The Reliability of Intelligence Tests," *New Republic*, 8 November 1922); 275–77; "Tests of Hereditary Intelligence," *New Republic*, 22 November 1922, 328–30; see also N. J. Block, & Gerald Dworkin, eds., *The IQ Controversy* (New York: Random House, 1976).

9. R. M. Yerkes, "Psychological Examining in the United States Army. Washington" *Memoir of the National Academy of Sciences* 15, pt. I (1922).

10. Stephen J. Gould, *The Mismeasure of Man* (New York: Norton, 1981).

11. A. Jacquard, *In Praise of Difference: Genetics and Human Affairs* (New York: Columbia University Press, 1984).

12. Elaine Mensh & Harry Mensh, *The IQ Mythology* (Carbondale: Southern Illinois University Press, 1991); C. G. Liungman, *What Is IQ?* (London: Gordon Cremonesi,1975).

13. W. H. Tucker, *The Science and Politics of Racial Research* (Urbana: University of Illinois Press, 1994); Richard E. Lewontin, Steven Rose, & Leon Kamin, *Not In Our Genes* (New York: Pantheon Books, 1984).

14. Ashley Montagu, *Man's Most Dangerous Myth: The Fallacy of Race*, 5th ed. (New York: Oxford University Press, 1974).

15. Martin Gilbert, *The Holocaust: A History of the Jews of Europe during the Second World War* (New York: Holt, Rinehart & Winston, 1986); Lucy S. Dawidowicz, *The War Against the Jews: 1933–1945* (New York: Holt, Rinehart & Winston, 1975).

16. *Crisis in Child Mental Health,* Joint Commission on Mental Health (New York: Harper & Row, 1970); C. V. Willie, B. M. Kramer, and B. S. Brown, eds., *Racism and Mental Health* (Pittsburgh:University of Pittsburgh Press, 1973).

17. Madison Grant, *The Passing of the Great Race* (New York: Scribner's, 1916): vii–ix, 14–15, 80–81.

18. Madison Grant, *Passing of the Great Race*, new edition (1918/19), 91–92.

19. Stefan Kühl, *The Nazi Connection: Eugenics, American Racism, and German National Socialism* (New York: Oxford University Press, 1994): 85–88; See most importantly also, R. Proctor, "From Anthropologie to Rassenkunde in the German Anthropological Tradition," in *Genes, Bodies and Behavior,* ed. G. W. Stocking Jr., (Madison, WI: University of Wisconsin Press, 1988), 138–79; R. N. Proctor, *Racial*

Hygiene: Medicine Under the Nazis (Cambridge: Harvard University Press, 1988); Benno Muller-Hill, *Murderous Science: Elimination by Scientific Selection of Jew, Gypsies, and Others* (New York: Oxford University Press, 1988).

20. Grant, ibid., 14.

21. H. F. Osborn, in Grant, *Passing of the Great Race,* xi–xiii.

22. Christine Bolt, *Victorian Attitudes to Race* (London: Routledge, 1971); L. Dumont, *Homo Hierarchicus* (Chicago: University of Chicago Press, 1970); George W. Stocking, Jr. *Victorian Anthropology* (New York: Free Press, 1987); J. W. Trent, Jr., *Inventing the Feeble Mind* (Berkeley: University of California Press, 1994); N. Wiener, *The Human Use of Human Beings* (Boston: Houghton-Mifflin, 1950).

23. Sander L. Gilman, *Difference and Pathology: Stereotypes of Sexuality, Race, and Madness* (Ithaca: Cornell University Press, 1985); Maurice Dumas, *A History of Technology and Invention: Progress Through the Ages* (New York: Crown, 1969); Ashley Montagu, *Culture and the Evolution of Man* (New York: Oxford University Press, 1962); Ashley Montagu, ed., *Culture, Man's Adaptive Dimension* (New York: Oxford University Press, 1968).

24. JoAnne Brown, *The Definition of a Profession: The Authority of Metaphor in the History of Intelligence Testing, 1890–1930* (Princeton: Princeton University Press, 1992); A. Alan Hanson, *Testing Testing: Social Consequences of the Examined Life* (Berkeley: University of California Press, 1993).

25. Ashley Montagu, "Education, Humanity, and Technology," in *Advances in Telematics,* ed. Jarice Hanson (Norwood, NJ: Ablex Publishing, 1994), 1–15; Ashley Montagu, *The Direction of Human Development* (New York: Harper & Row, 1955); Ashley Montagu, The Origin and Significance of Neonatal Immaturity in Man *Journal of the American Medical Association* 178 (1961): 156–57; William Stanton, *The Leopard's Spots: Scientific Attitudes Toward Race in America, 1815–1859* (Chicago: University of Chicago Press, 1960).

26. A. Montagu, *Growing Young,* 2nd ed. (Westport, CT: Bergin & Garvey, 1989).

Index